UFOs AR

Extraterrestrial Encounters
Documented by the
U.S. Government

Clifford E. Stone

S.p.i.
BOOKS

New York

For further information, contact:

SPI Books
136 West 22nd Street
New York, NY 10011
Tel: 212/633-2023
FAX: 212/633-2123

Library of Congress Cataloging-in-Publication Data available.

ISBN 1-56171-972-2

Dedicated, in loving memory,

to my son

Robert Francis Stone

November 13, 1975 to August 18, 1995.

We still love you, son,

forever and ever.

Contents

Table of Documents

Acknowledgments

In doing the research for this book, my superiors in the military became aware of my interest and activities involving UFOs. As a result, some members of my chain of command attempted to force my retirement from military service. As one official report on my situation put it, my superiors tried to get rid of me "through the use of pressure, intimidation, or insinuation."

My command also ordered me to undergo a mental health evaluation at Fort Bliss, Texas, because I was writing Freedom of Information Act requests concerning UFOs and talking to the media. My diagnosis was based upon interviews and testing, and reflected that I was "fully alert and oriented. Thinking was clear and coherently expressed. No psychotic processes noted....Memory intact...[my] mental status was found to be within normal limits. Problems appear to be related to situational stress manifested by interpersonal and occupational difficulties." The report further stated: "It appears the command may have overreacted to the newspaper article on UFOs [after the subject was interviewed by a reporter]." Finally, their report stated that my superiors felt I was "an 'embarrassment' to command."

After the psychiatric report, my case got kicked all the way up to the Army Inspector General's Office. In the final analysis, I was cleared of any wrongdoing, reinstated in my job, and I chose to remain on active duty with the United States Army.

An official investigation was made into this entire sordid affair which resulted in three members of my command being relieved of duty and reassigned for, among other things, their part in trying to force my retirement. I eventually retired from the Army in January 1990. However, this was my decision and retirement was not forced upon me.

With everything that was happening to me, I could have easily ended up getting kicked out of the Army, and then I probably would never have written this book. However, with the support of many friends and family members, I was able to overcome all of the hardships put before me and to prevail.

I wish to express my love and appreciation to my loving wife, Hanh, and my children, George, Julia, Robert, and John, who all stood beside me and were willing to undergo any hardship, no matter what the cost, to assist in my fight against the unjust actions taken by members of the military chain of command against me.

I also wish to express my thanks to Ralph Heick, who stood beside me in my time of need and supported me as a true friend and companion in my darkest hour. Further, I wish to express my appreciation to Major Earl A. Peterson, Captain Kenneth C. Ross, and Captain Michael V. Jernigan for their support, at the risk of their careers, in defending my right as a member of the armed services to express my personal viewpoints as a private citizen.

And I would especially like to express my appreciation to Larry W. Bryant of CAUS (Citizens Against UFO Secrets), whose support gave me the courage and spirit to dare to fight back and write this book.

While there exist many others who supported me—too many to name here—you all know who you are and I wish to express my thanks to you as well.

And lastly, I would like to thank my super agent Bill Birnes, my thoughtful editors at S.P.I. Books, Isaac Mozeson and Ian Shapolsky, and the editorial staff at S.P.I., including Jay Bond, Robin Souza, and Donn Teal. Without you all this book would still be just a work-in-progress instead of an important document that can be used to change our country's existing flawed systems for dealing with the UFO phenomena.

Preface

This book should not exist.

Why do I say this? Simply put, according to the U.S. Air Force, there is no government interest in the subject of UFOs. If this were truly the case, then the documents that make up the bulk of this book should have never been created by the various agencies of the U.S. Government. Furthermore, I myself could not have been assigned by the U.S. Army to the investigation of UFO debris for more than 22 years.

When I first wrote this book, it was my desire to provide the public with documented proof, with government records that clearly show that something we commonly refer to as UFOs actually exists. While many records have been declassified and released to the public, many other relevant records remain classified in the interests of national security. Even the documents I could not obtain, therefore, prove that UFOs represent a vital national security issue.

Parts of this book were included in a report I submitted to the U.S. Congress in the hope of getting a congressional hearing into two little-known military operations codenamed Project Moondust and Operation Blue Fly. You will learn in the chapters to come that the U.S. Air Force even lies to members of Congress to conceal the activities of these two missions. Recently, the Air Force has rehashed these old lies into a report called "The Roswell Report: Case Closed," conveniently timed to discredit the fiftieth anniversary commemoration of the Roswell Incident and, by extension, the belief in UFOs by the majority of the American people.

The Air Force states that no records exist—classified or otherwise—on these two missions. However, since December 13, 1994, the Air Force has not been able to explain why it still has classified documents on these nonexistent missions. (I can prove that they have at least such documents.)

On December 13, 1994, I filed an appeal for the release of the above-mentioned documents. As of June 1997, the U.S. Air Force has not responded to that appeal. They have yet to figure out a way to deny these records without admitting they knowingly lied to members of Congress about the existence of these same records.

As for me, I continue my search for answers to some of the many questions raised by the one truth I have come to know about all of this: MAN IS NOT ALONE IN THE UNIVERSE.

Clifford E. Stone
Roswell, New Mexico
June 25, 1997

Author's Introduction

The U.S. government, and specifically the Air Force's Declassification and Review team, released a preemptive attack on the 50th anniversary UFO activities in Roswell, NM on June 24, 1997. The Air Force timed the release of this previously prepared 1996 report in an attempt to strategically deflate what they fear is becoming a popular movement. If the government claims that UFOs don't exist, why should it bother to put the time and effort into creating a 231-page report that unsuccessfully attempts to disprove every bit of evidence supporting the likely scenario of a UFO crash at Roswell in 1947?

The "powers that be" in the Miltary and Intelligence agencies are not concerned with more Heaven's Gate-type victims, as they claim, but rather in quieting the charges of deliberate government cover-ups. So how did they deflect all that mistrust of the government? With another elaborate cover-up, of course.

"The Roswell Report: Case Closed" includes such convenient government explanations as balloon-dropped life-sized crash dummies, badly burned crash victims of a military plane, and round hovercraft, all of which must have been mistaken by hysterical civilian witnesses for alien corpses and flying saucers.

To briefly counter this clumsy deflection:

1) All the crucial sightings of dead, live and burnt aliens describe child-sized figures that were half the size of the government's crash dummies explanation. (The dummies were generally 5'4" to 6' in height.)

2) The datings of the Air Force incidents and exercises are *up to a decade after* Roswell's reports.

3) The slow hovercraft never got higher than several yards, while flying saucer reports by civilians ***and scores of Air Force pilots*** involve high altitude crafts with unprecedented speed and maneuverability.

Most important, all these attempts to "close" the Roswell case don't put a dent in the many decades of UFO data collected by civilians and military personnel—like myself—around the nation and world.

For many years now the American Intelligence Community has been charged with the alleged cover-up of UFO data and not releasing this information to the American public or to members of Congress. Worse than not releasing UFO information to Congress is the verifiable fact that the Intelligence Community regularly lied to Congress about this sensitive subject.

Congress serves as a weighty factor in our democracy's system of checks and balances. Our various Congressional Committees serve as significant watchdogs to oversee those government agencies entrusted with our national security. Because we have our U.S. Constitution and our Congress, we cannot have an all-powerful secret police force that is typical of autocratic nations. While various types of information must be protected (classified) and kept from the public in the legitimate interests of national security, we can never accept that such information may not be discreetly revealed to the relevant Congressional Committee in a closed executive session.

Over the years, Congress has held many open hearings on the subject of UFOs, but there has never been any mention of any executive sessions held on the subject. These hearings have always been based on the Project Blue Book files, with no mention of any other agencies' involvement. This is more than deceptive, since, as you shall read further on, Blue Book was conceived as a government smoke screen to keep the American people from the true depth and scope of its government's work on UFOs.

With the enactment of the Freedom of Information Act (FOIA) of 1974, documents were released alluding to more than a passive interest by the U.S. Military in UFOs. Exposing Blue Book for what it was, it then became clear that many government agencies other than merely the U.S. Air Force were involved in UFO work. These released documents were once classified and heavily censored. Also, there are strong indications that the Congress was never made aware of the existence of these documents, their classified nature, or even the other agencies' involvement in UFOs.

Not restricted to dramatic UFO events in the 1940s and '50s, many of these documents deal with incidents in the 1970s, '80s, and '90s. They also reflect a concern that UFOs are something real, not theoretical, and that they involve technologies far in advance of our own. If this is truly the case, it means that the Air Force purposely lied to the U.S. Congress and the American people about UFOs' not existing and not posing a potential threat to our security.

I am of the firm belief that Congress should hold a hearing on the involvement of various U.S. intelligence agencies concerning their past and present interest in UFO phenomena. This would not be held to determine, for example, whether discovered UFO debris is composed of materials not found on Earth, but rather to determine if information is being illegally kept from Congress and how we may guarantee that proper channels of information are kept open in the future.

The primary intent of this book is not to provide the American people and members of Congress with reliable documentary evidence of interplanetary spacecraft, even though I would question the reasoning powers of a reader who continues to doubt the reality of UFOs, given the documentation provided in this book. My main goal is to prove through documented evidence that many different government agencies are involved in serious UFO investigation—even though this fact has been expressly denied. In addition, this documentation clearly shows a high level of national security interest, often classified Top Secret; yet the appropriate members of Congress are not being kept informed about significant developments relating to the safety of their constituents.

Our nation is not a banana republic ruled by a military hunta. Congress must protect its own rights and powers, as well as the trust placed in it by the American People. Our senators and representatives who serve in the most significant committees overseeing our national security must be well informed of the activities of all other governmental agencies. We don't want our leaders to find out crucial information about UFOs when it is too late to do anything about this phenomenon. I'm a proud career soldier, but I don't want information of global importance restricted only to military minds.

While it is understood that some information must be kept out of the public domain to insure legitimate national security interests, no justification must ever be accepted for the exclusion of the U.S. Congress.

Planet Earth may have some serious decisions to make in the immediate future, and we'd better make sure that the leaders of its mightiest nation are involved in a manner that befits our world's primary democracy.

Don't just read this book. Act on it. Make certain that the *few* (key officers in the Air Force) do not bully the *many* (our nation's leading senators and congressmen), creating convenient Warren Commission-type reports, such as "The Roswell Report: Case Closed," keeping us in the dark when our skies are lit with vital questions.

Introduction by Stanton T. Friedman

As a nuclear physicist with a strong interest in flying saucers since 1958, and having lectured on the subject "Flying Saucers ARE Real" since 1967 in fifty states, nine provinces, and ten foreign countries, I have met many people who claim to be "UFO researchers." Often what they mean is that they are interested enough to have read several books, many newspaper articles, and seen a few TV shows on the topic. Usually, they have not seriously researched all aspects of the UFO phenomena and have made no objective attempt to evaluate what they have read, seen, or heard.

Most so-called documentaries on television are very short on documentation and very long on unsubstantiated opinion. Both sides of the discussion often seem to take the same approach: "Don't bother me with the facts; my mind is made up." Debunkers also seem to abide by another rule: "What the public doesn't know, I won't tell them."

Sergeant Clifford Stone (ret.), in contrast, has spent an enormous amount of time, energy, and money documenting the role of the U.S. Government with regard to the investigation of flying saucers. Stone risked his military career by trying to dig out the facts about highly classified USAF projects such as Moon Dust and Blue Fly. This truly dedicated researcher demonstrates throughout this book that the government agencies responding to his requests often gave contradictory testimonies. There clearly seems to be a certain level of incompetence demonstrated by those who responded to his requests under the Freedom of Information Act. More importantly, there is also a definite indication of intentional misrepresentation by official government agency spokesmen.

It is outrageous to consider that a serving member of our military forces is not entitled to exercise his rights as an U.S. citizen. To the best of my knowledge, the Freedom of Information Act and the various executive orders used to control dissemination, storage, declassification, etc., of government documents are not restricted to either civilians or the military. As an officer in the Armed Forces, SFC Stone's primary duty was the defense of this nation's citizens. Wasn't it his duty to do everything possible to inform members of Congress about visitations by aliens? This is especially important in view of the constant stance of government agencies who maintain that UFOs are not a threat to the security of the United States.

Sergeant Stone provides ample evidence of the willingness of our government agencies to lie to its citizens. Even worse, he demonstrates that lies are even told to members of Congress, such as New Mexico's Senator Bingaman.

As Clifford Stone lives in Roswell, New Mexico, he presents a number of documents dealing with the USAF's efforts to cover up the facts about the recovery of a crashed flying saucer near Roswell in July 1947. He includes the complete texts of the report on Roswell by the General Accounting Office and of the Air Force's attempted preemptive strike against the Federal Accounting Office. He points out the Air Force's deceptive and nasty tricks, such as leaving out a crucial phrase from an FBI memo and conveniently omitting a very important quote from the Roswell newspaper article about the crash.

Stone also documents from military sources the fact that Project Blue Book was not even the primary USAF group that concurred with investigation of flying saucer reports. The author describes and criticizes the activities of the other agencies that censored out reports which were often too sensitive to be included in Project Blue Book.

I am frequently surprised that most citizens aren't aware that the U.S. Government maintains special teams ready to retrieve components from interstellar objects that inadvertently crash on Earth. The vast technical resources we maintain for surveillance of the upper and lower atmosphere, including radar and orbital satellites, can trace those rare pieces of Russian (or old Soviet) payloads falling out of orbit and/or crashed flying saucers.

There is obviously a need to provide security as quickly as possible when a highly classified aircraft, such as a U2, goes down. When a strategic airborne or ground-based vehicle has an accident, a prompt response is necessary to seal off the crash site and to report the significant details. To recover classified components such as code books, sophisticated electronics, or nuclear warheads are obvious necessities.

It should further be noted that our primary sky and ground surveillance systems all produce data that is immediately classified rather that distributed to the news media. Every year our military and intelligence community agencies, such as the National Security Agency, the National Reconnaissance Office, the Air Defense Command, and others all detect and monitor flights of "uncorrelated targets."

Here is a very provocative quote from a November 1961 USAF document from this book:

> These three peacetime projects [UFO Investigation, Project Moon Dust, and Project Blue Fly] all involved a potential for employment of qualified field intelligence personnel on a quick-reaction basis to recover or perform field exploitation of unidentified flying objects, or known Soviet Bloc aerospace vehicles, weapons systems and or residual components of technical equipment.

This quote certainly indicates that there would have been standard procedures written for personnel carrying out these functions such as are described in "Majestic-12 Group Special Operations Manual SOM1-1 Extraterrestrial Entities and Technology, Recovery and Disposal," which is revealed in my own book, *Top Secret/Majic*.

Sergeant Stone is to be congratulated for providing a multitude of government documents, many never before published, for interested readers to evaluate on their own. Some will be especially shocking for those who think U.S. government agencies cannot keep secrets. The unwillingness of agencies to often say no more than "we cannot confirm nor deny" gives a clear indication of high security, and certainly establishes the sensitive nature of matters relating to Unidentified Flying Objects...long after the closure of Project Blue Book.

One can only hope that major media organizations such as the *New York Times*, the *Washington Post, Sixty Minutes, 20/20*, etc., will read this book and expend the same energy blowing the lid off this cosmic Watergate as they did concerning the political one.

The newly established (1995) Executive Order 12958 makes it much more difficult for military and intelligence organizations to keep any files classified for more than twenty-five years. The rule now is "If in doubt, declassify," rather than the reverse philosophy from our Cold War days. The government should justify maintaining Top Secret security status for UFO documents after so many years.

With the efforts of hard working, truth-seeking researchers like Clifford Stone, there is a chance that the truth will finally come out by the end of the century.

Stanton T. Friedman
June 19, 1997
Fredericton, NB, Canada

CHAPTER ONE

UFOs: The Beginning

On June 24, 1947, a civilian pilot flying over the Cascade Mountains in Washington State, spotted nine disc-shaped craft flying in formation at a high rate of speed. He radioed in his sightings, fully expecting a rational explanation about some sort of Air Force experiment. No explanation was forthcoming, and the eerie craft remained unidentified. Thus began the modern era of flying saucers.

For the next twenty-two years, the United States Air Force would study flying saucer reports. Later, the Air Force would change the term "flying saucer" to "Unidentified Flying Object (UFO)" as a more appropriate definition of the phenomena. These official studies were to be conducted under such names as Project Sign, Project Grudgeand, finally, Project Blue Book.

On December 17, 1969, the Secretary of the Air Force announced the termination of Project Blue Book, the AirForce's official and only publicly known program forinvestigating Unidentified Flying Objects (UFOs).

The decision to discontinue UFO investigationswas based on an evaluation of a report prepared by theUniversity of Colorado entitled, "Scientific Study of Unidentified Flying Objects," a review of the University of Colorado's report by the National Academy of Sciences, past UFO studies, and the Air Force's two decades of experience investigating UFO reports.

As a result of these investigations and studies, and of experience gained from investigating UFO reports since 1948, the conclusions of Project Blue Book were the following:

(1) no UFO reported, investigated, and evaluated by the Air Force has ever given any indication of threat to our national security,
(2) there has been no evidence submitted to or discovered by the Air Force that sightings categorized as "unidentified" represented technological developments or principles beyond the range of present day scientific knowledge, and
(3) there has been no evidence indicating that sightings categorized as "unidentified" are extraterrestrial vehicles.

In 1977, President Carter asked the National Aeronautics and Space Administration (NASA) to look into the possibility of resuming UFO investigations. After alleging to have studied all the facts available, NASA decided that nothing would be gained by further investigation. The Air Force agreed with that decision, stating that if firm evidence was found justifying further investigation, an appropriate agency would be directed to undertake the effort.

With the termination of Project Blue Book, the Air Force regulation establishing and controlling the program for investigating and analyzing UFOs was rescinded. All documentation regarding the former Blue Book investigation was permanently transferred to the National Archives and Records Service in Washington, D.C. where it is available for public review and analysis.

The termination of Project Blue Book, if we are to believe the stated conclusions of the Project itself, should have ended the U.S. Government's involvement and interest in UFOs. But did it? Or did government work with UFOs go underground?

We will investigate this crucial question further, but for now we will focus our analysis on the Air Force's conclusions which brought to an end the U.S. Government's "official" UFO investigative program, Project Blue Book.

For the purpose of this analysis I will limit my comments and references to documents known to have existed prior to the closure of Project Blue Book in 1969. Let's look at those incredible United States Air Force conclusions point by point.

(1) No UFO reported, investigated, and evaluated by the Air Force has ever given any indication of threat to our national security.

To this point I must retort that if an unknown flying object violates the air space of the United States then a potential (and I must stress potential) threat to our security does in fact exist. Who is to say that an object hurtling towards a major American city or defense facility is not carrying thermonuclear weapons from a hostile nation or rogue terrorist organization? Can we slouch back and relax at our radar scanners because we cannot identify the flying objects closing in on us. Should we take comfort that these craft are too fast and maneuverable to be known Soviet fighter jets or scud missiles?

Obviously, our armed forces have the primary role of defending our nation from attack. If scrambling fighter jets proves futile, then we, in my humble opinion, had better do what we can to gather information about such phenomena from scientists, aviators and air force personnel worldwide.

Conclusion number one, in short, is illogical and highly disturbing. After Pearl Harbor, the World Trade Center, Oklahoma City, and reports of unauthorized private sales of nuclear submarines and warheads from the corrupt former Soviet military, one would expect that our armed forces would be less cavalier about America's security.

Now we will look at some of the early government documents to see what they say about the Air Force's first conclusion.

In 1948, the Office of Naval Intelligence and the Directorate of Intelligence of the United States Air Force did a joint study of the UFO phenomena. Air Intelligence Report No. 100-203-79, entitled "Analysis of Flying Object Incidents in the U.S." and dated December 10, 1948, was the end result of that study. It concluded:

> Since the Air Force is responsible for control of the air in the defense of the U.S. it is imperative that all other agencies cooperate in confirming or denying the possibility that these objects have a domestic origin. Otherwise, if it is firmly indicated that there is no domestic explanation, the objects are a threat and warrant more active efforts of identification and interception.
>
> It must be accepted that some type of flying objects have been observed, although their identification and origin are not discernible. In the interest of national defense it would be unwise to overlook the possibility that some of these objects may be of foreign origin. (See doc. 1-17.)

The above report was classified, "TOP SECRET." Also, the Air Force did not intend for the American Public to ever find out about this report. The Air Force even ordered the report's destruction in an official memorandum dated September 25, 1950. The memo stated:

> It is requested that action be taken to destroy all copies of Top Secret Air Intelligence Report Number 100-203-79, subject: "Analysis of Flying Object Incidents in the U.S."

This memo to destroy the report was dated September 25, 1950, and was fortunately lost in a bureaucratic oversight (or, perhaps rescued by some patriotic and concerned officer). The crucial report maintaining the strategic importance of UFO intelligence gathering was thus never destroyed. Through the diligent efforts of Mr. Robert Todd, the document was located and eventually declassified on March 5, 1985.

Again, the importance of this report cannot be overstated. We have official government reportage contradicting the notion that the UFO issue does not impact upon national security. The first conclusion of the government's document is thus highly suspect. We can conclude that our government wants to make the public think that we have discontinued to investigate UFOs, and that the public is supposed to accept the flimsy thinking that UFOs can not pose a security problem.

Where there's smoke there's fire, and where there's a government smoke-screen in the world's most open democracy there is surely a burning conflagration. If the government is lying to us to soothe our nerves, the strategy is backfiring.

On July 26, 1952, the plot thickened. The Air Force issued orders to its interceptor pilots to scramble and shoot down UFOs which refused to land when ordered to do so. Obviously, the unidentified craft were within the pilots' visual and radio range. This was no drunken farmer raving about flying saucers during a full moon. The United States faced its greatest security crisis since World War II, and the enemy was not even known! While our fighters were frustrated in their attempt to get close enough to fire, the shooting orders were rescinded by order of the Commander-in-Chief himself.

Why was the President involved in something as remote and irrelevant as another UFO sighting over some godforsaken wilderness? Because, this time, the UFOs were overflying the White House itself!

The President and military chiefs of staff wisely decided not to engage in combat this unknown force displaying vastly superior aerospace technology. Until forced to fire in self-defense, why start a shooting confrontation when the nation's capital lay directly below? The decision not to act aggressively represented neither cowardice nor lack of interest in the UFOs. Many thousands of lives in the sprawling metropolis below were at stake. Who knew for sure if the very planet's fate may have hung in the balance?

Unfortunately, this same concern for the welfare of the American public may be overextended and misused with regard to the public's right to know. Perhaps the President and military brass that same fateful day in 1952 decided that the American public "did not need to know" what the Air Force pilots and air defense personnel learned about the unimagined power of the UFOs. The gag order may have started as a temporary measure to calm a frightened nation. A half century later, however, we are still forced to obtain our government's military information about UFOs with long and painful ordeals such as the one I have lived through to write this book.

I understand why none of our current history books mark that July day in 1952 as the greatest threat to our nation's capitol since the British invaded in Colonial times. After all, no matter how many fighter planes were involved, no casualties were suffered on either side. Nonetheless, the near confrontation with this unknown threat rocked the nation. July 1952 forever changed the UFO question, no matter how long and hard the nay-sayers have worked to smooth over the incident. The overflights by unidentified craft so alarmed the American public that on July 29, 1952, the Pentagon held the largest press conference since the end of World War Two. The subject: UFOs. (See doc. 1-2.)

This press conference was held in room 3E-869 of the Pentagon at 4:00 P.M. on July 29, 1952. In attendance were Major General Roger M. Ramey, Director of Operations, United States Air Force; Colonel Donald L. Bower, Technical Analysis Division, Air Technical Intelligence Center; Captain Roy L. James, Electronics Branch, Air Technical Intelligence Center; Captain Edward J Ruppelt, Aerial Phenomenon

Branch, Air Technical Intelligence Center; and Mr. Burgoyne L. Griffing, Electronics Branch, Air Technical Intelligence Center.

Of course, this press conference was designed to downplay the public's fears and to allay any security concerns about the inadequacy of our air defenses. These heavy hitters were brought out to practice that great American art of plausible deniability. They tried to explain all of the elaborate and firsthand sightings as misidentifications of known objects and the interaction of unusual weather phenomenon with our defense instrumentation.

Most thinking Americans weren't buying this dog and pony show. We don't call in the President for runaway weather balloons or temporary blips on a radar screen. This wasn't happening within easy bombing range of Walla Walla, Washington, but Washington, DC—the new capital of the Free World. Americans were not as cynical as they would become after Vietnam and the wave of historic assassinations, but even then they were not willing to let the men in the shiny brass buttons overrule our flyboys' testimony in the cockpits. Those Americans who were concerned with bigger things than the pennant race would not allow sightings of this quantity and quality to be conveniently explained away.

It is interesting to note that on the same day as the press conference (July 29, 1952) the FBI was advised, through Major General Samford's Office (Director of Air Intelligence), that it was, "not entirely impossible that the objects sighted may possibly be ships from another planet such as Mars." The FBI was further advised, "that at the present time there is nothing to substantiate this theory, but the possibility is not being overlooked." (See doc. 1-3.) This same message was again relayed to the FBI in a memorandum, dated October 27, 1952, in which Air Intelligence stated, "Air Intelligence still feels flying saucers are optical illusions or atmospheric phenomena, but some Military officials are seriously considering the possibility of interplanetary ships." (See doc. 1-4.)

Of course, before Voyager missions and the Hubble telescope we had all kinds of incorrect theories about artificially dug canals on Mars, but could it be that "some military officials" knew something than the people at Air Intelligence did not know or could not say? The FBI was not in the habit of making fools of itself, and obviously they felt true concern about the possibility of interstellar interference or invasion.

After July 1952, the term "flying saucer" would forever enter our vocabulary. The phenomenon also impacted upon official military policy. Since 1954 an official military directive called Joint Army, Navy, Air Publication 146 (JANAP 146) has required pilots in flight and ships at sea that observe UFOs to report them immediately as a matter of vital national security interest. (See doc. 1-5.) Of course, the justification for this requirement is significant for routine security measures. An enemy bomber or missile might first be reported as an UFO until clarification and identification can be made. Sightings reported under this regulation are known as CIRVIS reports. CIRVIS is the acronym for Communication Instructions For Reporting Vital Intelligence Sightings. While UFO denial has become entrenched in the military, it is significant that this security directive is still in force today. Obviously, the government is still researching UFO sightings as a crucial component of our security gathering information. Any official words to the contrary are just that—contrary words.

CIVRIS reports do not necessarily require top secret security classification. However, anyone leaking information about a CIVRIS report runs the risk of facing a $10,000.00 fine and/or 10 years in prison. This same penalty applies to those who fail to file CIVRIS reports due to a reluctance on the part of Air and Naval personnel to report sightings of UFOs. To quote one Air Force pilot, "If a space ship flew wing-tip to wing-tip formation with me, I would not report it." This attitude, of course, is disconcerting to the U.S. Air Force in that if any unconventional craft existed, its detection would be hampered by the reluctance to report sightings of any unusual aerial objects.

The government can't have it both ways. They want our men and women in the armed forces to report what they see when in uniform, but to withhold information to the civilian world when they see something that is not supposed to exist. It is easy to see how the government's close-mouthed attitude towards UFOs clearly intimidates our military personnel, preventing them from doing their best to defend our sovereign territory, skies and seas.

Let's investigate the operative up close, as this book is all about giving readers a firsthand experience with the government's UFO-related documents. Section III, paragraph 208 states in part:

> Transmission of CIVRIS reports are subject to the U.S. Communications Act of 1934, as amended, and the Canadian Radio Act of 1938, as amended. Any person who violates the provisions of these acts may be liable to prosecution thereunder. These reports contain information affecting the National Defense of the United States and Canada.... This should not be construed as requiring classification of CIVRIS messages.

★★★

The U.S. Air Force's next major, documented encounter with an UFO occurred in the early morning hours of July 17, 1957. A U.S. Air Force RB-47, equipped with electronic countermeasures (ECM Equipment), was followed by an UFO for one and one half hours, covering a distance of more than 700 miles. This object was observed visually by the crew, tracked by ground radar, and detected by the on-board ECM equipment of the RB-47. Once again, the pilots were not following a suspicious phenomenon (that might be an aberrant weather condition or apparatus), the RB-47 was being followed and observed by the UFO. Moreover,

the data could not be dismissed as an optical illusion or faulty instrument reading, because eye witnesses plus two different tracking devices confirmed the same thing.

This airtight case was brought to the attention of the Condon Committee for its consideration in the so-called "Scientific Study of Unidentified Flying Objects." After studying the case, the Condon Committee concluded:

> If a report of this incident, written either by the RB-47 crew or the Wing Intelligence personnel, was submitted in 1957, it apparently is no longer in existence. Moving pictures of radar scope displays and other data said to have been recorded during the incident apparently never existed. Evaluation of the experience must, therefore, rest entirely on the recollection of the crew members ten years after the event. These descriptions are not adequate to allow identification of the phenomenon encountered."

No, I have not inadvertently quoted from the former Soviet newspaper *Pravda* or the KGB. This disinformative double-talk is the voice of the so-called Free World, in a published report that makes the Warren Commission look highly reliable. In fact, later in this book you will be able to examine documents I was able to secure from the Soviet military and decide for yourself which of the Cold War superpoweres was more paranoid about UFOs.

Thanks to the efforts of the late Dr. James E. McDonald, several military records dealing with the above case were uncovered in the files of Air Force Intelligence. This case and others like it, were never meant to be part of the government's Blue Book Files. These cases were classified as, "Vital Intelligence Information," given a classified status and forwarded, as per routine procedure, to the National Security Agency.

On October 20, 1989, the paper file pertaining to four other such cases, involving RB-47 aircraft, was released to me by Air

Force Intelligence. (See doc. 1-6.) This file, which includes the statements of the RB-47 crew members, may be viewed at the end of this chapter. However, the other evidence known to exist remains classified by the National Security Agency at the Top Secret/ UMBRA level to this very day (I will explain the government's classification system in the next chapter). Once again, one can only wonder why this is so if, as the U.S. Air Force states, there is nothing to UFOs, and certainly nothing to be concerned about regarding national security.

The Condon Committee was limited to the Blue Book Files and not made aware of any other files existing within any other government agency. They were limited to only "Secret" material and not aware that much of the information the U.S. Government has on UFOs is classified at the "Top Secret" level and in many cases requires a Special Access Clearance to be viewed. Therefore, the Condon Committee did not get to view the best and most compelling UFO cases with which to base their findings. To be sure, all the Condon Committee received were those cases that the U.S. military and intelligence brass wanted the Committee to view, and those cases that supported the military's point of view.

Compare this backhanded cover-up activity with the straightforwardness of the Operations and Training Order issued by the Inspector General of the Air Force dated December 24, 1959. It stated that, "Unidentified Flying Objects—sometime treated lightly by the press and referred to as "flying saucers"— must be rapidly and accurately identified as serious Air Force business in the ZI (Zone of the Interior)."

A memo from General Carroll Bolender, USAF, dated October 20, 1969, states: "Reports of unidentified flying objects which could affect national security are made in accordance with JANAP 146 or Air Manual 55-11, and are not part of the Blue Book System." (See Report to Congress in Appendix.) Does this mean that some UFO reports (those involving matters of national security) were never part of the Project Blue Book Files and were never meant to be? Unfortunately, it does. We can be further convinced that the government is concealing far more than in reveals about this topic of vital importance.

The Air Force's second conclusion was: "There has been no evidence submitted to or discovered by the Air Force that sightings categorized as 'unidentified' represent technological developments or principles beyond the range of present day scientific knowledge."

Once again we must go to Air Intelligence Report No. 100-203-79, which states: "It is evident from the performance characteristics attributed to the unidentified objects at this time that if they are foreign, they involve efficiencies of performance which have not been realized in any operational airborne device in this country. It would, therefore, be a mistake to analyze the technical aspects of the situation within the limits of our own knowledge of practical developments."

A perusal of many other documents here will confirm that these flying objects are clearly not limited to speeds and maneuvers now available to even our most sophisticated experimental craft. Again, we can only conclude that the government has made a strategic decision (and, I believe, a mistaken one) to be less than truthful with the taxpaying public whom it serves.

Flying disks that registered on radar or, in several celebrated cases, appeared in eyewitness pilot reports, were not the only strange fish in the stratospheric sea. Starting in 1947, the southwestern part of the United States began experiencing a phenomena known as "green fireballs." Disturbing for our national security agencies, most of these sightings were taking place in the State of New Mexico in the vicinity of key military installations. The situation was the cause of such concern that a special secret project was established to investigate the Green Fireball Phenomena. This project was known as Project Twinkle. (See doc. 1-7.) The conclusions of the Project were inconclusive.

The Air Force was trying to "prove" that the Green Fireballs were natural phenomena, yet the final Project Twinkle Report was not able to support such a conclusion. To compound matters, many reputable scientists believed, "that the observed phenomena are man-made."

The final report reflected the security concerns of Dr. Lincoln La Paz. To quote from a key passage, "Dr. La Paz expressed the opinion that the fireballs may be of our own military origin, but if not, they are a matter of serious concern."

In short, Dr. La Paz was stating that the phenomena was "man-made" in the sense that they did not at all resemble meteor showers or any other known natural phenomena. The term "man-made," by the way, did not mean that the production of these flying devices were within the technological range of present-day denizens of our planet. The report's rejection of their preferred conclusion was so upsetting to the Air Force that in 1952, when asked to reclassify the final secret report, they refused to do so, stating:

> The Scientific Advisory Board Secretariat has suggested that this project not be declassified for a variety of reasons, chief among which is that no scientific explanation for any of the "fireballs" and other phenomena was revealed by the report and that some reputable scientists still believe that the observed phenomena are man-made.

If science won't conform to Air Force directives, then damn the science. Any sort of natural cause, no matter how far-fetched, would have been acceptable to the military. After all, if the reported phenomena were man-made and not of American origin, they would have to be secret Soviet intelligence gathering devices. This would mean that the U.S. faced imminent Soviet attack or atomic blackmail. If, despite paranoia about the capabilities of Russian space technologists and their captive East German physicists,

these fiery craft were not Soviet, then who did make them? We had ourselves an interstellar threat that made the designers of Sputnik look like kids with an erector set! The possibilities were, to the U.S. Air Force, just too horrifying to discuss with the excitable American people.

The once Top Secret memo dated November 21, 1950, from a Mr. Wilbert B. Smith, a Canadian Government official and UFO Researcher, to the Controller of Telecommunications states the following:

> I made discreet inquiries through the Canadian Embassy staff in Washington who were able to obtain for me the following information: (a) The matter is the most highly classified subject in the United States Government, rating higher even that the H-Bomb. (b) Flying saucers exist. (c) Their modus operandi is unknown but concentrated effort is being made by a small group headed by Doctor Vannevar Bush. (d) The entire matter is considered by the United States authorities to be of tremendous significance. (See doc. 1-8.)

This once-suppressed document from Ottawa reveals that the Canadians were more interested in harnessing geo-magnetism to create a new technology than concerned about potential security issues. It states:

> The existence of a different technology is borne out by the investigations which are being carried on at the present time in relation to flying saucers.

This was also writen by Wilbert Smith, a Canadian official without the least self-consciousness, fear or surprise concerning UFOs.

Granted, Canada was not dueling the USSR for global supremacy and the "fireballs" were not appearing beside her most sensitive military installations. Nonetheless, the Canadian attitude towards UFOs was refreshingly different. Contact with a superior, probably extraterrestrial technology to them simply meant an epochal opportunity to advance humankind.

Compare this attitude to the third and final conclusion reached by the U.S. Air Force:

> There has been no evidence indicating that sightings categorized as "unidentified" are extraterrestrial vehicles.

In July or August of 1948, the Air Technical Intelligence Center published a Top Secret "Estimate of the Situation." The unmentionable "situation" involved those pesky UFOs. The informed opinion presented in this report was that UFOs were interplanetary. The late General Hoyt S. Vandenberg, then Chief of Staff, felt the report lacked proof. As a result, the report was later declassified only to be immediately destroyed.

Why did the U.S. Air Force, in the person of General Vandenberg, feel that they had to declassify the report before destroying it? No such requirements existed then or now. They could have destroyed it as a classified document, with no need for declassification. To be sure, once a document is declassified, there exist no national security concerns and the contents of the document should be available to the public at large. The Air Force wanted the document to sound unimportant, thus declassified, but without the accessibility of declassification. By ordering the destruction of the document, General Vandenberg was ensuring that the document, with its conclusion that UFOs were, in fact, interplanetary spaceships, would not become public knowledge.

The world, least of all the American Public, was to never know that the U.S. Air Force ever considered planetary defense strategies to face the threat of spaceships, UFOs or flying saucers. You see, if a classified document is ordered destroyed, a classified document record of destruction is created on the destroyed document and one copy is usually retained for historical reference. This is not the case with an unclassified document, and no records are required to be retained on its destruction. So declassification was merely a ploy to keep embarrassing vital information away from the people of the land of the free and the home of the brave.

Project Magnet, a formerly classified 1952 Canadian Government report on UFOs concluded:

> It appears then, that we are faced with a substantial probability of the real existence of extra-terrestrial vehicles, regardless of whether or not they fit into our scheme of things. Such vehicles of necessity must use a technology considerably in advance of what we have. It is therefore submitted that the next step in this investigation should be a substantial effort towards the acquisition of as much as possible of this technology, which would without doubt be of great value to us. (See doc. 1-9.)

As reinforced by the documents provided here, the U.S. Government was too busy telling the general public there was no such thing as UFOs therefore they did not discuss the subject of possible technological progress that could be learned from UFOs. Behind the scenes, they not only believed UFOs were something real, they were also quite concerned about UFOs presenting a national security threat. After all, the only justification the U.S. Government can use for classifying material Secret and Top Secret is national security concerns. Could the difference in attitude between the American and Canadian governments have anything to do with the fact that the self-declared kings of the Free World were not ready to admit to being helplessly inferior to another, albeit unknown, power.

All the documents that we have discussed so far have been documents generated during the existence of the Air Force sponsored UFO investigations. Let us assume for the moment that the U.S. Government believes the basic "official" conclusions of the Air Force investigations. Should it not stand to reason that if the U.S. Government is no longer interested in conducting any "official" investigations into the matter of UFOs, that the intelligence community would not collect intelligence and field data concerning UFOs? Remember, the U.S. Government officially stopped investigating UFOs in December 1969.

But, what if the U.S. Government did not stop having an interest in UFOs in 1969, which is the more likely scenario? Would the information the intelligence community gathers on UFOs need to be classified in the interest of national security? If so, why?

It shall be proven to you in the following chapters of this book that the U.S. Government still does has an interest in UFOs and requires careful collection of data. The fact that these reports are not known to the public should indicate that some national security interest or concern is definitely involved.

Furthermore, most of the material on UFOs the U.S. Government has collected since 1969 is once again classified in the interest of national security. We will also see, from the information that has been released, why UFOs present a potential threat to our national security, and specifically to our national defense infrastructure and capabilities.

★★★

Along with Operation Blue Fly, involving UFO sightings and overflights, you will be hearing about Project Moondust which involved the collection of space debris and other physical evidence that was used in the investigations regarding suspected UFO activity. The typical investigation often took fourteen days and, in some cases, lasted months. The Defense Intelligence Agency (DIA) would direct the U.S. Air Force to appoint a Project Moondust officer to serve as a contact within the area of investigation. After the "mission window" had closed, the assigned Project Moondust officer's duty would be terminated.

I wish to remind the reader that Project Moondust was to deal only with objects of non-U.S. origin or objects of unknown origin. While some of our own "space junk" (such as booster rocket fragments) might have initially come under Moondust investigation, such debris would have been quickly indentified. Space objects of domestic origin, in fact, came under the jurisdiction of NASA rather than the Department of Defense. Moondust was a primary concern of the Department of Defense and not NASA because of the very real foreign intelligence interest in these items.

Whether or not the Canadians were right about potential technological benefits from such investigations, the security (or insecurity) apparatus of the Defense Department overshadowed the NASA scientists at Moondust sites. From its inception, Moondust was in the hands of soldiers rather than scientists. Project Moondust was established for the sole "peacetime mission" of locating, recovering, and delivering "descended foreign space vehicles." This included objects of unknown origin. Also, Moondust involved the gathering of technical intelligence data on the development of the Soviet space programs and their intended purposes. In the charged atmosphere of the Cold War, losing the Space Race was akin to losing any claims to the possible riches of the solar system.

In 1973, the DIA had the State Department inform all of its Embassies and Consular Posts to use the code word "Moondust" when reporting "cases involving the examination of non-U.S. space objects or objects of unknown origin." Based upon the information provided, "the Department of State in conjunction with other interested agencies will determine subsequent action required."

On August 28, 1970, a Soviet satellite (COSMOS 316) broke up upon re-entering the earth's atmosphere and crashed across the American Midwest. Six fragments of this satellite were recovered in Texas,

Oklahoma, and Kansas. We were able to ascertain the origin of the objects through tracking data and by analysis of the fragments themselves. We now had samples of foreign debris to compare with physical evidence that was much more difficult to identify. In brief, earth-made space junk burns up so much on the way down that the remnants are never very large. This is why the proceedings of 1972 Senate hearings on the topic are of special interest, especially the answer to the ninth question that was asked.

The question: "Have any fragments as large as these ever come back to earth from U.S. or other Soviet satellites?"
The answer: "We do not have any record of a NASA fragment or of another Soviet fragment as large as the largest COSMOS 316 fragment surviving re-entry. The largest COSMOS 316 fragment is approximately 4 ft. X 4 ft. and weighs 640 lbs." (See Report to Congress in Appendix.)

Compare those numbers to a once classified DIA document dated August 17, 1967, out of Sudan:

Local press, 17 August, 1967, reported that a satellite, cube shaped, weighing approximately three tons, discovered 3 August, 50 miles from Kutum... Satellite described as made of soft metal, presumably light aluminium, in oblong cubes measuring two inches by one inch tightly fastened together and covered by a silky material. Nationality not identified, as no inscriptions evident on outer surface. Local authorities in El Fasher have photographs and, with difficulty, cut samples.

Could it be that the State Department forgot about the object found in Sudan on August 17, 1967, and the fact it weighed about three tons? Or could it be that the State Department was, in fact, very truthful and that no space fragment of U.S. or Soviet origin had been recovered weighing more than 640 lbs.? If the object recovered in Sudan, weighing three tons, was not from the American or Soviet space program, from which nation or planet did it originate?

Neither NASA, the DIA, nor the State Department are willing to release any other information on the Sudan case. As it is with similar cases, they consider this information to be classified and not releaseable under criteria provided by Executive Order 12356.

When it comes to the Air Force's Operation Blue Fly recovery of such objects, the Air Force swears by Executive Order 12356. When confronted with their own documentation as to the existence of Operation Blue Fly, they still respond that they may neither deny nor confirm the existence or non-existence of any such records under the criteria provided by Executive Order 12356, not even to members of Congress.

It is this kind of resistance that I had to battle in my career-long struggle to uncover what the government really knows about UFOs. At one point I even wrote to my Commander in Chief, President George Bush, to complain about armed forces irregularities. This so upset my superiors that I got slapped into solitary, being confined in a small room of the building I worked in. This was done in an effort to keep me from contacting members of Congress regarding my concerns over the Intelligence Community's withholding of information on UFOs from the Congress. However, during my lunch hours I was able to make those calls that I was "ordered" not to make, and in the evenings I wrote those letters I was "ordered" not to write. I was reinstated to my duties, and three field-grade officers over me were relieved of their duties pending transfers. I have paid a high price for my continued crusade for the truth, as you will learn later in this book.

As you now turn to the documents that pertain to this chapter, please know that every page, every line not crossed out by the military censor, came at a great price. Why am I prepared to pay such prices? Why am I on this strange personal mission? Because I saw an UFO at close range as a child and subsequently dedicated my life to studying UFOs for the Armed Forces of my country. One day the whole truth will be open to us, the regular working people of this world, and all my efforts—and your support—will have been worthwhile.

Doc. 1-1a Air Intelligence Study 203

AIR INTELLIGENCE DIVISION STUDY
(DI/USAF-ONI)

2 6107

ANALYSIS OF FLYING OBJECT INCIDENTS
IN THE UNITED STATES

STUDY NO. 203   10 DECEMBER 1948

Doc. 1-1b Air Intelligence Study 203

Air Intelligence Report No. 100-203-79

ANALYSIS OF FLYING OBJECT INCIDENTS IN THE U. S.

Air Intelligence Division Study No. 203
10 December 1948

Directorate of Intelligence and Office of Naval Intelligence

DISTRIBUTION "C"

Directorate of Intelligence
Headquarters United States Air Force

Office of Naval Intelligence
Navy Department

Washington, D. C.

DECLASSIFIED

Authority AF INA Memo 5/April 85

By _____ NARS Date 3/2/85

~~TOP SECRET~~

ANALYSIS OF FLYING OBJECT INCIDENTS IN THE U. S.

INDEX

~~TOP SECRET~~

TOP SECRET

ANALYSIS OF FLYING OBJECT INCIDENTS IN THE U. S.

SUMMARY AND CONCLUSIONS

PROBLEM

1. TO EXAMINE pattern of tactics of "Flying Saucers" (hereinafter referred to as flying objects) and to develop conclusions as to the possibility of existence.

FACTS AND DISCUSSION

2. A DETAILED discussion of information bearing on the problem as set forth above is attached as Appendix "A". The main points established therein are summarized below.

3. THE FREQUENCY of reported incidents, the similarity in many of the characteristics attributed to the observed objects and the quality of observers considered as a whole, support the contention that some type of flying object has been observed. Approximately 210 incidents have been reported. Among the observers reporting on such incidents are trained and experienced U.S. Weather Bureau personnel, USAF rated officers, experienced civilian pilots, technicians associated with various research projects and technicians employed by commercial airlines.

4. THE POSSIBILITY that reported observations of flying objects over the U.S. were influenced by previous sightings of unidentified phenomena in Europe, particularly over Scandinavia in 1946, and that the observers reporting such incidents may have been interested in obtaining personal publicity have been considered as possible explanations. However, these possibilities seem to be improbable when certain selected reports such as the one from U.S. Weather Bureau at Richmond are examined. During observations of weather balloons at the Richmond Bureau, one well trained observer has sighted strange metallic disks on three occasions and another observer has sighted a similar object on one occasion. The last observation of unidentified objects was in April, 1947. On all four occasions the weather balloon and the unidentified objects were in view through the theodolite. These observations at the Richmond Bureau occurred several months before publicity on the flying saucers appeared in a U.S. newspaper.

5. DESCRIPTIONS OF the flying objects fall into three configuration categories: (1) disk-shaped (2) rough cigar-shaped (3) balls of fire. Varying conditions of visibility and differences in angles at which the objects may have been viewed introduces a possibility that a single type object may have been observed rather than three different types. This possibility is further substantiated by the fact that in the areas where such objects have been observed the ratio of the three general configurations is approximately the same.

6. THEREFORE, IT appears that some object has been seen; however, the identification of that object cannot be readily accomplished on the basis of information reported on each incident. It is possible that the object, or objects, may have been domestically launched devices such as weather balloons, rockets, experimental flying wing aircraft, or celestial phenomena. It is necessary to obtain information on such domestic activity to confirm or deny this possibility. Depending upon the degree with which this may be accomplished, foreign devices must then be considered as a possibility.

7. THE PATTERN of sightings is definable. Sightings have been most intense throughout the states bordering the Atlantic and Pacific coast lines, and the central states of Ohio and Kentucky. A map showing location of sightings is attached as Appendix "B"

~~TOP SECRET~~

8. THE ORIGIN of the devices is not ascertainable. There are two reasonable possibilities:
(1) The objects are domestic devices, and if so, their identification or origin can be established by a survey of all launchings of airborne objects. Domestic flying wing type aircraft observed in various aspects of flight might be responsible for some of the reported flying objects, particularly those described as disks and rough cigar shapes. (See Appendices "C" and "D".) Among those which have been operational in recent years are the XF5U-1 ("Flying Flapjack") developed by Chance-Vaught, the Northrup B-35, and the turbo-jet powered Northrup YB-49. The present existence of any privately developed flying-wing type aircraft has not been determined but one such aircraft, the Arup tailless monoplane, was operational at South Bend, Indiana, prior to 1935. (2) Objects are foreign, and if so, it would seem most logical to consider that they are from a Soviet source. The Soviets possess information on a number of German flying-wing type aircraft such as the Gotha P60A, Junkers EF 130 long-range, high-speed jet bomber and the Horten 229 twin-jet fighter, which particularly resembles some of the description of unidentified flying objects (See Appendix "D"). As early as 1924 Tscheranowsky developed a "Parabola" aircraft, an all wing design, which was the outcome of considerable Soviet experimentation with gliders of the same general form. Soviet aircraft based on such designs might have speeds approaching transsonic speeds attributed to some flying objects or greater over-all performance assuming the successful development of some unusual propulsion device such as atomic energy engine.

9. THAT THE Soviets have a current interest in flying-wing type aircraft is suggested by their utilization of Dr. Guenther Bock who, at the end of World War II, was in charge of the flying-wing program in Germany (See Appendix "A", paragraph 3, page 4). Achievements satisfactory to the U.S.S.R. are indirectly indicated by the personal recognition he is reported to be receiving in the U.S.S.R. Recently it has been reported that the U.S.S.R. is planning to build a fleet of 1,800 Horten flying-wing aircraft. Information of low evaluation has been received stating that a regiment of jet night fighters, Model Horten XIII, is at Kuzmikha, an air base two miles southwest of Irkutsk. Kuzmikha is identified as one of a number of airfields for the protection of an atomic energy plant at Irkutsk. The Horten XIII as developed by Germany was a glider.

10. ASSUMING THAT the objects might eventually be identified as foreign or foreign-sponsored devices, the possible reason for their appearance over the U.S. requires consideration. Several possible explanations appear noteworthy, viz:

    a. To negate U.S. confidence in the atom bomb as the most advanced and decisive weapon in warfare.

    b. To perform photographic reconnaissance missions.

    c. To test U. S. air defenses.

    d. To conduct familiarization flights over U.S. territory.

CONCLUSIONS

11. SINCE the Air Force is responsible for control of the air in the defense of the U.S., it is imperative that all other agencies cooperate in confirming or denying the possibility that these objects have a domestic origin. Otherwise, if it is firmly indicated that there is no domestic explanation, the objects are a threat and warrant more active efforts of identification and interception.

12. IT MUST be accepted that some type of flying objects have been observed, although their identification and origin are not discernable. In the interest of national defense it would be unwise to overlook the possibility that some of these objects may be of foreign origin.

~~TOP SECRET~~

TOP SECRET

APPENDIX "A"

ANALYSIS OF FLYING OBJECT INCIDENTS IN THE U. S.

AND HYPOTHETICAL TACTICS EMPLOYED

1. INTRODUCTION. To formulate the possible tactics of flying objects reported over the U. S. assumes from the outset that firm conclusions have been reached on both the existence and origin of the reported flying objects. The current status of information on such incidents and over-all analysis does not allow substantiation for such conclusions. However, the lack of such firm conclusions points to the necessity for an immediate and sound statistical analysis of every aspect of the situation and does not preclude a concurrent examination of the reported incidents to develop explanations of their possible tactics. The latter will be useful at some future date should the existence and origin of the flying objects be definitely established. Therefore, the following analysis of available information is advanced in order to present evidence on the actual existence of some type flying object and to relate same to tactical purposes for which the objects are possibly designed. The following discussion must be considered a provisional analysis, pending a further detailed analysis of all aspects of the problem.

2. SOME ASPECTS REGARDING FLYING OBJECT INCIDENTS. A cursory examination of evidence on reported incidents has been made and it is possible to cite certain generalities which it appears may be borne out when detailed analyses have been completed.

Among the incidents reported there are many statements by reliable and experienced persons which tend to confirm that flying objects have been seen. The description of such objects seems to fall roughly into three categories: (1) Silver disks or balls, approximating a Horten wing type aircraft; (2) Balls of fire of various colors and intensities; (3) Cigar or pencil-shaped objects similar in appearance to V-2 type rockets in horizontal flight. The numbers of configurations might be further reduced with the following considerations in mind: Silver disks or balls have, for the greater part, been observed in daylight and a number under clear weather conditions with visibility unlimited. In most instances, balls of fire have been observed at night. Cigar, or pencil-shaped objects have been sighted in fewer numbers but with about equal distribution in daylight and at night. A few accounts tell of the disks having a rough cigar-shape when viewed while maneuvering. Some of the disks are described as having luminosity in daylight. It therefore is possible that a single type of object may be involved in all sightings, and differences in description may result from viewing the objects at various angles and under differing conditions of visibility.

The above tends to indicate that some type object has been seen and the possibility exists that the object or objects seen are conventional domestic devices, such as weather balloons, test rockets, or jet-equipped aircraft with pancake or flying wing configurations.

The possibility exists that the reporting of flying objects may have been influenced by earlier reports on similar incidents in Scandinavia and Central Europe. The publication in newspaper of details on such incidents, both foreign and domestic, may have induced some of the description provided in reported domestic incidents. However, one of the earliest reported sightings in the U.S. was the one observed by U.S. Weather Bureau personnel in April 1947, at Richmond, Virginia, and on the basis of this one report it appears that the disks are not balloons. It would seem that this sighting was not influenced by the reports of foreign incidents, the newspaper accounts of domestic incidents, nor by misidentification of a conventional object.

TOP SECRET

Although reported domestic incidents are widely scattered throughout the U.S., frequency of sighting and number of observers per sighting assumes a definable pattern. There is a large concentration of sightings along the Eastern Seaboard; another large concentration throughout the Western Coast states, and a few sightings in the Middle West. Distribution of incidents by configuration of object and description of maneuverability is approximately equal in each of these areas and this is believed to further substantiate the possibility that one type of object might have been observed in different aspects of flight.

If sightings are induced by rumor, it seems unusual that more incidents have not been reported from the areas with high concentration of population. Reports from such areas would also have greater facility in channeling either to newspaper or official reporting agencies. For the most part, sightings have been made in fairly open country where there are few restrictions to visibility, which may indicate that obstructed vision has reduced sightings in built-up areas.

It therefore seems that some type of flying object has been observed; the identification of its origin requires the completion of other analyses.

3. POSSIBLE ORIGIN OF UNUSUAL FLYING OBJECTS. Provided, upon the completion of analyses, it is indicated that some or all of the reported flying objects over the U.S. are of foreign origin, the objects could from a logical viewpoint, be considered Soviet. It is evident from the performance characteristics attributed to the unidentified objects at this time that if they are foreign, they involve efficiencies of performance which have not been realized in any operational airborne device in this country. It would, therefore, be a mistake to analyze the technical aspects of the situation within the limits of our own knowledge of practical developments. It is more desirable to consider then the outer limits of possible Soviet developments and objectives in attempting to formulate some idea of the tactics which might be involved.

First of all, the scientific objectives of the U.S.S.R. have been stated many times and indicated in many forms. The most clearcut statement of this objective is probably the one contained in the preamble to the Fourth Five-year Plan (1946-1950) which states that the objective of Soviet science is to overtake and surpass the scientific and technical developments of the capitalist nations. It apparently would be an impossible task for the Soviet Union to accomplish such an objective by proceeding step-by-step along the same lines of development already achieved in the capitalist nations. This would mean that it would be necessary to rapidly proceed through each phase of aeronautical development that has already been accomplished in this country, and this probably would never have any prospects of accelerating Soviet development beyond any point reached by the U.S. The obvious answer to accomplish their objective of not only overtaking, but surpassing the capitalist countries would be a scientific shortcut. This possibility is not so remote when examined on the basis of our knowledge of the current situation in the U.S.S.R. Provided Soviet emphasis was given to the most promising and advanced ideas acquired from Germany in 1945 and the work aided by German scientists, the possibility of catching up and possibly surpassing other nations in technical developments becomes more realistic. It becomes even more realistic if the Soviets have shown a tendency to concentrate on certain developments which have still not received a maximum of priority in our own programs.

It is known that the U.S.S.R. has since 1945 enlisted the services of Dr. Guenther Bock, a German who headed all development of low aspect ratio (flying wing) type aircraft in Germany. Dr. Bock is believed to be the top German scientist in charge at TSAGI and TSIAM which are "Air Materiel Command" type organizations in the U.S.S.R. Further, it is believed that Dr. Bock has made available all German plans for flying wing type aircraft to the Soviets. Among the designs considered by the Germans and possibly exploited by the U.S.S.R., are jet-propelled, flying wing type aircraft whose configuration would be similar to descriptions of certain objects reported flying over the U.S. The estimated speeds of such aircraft are within range of the lower limits of speed attributed to flying objects over the U.S. It is not impossible that emphasis on surpassing foreign developments has led to unusual progress in fuels and propulsion by the U.S.S.R. In connection with possible advancements in the field of fuels and propulsion, it should be observed that

TOP SECRET

the Russian oil situation (regardless of estimated oil reserves) is quite different from that in the U.S. For example, U.S. oil industry is prepared to turn out tremendous quantities of highly frac- tionated petroleum products, while the U.S.S.R. cannot reasonably approach such capabilities. This consideration dictates different solutions on fuels for propulsion in the two countries and in turn, dictates the direction taken in development of jet motors or the use of other propulsive devices. We must therefore, arrive at the conclusion that any Soviet device which may have made its appearance over the U.S. as described, would possess unusual performance characteristics which, in all probability, would include unusual range. The possibility that they could have been launched at fairly close range should not be discarded.

4. POSSIBLE REASONS OR TACTICS FOR THE USE OF SOVIET UNCONVENTIONAL AIRCRAFT OVER THE U.S. Predicated on all the foregoing assumptions, Soviet unconventional aircraft may have been flown over the U.S. for one, all, or a combination of the following reasons:

a. TO NEGATE U.S. CONFIDENCE IN ATOM BOMB AS THE MOST ADVANCED AND DECISIVE WEAPON. If the objects have been used in a propaganda sense, it would be reasonable to assume that the Soviets would choose first to frighten pro-American nations in Europe with the appearance of a radically new weapon to counteract the ability of the U.S. to obtain full propaganda effective- ness with the atom bomb. It will be remembered that strange objects first appeared over the Scandinavian countries in 1946. The objects observed there had unusual range and unusual per- formance characteristics. As this demonstration over the Scandinavian countries occurred the U.S. was making a vigorous campaign for the economic and political alignment of these nations with other pro-American Western European nations. When these incidents subsided, strange flying objects began to be observed at an increasing rate over the U.S. The conclusion on this point is that flying objects may have been used to frighten both European nations and the U.S. by the appear- ance of a new device, and that failure to identify such a Soviet object would give them invaluable indication that U.S. development is far behind that of the Soviets. Except for this indication, it is believed that the use of the objects to promote fear has been worthless in that the U.S. public has tended to characterize these incidents entirely as hallucinations by "crack pots", misidentification of conventional objects, or that they represent a secret American project which should not be pub- licized. Any fear that might result from Soviet use will come only by a discovery that the objects have been Soviet aircraft and that they involve radical developments which are in advance of our own accomplishments.

b. FOR PHOTOGRAPHIC RECONNAISSANCE. It is possible that the Soviets have employed the flying objects for the collection of photographic intelligence or the mapping of certain areas in the U.S. The evasive action employed by all objects sighted indicates not so much an attempt to avoid being sighted, as an attempt to prevent disclosure of the exact type of flying craft and its mission. The sighting of objects over the U.S. has been most intense in Eastern and Western Coastal States. In addition, sightings of flying objects have been made near Oak Ridge, Tenn., Las Cruces, N. M., and in the general area of the Hanford Works in Oregon. Generally, sightings have not been made over what we consider strategic industrial areas. The reason for this might be either that the flying objects have been observed only enroute to or from missions over these more concentrated strategic areas, or that the Soviets obtained sufficient information during their World War II liaison with U.S. industry to satisfy their intelligence requirements and have a more active requirement for information on industries and areas which were not available to them during World War II con- tacts. This is of interest in connection with the sightings near Oak Ridge, Las Cruces, and in the general area of the Hanford Works since these establishments were not, and are not, accessible to Soviet collectors of photographic intelligence.

c. TEST OF U. S. DEFENSES. It is possible that the use of Soviet flying objects over the U.S. is intended only to determine the ability of the U.S. defenses to spot foreign aircraft. This would be of extreme importance to the U.S.S.R. in the event that a one-way all-out attack of Soviet strate- gic bombers is planned. Ability to operate over the U.S. uninhibited at a time when the U. S. is supposedly re-arming and putting great stress on defenses would provide valuable information on which to base estimates for probability of success in bombing strategic objectives in the U. S.

TOP SECRET

~~TOP SECRET~~

d. FAMILIARIZATION FLIGHTS OVER U.S. TERRITORY. This possible reason is perhaps the most improbable. It is assumed that, should this purpose be involved, other purposes are probably also accomplished in its execution. Provided the U.S.S.R. has unusually high performance aircraft they might find it advantageous to familiarize themselves with the topography of the U.S. in anticipation of future combat missions to strategic targets.

5. CONCLUSION. The conclusion that some type of flying object has been observed over the U.S. seems to be substantiated. It is not known at this time whether these observations are misidentifications of domestically launched devices, natural phenomena, or foreign unconventional aircraft. It is, therefore, impossible to make any reliable explanation for their appearance over the U.S. or the tactics which they may employ if the objects observed include any foreign developments in aeronautical fields. It is likewise impossible at this time to contain discussions of possible performance characteristics or tactics within limits of practical reason, if for no other reason than the fact that proof of the existence of a foreign development of this type would necessarily introduce considerations of new principals and means not yet considered practical possibilities in our own research and development.

~~CONFIDENTIAL~~

APPENDIX "B"

REPORTED SIGHTINGS OF FLYING OBJECTS

AS OF 1 AUGUST 1948

~~TOP SECRET~~

~~SECRET~~

APPENDIX "C"

SELECTED REPORTS OF FLYING OBJECT INCIDENTS

1. A NUMBER of reports on unidentified flying objects come from observers who, because of their technical background and experience do not appear to be influenced by unfounded sensationalism nor inclined to report explainable phenomena as new types of airborne devices. Some of the details of their reports are presented in this appendix, along with those from possibly less reliable sources who have reported evidence which is of such a nature that it cannot be entirely ignored.

2. DESCRIPTIONS OF significant incidents, arranged chronologically, follow:

a. During April 1947, two employees of the Weather Bureau Station at Richmond, Virginia reported seeing a strange metallic disk on three occasions through the theodolite while making PIBAL observations. One observation was at 15,000 feet when a disk was followed for 15 seconds. The disk appeared metallic, shaped something like an ellipse with a flat bottom and a round top. It appeared below the balloon and was much larger in size. The disk appeared to be moving rather rapidly, although it was impossible to estimate its speed. The other observations were made at 27,000 feet in like manner.

b. The following month, ███████████ a field engineer for Radio Corporation of America, reported a disk flying near his home in Oklahoma City, Oklahoma. The object was thought to be at an altitude between 10,000 feet and 18,000 feet, and was moving toward the north at a high rate of speed, leaving no trailing effects.

c. While flying at 10,000 feet on a course of 300 degrees, 30 miles northwest of Lake Meade, Nevada, an Air Force lieutenant reported seeing five or six white circular objects in close formation and traveling at an estimated speed of 285 miles per hour. This sighting occurred on 28 June 1947.

d. The following day a party of three, two of them scientists, were motoring along Highway 17 toward the White Sand, New Mexico, V-2 firing grounds and reported seeing a large disk or sphere moving horizontally at a high speed and an estimated altitude of 10,000 feet. It was of uniform shape and had no protruding surfaces such as wings. The object was in sight for about 60 seconds before it disappeared to the northeast. The three observers agreed on the details of the sighting except that one thought he had seen vapor trails.

e. On 7 July 1947, five Portland, Oregon police officers reported varying numbers of disks flying over different parts of the city. All observations were made within a minute or two of 1305 hours.

f. On the same day, ███████████ of Phoenix, Arizona allegedly saw a disk circling his locality during sunset and took two photographs. The resulting pictures (page 9) show a disk-like object with a round front and a square tail in plan form. These photographs have been examined by experts who state they are true photographic images and do not appear to be imperfection in the emulsion or imperfections in the lens. (See Figs. 1, 2, 3 and 4.)

~~SECRET~~

~~SECRET~~

ORIGINAL PHOTOGRAPHS BY MR. ▆▆▆▆▆

~~SECRET~~

g. On 10 July 1947, Mr. ▆▆▆▆ a Pan-American Airways mechanic reported a circular object flying at high velocity, paralleling the earth's surface and leaving a trail which appeared as a "burning up" of the cloud formation. The sighting occurred near Harmon Field, Newfoundland. Two other persons also saw the trail which remained in the sky for about an hour and was photographed by another PAA employee. The resulting photographs support Mr. Woodruff's observation as far as the sky cleavage is concerned. (See Figs. 5 and 6.)

Fig. 6

h. On 29 July 1947, ▆▆▆▆▆▆▆ while flying near Tacoma, Washington, reported a formation of flying objects. His sketch of their shape corresponds closely to that shown in the photographs made by Mr. ▆▆▆. On the same day, two U. S. Air Force pilots at Hamilton Field reported two flying disks trailing a P-80, following it toward Oakland, California.

i. On 4 August 1947, the pilot and co-pilot of a DC-3, flying for one Al Jones, near Bethel, Alaska, reported a flying disk larger than their aircraft. This disk crossed their path at about 1,000 feet and they turned to give chase. The DC-3 was flying at 170 mph, but the disk flew out of sight in four minutes.

j. On 12 November 1947, two flying disks trailing jet-like streams of fire were reportedly sighted from the bridge of the tanker Ticonderoga, according to the second officer. The Ticonderoga was 20 miles off the Oregon shore. This officer said the disks were in sight 45 seconds, moving at a speed estimated at 700-900 mph, curving in a long, low arc.

~~SECRET~~

~~SECRET~~

k. On 7 January 1948, a National Guard pilot was killed while attempting to chase an unidentified object up to 30,000 feet.. While it is presumed that this pilot suffered anoxia, resulting in his crash, his last message to the tower was, "it appears to be metallic object....of tremendous size....directly ahead and slightly above....I am trying to close for a better book."

l. On 5 April 1948, three trained balloon observers from the Geophysics Laboratory Section, Watson Laboratories, N.J. reported seeing a round, indistinct object in the vicinity of Hollman Air Force Base, New Mexico. It was very high and fast, and appeared to execute violent maneuvers at high speed. The object was under observation for approximately 30 seconds and disappeared suddenly.

m. A yellow or light colored sphere, 25 to 40 feet in diameter was reported by Lt. Comdr. Marcus L. Lowe, USN, just south of Anacostia Naval Air Station, D.C., while he was flying on 30 April 1948. It was moving at a speed of approximately 100 miles per hour at an altitude of about 4,500 feet. Although winds aloft were from the north-northwest, its course was to the north.

n. On 1 July 1948, twelve disks were reported over the Rapid City Air Base by Major Hammer. These disks were oval-shaped, about 100 feet long, flying at a speed estimated to be in excess of 500 mph. Descending from 10,000 feet, these disks made a 30-degree to 40-degree climbing turn accelerating very rapidly until out of sight.

o. On 17 July 1948, a report from Kirtland Air Force Base describes a sighting in the vicinity of San Acacia, New Mexico, of seven unidentified objects flying in a "J" formation at an estimated height of 20,000 feet above the terrain. The formation varied from "J" to "L" to circle after passing the zenith. Flashes from the objects were observed after passing 30 degrees beyond the zenith, but there was no smoke or vapor trail. If the reported altitude is correct the speed was estimated at 1,500 miles per hour, according to the report.

p. Other sightings of lights and trails, rather than disks, have been reported, viz:
(1) On 12 September 1947, the pilot and co-pilot of a Pan American aircraft, en route from Midway to Honolulu, saw a blue-white light approaching, changing to twin reddish glows upon withdrawal. The pilot estimated the speed of the light at about 1,000 knots.

(2) On 15 June 1948, Mr. ███████ territory manager for the B.F. Goodrich Company, observed a reddish glow with a jet exhaust in the vicinity of Miles City, Montana. This glowing light made no sound, traveled about twice the speed of a conventional aircraft and flew from noth to south several times in a wide arc, finally disappearing over the horizon.

q. During the early morning of 25 July 1948, two Eastern Airlines pilots reported having seen a huge flying craft similar to a V-2 pass their aircraft in flight. (See Figs. 7 and 8.) The attached drawings made by these two observers very closely resemble a flying object reported to have been seen on 20 July 1948, by ███████ chief investigator of Court of Damage Inquiry, and his daughter at Arnham, Netherlands. This object appeared to be a wingless aircraft having two decks. The craft, sighted four times through scattered clouds and unlimited visibility, was traveling at high speed at a high altitude. A sound similar to that made by a V-2 was reported.

r. An object, similar in shape to the one in the preceding incident was reported by an experienced American newspaper reporter about 25 kilometers northeast of Moscow on 3 August 1948. A Russian acquaintance identified it as a rigid airship but the reporter disagrees because it flew at a high, but not excessive speed.

s. On 1 October 1948 at approximately 2030 hours the pilot of a F-51 aircraft, 2nd Lt. George F. Gorman (North Dakota Air National Guard), flying near Fargo, North Dakota, sighted an intermittent white light about 3,000 feet below his 4,500 feet cruising altitude. The pilot pursued the light which appeared to then take evasive tactics. The object or light out-turned, out-speeded, and out-climbed the F-51 in every instance during the attempt to intercept. The pilot lost contact 27

~~SECRET~~

Doc. 1-1q Air Intelligence Study 203

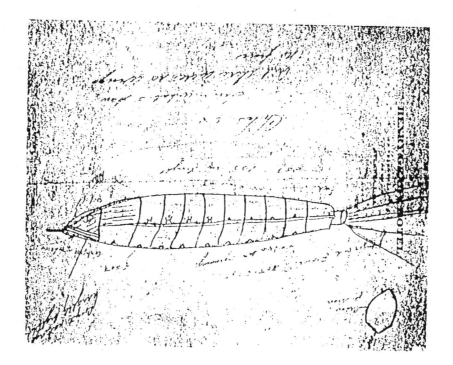

Doc. 1-1r Air Intelligence Study 203

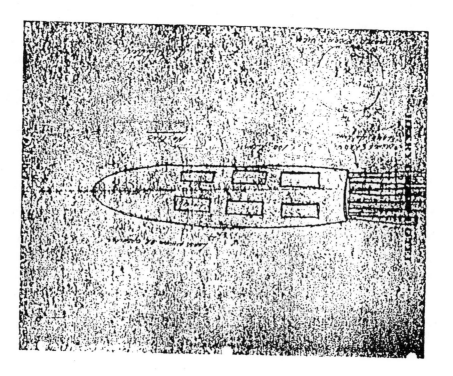

minutes after the initial sighting. The same light was observed by three other witnesses from the ground: Mr. ██████████, Air Traffic Controller, Mr. ██████████ Assistant Traffic Controller, and Dr. ██████████, Oculist. A comparison of all testimony revealed that one object was sighted and that it consisted only of a small round ball of clear white light with no apparent shape attached. It was about 6 to 8 inches in diamter. At times it traveled faster than the F-51 and performed maneuvers in an evasive manner. When first sighted the ball of light was traveling at an estimated 250 miles per hour. Under this condition, the light was not continuous but blinked off and on. At high performance the white light was continuous. Subsequent investigation eliminated the possibility that this incident may have been another aircraft or a meteorological balloon.

t. On 18 November 1948 at approximately 2145 hours, three reserve pilots, 2nd Lt. Kenwood W. Jackson, 2nd Lt. Glen L. Stalker, and 2nd Lt. Henry G. Combs, flying near Andrews Field, Maryland, encountered an unidentified flying object. When first sighted, it appeared to be lighted and flying at about 1,700 feet. Three or four passes were made in an attempt to identify it. The pilot of the aircraft stated that while diving his aircraft at approximately 240 miles per hour, the object would climb vertically and then would drop below the aircraft from behind and continue to circle. On the last pass, the landing light was switched on and momentarily a dull gray glow from the object was observed. Lt. Combs stated he maintained contact for about ten minutes with the object flying between the lights of Washington, D. C. and his aircraft. All that could be observed was an oblong ball with one light, no wings and no exhaust flame. It finally made a very tight turn and headed toward the east coast at an estimated 500 to 600 miles per hour. At the same time Staff Sergeant John J. Kushner observed from the ground an unusual object in the air over Andrews Field. He stated that it was not very high and that it did not look like an aircraft.

3. REPORTS OF radar intercepts point to unusual air activity which may be related to flying objects.
    a. On 1 July 1947, a GCA radar at Hokkaido, Japan picked up an unidentified target at 16 miles, with a speed in excess of 500 mph. This target split into two targets, each estimated to be larger than a P-51.

    b. On 16 September 1947, an MEW radar at Fukuoka, Japan, picked up a target at 89 miles and trailed it to 19 miles, where it faded. Speed was 840-900 mph. The speed measurement, made by a good crew through a 70-mile track, is believed accurate.

4. Investigations conducted by Headquarters, Air Materiel Command, have definitely established the identification of 18 of approximately 210 so-called flying saucers which have been reported. Approximately nine per cent of the total number of incidents are, therefore, eliminated from further specific consideration. Among those incidents positively explained, three were hoaxes, two were from unreliable witnesses. In the remaining 13 eliminated incidents, objects were actually seen but investigation has shown that they were celestial bodies or phenomena, meteorological and carnival balloons, and airborne cosmic ray experimental equipment. The following examples are presented for comparison of the information reported by witnesses and true identification of the object involved:
    a. On 22 July 1948, Captain Henry Glover (Ordnance Reserve) and his wife observed at Van Nuys, California, an object which they were unable to positively identify. Object at first appeared to be round and looked like a weather balloon at about 2,000 feet but there was no characteristic bobbing. The wind was blowing on the ground but the object was quite steady. During the time it was under observation, about an hour, it traveled through a vertical arc of about twenty-five (25°) degrees or more. The observer concluded that it was not a celestial body. It has a bluish luminescence and as the sun set, the object's color gradually changed to orange at dusk and ceased to be illuminated almost instantaneously. The outline was clear and the air was clear with visibility unlimited. The object traveled from the east to the west.

This object was determined by investigation to have been a balloon carrying cosmic ray equipment.

SECRET

b. On 19 August 1948, at approximately 1050 hours an unidentified flying object was visible from the ground at Godman Air Force Base, Kentucky. This object was estimated to be at about 30,000 to 40,000 feet altitude, spherical in shape, bright silver color and gave a bright reflection from the sun. An F-51 was dispatched from Standiford Air Force Base, Kentucky, to observe the object. During observation from the ground, there was no change in the elevation of the object and it seemed to be moving southwest from Godman Air Force Base. The F-51 which was flying over Godman AFB at an altitude of 30,000 to 35,000 feet reported that it was unable to locate the object although it was still visible from the ground with the naked eye. Azimuth and elevation readings were taken by theodolite every minute and the path of the object was charted.

The object was determined to be the planet Venus by Mr. Moore, the head astronomer at the University of Louisville, Louisville, Kentucky. It is believed that earlier incidents at Godman Field (reference paragraph 2k, page 12, Appendix "C") may also have been observations of the planet Venus.

5. AMONG THOSE incidents still not positively explained, reported observations differ to some extent, but three general categories of sightings emerge -- the flying disk, the ball of fire and the large jet rocket. Interesting observations that were noted are:
   a. Most of the objects are a thin disk, round on top and flat on the bottom. The front half of the disk is often circular, sweeping back to a square tail across the full width.

   b. A high rate of climb as well as the apparent ability to remain motionless or hover for a considerable length of time is indicated.

   c. Reported sizes have varied from that of a 25-cent piece to 250 feet in diameter, and from the size of a pursuit plane to the bulk of six B-29 airplanes.

   d. Speeds have been estimated throughout the entire range from very slow or hovering to supersonic.

   e. Sounds and visual trails are not normally associated with the sightings.

SECRET

~~CONFIDENTIAL~~

APPENDIX "D"

FLYING WING TYPE AIRCRAFT

1. AERONAUTICAL ENGINEERS in several countries have been engaged for some time in the design, construction, and flight of flying wing type aircraft. The study of flying objects requires, at least, a brief examination of proposed and existing unconventional aircraft whose configurations, when seen by the uninitiated, could lead to reports of strange flying devices. A description of some of the more significant types by country follows.

2. GERMANY. At the end of World War II, German aircraft designers had numerous projects under way concerning tailless aircraft which conceivably could be mistaken for "Flying Saucers" or disc-like objects. It is not clear just what the Soviets are doing in the way of developing these projects but it is considered that German studies on tailless, delta-wing, and related configurations are available to the U.S.S.R.

    a. ARADO NIGHT AND BAD WEATHER FIGHTER, PROJECT I. This is a tailless, low-wing monoplane with swept-back wing of large root chord and having a long, narrow fuselage.

Span	60.3 feet
Length	42.5 feet
Power Plant	2 HeS 011 turbo jet units
Max. Speed (sea level)	441 mph
Max. Speed (29,500 feet)	503 mph

    b. ARADO E 581-4. A high-wing tailless single-seater with a single jet unit mounted in the fuselage. Fin and rudder units are mounted on the wing midway between fuselage and wing tip at the trailing edge.

Span	29.3 feet
Length	18.4 feet
Power Plant	1 HeS 011 turbo jet unit
Max. Speed (sea level)	--
Max. Speed (service ceiling)	--

    c. GOTHA P 60 A. This was the first of the P 60 series of jet fighters. It is a flying wing type and, since the pilot and observer lie prone, there is no projecting canopy, thus permitting a particularly clean design. The jet units are mounted at the rear of the center section, one above and one below.

Span	40 feet 8 1/2 in.
Wing Area	504 square feet
Power Plant	2 BMW 003 turbo jet units
Max. Speed (23,000 feet)	596 miles per hour

    d. HEINKEL P 1080. This is a single-seat fighter with a sharply swept-back wing, resembling a flying wing type, but having a single fin and rudder with no tail plane.

Span	29.2 feet
Wing Area	218 square feet

No performance estimates are available.

~~CONFIDENTIAL~~

CONFIDENTIAL

e. JUNKERS EF 130. Of the flying wing type, this project was established as a long-range, high-speed jet bomber.

Span	78.8 feet
Wing Area	1290 square feet
Power Plant	4 HeS 011 turbo jet units
Max. Speed	620 miles per hour
Range	3700 miles

f. ME 329. This is a tailless mid-wing monoplane driven by two pusher propellers with the engines centrally located in the wings on each side of the stubby rounded fuselage.

Span	56 feet
Length	25.4 feet
Max. Speed	455-465 miles per hour
Power Plant	2 DB 603 reciprocating engines

g. HORTEN WING. The closest resemblance to the estimated configuration of "Flying Disks" is represented by the Horten Wing aircraft. Work on the Horten 229, a twin jet fighter, had progressed to the final stages at the end of World War II. Its prototype, a Horten glider, successfully soared to an altitude of 14,200 feet as early as 1938, proving the soundness of this design. (Figs. 1, 2 and 3)

Doc. 1-1w Air Intelligence Study 203

CONFIDENTIAL

Photograph is illegible.

Doc. 1-1x Air Intelligence Study 203

CONFIDENTIAL

Photograph is illegible.

Doc. 1-1y Air Intelligence Study 203

CONFIDENTIAL

3. GREAT BRITAIN.

a. THE ARMSTRONG WHITWORTH. The AW 52 G, a glider, and the AW 52, a twin-jet airplane, are British designs of tailless aircraft. The vertical stabilizers are located at the tips of the swept-back wing. (Figs. 4 and 5) Data on the AW 52 appear below.

Span	90 feet
Length	37 feet
Max. Speed (sea level)	435 knots
Max. Speed (20,000 feet)	435 knots
Max. Speed (36,000 feet)	417 knots
Range	1300 nautical miles
Power Plant	2 Nene II turbo jet units

Photograph is illegible.

~~CONFIDENTIAL~~

Photograph is illegible.

~~CONFIDENTIAL~~

4. UNITED STATES.
   a. NORTHROP B-35. This is a flying wing type aircraft, powered by four reciprocating engines and has a wing span of 172 feet and a length of only 53 feet. (See Fig. 6)

Photograph is illegible.

~~CONFIDENTIAL~~

   b. NORTHROP YB 49. Powered by eight turbo-jet engines, this airplane is the jet-propelled version of the Northrop Flying Wing (B 35). (See Fig. 7)

~~CONFIDENTIAL~~

   c. CHANCE-VAUGHT XF5U-1. Developed by Chance-Vaught Aircraft, this radical design promises the reality of high and low speed performance. Powered by two R-2000-2 engines, the airplane will have a speed range of from 40 to 425 miles per hour. (See Fig. 8)

Photograph is illegible.

~~CONFIDENTIAL~~

   d. ARUP TAILLESS MONOPLANE. Jane's "All the World's Aircraft" (1935 edition) describes this airplane as "a two-seat machine with a 70 h.p. LeBlond engine.... This has a high aspect ratio wing with straight leading-edge and built in nacelle...." In plan form, the wing is almost semi-circular.

   An Air Force film, "Aeronautical Oddities", shows this airplane in flight at South Bend, Indiana and in some attitudes appears identical to the photograph included in Appendix "C" as Figure 4. Although it is believed that the ARUP Manufacturing Co. is no longer in existence, it is possible that later models of this or similar U.S. civil aircraft may have been observed.

Span	22 feet
Length	19 feet
Power Plant	1 LeBlond engine
Max. Speed	86 miles per hour

5. ALTHOUGH APPENDIX "D" is not intended to explain conclusively the phenomenc of "Flying Saucers" the possibility of unconventional type aircraft being the cause of flying disk eports must not be overlooked.

Photograph is illegible.

DECLASSIFIED PER EXECUTIVE ORDER 12356, Section 3.3, *NND 841508*

By *W G Lewis*   MARS, Date   *Jan 29, 1985.*

312.11 Declassification

CONFIDENTIAL

313.6   Records Destruction of

FROM: AFOIV-TC

350.05 T/O & AF

TO: CG, Alaskan Air Command,   11 Aug 1950

1st Ind

SUBJECT: "Downgrading of Air Intelligence Report No. 100-203-79"

1. Subject document, for which your Command requests downgrading action, contains info and speculation on the "flying saucer" situation which have never been released or intimated publicly by the Air Force.

FILED UNDER: 319.1 Air Intelligence Division Studies

DECLASSIFIED PER EXECUTIVE ORDER 12356, Section 3.3, *NND 841508*

By *W G Lewis*   MARS, Date   *Jan 29, 1985.*

000.9 Flying Discs

NFIDENTIAL

319.1   Air Intelligence Division Stud

25 Sept 1950

FROM: Dept of the Air Force Hqs U.S. Air Force

TO: See below

Ltr

SUBJECT: Destruction of Air Intelligence Report Number 100-203-79

1. It is requested that action be taken to destroy all copies of Top Secret Air Intelligence Report Number 100-203-79, subject, "Analysis of Flying Object Incidents in the U.S.," dtd 10 Dec 1948.

*   *   *

FILED UNDER: 313.6 Records, Destruction of *17 Oct 50*

CONFIDENTIAL

...distribution)

DEPARTMENT OF DEFENSE

MINUTES OF PRESS CONFERENCE HELD BY

MAJOR GENERAL JOHN A. SAMFORD

DIRECTOR OF INTELLIGENCE, U. S. AIR FORCE

29 July 1952 - 4:00 p. m. - Room 3E-869, The Pentagon

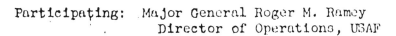

Participating: Major General Roger M. Ramey
Director of Operations, USAF

Colonel Donald L. Bower, Technical Analysis
Division, Air Technical Intelligence Center

Captain Roy L. James, Electronics Branch,
Air Technical Intelligence Center

Captain Edward J. Ruppelt, Aerial Phenomenon
Branch, Air Technical Intelligence Center

Mr. Burgoyne L. Griffing, Electronics Branch,
Air Technical Intelligence Center

MR. SCHOOLEY: Ladies and gentlemen, let me remind
the military that, while they are welcome here, this is a
press conference and let's be sure that the press is all
seated before the conference begins.

Let me introduce General Samford, Air Force Director
of Intelligence, and General Ramey, Director of Operations.
General Samford.

MAJOR GENERAL SAMFORD: I think the plan is to have
very brief opening remarks and then ask for such questions as
you may want to put to us for discussion and answer. In so
far as opening remarks is concerned, I just want to state our
reason for concern about this.

The Air Force feels a very definite obligation to
identify and analyze things that happen in the air that may
have in them menace to the United States and, because of that
feeling of obligation and our pursuit of that interest, since
1947, we have an activity that was known one time as Project
Saucer and now, as part of another more stable and integrated
organization, have undertaken to analyze between a thousand

and two thousand reports dealing with this area. And out of that mass of reports that we've received we've been able to take things which were originally unidentified and dispose of them to our satisfaction in terms of bulk where we came to the conclusion that these things were either friendly aircraft erroneously recognized or reported, hoaxes, quite a few of those, electronic and meteorological phenomena of one sort or another, light aberrations, and many other things.

However, there have remained a percentage of this total, in the order of twenty per cent of the reports, that have come from credible observers of relatively incredible things. And because of these things not being possible for us to move along and associate with the kind of things that we've found can be associated with the bulk of these reports, we keep on being concerned about them.

However, I'd like to say that the difficulty with disposing of these reports is largely based upon the lack of any standard measurement or any ability to measure these things which have been reported briefly by some, more elaborately by others, but with no measuring devices that can convert the thing or the idea or the phenomenon into something that becomes manageable as material for any kind of analysis that we know. We take some of these things and we try to get the best professional advice, if we can, from them, about them, and we're in much the same position of trying to bring to the good honest workmen of science a piece of material that has no utility because it doesn't have the kind of measurements on it that he can use. And, as a consequence, he has to reject these things and say, "Until you can bring me something more substantial than that, I can't make any progress."

So our need, really, is to get the measurement value on these and, in the interim, lacking sufficient measure of these things to make them amenable to real analysis, we have to say that our real interest in this project is not one of intellectual curiosity but is in trying to establish and appraise the possibility of a menace to the United States. And we can say, as of now, that there has been no pattern that reveals anything remotely like purpose or remotely like consistency that we can in any way associate with any menace to the United States.

Now, we do want to continue in the interests of intellectual curiosity or the contributions to be made to scientific measurements, but our main interest is going to

have to continue in the problem of seeing whether the things
have possibility of hurt to the United States, and our present
dilemma of lack of measurement that can be turned to analysis
and a complete lack of pattern in any of these things which
gives any clue to possible purpose or possible use, leaves us
in some dilemma as to what we can do about this remaining twenty
per cent of unidentified phenomena.

The volume of reporting is related to many things.
We know that reports of this kind go back to Biblical times.
There have been flurries of them in various centuries. 1846
seems to have had a time when there was quite a flurry of reporting of this kind. Our current series of reports goes
back, generally, to 1946 in which things of this kind were
reported in Sweden.

There are many reasons why this volume goes up and
down, but we can't help but believe that, currently, one of the
reasons for volume is that man is doing a great deal more.
There's more man-made activity in the air now than there was,
certainly, in Biblical times or in 1846. In addition to that,
our opportunities to observe have been enhanced greatly.

The difficult part of it, as far as advancing the
program is concerned, is that our ability to measure doesn't
seem to have advanced in any way as well as our opportunity
to observe and the greater recurrence of more disturbing things
of this sort that are actually in existence from man-made air
participation that we know about.

So our present course of action is to continue on this
problem with the best of our ability, giving to it the attention
that we feel it very definitely warrants in terms of identifying
adequately the growing or possible or disappearing, if it turns
out to be that, menace to the United States to give it adequate
attention but not frantic attention.

Now, I think with those opening remarks I could invite
questions. Question, yes, sir?

THE PRESS: Have there been more than one radar sighting
simultaneously -- that is, blips from several stations all concentrating on the same area?

MAJOR GENERAL SAMFORD: You mean in the past?

THE PRESS: Yes, sir.

TO   :   MR. A. H. BELMONT   TE: July 29, 1952

FROM   :   V. P. KEAY

SUBJECT: FLYING SAUCERS

PURPOSE:

To advise at the present time the Air Force has failed to arrive at any satisfactory conclusion in its research regarding numerous reports of flying saucers and flying discs sighted throughout the United States.

DETAILS:

Mr. N. W. Philcox, the Bureau's Air Force Liaison Representative, made arrangements through the office of Major General John A. Samford, Director of Air Intelligence, U.S. Air Force, to receive a briefing from Commander Randall Boyd of the Current Intelligence Branch, Estimates Division, Air Intelligence, regarding the present status of Air Intelligence research into the numerous reports regarding flying saucers and flying discs.

Commander Boyd advised that Air Intelligence has set up at Wright Patterson Air Force Base, Ohio, the Air Technical Intelligence Center which has been established for the purpose of coordinating, correlating and making research into all reports regarding flying saucers and flying discs. He advised that Air Force research has indicated that the sightings of flying saucers goes back several centuries and that the number of sightings reported varies with the amount of publicity. He advised that immediately if publicity appears in newspapers, the number of sightings reported increases considerably and that citizens immediately call in reporting sightings which occurred several months previously. Commander Boyd stated that these reported sightings of flying saucers are placed into three classifications by Air Intelligence:

(1) Those sightings which are reported by citizens who claim they have seen flying saucers from the ground. These sightings vary in description, color and speeds. Very little credence is given to these sightings inasmuch as in most instances they are believed to be imaginative or some explainable object which actually crossed through the sky.

(2) Sightings reported by commercial or military pilots. These sightings are considered more credible

- RECORDED-1 6

NWP:hke

67-23894-281

by the Air Force inasmuch as commercial or military
pilots are experienced in the air and are not
expected to see objects which are entirely imaginative.
In each of these instances, the individual who reports
the sighting is thoroughly interviewed by a representative
of Air Intelligence so that a complete description of
the object sighted can be obtained.

(3) Those sightings which are reported by pilots and
for which there is additional corroboration, such as
recording by radar or sighting from the ground.
Commander Boyd advised that this latter classification
constitutes two or three per cent of the total number
of sightings, but that they are the most credible
reports received and are difficult to explain. Some
of these sightings are originally reported from the
ground, then are observed by pilots in the air and then
are picked up by radar instruments. He stated that in
these instances there is no doubt that these individuals
reporting the sightings actually did see something in
the sky. However, he explained that these objects could
still be natural phenomena and still could be recorded
on radar if there was some electrical disturbance in the
sky.

He stated that the flying saucers are most frequently
observed in areas where there is heavy air traffic, such as
Washington, D.C., and New York City. He advised, however, that
some reports are received from other parts of the country
covering the entire United States and that sightings have also
recently been reported as far distant as Acapulco, Mexico;
Korea and French Morocco. He advised that the sightings
reported in the last classification have never been satisfactorily
explained. He pointed out, however, that it is still possible
that these objects may be a natural phenomenon or some type
of atmospherical disturbance. He advised that it is not
entirely impossible that the objects sighted may possibly be
ships from another planet such as Mars. He advised that at
the present time there is nothing to substantiate this theory
but the possibility is not being overlooked. He stated that
Air Intelligence is fairly certain that these objects are not
ships or missiles from another nation in this world. Commander
Boyd advised that intense research is being carried on presently
by Air Intelligence, and at the present time when credible
reportings of sightings are received, the Air Force is attempting
in each instance to send up jet interceptor planes in order to

obtain a better view of these objects. However, recent attempts
in this regard have indicated that when the pilot in the jet
approaches the object it invariably fades from view.

RECOMMENDATION:

None. The foregoing is for your information.

Office Memorandum • UNITED STATES GOVERNMENT

TO : MR. A. H. BELMONT   DATE: *October 27, 1952*

FROM : V. P. KEAY

SUBJECT: *FLYING SAUCERS*

SYNOPSIS:

Air Intelligence advised of another creditable and unexplainable sighting of flying saucers. Air Intelligence still feels flying saucers are optical illusions or atmospherical phenomena but some Military officials are seriously considering the possibility of interplanetary ships.

BACKGROUND:

You will recall that Air Intelligence has previously kept the Bureau advised regarding developments pertaining to Air Intelligence research on the flying saucer problem. Air Intelligence has previously advised that all research pertaining to this problem is handled by the Air Technical Intelligence Center located at Wright-Patterson Air Force Base, Dayton, Ohio; that approximately 90 per cent of the reported sightings of flying saucers can be discounted as products of the imagination and as explainable objects such as weather balloons, etc., but that a small percentage of extremely creditable sightings have been unexplainable.

DETAILS:

Colonel C. M. Young, Executive Officer to Major General John A. Samford, Director of Intelligence, Air Force, advised on October 23, 1952, that another recent extremely creditable sighting had been reported to Air Intelligence. A Navy photographer, while traveling across the United States in his own car, saw a number of objects in the sky which appeared to be flying saucers. He took approximately thirty-five feet of motion-picture film of these objects. He voluntarily submitted the film to Air Intelligence who had it studied by the Air Technical Intelligence Center. Experts at the Air Technical Intelligence Center have advised that, after careful study, there were as many as twelve to sixteen flying objects recorded on this film; that the possibility of weather balloons, clouds or other explainable objects has been completely ruled out; and that they are at a complete loss to explain this most recent creditable sighting. The Air Technical Intelligence Center experts pointed out that they could not be optical illusions inasmuch as optical illusions could not be recorded on film.

162-83894-323

21   OCT 30 1952

NWP/SJD

67

Memo to Mr. A. H. Belmont   RE: *FLYING SAUCERS*
from V. P. Keay

Colonel Young advised that Air Intelligence still feels that the so-called flying saucers are either optical illusions or atmospherical phenomena. He pointed out, however, that some Military officials are seriously considering the possibility of interplanetary ships.

ACTION:

None. This is for your information.

JANAP 146(D)

CANADIAN - UNITED STATES
COMMUNICATIONS INSTRUCTIONS
FOR REPORTING VITAL
INTELLIGENCE SIGHTINGS
(CIRVIS / MERINT)

JANAP 146 (D)

THE JOINT CHIEFS OF STAFF
MILITARY COMMUNICATIONS - ELECTRONICS BOARD
WASHINGTON 25, D.C.
February 1959

ORIGINAL

(Reverse Blank)

JANAP 146(D)

MILITARY COMMUNICATIONS-ELECTRONICS BOARD
WASHINGTON 25, D.C.

1 February 1959

<u>LETTER OF PROMULGATION TO:</u>

        The Department of the Army
        The Department of the Navy
        The Department of the Air Force

Subject: JANAP 146(D)

1. JANAP 146(D), CANADIAN-UNITED STATES COMMUNICATIONS INSTRUCTIONS FOR REPORTING VITAL INTELLIGENCE SIGHTINGS, is an unclassified non-registered publication, prepared by the US Military Communications-Electronics Board in conjunction with the Canadian JCEC(W), for Joint and Canadian use.

2. JANAP 146(D) supersedes JANAP 146(C), and is effective upon receipt for the U.S. JANAP 146(D) will become effective for the Canadian Forces when directed by the appropriate implementing agency.

3. This publication contains military information and is for official use only.

4. Copies and extracts may be made from this publication in the preparation of official publications.

5. Comments and recommendations concerning this publication should <u>not</u> be addressed to the Military Communications-Electronics Board, but to one of the following, as appropriate:

    a. Chief Signal Officer, U.S. Army.
    b. Chief of Naval Operations (DNC), U.S. Navy.
    c. Director of Communications-Electronics, U.S. Air Force.

  FOR THE CHAIRMAN, MILITARY COMMUNICATIONS-ELECTRONICS BOARD:

JOSEPH BUSH
Colonel, USAF

E. H. FARRELL
Commander, USN

Secretaries

III

ORIGINAL
(Reverse Blank)

LIST OF EFFECTIVE PAGES

Subject Matter	Page Numbers	Change in Effect
Title Page	I (Reverse Blank)	Original
Letter of Promulgation to JANAP 146(D) dated 1 February 1959	III (Reverse Blank)	Original
List of Effective Pages	V (Reverse Blank)	Original
Record of Changes	VII (Reverse Blank)	Original
Table of Contents	IX , X	Original
Text		
Chapter 1	1-1 (Reverse Blank)	Original
Chapter 2	2-1 to 2-9 (Reverse Blank)	Original
Chapter 3	3-1 to 3-8	Original

RECORD OF CHANGES

Identification of Change or Correction and date of same	Date Entered	By whom entered (Signature; rank, grade or rate; name of command)

GENERAL DESCRIPTION AND PURPOSE OF COMMUNICATION
INSTRUCTIONS FOR REPORTING VITAL INTELLIGENCE SIGHTINGS

TABLE OF CONTENTS

IX   ORIGINAL

TABLE OF CONTENTS (Cont'd)

CHAPTER III

MERINT REPORTS

CHAPTER I

GENERAL DESCRIPTION AND PURPOSE OF COMMUNICATION INSTRUCTIONS FOR REPORTING VITAL INTELLIGENCE SIGHTINGS

101. <u>Purpose</u>. - The purpose of this publication is to provide uniform instructions for the peacetime reporting of vital intelligence sightings and to provide communication instructions for the passing of these intelligence reports to appropriate military authorities.

102. Scope. -

a. This publication is limited to the reporting of information of <u>vital importance</u> to the security of the United States of America and Canada and their forces, which in the opinion of the observer, requires very urgent defensive and/or investigative action by the US and/or Canadian Armed Forces.

b. The procedures contained in this publication are provided for:

(1) US and Canadian civil and commercial aircraft.

(2) US and Canadian government and military aircraft other than those operating under separate reporting directives.

(3) US and Canadian merchant vessels operating under US and Canadian registry.

(4) US and Canadian government and military vessels other than those operating under separate reporting directives.

(5) Certain other US and Canadian vessels including fishing vessels.

(6) Military installations receiving reports from civilian or military land based or waterborne observers unless operating under separate reporting directives.

(7) Government and civilian agencies which may initiate reports on receipt of information from land-based, airborne or waterborne observers.

103. Message Identification. -

a. Reports made from airborne and land-based sources will be identified by CIRVIS pronounced <u>SUR VEES</u> as the first word of the text. (Refer Chapter II).

b. Reports made by waterborne sources will be identified by MERINT pronounced as <u>MUR ENT</u> as the first word of the text. (Refer Chapter III).

CHAPTER II

CIRVIS REPORTS

SECTION I - GENERAL

201. **Information to be Reported and When to Report.** -

a. Sightings within the scope of this chapter, as outlined in Article 102b(1), (2), (6) and (7), are to be reported as follows:

(1) While airborne (except over foreign territory - see paragraph 210) and from land based observers. NOTE: Canada and the United States are not considered foreign territory for either country-for the purposes of this publication.

  (a) Hostile or unidentified single aircraft or formations of aircraft which appear to be directed against the United States or Canada or their forces.

  (b) Missiles.

  (c) Unidentified flying objects.

  (d) Hostile or unidentified submarines.

  (e) Hostile or unidentified group or groups of military surface vessels.

  (f) Individual surface vessels, submarines, or aircraft of unconventional design, or engaged in suspicious activity or observed in a location or on a course which may be interpreted.as constituting a threat to the United States, Canada or their forces.

  (g) Any unexplained or unusual activity which may indicate a possible attack against or through Canada or the United States, including the presence of any unidentified or other suspicious ground parties in the Polar region or other remote or sparsely populated areas.

(2) Upon landing.

  (a) Reports which for any reason could not be transmitted while airborne.

  (b) Unlisted airfields or facilities, weather stations, or air navigation aids.

  (c) Post-landing reports.

SECTION II - PROCEDURES

202. <u>General.</u> - Communications procedures to be employed will be basically those prescribed for the communications system or service used. Continuing efforts will be made by an aircraft originating a CIRVIS report to insure that each CIRVIS message is received by an appropriate station.

203. <u>Precedence (priority or transmission).</u> -

a. To avoid delays by aircraft in rendering a CIRVIS report to a ground facility, the word "CIRVIS" spoken three (3) times will be employed, preceding the call, to clear the frequency(ies) over all other communications, except DISTRESS, URGENCY and SAFETY, to insure its expeditious handling.

b. Should instances occur, when use of the above procedure fails to clear the frequency(ies) over all other communications in progress except as provided for in 203a, the International Urgency Signal "XXX" transmitted three (3) times or "PAN" spoken three (3) times will be employed to facilitate disposition of the message to the receiving facility.

c. The following precedence will be employed in the transmission of all CIRVIS reports, as appropriate, commensurate with the communications facilities used:

Tabulation

Circuit clearance	CIRVIS CIRVIS CIRVIS
International Urgency Signal (alternate)	XXX XXX XXX or PAN PAN PAN
Military precedence	Y or Emergency
Commercial class of service Indicator	RAPID US GOVT for US Government activities or RUSH for Canadian Government activities (to be used only when refiled with commercial companies)

204. <u>Contents of CIRVIS Reports.</u> -

a. Airborne CIRVIS reports will be similar to routine aircraft position reports transmitted by either radiotelephone or radiotelegraph. The appropriate procedures to be employed will be those applicable to communications facilities utilized. The reports should contain the following information, when appropriate, in the order listed:

(1) CIRVIS Report.

(2) Identification of reporting aircraft or observer as appropriate.

(3) Object sighted. Give brief description of the sighting which should contain the following items as appropriate.

    (a) Number of aircraft, vessels, missiles, submarines, etc.

    (b) Category of object, general description, e.g., size, shape, type of propulsion, etc.

(4) The position of the object. This can be indicated by any of the following methods:

    (a) Latitude and Longitude.

    (b) Over a radio fix.

    (c) True bearing and distance from a radio fix.

    (d) Over a well-known or well-defined geographic point.

    (e) True bearing and distance from a geographic point.

(5) Date and time of sighting (GMT).

(6) Altitude of object.

(7) Direction of travel of object.

(8) Speed of object.

(9) Any observed identification, insignia, or other significant information. Every reasonable effort should be made to positively identify the object sighted.

Example of an air/ground radiotelephone transmission:

(Aircraft)   CIRVIS CIRVIS CIRVIS - KINDLEY THIS IS AIR FORCE TWO FIVE NINE THREE SIX - CIRVIS REPORT - OVER

(Aeronautical Station)   AIR FORCE TWO FIVE NINE THREE SIX THIS IS KINDLEY - GO AHEAD

(Aircraft)   EMERGENCY - CIRVIS REPORT - AIR FORCE TWO FIVE NINE THREE SIX SIGHTED FORMATION OF SIX JET BOMBERS - CONFIGURATION IS SWEPT WING WITH EIGHT JET ENGINES - TWO HUNDRED MILES EAST OF BERMUDA ON THIRTEEN MAY AT ONE THREE FIVE ZERO ZULU - ALTITUDE THREE FIVE THOUSAND - HEADING TWO SEVEN ZERO DEGREES - NO MARKINGS OBSERVED - OVER

(Aeronautical Station)   KINDLEY - ROGER - OUT

    ORIGINAL

Example of an air/ground radiotelegraph transmission:

(Aircraft)   XXX XXX XXX AFA3 DE A48207

(Aeronautical
   Station)   A48207 DE AFA3 K

(Aircraft)   Y - CIRVIS REPORT. A48207 SIGHTED ....ETC.

(Aeronautical
   Station)   A48207 DE AFAR AR

205.   Additional CIRVIS Reports. -

       a.   Additional reports should be made if more information
becomes available concerning a previously sighted object. These reports should contain a reference to the original report sufficient
to identify them with the original sighting.

Example of an air/ground radiotelephone transmission:

(Aircraft)   CIRVIS CIRVIS CIRVIS - KINDLEY THIS IS AIR FORCE TWO
                   FIVE NINE THREE SIX - CIRVIS REPORT - OVER

(Aeronautical
   Station)   AIR FORCE TWO FIVE NINE THREE SIX - THIS IS KINDLEY -
                   GO AHEAD

(Aircraft)   EMERGENCY - THE SIX JET BOMBERS PREVIOUSLY REPORTED AT
                   ONE THREE FIVE ZERO ZULU BY AIR FORCE TWO FIVE NINE
                   THREE SIX ARE NOW ONE THREE ZERO MILES WEST OF BERMUDA
                   AT ONE FOUR THREE FIVE ZULU - HEADING TWO SEVEN ZERO
                   DEGREES - OVER

(Aeronautical
   Station)   KINDLEY - ROGER - OUT

NOTE: In radiotelegraph transmission, the same procedures would apply
       as prescribed in para 204.

       b.   Cancellation reports should be made in the event a previously
reported sighting is positively identified as friendly or that it has
been erroneously reported. Such reports should be transmitted as a
brief message cancelling the previous report(s).

Example of an air/ground radiotelephone transmission:

(Aircraft)   CIRVIS CIRVIS CIRVIS - KINDLEY THIS IS AIR FORCE TWO
                   FIVE NINE THREE SIX - CIRVIS REPORT - OVER

(Aeronautical
   Station)   AIR FORCE TWO FIVE NINE THREE SIX THIS IS KINDLEY -
                   GO AHEAD

(Aircraft)   EMERGENCY - CANCEL CIRVIS REPORT OF ONE THREE FIVE ZERO
ZULU BY AIR FORCE TWO FIVE NINE THREE SIX - SIX JET
BOMBERS POSITIVELY IDENTIFIED AS AIR FORCE BRAVO FORTY
SEVENS AT ONE FOUR FOUR SIX ZULU - OVER

(Aeronautical
  Station)   KINDLEY - ROGER - OUT

NOTE: In radiotelegraph transmission, the same procedures would apply
as prescribed in para 204.

     c. A post-landing report is desired immediately after landing
by CINCNORAD or RCAF-ADC to amplify the airborne report(s). This may
be filed with either the military or civil communications facility
located at the place of landing. If the landing is not made in Canadian or United States territory the report should be made to the nearest
Canadian or United States military or diplomatic representative in that
area. The post-landing report will refer to the airborne report(s) and,
in addition, contain a brief resume of weather conditions at the time
of sighting(s), verification of the sighting(s) by other personnel and
any other information deemed appropriate. If the sighting was identified
as friendly, and a report so stating was filed while airborne, no post-
landing report is required.

          (1) If no airborne report was made as a result of inability
to reach a communications station or due to being over
foreign territory (see paragraph 210), the post-landing
report will contain all the information available concerning the sighting.

206. Addressing. -

     a. Aircraft. - It is imperative that all CIRVIS reports reach
the appropriate military commands as quickly as possible. The reports,
therefore, shall be transmitted as soon as possible after the sighting.
Ground procedures have been established to handle CIRVIS reports by
either military or civil facilities, so the same procedures as those
now established and in use by pilots for air traffic control shall be
followed. When contact by civil or military pilots cannot be established with any ground communications station, maximum effort shall be
made to relay the CIRVIS reports via other aircraft with which communication is possible.

          (1) Post-landing reports should be addressed to CINCNORAD,
Ent AFB, Colorado Springs, Colorado, or RCAF-ADC, St.
Hubert, Quebec whichever is the more convenient if the
sighting occurred within or adjacent to the North
American continent. Whichever of these headquarters
receives the report will immediately notify the other
and also all other addressees of the original report(s).
If the sighting(s) occurred in other areas, the post-
landing report should be made to the nearest US or

434415 O - 59 - 2

Canadian military or diplomatic representative in that area who will forward the report as prescribed in subparagraph 206b(1)(a).

b. Communications Stations. - Communications stations (to include any civil or military facility such as control tower, naval shore radio station, approach control, ARTC center, or any other communications facility) receiving CIRVIS reports will immediately after receipting process the report as follows (for <u>additional</u> instructions to US military fixed communications stations in Canada, Alaska and Greenland see subparagraph (2) (a) below):

    (1) US military fixed communications stations will multiple-address the CIRVIS report to the following address designations:

      (a) For sightings in overseas areas - reports will be forwarded to:

         <u>1</u>. Addressees as prescribed by Area Commanders. (Normally, these addressees are the operating service commands concerned).

         <u>2</u>. Commander-in-Chief, North American Air Defense Command (CINNORAD), Ent AFB, Colorado Springs, Colorado.

         <u>3</u>. Chief of Staff, United States Air Force (COFS, USAF), Washington, D. C.

    (2) Canadian and US military fixed communications stations will multiple address the CIRVIS reports to the following address designations:

      (a) For sightings within or adjacent to the North American continent, reports will be forwarded to:

         <u>1</u>. Commander of the nearest joint air defense division, command or group.

         <u>2</u>. CINCNORAD, Ent AFB, Colorado Springs, Colorado.

         <u>3</u>. Appropriate Sea Frontier Command:

            <u>a</u>. Commander, Western Sea Frontier (COMWEST-SEAFRON), San Francisco, California.

            <u>b</u>. Commander, Eastern Sea Frontier (COMEAST-SEAFRON), New York, N. Y.

         <u>4</u>. Chief of Staff, United States Air Force (COFS, USAF) Washington, D. C.

ORIGINAL

<u>5</u>. RCAF Air Defense Command (CANAIRDEF) St. Hubert, Montreal, Canada.

<u>6</u>. Appropriate Flag Officer in Command:

<u>a</u>. Canadian Flag Officer, Atlantic Coast, (CANFLAGLANT), Halifax, Nova Scotia.

<u>b</u>. Canadian Flag Officer, Pacific Coast, (CANFLAGPAC), Esquimalt, British Columbia.

(3) Civil communications stations will handle CIRVIS reports received from either aircraft or other communications stations as follows:

(a) Air Carrier company stations will pass the CIRVIS report, exactly as received, to the nearest CAA or DOT ARTC center in the same manner as air traffic control information.

(b) CAA or DOT communications stations, upon receipt of a CIRVIS report will immediately pass the report to the appropriate ARTC center.

(c) CAA or DOT ARTC Centers. Upon receipt of CIRVIS reports, ARTC centers will forward them immediately to the appropriate military facility as prescribed by agreement with the appropriate military commander.

207. <u>Acceptance of and Responsibility for CIRVIS Reports.</u> -

a. The following activities have responsibilities as follows:

(1) CONCNORAD or RCAF-ADC will review all CIRVIS reports to ascertain that they have been addressed in accordance with paragraph 206 and forward reports to any omitted addressees in the United States and Canada respectively. These headquarters are the normal points of contact between the two countries and are responsible for passing CIRVIS reports of interest, including post-landing reports, to each other.

(2) United States or Canadian military or diplomatic author- ities in receipt of CIRVIS reports that have not been previously forwarded should take the action indicated in paragraph 206 without delay by the most rapid means available.

(3) Chief of Staff, USAF, will disseminate CIRVIS reports to appropriate agencies in the Washington, D. C. area.

(4) RCAF-ADC and the Canadian Flag Officers will be respon- sible for notifying Canadian military headquarters in Ottawa concerning CIRVIS reports.

(5) Sea Frontier Commanders will be responsible for notifying Chief of Naval Operations and appropriate Fleet Commanders concerning CIRVIS reports.

b. Fixed and mobile military communications facilities and military personnel having occasion to handle CIRVIS reports must lend assistance in all cases required in expediting CIRVIS reports. All civilian facilities and personnel are also urged to do so. Maximum effort must be made by all persons handling CIRVIS reports to insure positive immediate delivery.

c. WHEN A STATION RECEIVES A PARTIAL CIRVIS REPORT AND THE REMAINDER IS NOT IMMEDIATELY FORTHCOMING, IT WILL BE RELAYED OR DELIVERED IN THE SAME MANNER AS A COMPLETE REPORT.

SECTION III - SECURITY

208. Military and Civilian. - Transmission of CIRVIS reports are subject to the U. S. Communications Act of 1934, as amended, and the Canadian Radio Act of 1938, as amended. Any person who violates the provisions of these acts may be liable to prosecution thereunder. These reports contain information affecting the National Defense of the United States and Canada. Any person who makes an unauthorized transmission or disclosure of such a report may be liable to prosecution under Title 18 of the US Code, Chapter 37, or the Canadian Official Secrets Act of 1939, as amended. This should not be construed as requiring classification of CIRVIS messages. The purpose is to emphasize the necessity for the handling of such information within official channels only.

SECTION IV - EVALUATION REPORTS

209. Action by Activities. -

a. All investigative measures and evaluation processes instituted by addressees, and by originating authorities where applicable, will be handled in accordance with existing procedures and reported in accordance with these instructions, insuring that appropriate commands as listed in paragraph 206 are kept fully informed of investigative results and evaluations. These evaluations shall be expressed in terms indicating the reported sighting as being Positive, Probable, Possible, or No Threat insofar as being a threat to the security of the United States of America or Canada or their forces, or an explanation of the subject reported when known.

b. The first two words of the text of an evaluation report shall be "CIRVIS EVALUATION" followed by the date-time-group and/or other identification of the CIRVIS report(s) being evaluated.

SECTION V - SPECIAL CONSIDERATIONS

210. <u>Radio Transmission Restrictions</u>. - CIRVIS reports will not be transmitted by radio while over foreign territory, other than Greenland or Iceland, but will be transmitted as soon as practicable upon leaving foreign territorial boundaries. In accordance with special permission from the Danish government, reports may be transmitted while traversing Greenland. Foreign territory includes all territory except international water areas and territory under the jurisdiction of the United States of America and Canada.

SECTION VI - COMMERCIAL CHARGES

211. <u>Charges</u>. -

a. All charges incurred in handling CIRVIS reports through U. S. facilities will be charged to the U. S. Department of the Air Force (accounting symbol "AF"). Insofar as practicable, CIRVIS reports so handled should be forwarded <u>RAPID US GOVT COLLECT</u>.

b. All charges incurred in handling CIRVIS reports through Canadian facilities will be charged to the Royal Canadian Air Force. Insofar as practicable, CIRVIS reports so handled will be forwarded "RUSH COLLECT".

c. Any or all questions of charges will be resolved after traffic has been handled. In no case should CIRVIS reports be delayed because of communication handling charges.

ORIGINAL
(Reverse Blank)

CHAPTER III

MERINT REPORTS

SECTION 1 - GENERAL

301. Information to be Reported and When to Report. -

a. Sightings within the scope of this chapter, as outlined in Article 102b, (3), (4), (5) and (6) are to be reported as follows:

    (1) Immediately (except when within territorial waters of nations other than Canada or the USA as prescribed by International Law).

        (a) Hostile or unidentified single aircraft or formation of aircraft which appear to be directed against Canada or the United States or their forces.

        (b) Missiles.

        (c) Unidentified flying objects.

        (d) Hostile or unidentified submarines.

        (e) Hostile or unidentified group or groups of military surface vessels.

        (f) Individual surface vessels, submarines, or aircraft of unconventional design, or engaged in suspicious activities or observed in an unusual location.

        (g) Any unexplained or unusual activity which may indicate possible attack against or through Canada or the United States, including the presence of any unidentified or other suspicious ground parties in the Polar Region or other remote or sparsely populated areas.

SECTION II - PROCEDURES

302. General. - Communication procedures to be employed will be basically those prescribed for the communications system or services used. Merchant ships will employ normal international commercial communication procedures and utilize existing commercial or military facilities as appropriate. Every effort will be made to obtain an acknowledgment for each MERINT message transmitted. Canadian or U. S. vessels which are manned by military or civil service personnel will use military communication procedure.

ORIGINAL

303. <u>Precedence (priority of transmission)</u>. - Transmission of MERINT reports shall be preceded by the word "MERINT" spoken three times OR by its alternate, the international "Urgency Signal". Additionally, the military precedence of "Emergency" shall be used if the report is addressed to military activities. Governmental precedence of "Rapid U. S. Government" for reports addressed to other U. S. Government activities, or Canadian "Rush", for reports addressed to Canadian Government activities shall be used:

<u>Tabulation</u>

Circuit clearance	MERINT MERINT MERINT
International Urgency Signal (Alternate)	XXX XXX XXX or PAN PAN PAN
Military Precedence	Y or Emergency
Commercial Class of Service Indicator	RAPID US GOVT for US Government activities or RUSH for Canadian Government activities (to be used only when refiled with commercial companies)

304. <u>Contents of MERINT Reports</u>. -

a. MERINT reports should contain the following as applicable in the order listed:

(1) "MERINT" will always be the first word of the text.

(2) Name and call letters of reporting ship.

(3) Object sighted. Give brief description of the sighting which should contain the following items as appropriate:

(a) Number of aircraft, vessels, missiles, submarines, etc.

(b) Category of object, general description, e.g., size, shape, type of propulsion, etc.

(4) Ship's position at time of sightings.

(5) Date and time of sighting (GMT)*

(6) Altitude of object expressed as Low, Medium or High.

(7) Direction of travel of object.

(8) Speed of object.

(9) Any observed identification, insignia, or other significant information. Every reasonable effort should be made to positively identify the object sighted.

(10) Conditions of sea and weather.

* "071430Z" is an example of a complete date-time group (DTG). When broken into component parts (07) is the day of the month, followed by (14) the hour in 24 hour time, followed by (30) the minutes of the hour, followed by (Z) the time zone. "Z" signifies that Greenwich Mean Time has been used in composing the date-time group.

Day of Month   Hour Expressed   Minutes of   Indication that
             in 24 hour time   the hour   GMT is being used

EXAMPLE of a Radiotelephone Transmission:

MERINT MERINT MERINT - WHISKEY ZULU TANGO - THIS IS KILO HOTEL
WHISKEY MIKE - OVER
KILO HOTEL WHISKEY MIKE - THIS IS - WHISKEY ZULU TANGO - OVER
WHISKEY ZULU TANGO - THIS IS - KILO HOTEL WHISKEY MIKE
MERINT SS TUNA KILO HOTEL WHISKEY MIKE SIGHTED FORMATION OF SIX
JET BOMBERS LAT 40N 50E AT 211500Z ALTITUDE MEDIUM HEADING
270 DEGREES TYPE OF AIRCRAFT NOT OBSERVED BEFORE WIND FORCE
3 SEA CALM -
OVER

EXAMPLE of a Radiotelegraph Transmission:

MERINT MERINT MERINT CFH DE KHWM K
KHWM DE CFH K
CFH DE KHWM
"RAPID U S GOVERNMENT" or CANADIAN "RUSH"
MERINT (REMAINDER OF TEXT)
211513Z JONES KHWM
K

305. Additional MERINT Reports. -

   a. Amplifying Reports. -

     (1) When additional information becomes available to any observer and is of importance, it is to be transmitted as a "MERINT AMPLIFY" report.

     (2) Amplifying reports are to be handled in the same way as the original report except that the first two words of the text will be "MERINT AMPLIFY" followed by the date and time of filing of the MERINT report being amplified.

     (3) Amplifying reports on aerial objects normally consist of additional information pertaining to the sighted object's size, shape; description of jet or rocket streams; color, sound; if multiple objects, the number; type; method of propulsion; number of engines; insignia and estimated speed.

(4) Amplifying reports on submarines or surface sightings
normally consist of additional information on the state
of sea and weather, including visibility; actions of
object (course, speed, evasive maneuvers, etc.) identification marks, (flags, signals, numbers, exchange of
communication); closest range at which object observed;
any further remarks, (dived, surfaced, commenced snorkling, stopped snorkling, etc.)

b. Cancallation Reports. -

(1) Cancellation reports should be made in the event a
previously reported sighting is positively identified
as friendly, erroneous or false.

(2) MERINT cancellations are to be handled in the same
manner as the original MERINT report except that the
first two words shall be "MERINT CANCEL" followed by
the date and time of filing of the MERINT report being
cancelled and, in brief, the information on which the
cancellation is based.

c. Delayed Reports. - In the event a MERINT report cannot be
made by radio, the Master is requested to report the details of the
MERINT sightings to the appropriate Canadian or United States military
authorities. If the port of arrival is outside of Canada or USA, the
report is to be made to the nearest Canadian or US military or diplomatic representative in the area. This report should be submitted
immediately upon arrival in port by any available means and should be
in the format prescribed in paragraph 304.

306. Addressing. -

a. Vessels. -

(1) It is imperative that all MERINT reports reach the
appropriate military commands as quickly as possible.
The reports, therefore, shall be transmitted as soon
as possible after the sighting. All Canadian or U.S.
vessels listed under Para 102b, (3), (4), and (5) are
to transmit in plain language all MERINT reports to
the nearest Canadian or U. S. military, government or
commercial radio station, regardless of whether the
vessel is Canadian or U. S. registered.

(2) Naval vessels which intercept MERINT reports from
merchant vessels shall copy the report and immediately
relay EXACTLY AS RECEIVED to the appropriate Canadian
or U. S. Navy-Shore Radio Station with relay instructions.

b. Communications Stations. - Communications Stations (to include any commercial, government or military facility such as coastal marine radio station, telegraph offices, naval or coast guard shore radio station or any other communication facility) receiving MERINT reports will immediately after receipting process the report as follows:

 (1) Canadian or U. S. commercial or government communications stations will handle MERINT reports received from either vessels or other communications stations by immediately forwarding them to a Canadian or U. S. military fixed communication facility as prescribed by agreement with the appropriate military commander.

 (2) U. S. military fixed communications stations will multiple-address the MERINT report to the following address designations:

  (a) For sightings in overseas areas - reports will be forwarded to:

   1. Addressees as prescribed by Area Commanders. (Normally, these addressees are the operating Service commands concerned).

   2. Commander-in-Chief, North American Air Defense Command (CINCNORAD), Ent AFB, Colorado Springs,

   3. Chief of Staff, United States Air Force (COFS, USAF), Washington, D. C.

 (3) Canadian and U. S. military communications stations will multiple-address the MERINT reports to the following address designations:

  (a) For sightings within or adjacent to the North American continent, reports will be forwarded to:

   1. Commander of the nearest joint air defense division, command or group.

   2. CINCNORAD, Ent AFB, Colorado Springs, Colorado.

   3. Appropriate Sea Frontier Command:

    a. Commander, Western Sea Frontier (COMWESTSEAFRON), San Francisco, Calif.

    b. Commander, Eastern Sea Frontier (COMEASTSEAFRON), New York, N. Y.

   4. Chief of Staff, United States Air Force, (COFS USAF), Washington, D. C.

<u>5</u>. RCAF Air Defense Command (CANAIRDEF), St. Hubert, Montreal.

<u>6</u>. Appropriate Flag Officer in Command:

    <u>a</u>. Canadian Flag Officer, Atlantic Coast, (CANFLAGLANT), Halifax, Nova Scotia.

    <u>b</u>. Canadian Flag Officer, Pacific Coast, (CANFLAGPAC), Esquimalt, British Columbia.

307. <u>Acceptance of and Responsibility for MERINT Reports.</u> -

a. The following activities have responsibilities as follows:

(1) CINCNORAD or RCAF-ADC will review all MERINT reports to ascertain that such reports have been addressed in accordance with paragraph 306 and forward reports to any omitted addressees in U. S. and Canada respectively. These headquarters are the normal points of contact between the two countries and are responsible for passing MERINT reports of interest, including delayed reports, to each other.

(2) Canadian or United States military or diplomatic authorities in receipt of MERINT reports will take the action indicated in paragraph 306 without delay by the most rapid means available.

(3) Chief of Staff, USAF, will disseminate MERINT reports to appropriate agencies in the Washington, D. C. area.

(4) RCAF-ADC and the Canadian Flag Officers will be responsible for notifying Canadian military headquarters in Ottawa concerning MERINT reports.

(5) Sea Frontier Commanders will be responsible for notifying Chief of Naval Operations and the appropriate Fleet Commanders concerning MERINT reports.

b. Fixed and mobile military communications facilities and military personnel having occasion to handle MERINT reports must lend assistance in all cases required in expediting MERINT reports. All civilian facilities and personnel are also urged to do so. Maximum effort should be made by all persons handling MERINT reports to insure positive immediate delivery.

c. WHEN A STATION RECEIVES A PARTIAL MERINT REPORT AND THE REMAINDER IS NOT IMMEDIATELY FORTHCOMING, IT WILL BE RELAYED OR DELIVERED IN THE SAME MANNER AS A COMPLETE REPORT:

ORIGINAL

SECTION III - SECURITY

308. **Military and Civilian.** - Transmission of MERINT reports are subject to the Communications Act of 1934, as amended, and the Canadian Radio Act of 1938, as amended. Any person who violates the provisions of these acts may be liable to prosecution thereunder. These reports contain information affecting the National Defense of the United States and Canada. Any person who makes an unauthorized transmission or disclosure of such a report may be liable to prosecution under Title 18 of the US Code, Chapter 37, or the Canadian Official Secrets Act of 1939, as amended. This should not be construed as requiring classification of MERINT messages. The purpose is to emphasize the necessity for the handling of such information within official channels only.

SECTION IV - EVALUATION REPORTS

309. **Action by Activities.** -

    a. All investigative measures and evaluation processes instituted by addressees, and by originating authorities, where applicable, will be handled and reported in accordance with existing procedures, insuring that appropriate commands as listed in paragraph 306 are kept fully informed of investigative results and evaluations. These evaluations shall be expressed in terms indicating the reported sighting as being Positive, Probable, Possible or No Threat insofar as being a threat to the security of the United States of America or Canada or their forces, or an explanation of the subject reported when known.

    b. The first two words of the text of an evaluation report shall be "MERINT EVALUATION" followed by the date-time-group and/or other identification of the MERINT report(s) being evaluated.

SECTION V - SPECIAL CONSIDERATIONS

310. **Radio Transmission Restrictions.** - MERINT reports will not be transmitted by radio other than Canadian or U. S. or international waters.

SECTION VI - COMMERCIAL CHARGES

311. **Charges.** -

    a. All charges incurred in handling MERINT reports through U. S. facilities will be charged to the U. S. Department of the Navy (accounting symbol NAVY). Insofar as practicable, MERINT reports so handled should be forwarded RAPID US GOVT COLLECT.

    b. All charges incurred in handling MERINT reports through facilities will be charged to the Royal Canadian Navy. Insofar

JANAP 146(D)

as practicable, MERINT reports so handled will be forwarded "RUSH COLLECT".

    c. Any or all questions of charges will be resolved after traffic has been handled. In no case should MERINT reports be delayed because of communication handling charges.

DEPARTMENT OF THE AIR FORCE
WASHINGTON DC 20330-1000

OCT 2 0 1989

OFFICE OF THE SECRETARY

Sergeant First Class Clifford E. Stone
HHC, USMCA, WRZ
ATTN: Adj Ofc
APO New York 09801

Dear Sergeant Stone:

We are responding to your August 13, 1989 Freedom of
Information Act request.

We determined portions of the attached documents are exempt
from disclosure because they contained information that, if
disclosed to the public would result in a clearly unwarranted
invasion of personal privacy. The authority for this exemption is
the United States Code Title 5, Section 552(b)(6) and Air Force
Regulation 12-30, paragraph 10f.

The denial authority is C. Norman Wood, MG, USAF, Asst. Chief
of Staff, Intelligence.

Should you decide to appeal this decision, you must write to
the Secretary of the Air Force within 60 days from the date of
this letter. Include in the appeal your reasons for
reconsideration and attach a copy of this letter. Mail it to:

> Secretary of the Air Force
> Thru: SAF/AADS (FOIA)
> Washington, DC 20330-1000

We are attaching the releasable records.

We surfaced other records responsive to your request. We do
not have the authority to deny or release them. We forwarded your
letter and the records to Military Airlift Command/IMD (FOIA),
Scott AFB, IL 62225. They will reply directly to you.

We do not have records responsive to item 2 of your request.
We also forwarded it to 544 CSG/IMD (FOIA), Nelis AFB, NV 89191-
5000. They will reply directly to you.

Sincerely,

BARBARA A. CARMICHAEL
Freedom of Information Manager

1 Atch
Releasable records
89-0923

AIR FORCE SPECIAL SECURITY OFFICE
Headquarters, Northeast Air Command
APO 862 New York, N.Y.

SSO   18 July 1955

SUBJECT: (UNCLASSIFIED) UFOB NEAC Area

TO: Commander
           USAF Security Service
           San Antonio, Texas

    1. Reference to SSO NEAC message, Cite SONEC-13, DTG 031200Z July
and your message Cite OOP-X5547, DTG 122311Z July 1955. Following is
more detailed information on sighting in the NEAC area in June and July
as requested in your message.

    2. Inclosures 1, 2, 3, and 4 are detailed reports prepared by
Watch Division, NEAC, on the 1 to 8 July sightings made by RB-47 crews.
D/I NEAC has not correlated these sightings with any known activity.

    3. Inclosures 5, 6, and 7 are detailed reports on the 7 July
sighting near Harmon AFB, Nfld. Inclosure 6 contains the interrogation
reports of the crews involved in the sighting. Inclosure 7, NEAC
Weekly Intelligence NOFORN Digest contains a resume of the 7 July
sighting and subsequent evaluation by D/I NEAC. Copies of all inclosures
forwarded to DIRNSA.

7 Incls
    1. RB-47 sighting #1
    2. RB-47 sighting #2
    3. RB-47 sighting #3
    4. RB-47 sighting #4
    5. 64th Air Div Msg DTG 0612ADZ Jul 55
    6. 64th Air Div Msg DTG 0701DDZ Jul 55
    7. Weekly Intell NOFORN Digest

DECLASSIFIED BY: ACS/Intelligence on 7 Sep 89.

C. NORMAN WOOD, Maj Gen,
Asst Chief of Staff, Intelligence

55-544

ITEM 1. At 2100Z on 1 June, an eastbound RB-47 experienced electronic
contact with an unknown aircraft or object in the area of Devon Island.
A bright return was received on the APG-32 set for 20 minutes and the
warning light flashed intermittently. The RB-47's K-system recorded
what was possibly the sweep of another radar nearby. Contact was lost
at 2120Z. No visual contact established.

On the return westbound flight, the APG-32 again had a contact
for 30 minutes duration at approximately 8,000 yards. This time no
indication was registered by the warning light. No visual contact
made. ****

Coordinates and times as follows:

First contact (estimate)	74°40'N-105°00'W	2100Z	1 June
Contact lost	76°15'N-31°00'W	2120Z	1 June
Second contact (estimate)	74°30'N-90°30'W	2400Z	1 June
Contact lost	74°10'N-31°00'W	0030Z	2 June

ITEM 2

At 0030Z on 4 June, a westbound RB-47 experienced electronic
and visual contact with an unknown aircraft or object in the Mel-
ville Sound area. The RB-47 gun warning light was flashing intermittently and the S radar had a contact at 7,000 yards range. Visual
contact was made by crew chief, who describes aircraft as glistening
silver metallic. The aircraft was first seen low and to the rear of
the RB-47. It maintained a position low and to the rear and slightly
right of the RB-47. The configuration of the aircraft was obscured
by contrails. The aircraft broke off contact to the north with an
increase in speed. The RB-47 was at 32,000, indicating Mach .735.
Although gun camera films are available, they are of such poor quality
that no information can be obtained from them. The radar and visual
contacts were maintained for a total of 9 minutes.****

Coordinates and times are as follows:

Contact established	74°10'N - 107°10'W	0030Z	4 June
Contact lost	73°45'N - 111°35'W	0049Z	4 June

ITEM 3

At 0050Z on 7 June, a westbound RB-47 enroute to Eilson AFB,
Alaska, at 35,000 feet experienced electronic contact southeast of
Banks Island. The RB-47's APG-32 detected an aircraft/object at
3,500 yards and at the same level as the aircraft. The scope return
was small and rectangular. The pilot interpreted it to be a form of
jamming. The target warning light went on and off 3 times in as
many minutes. No visual or K-system contacts.****

Coordinates and times are as follows:

Contact established   71°02'N - 127°00'W   0050Z   7 June
Contact lost   0053Z   7 June
                                                      (possibly later)

ITEM 4

At 2044Z on 8 June, an eastbound RB-47 flying at 30,000 feet
experienced electronic and visual contact with an unknown aircraft
south of Bathurst Island. The RB-47 was flying at 30,000 and indicating 450 knots. The warning light flashed and 2 indications were
observed on APG-32 scope. The K-system scope showed indications of
sweeping by another radar. Visual contact indicates aircraft was 5
to 10,000 feet above RB-47 and approximately 5-10 miles behind for
approximately 20 minutes. The co-pilot of RB-47 states aircraft had
fighter configuration. Contrail was observed as aircraft disappeared.
Contrail also sighted by 2nd RB-47 approximately 80 miles behind 1st;
therefore, about 70 miles behind the sighted aircraft. Distance
suggests contrails remain visible for some time.****

Coordinates and times are as follows:

Contact established   74°26'N - 103°25'W   2044Z   8 June
Contact lost   2140Z   8 June

UNCLASSIFIED

PROJECT TWINKLE

FINAL REPORT

L. ELTERMAN

27 November 1951 **SMC**

APPROVED:

I. TWINKLE, Project

P. H. WYCKOFF
Chief, Atmospheric Physics Laboratory

UNCLASSIFIED

1003284

UNCLASSIFIED

ion

ABSTRACT

Early in 1950 the Geophysics Research Division received a directive to investigate peculiar light phenomena that had been observed in the skies of the southwestern United States. Project Twinkle was established to check into these phenomena and their explanation.

The gist of the findings is essentially negative. The period of observations covers a little over a year. Some unusual phenomena were observed during that period, most of them can be attributed to such man-made objects as airplanes, balloons, rockets, etc. Others can be attributed to natural phenomena such as flying birds, small clouds, and meteorites. There has been no indication that even the somewhat strange observations often called "Green Fireballs" are anything but natural phenomena.

Our recommendations are in essence that there is no use in sinking any more funds into this at the present time and that we will keep in connection with one of our meteor studies a sharp eye on anything unusual along this line.

UNCLASSIFIED

1. Background

In accordance with instructions contained in a classified letter
from Chief of Staff, USAF to CG, AMC, subject "Light Phenomena", on
14 September 1949, Lt. Col. Frederic C.E. Oder of CRD attended a conference at Los Alamos, 14 October 1949 on the subject of "Green Fireballs"
observed in the Northern New Mexico area. Since the phenomena had been
observed only in this area and only since 1947, it had caused considerable
concern among security agencies in the area. It was the conclusion of
the scientists present at this meeting that the information available
was not sufficiently quantitative. Instrumental observations - photographic, triangulation, and spectroscopic were considered essential.

Dr. L. La Paz of the Department of Meteoritics of Univ. of New
Mexico was present at the Los Alamos meeting and subsequently was invited to submit proposals for studying this phenomena under GRD spon-
sorship. On 2 February 1950, Dr. La Paz advised that due to difficulties with academic arrangements, he was unable to undertake this
study.

During February 1950, the frequent reports of unexplained aerial
phenomena in the vicinity of Holloman Air Force Base and Vaughn, New
Mexico prompted the Commanding Officer of Holloman Air Force Base to
initiate a program to gather factual data.

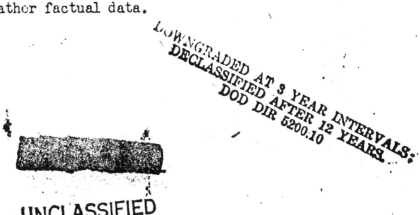

These data then would be used to demonstrate the need for initiating a study of the phenomena. On 21 February 1950, an observation outlook post was set up at Holloman Air Force Base manned by two personnel. Observations with theodolight, telescope and camera were undertaken between the hours of sunrise and sunset.

On 5 March 1950 a conference was held at Wright-Patterson Air Force Base which included Holloman Air Force Base and GRD personnel. Action was taken to initiate a three point program which was confirmed by AMC in the form of a letter directive on 16 March 1950, subject "Light Phenomena".

  a. Askania instrument triangulation by Land-Air Inc.

  b. Observations with Mitchell camera using spectrum
    grating by Holloman Air Force Base personnel.

  c. Electromagnetic frequency measurements using Signal
    Corps Engineering Laboratory equipment.

Under contract to GRD, Land-Air Inc. was required to maintain constant watch at two Askania stations for a six-month period. Since an abnormal number of reports had been received from Vaughn, New Mexico, it was decided to install the instrumentation at Vaughn.

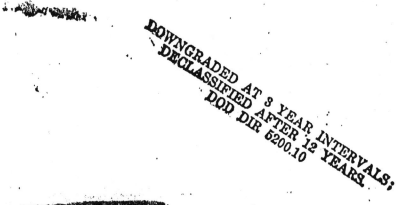

DOWNGRADED AT 8 YEAR INTERVALS;
DECLASSIFIED AFTER 12 YEARS.
DOD DIR 5200.10

2. Contractual period - 1 April 1950 to 15 September 1950.

Some photographic activity occurred on 27 April and 24 May, but simultaneous sightings by both cameras were not made, so that no information was gained. On 30 August 1950, during a Bell aircraft missile launching, aerial phenomena were observed over Holloman Air Force Base by several individuals; however, neither Land-Air nor Project personnel were notified and, therefore, no results were acquired. On 31 August 1950, the phenomena were again observed after a V-2 launching. Although much film was expended, proper triangulation was not effected, so that again no information was acquired. On 11 September, arrangements were made by Holloman AFB for Major Gover, Commander 93rd Fighter Squadron at Kirtland AFB, to be on call so that aerial objects might be pursued. This would make possible more intimate visual observation and photography at close range. Major Gover was not authorized to shoot at the phenomena.

Generally, the results of the six-month contractual period may be described as negative. Although the photographic theodolites functioned continuously, the grating cameras functioned very little, since the military personnel assigned to operate them had been withdrawn due to the needs concerned with the Korean situation. The

facilities for the electromagnetic frequency measurements that were
to be provided by the Signal Corps Engineering Laboratories were not
utilized due to the fact that the frequency of occurrence of these
phenomena did not justify the $50,000 a year transfer of funds to the
Signal Corps which would be required to carry out such a monitoring
facility. However, the phenomena activity over Holloman AFB 150 miles
south of Vaughn, N. Mexico during the latter part of August 1950 was
considered sufficiently significant so that the contract with Land-Air
(Askania cameras only) was extended for six months ending 31 March 1951.

3. Contractual Period - 1 October 1950 to 31 March 1951

Because of the diminution of phenomena activity in the vicinity
of Vaughn and the resumption of activity near HAFB, the Askania cameras
again were overhauled and installed at HAFB. This installation was
completed about 5 November 1950. On 16 October 1950, arrangements
were made by Lt. Albert of HAFB that Northrup Aircraft pilots engaged
in frequent flying of B-45 and QF-80 aircraft in the Holloman vicinity
would report all observations of aerial phenomena.

During this period, occasional reports were received of individuals
seeing strange aerial phenomena, but these reports were sketchy, inconclusive, and were considered to be of no scientific value. No
sightings were made by the Askania cameras. Nothing whatsoever was
reported by the Northrup pilots. Popular interest seemed abated,
at least in the southwest. On 31 March 1951, due to the expiration
of the contract, Land-Air ceased constant vigilance at the two Askania stations. In summary, the results during this period were negative.

Doc. 1-7g Project Twinkle Final Report, Nov 27, 1951

4. Post Contractual Inquiry

In view of the unproductive nature of the contract with Land-Air, it was decided to make further inquiry concerning recent aerial object developments in New Mexico. On 9 August 1951, the situation was discussed with Lt. Col. Cox of the 17th OSI District (Kirtland AFB). Until 15 March 1950 the District had been diligent in forwarding copies of their reports on aerial object phenomena. Since then, no reports have been received by the Geophysics Research Division. Colonel Cox advised that reports of strange aerial phenomena were still received by the 17th OSI office, at the rate of once or twice a month but little attention was being given to this matter. Most of the reports originated from personnel at Los Alamos. The OSI files were reviewed. (A summary covering recent reports is attached.) It was learned that representatives from LIFE and also from ARGOSY were interested in publishing articles on aerial object phenomena.

On 27 August 1951, developments concerning aerial phenomena were discussed at Holloman AFB. Lt. John Albert previously associated with the project had now been transferred from Holloman. Therefore, the project was discussed with Major Edward A. Doty who had assumed responsibility. Major Doty, who seemed to be thoroughly acquainted with the situation, advised that there have been very few reports of

aerial phenomena in the vicinity of Holloman since September 1950. The populace around HAFB seem to have lost their sensitivity as observers. Even during the meteor shower of 11-12 August 1951, no alarming reports were received. However, on 14 March 1951, nine Bell personnel reported sighting between fourteen and twenty bodies "not unlike a flock of geese". On 9 July a "red glowing ball" was sighted by a sergeant stationed at the Corona Experimental Radar Site at Corona, New Mexico. (Copies of both reports are attached). More recently, a pilot reported some aerial objects which, after investigation, were identified as planets.

Mr. B. Guildenberg, who is an assistant to Major Doty and an active amateur astronomer, commented that he has been spending several hours at his telescope almost every night for the past few years and never once observed an unexplainable object; that on one occasion, an excited acquaintance was pacified when a "strange object" showed up as an eagle in the telescope; that Clyde Tombaugh, discoverer of the planet Pluto and now engaged in activities at White Sands, never observed an unexplainable aerial object despite his continuous and extensive observations of the sky; that Fred Whipple in his work photographing meteors at Las Cruces, never detected a strange aerial object with his Schmidt cameras; and that the A and M College at Las Cruces engages in astronomical observations but had never observed strange aerial phenomena.

It was learned from Major Doty, that Col. Baynes, C. O. at HAFB, no longer felt there was any justification for the allocation of funds for maintaining systematic investigation. Rather, he provided that the project be maintained on a standby basis and without official Air Force status. This entails assignment of an officer (Major Doty) to collect incoming reports, make periodic review of the files "for patterns or persistent characteristics in the reports", maintain liaison with OSI, Provost Marshall's Office and any other agencies whose activities may serve to provide information concerning future aerial phenomena developments. Land-Air has agreed to report and if possible photograph any abnormal sightings made during their scheduled periods of operation (about eight hours each day). The weather station will function similarly. Also, all pilots have been briefed to report any unusual observations. If necessary, the project can be activated very quickly, even to the extent where funds will be made available, for the purchase of equipment.

Major Doty also arranged a conference with Mr. Warren Kott, who is in charge of Land-Air operations. Mr. Kott pointed out that a formal report covering the year's vigilance period had not been issued since the contract contained no such provision. Actually, a time correlation study should be made covering the film and verbal recordings at both Askania stations. This would assure that these records did not contain significant material. However, such a study is quite laborious, and would require about thirty man days to complete. Again, no provisions are contained in the contract for this study, but Mr. Kott felt that

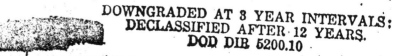

this could be done by Land-Air at the additional expense in the near future when the work load diminished. Mr. Kott requested formal authorization to do this and Major Doty agreed to issue this letter of authorization. It was arranged further that at such time when the study is completed all photographic and tape recordings would be sent to the Geophysics Research Division. Prior to departing HAFB, the project files were reviewed. Major Doty advised that access to the files had not been requested by any periodicals.

On 28 August 1951, the subject was discussed informally with Dr. Lincoln La Paz, who expressed disbelief in all aerial phenomena except for the green fire-balls. The red fire-ball occasionally reported he believed was the visual after-effect of the green. Their recent origin (1947) and peculiar trajectories did not permit, according to Dr. La Paz, them to be classed as natural phenomena. The most recent that has come to his attention occurred over Detroit on 7 July 1951. It crossed the city from Northwest to Southeast with a sharply descending trajectory which leveled out and was observed by many residents of the city. Dr. La Paz expressed the opinion that the fireballs may be of our own military origin, but if not, they are a matter of serious concern.

5. Conclusions

Undoubtedly, a good many of the observations reported are attributable to ordinary man-made objects such as airplanes, balloons, smoke rockets, etc. It appears that balloon observations especially are responsible for a large number of the reports. The possibility of small

DOWNGRADED AT 3 YEAR INTERVALS;
DECLASSIFIED AFTER 12 YEARS,
DOD DIR 5200.10

UNCLASSIFIED

emissive clouds issuing from atomic installations also has been proposed.

Many of the sightings are attributable to natural phenomena such as flight of birds, planets, meteors, and possibly cloudiness. Dr. Fred L. Whipple of Harvard, in a memorandum to this laboratory dated 9 August 1950 relative to this problem, indicated that he had observed a tendency for the occurrence of small detached clouds in New Mexico which might have been mistaken for an aerial object when illuminated by the reflected light of the moon. Dr. Whipple investigated the possibility of a correlation between the frequency of aerial phenomena observations and weather conditions -- specifically cloudiness. A rough analysis of available weather data, indicated that on the 53 nights (between 5 December 1948 and 5 March 1951) when observations were reported, 10 were clear, 24 partially cloudy, 5 completely overcast and 14 had no record. The number of cloudy nights involved seems unusually high for New Mexico. The weather reports were for the Las Cruces Area only whereas many of the observations were a considerable distance from Las Cruces. Further investigation is therefore necessary to determine correlations with cloudiness.

Dr. Whipple also conducted a study as to whether the age of the moon was related to the frequency of aerial phenomena observations. The results did not indicate that the phenomena were observed largely at full moon. The statistics show that of the 72 observations reported, 45 occurred when the moon was up and 27 when it was down with many of the observations occurring at the time of the moon's first quarter. From the statistical study, Dr. Whipple suggests that the existence of moonlight is correlated with the phenomena. Dr. Whipple's frequency diagram of observations vs. age of moon is included in this report.

UNCLASSIFIED

UNCLASSIFIED

It should be noted that Dr. Whipple made a careful study of meteor photographs taken in New Mexico on 35 nights when observations were reported. None of the photographs revealed the presence of un-usual sky phenomena.

Finally, the overall picture obtained from the year of vigilance and inquiry does not permit a conclusive opinion concerning the aerial phenomena of interest. The comparatively high incidence of the pheno-mena since 1948 does not necessarily indicate that the objects are man-made. It is conceivable that the earth may be passing through a region in space of high meteoric population. Also, the sun-spot maxima in 1948 perhaps in some way may be a contributing factor.

6. Recommendations

Since the findings to date cannot be considered conclusive, it appears that the following recommendations would be pertinent:

UNCLASSIFIED

UNCLASSIFIED

(1) No further fiscal expenditure be made in pursuing the problem.
This opinion is prompted partly by the fruitless expenditure during
the past year, the uncertainty of existence of unexplainable aerial
objects, and by the inactive position currently taken by Holloman
AFB as indicated by the "stand-by status" of the project. The
arrangements by HAFB for continued vigilance by Land-Air, the
weather station as well as the briefing of pilots on the problem
in part relieves the need for a systematic instrumentation program.

(2) Within the next few months, Dr. Whipple will have completed
the installation of two 18-inch Schmidt cameras for meteor studies.
The cameras will be stationed about 20 miles apart in the vicinity
of Las Cruces, New Mexico. Since these studies will be sponsored
by the GRD, arrangements can be made for examining the film for
evidence of aerial object phenomena.

LOUIS ELTERMAN
Project Scientist
Atmospheric Physics Laboratory
Geophysics Research Division

11

UNCLASSIFIED

Doc. 1-7n Project Twinkle Final Report, Nov 27, 1951

UNCLASSIFIED

Summary of Recent Aerial Phenomena Reports from 17th OSI District

11 Nov. 1950 - Reports of a large-sized balloon. It was determined that this was released by General Mills. The balloon subsequently was recovered.

12 Jan. 1951 - Report from ten Los Alamos employees. Tear shaped object with small tail; very bright appearance; descended slowly; sky lighted up for about 1 sec; observation time 05:00. Unconfirmed sights flare dropped by military pilot who sometimes lost his bearings.

16 Feb. 1951 - Aerial object reported in the vicinity of Holloman AFB. This turned out to be a General Mills balloon functioning for Project "Skyhook".

19 Feb. 1951 - A C-54 pilot reported a green flare or rocket observed in the vicinity of Rodeo, N.M. Its motion was vertical and passed the plane at 9000 ft. Investigators believed this to be a meteor.

6 Mar. 1951 - Report from four Los Alamos personnel of very bright object crossing sky. Also observed by two Kirtland AFB pilots who reported this as a meteor; time - 14:30; reported by Dr. La Paz to be a detonating fire-ball. No fragments recovered.

DOWNGRADED AT 3 YEAR INTERVALS;
DECLASSIFIED AFTER 12 YEARS.
DOD DIR 5200.10

UNCLASSIFIED

12 Mar. 1951 — Report from Albuquerque, N.M. by two individuals of ball-shaped object, shining-white appearance. The object descended rapidly to the horizon.

1 April 1951 — Report from a Los Alamos employee. Oblong shaped object moving slowly both in horizontal and vertical directions. Bright appearance.

7 June 1951 — Report from a Los Alamos employee. Pointed cylinder in vertical position. Cloth-like construction. Fell in canyon at 11:10 A.M. Search party was unable to find the object or any remains.

8 June 1951 — Report from a Los Alamos employee. Large reddish dot, dull appearance which turned bright green. Observed for three seconds.

~~SECURITY INFORMATION~~

CONFIDENTIAL

UNCLASSIFIED

(UNCLASSIFIED)   Project TWINKLE

Directorate of Intelligence
Attention: Colonel John G. Ericksen, Chief   19 Feb 1952
            Technical Capabilities Branch   1
Research Division, Directorate of Research and   Lt Col Clayton/djh/5..07
Development, Office, DCS/Development   AFDRD-RE

1.   Attached is a copy of a letter from the Air Research and Development
Command requesting declassification of Project TWINKLE, a project which was
carried out by AMC and ARDC for investigation of unusual light phenomena in
the general area of Holloman Air Force Base and Vaughn, New Mexico.

2.   The Scientific Advisory Board Secretariat has suggested that this
project not be declassified for a variety of reasons, chief among which is
that no scientific explanation for any of the "fireballs" and other phenomena
was revealed by the report and that some reputable scientists still believe
that the observed phenomena are man-made.

3.   In view of the great interest of the Directorate of Intelligence
in such phenomena and the related manifestations, evaluation of the final
report of Project TWINKLE with a view to its declassification is requested.

2 Incls   ALBERT E. LOMBARD, JR.
   1. cy ltr fr ARDC   Chief, Research Division
      to Hq 14 Jan 52   Directorate of Research and Development
   2. cy of Proj TWINKLE   Office, Deputy Chief of Staff, Development
      Final Report

                                 JOHN H. CLAYTON
                                 Lt Colonel, USAF

CONFIDENTIAL   UNCLASSIFIED

Doc. 1-8a Smith Memorandum, Nov 21, 1950

TOP SECRET

CONFIDENTIAL

DEPARTMENT OF TRANSPORT

INTRA-DEPARTMENTAL CORRESPONDENCE

"Smith" memo.

OTTAWA, Ontario, November 21, 1950.   ①

PLACE   DATE

SUBJECT		OUR FILE	
Geo-Magnetics			(R.ST.)

Downgraded to CONFIDENT SEE MEMO 15/9/69 CR?

MEMORANDUM TO THE CONTROLLER OF TELECOMMUNICATIONS:

For the past several years we have been engaged in the study of various aspects of radio wave propagation. The vagaries of this phenomenon have led us into the fields of aurora, cosmic radiation, atmospheric radio-activity and geo-magnetism. In the case of geo-magnetics our investigations have contributed little to our knowledge of radio wave propagation as yet, but nevertheless have indicated several avenues of investigation which may well be explored with profit. For example, we are on the track of a means whereby the potential energy of the earth's magnetic field may be abstracted and used.

On the basis of theoretical considerations a small and very crude experimental unit was constructed approximately a year ago and tested in our Standards Laboratory. The tests were essentially successful in that sufficient energy was abstracted from the earth's field to operate a volt-meter, approximately 50 milliwatts. Although this unit was far from being self-sustaining, it nevertheless demonstrated the soundness of the basic principles in a qualitative manner and provided useful data for the design of a better unit.

The design has now been completed for a unit which should be self-sustaining and in addition provide a small surplus of power. Such a unit, in addition to functioning as a 'pilot power plant' should be large enough to permit the study of the various reaction forces which are expected to develop.

We believe that we are on the track of something which may well prove to be the introduction to a new technology. The existence of a different technology is borne out by the investigations which are being carried on at the present time in relation to flying saucers.

While in Washington attending the NARB Conference, two books were released, one titled "Behind the Flying Saucer" by Frank Scully, and the other "The Flying Saucers are Real" by Donald Keyhoe. Both books dealt mostly with the sightings of unidentified objects and both books claim that flying objects were of extra-terrestrial origin and might well be space ships from another planet. Scully claimed that the preliminary studies of one saucer which fell into the hands of the United States Government indicated that they operated on some hitherto unknown magnetic principles. It appeared to me that our own work in geo-magnetics might well be the linkage between our technology and the technology by which the saucers are designed and operated. If it is assumed that our geo-magnetic investigations are in the right direction, the theory of operation of the saucers becomes quite straightforward, with all observed features explained qualitatively and quantitatively.

I made discreet enquiries through the Canadian Embassy staff in Washington who were able to obtain for me the following information:

a. The matter is the most highly classified subject in the United States Government, rating higher even than the H-bomb.

b. Flying saucers exist.

c. Their modus operandi is unknown but concentrated effort is being made by a small group headed by Doctor Vannevar Bush.

d. The entire matter is considered by the United States authorities to be of tremendous significance.

I was further informed that the United States authorities are investigating along quite a number of lines which might possibly be related to the saucers such as mental phenomena and I gather that they are not doing too well since they indicated that if Canada is doing anything at all in geo-magnetics they would welcome a discussion with suitably accredited Canadians.

While I am not yet in a position to say that we have solved even the first problems in geo-magnetic energy release, I feel that the correlation between our basic theory and the available information on saucers checks too closely to be mere coincidence. It is my honest opinion that we are on the right track and are fairly close to at least some of the answers.

Mr. Wright, Defence Research Board liaison officer at the Canadian Embassy in Washington, was extremely anxious for me to get in touch with Doctor Solandt, Chairman of the Defence Research Board, to discuss with him future investigations along the line of geo-magnetic energy release.

.... 3

- 3 -

I do not feel that we have as yet sufficient data to place before Defence Research Board which would enable a program to be initiated within that organization, but I do feel that further research is necessary and I would prefer to see it done within the frame work of our own organization with, of course, full co-operation and exchange of information with other interested bodies.

I discussed this matter fully with Doctor Solandt, Chairman of Defence Research Board, on November 20th and placed before him as much information as I have been able to gather to date. Doctor Solandt agreed that work on geo-magnetic energy should go forward as rapidly as possible and offered full co-operation of his Board in providing laboratory faciliti acquisition of necessary items of equipment, and specialised personnel for incidental work in the project. I indicated to Doctor Solandt that we woul prefer to keep the project within the Department of Transport for the time being until we have obtained sufficient information to permit a complete assessment of the value of the work.

It is therefore recommended that a PROJECT be set up within the frame work of this Section to study this problem and that the work be carried on a part time basis until such time as sufficient tangible results can be seen to warrant more definitive action. Cost of the program in its initial stages are expected to be less than a few hundred dollars and can be carried by our Radio Standards Lab appropriation.

Attached hereto is a draft of terms of reference for such a project which, if authorized, will enable us to proceed with this research work within our own organization.

(W.B. Smith)
Senior Radio Engineer

WBS/CC

PROJECT MAGNET REPORT

During the past five years there has been accumulating
in the files of the United States Air Force, Royal Canadian Air
Force, Department of Transport, and various other agencies, an
impressive number of reports on sightings of unidentified flying
objects popularly known as "Flying Saucers". These files contain
reports by creditable people on things which they have seen in
the sky, tracked by radar, or photographed. They are reports
made in good faith by normal, honest people, and there is little
if any reason to doubt their veracity. Many sightings undoubtedly
are due to unusual views of common objects or phenomenae, and
are quite normal, but there are many sightings which cannot be
explained so easily.

Project Magnet was authorized in December, 1950, by
Commander C. P. Edwards, then Deputy Minister of Transport for
Air Services, for the purpose of making as detailed a study of
the saucer phenomenae as could be made within the framework of
existing establishments. The Broadcast and Measurements
Section of the Telecommunications Division were given the
directive to go ahead with this work with whatever assistance
could be obtained informally from outside sources such as
Defence Research Board and National Research Council.

- 2 -

It is perfectly natural in the human thinking mechanism to try and fit observations into an established pattern. It is only when observations stubbornly refuse to be so fitted that we become disturbed. When this happens we may, and usually do, take one of three courses. First, we may deny completely the validity of the observations; or second, we may pass the whole subject off as something of no consequence; or third, we may accept the discrepancies as real and go to work on them. In the matter of Saucer Sightings all three of those reactions have been strikingly apparent. The first two approaches are obviously negative and from which a definite conclusion can never be reached. It is the third approach, acceptance of the data and subsequent research that is dealt with in this report.

The basic data with which we have to work consist largely of sightings reported as they are observed throughout Canada in a purely random manner. Many of the reports are from the extensive field organization of the Department of Transport whose job it is to watch the sky and whose observers are trained in precisely this sort of observation. Also, there are in operation a number of instrumental arrangements such as the ionospheric observatories from which useful data have been obtained. However, we must not expect too much from these field stations because of the very sporadic nature of the sightings. As the analysis progresses and we know more about what to look for we may be able to obtain and make much better use of field data. Up to the present we have been prevented from using conventional laboratory methods owing to the complete lack of any sort of specimens with which to experiment, and our prospects of obtaining any in the immediate future are not very good. Consequently, a large part of the analysis in these early stages will have to be based on deductive reasoning, at least until we are able to work out a procedure more in line with conventional experimental methods.

The starting point of the investigation is essentially the interview with an observer. A questionnaire form and an instructional guide for the interrogator were worked out by the Project Second Storey Committee, which is a Committee sponsored by the Defence Research Board to collect, catalogue and correlate data on sightings of unidentified flying objects. This questionnaire and guide are included as Appendix I, and are intended to get the maximum useful information from the observer and present it in a manner in which it can be used to advantage. This form has been used so far as possible in connection with the sightings investigated by the Department of Transport.

A weighting factor is assigned to each sighting according to a system intended to minimize the personal equation. This weighting system is described in Appendix II. The weighting factor may be considered as the probability that the report contains the truth, the whole truth and nothing but the truth, so far as the observer and interrogator are aware. It has nothing to do with the nature of the object claimed to be seen. It is in a sense analagous to the order of precision with which a measurement may be made, and for the purpose of this analysis this is precisely the manner in which it is used.

Sightings may be grouped according to certain salient features, and the combined weight of all pertinent observations with respect to these features may be determined by applying Peter's formula, which is a standard mathematical technique for determining probable error.

$$r_o = \frac{.8453}{n\sqrt{n-1}} (v_1 + v_2 + v_3 + \ldots v_n)$$

where r_o is the probable error of the mean, n is the number of observations and v is the probable error of each observation, that is, unity minus the weighting factor. This method has the advantage of being simple and easy to use and enables a number of mediocre observations to be combined effectively into the equivalent of one good one.

The next step is to sort out the observations according to some pattern. The particular pattern is not so important as the fact that it should take account of all contingencies

however improbable they may appear at first sight. In other
words, there must be a compartment somewhere in the scheme of
things into which each sighting may be placed, comfortably, and
with nothing left over. Furthermore, it must be possible to
arrive at each appropriate compartment by a sequence of logical
reasoning taking account of all the facts presented. If this
can be done, then the probability for the real existence of the
contents of any compartment will be the single or combined
weighting factor pertinent to that single or group of sightings.
The charts shown in Appendix III were evolved as a means for
sorting out the various sightings and provide the pattern which
was used in the analysis of those sightings reported to and
analysed by the Department of Transport.

Most sightings fit readily into one of the classifications shown, which are of two general types; those about which
we know something and those about which we know very little.
When the sightings can be classified as something we know about,
we need not concern ourselves too much with them, but when they
fit into classifications which we don't understand we are back
to our original position of whether to deny the evidence, dismiss
it as of no consequence, or to accept it and go to work on it.
The process of sorting out observations according to these charts
and fitting them into compartments can hardly by considered an

end in itself. Rather, it is a convenience to clarify thinking
and direct activity along profitable channels. It shows at
once which aspects are of significance and which may be bypassed.
Merely placing a sighting under a certain heading does not
explain it; it only indicates where we may start looking for an
explanation.

Appendix IV contains summaries of the 1952 sightings
as investigated by the Department of Transport. Considerably
more data exists in the files of other agencies, and more is
being collected as the investigations proceed. While it is not
intended to make any reference to an analysis of the records of
other agencies, it may be said that the Department of Transport
sightings are quite representative of the sightings reported
throughout the world. The following is a table of the breakdown
of the 25 proper sightings reported during 1952.

NATURE OF SIGHTING	NUMBER	WEIGHT
Probably meteor	4	91%
Probably aircraft	1	69%
Probably balloons	1	74%
Probably marker light	1	64%
Bright speck at night, not star or planet	3	75%
Bright speck daylight, not star or planet	1	68%
Luminous ring	1	68%
Shiny cone	1	53%
Circular or elliptical body, shiny day	5	88%

NATURE OF SIGHTING	NUMBER	WEIGHT
Circular or elliptical body luminous night	5	90%
Unidentified lights of various kinds	2	77%
TOTAL NUMBER OF PROPER SIGHTINGS	25	96%

With reference to the above table, of the four cases identified as probably meteors, their weight works out at 91%, which is the probability that the observers actually did see meteors which appeared as they described them. Considering the circular or elliptical bodies together, their weight works out at 91% for the ten sightings, from which we may conclude that SOMETHING answering this description was actually observed. Similarly we may consider each of the other groups of sightings, taking account of the probability that the observations are reliable.

It is not intended to describe here in detail the intricate and tedious processes by which the sightings are evaluated, beyond the fact that the pattern set forth in the charts in Appendix III is followed. The cardinal rule is that a sighting must fit completely under one or more of the chart headings, with nothing left over and without postulating any additions, deletions, or changes in the facts as reported. Should there be no suitable heading, then obviously the charts must be expanded to provide one, in fact this was the evolution of these charts. Where a sighting may be fitted under more than one heading an arbitrary division of the probability of finding it under each applicable heading is assigned. The sum of such

probability figures must of course be unity, and the probability
for the real existence under any particular heading is the product
of this probability figure and the reliability or weighting factor
for the sighting concerned.

It is apparent that the judgement of the people doing
the evaluating is bound to enter the picture and may produce
substantial numerical differences with reference to sightings
listed under certain headings. However, since many headings are
automatically eliminated by the nature of the facts available,
the discrepancies are confined to the probability figures for
the distribution under the remaining headings which are
considered eligible, and we end up with definite classifications
for the sightings with SOME probability figure for the reality
of each group. This has the effect of forcing those who are
doing the evaluating to face the reported facts squarely, pay
meticulous attention to them, and place each sighting honestly
under the only headings where it will fit.

In working through the analysis of the proper sightings
listed, we find that the majority of them appear to be of some
material body. Of these, seven are classed as probably normal
objects, and eleven are classed as strange objects. Of the
remainder, four have a substantial probability of being material,
strange, objects, with three having a substantial probability
of being immaterial, electrical, phenomenae. Of the eleven
strange objects the probability definitely favours the alien

vehicle class, with the secret missile included with a much lower probability.

The next step is to follow this line of reasoning as far as possible so as to deduce what we can from the observed data. Vehicles or missiles can be of only two general kinds, terrestrial and extra-terrestrial, and in either case the analysis enquires into the source and technology. If the vehicles originate outside the iron curtain we may assume that the matter is in good hands, but if they originate inside the iron curtain it could be a matter of grave concern to us.

In the matter of technology, the points of interest are: - the energy source; means of support, propulsion and manipulation; structure; and biology. So far as energy is concerned we know about mechanical energy and chemical energy, and a little about energy of fission, and we can appreciate the possibility of direct conversion of mass to energy. Beyond this we have no knowledge, and unless we are prepared to postulate a completely unknown source of energy of which we do not know even the rudiments, we must conclude that the vehicles use one of the four listed energy sources. Unless something we do not understand can be done with gravitation, mechanical energy has little use beyond driving model aircraft. We use chemical energy to quite an extent, but we realize its limitations, so if the energy demands of the vehicles exceed what we consider to be the reasonable capabilities of chemical fuels, we are forced to the conclusion that such vehicles must get their energy from either fission or mass conversion.

With reference to the means for support, propulsion and manipulation, unless we are prepared to postulate something else quite beyond our knowledge, there are only the two groups of possibilities, namely the known means and the speculative means. Of the known means there is only physical support through the use of buoyancy or airfoils, the reaction of rockets and jets, and centrifugal force, which is what holds the moon in position. Of the speculative means we know only of the possibility of gravity waves, field interaction and radiation pressure. If the observed behaviour of the vehicles is such as to be beyond the limitations which we know apply to the known means of support, then we are forced to the conclusion that one of the speculative means must have been developed to do the job.

From a study of the sighting reports (Appendix IV), it can be deduced that the vehicles have the following significant characteristics. They are a hundred foot or more in diameter; they can travel at speeds of several thousand miles per hour; they can reach altitudes well above those which would support conventional aircraft or balloons; and ample power and force seem to be available for all required manoeuvres. Taking these factors into account, it is difficult to reconcile this performance

with the capabilities of our technology, and unless the
technology of some terrestrial nation is much more advanced
than is generally known, we are forced to the conclusion that
the vehicles are probably extra-terrestrial, in spite of our
prejudices to the contrary.

It has been suggested that the sightings might be
due to some sort of optical phenomenon which gives the appearance
of the objects reported, and this aspect was thoroughly
investigated. Charts are shown in Appendix III showing the
various optical considerations. Enticing as this theory is,
there are some serious objections to its actual application, in
the form of some rather definite and quite immutable optical
laws. These are the geometrical laws dealing with optics generally
and which we have never yet found cause to doubt, plus the wide
discrepancies in the order of magnetude of the light values which
must be involved in any sightings so far studied. Furthermore,
introducing an optical system might explain an image in terms of
an object, but the object still requires explaining. A particular
effort was made to find an optical explanation for the sightings
listed in this report, but in no case could one be worked out.
It was not possible to find so much as a partial optical
explanation for even one sighting. Consequently, it was felt
that optical theories generally should not be taken too seriously
until such time as at least one sighting can be satisfactorily
explained in such a manner.

- 12 -

It appears then, that we are faced with a substantial
probability of the real existence of extra-terrestrial vehicles,
regardless of whether or not they fit into our scheme of things.
Such vehicles of necessity must use a technology considerably in
advance of what we have. It is therefore submitted that the
next step in this investigation should be a substantial effort
towards the acquisition of as much as possible of this technology,
which would without doubt be of great value to us.

W. B. Smith,
Engineer-in-Charge,
Project Magnet.

CHAPTER TWO

UFOs and National Security

As we have seen from Chapter One of this book, the United States Government apparently had considered the subject of UFOs a matter of national security, at the same time telling the American public that there was no need for alarm because UFOs just did not exist.

In addition, the very first conclusion of every government UFO investigation was that UFOs did not represent a threat to our national security. This, in my opinion, is the most important conclusion reached by the Air Force: It would justify no further investigation, as far as the military and intelligence communities were concerned, into the matter of UFOs.

So, after December 17, 1969, the U.S. Government should have been out of the UFO business forever; that is, if they really and truthfully believed their own conclusions. But did they really believe them?

I feel that it is important, before we continue, to define some key terms in order to better understand the meaning of the classification system used by the U.S. Government. What superior source could we use for these definitions than our own government?

The following definitions are taken directly from the United States Army, Army Regulation (AR) 380-5, entitled "Department of the Army Information Security Program":

SENSITIVE COMPARTMENTED INFORMATION—Information and material that requires special controls for restricted handling within compartmented intelligence systems and for which compartmentation is established.

SPECIAL ACCESS PROGRAM— Any program imposing need-to-know or access controls beyond those normally required for access to Confidential, Secret, or Top Secret information. Such a program includes, but is not limited to, special clearance, adjudication, or investigative requirements; special designation of officials authorized to determine need-to-know; or special lists of persons determined to have a need-to-know.

CONFIDENTIAL—Shall be applied only to information or material the unauthorized disclosure of which reasonably could be expected to cause damage to the national security.

SECRET—Shall be applied only to information or material the unauthorized disclosure of which reasonably could be expected to cause serious damage to the national security.

TOP SECRET—Shall be applied only to information or material the unauthorized disclosure of which reasonably could be expected to cause exceptionally grave damage to the national security.

The above terms were taken directly from official Army sources (AR) 380-5. They are important because they clearly define the classification system and show that the highest classification is Top Secret. They also show that in some programs known to exist you need more than a Top Secret Clearance. Keep these terms in mind for this and the other chapters of this book.

Several other terms should be defined here. However, I could not find the official definitions for those terms in any unclassified government documents that I had access to. Therefore, I trust that the reader will accept the following generally accepted definitions:

> NATIONAL SECURITY INFORMATION—Any information or material the unauthorized disclosure of which reasonably could be expected to cause serious or exceptionally grave damage to the security of the United States of America.

> NATIONAL INSECURITY—Any information or material the unauthorized disclosure of which reasonably could be expected to cause serious or exceptionally grave damage to the censors who wish to keep the truth from the General Public.

Now that we have seen the definitions and have a better understanding of what they mean, keep these terms in mind as we continue with this chapter.

We have seen that the U.S. Government stopped investigating UFOs in December 1969. Officially, the U.S. Government does not have any interest in UFOs. But is this really the case?

We are going to look at some UFO events in which apparently there was some government interest. These events took place after the closure of Project Blue Book, and in these cases the government documents dealing with them were initially classified, in the interests of national security.

All of the cases we are about to discuss are military cases, involving either the U.S. Military or the military of a foreign government. I have chosen these cases because I feel they can best illustrate what is meant by a matter of national security. To be sure, there are many other such examples—many still highly classified—in the interests of national security, of course.

During late October and early November 1975, various U.S. Air Force bases across the northern United States and Canada were picking up UFOs both on radar and visually. UFO sightings were reported by such bases as Loring, Wurtsmith, Minot, and others.

At the times of these sightings, the official documentation covering them was classified from Confidential to at least Secret. I presently have over 300 pages of documents dealing with these sightings from various government agencies released through the Freedom of Information Act (FOIA). Once these sightings became public knowledge, the U.S. Air Force attempted to dismiss them as helicopters and temperature inversions. If they were helicopters, then we have a very serious problem in that the Air Force was powerless to prevent these "helicopters" from "landing" inside nuclear weapons storage areas.

Furthermore, no arrests were ever made. Do you, the reader, really believe that our military is that helpless against this type of intrusion by helicopters?

In the U.S. Air Force there exists a reluctance among its personnel to use such terms as "UFOs" or "flying saucers." It is preferred that the term "unknown" be used, as opposed to "UFO."

To illustrate my point, let me quote from two official documents concerning the 1975 overflights dealing with the same incident. The first quote is from the NORAD Command Director's Log. The second quote is from the 24th NORAD Region Senior Director's Log. (See doc. 2-17.)

> 8 Nov 75/0753Z: 24th NORAD region unknown track J330, heading SSW, 12000 feet. 1 to 7 objects, 46.46 (degrees) N x 109.23W. Two

F-106 scrambled out of Great Falls at 0754Z. SAC reported visual sighting from Sabotage Alert Teams (SAT) K1, K3, L1 and L6 (lights and jet sound). Weather section states no anomalous propagation or northern lights. 0835Z SAC SAT Teams K3 and L4 report visual, K3 reports target at 300 feet altitude and L4 reports target at 5 miles. Contact lost at 0820Z. F-106's returned to base at 0850Z with negative results. 0905Z Great Falls radar search and height had intermittent contact. 0910Z SAC teams again had visual (Site C-1, 10 miles SE Standford, Montana). 0920Z SAC CP reported that when F-106's were in area, targets would turn out lights, and when F-106's left, target would turn lights on. F-106's never gained visual or radar contact at anytime due to terrain clearance. This type of activity has been reported in the Malmstrom area for several days although previous to tonight no unknowns were declared. The track will be carried as a remaining unknown.

And now, the extract from the 24th NORAD Region Senior Director's Log:

8 Nov 75 (0635Z)—A security camper team at K-4 reported UFO with white lights, one red light 50 yards behind white. Personnel at K-1 seeing same object.
8 Nov 75 (0645Z)—Height personnel picked up objects 10 - 13,000 feet, Track J330, EKLB 0648, 18 knots, 9,500 feet. Objects as many as seven, as few as two A/C.
8 Nov 75 (0745Z)—Conversation about the UFOs; Advised to go ahead and scramble; but to be sure and brief pilots, FAA. Go easy and the fighters will not descend below 12,000 ft.
8 Nov 75 (0753Z)—J330 unknown 0753. Stationary/seven knots/ 12,000. One (varies to seven) object. None, no possibility, EKLB

3746, two F-106, GTF, SCR 0754. NCOC notified.
8 Nov 75 (0820Z)—Lost radar contact, fighters broken off at 0825, looking in area of J331 (another height finder contact).
8 Nov 75 (0850Z)—Directed Ftrs to RTB (return to base).
8 Nov 75 (0905Z)—From SAC CP; L-sites had fighters and objects; fighters did not get down to objects.
8 Nov 75 (0953Z)—From SAC CP: From four different points; Observed objects and fighters; when fighters arrived in the area, the lights went out; when fighters departed, the lights came back on; to NCOC.
8 Nov 75 (0953Z)—From SAC CP: L-5 reported object increased in speed - high velocity, raised in altitude and now cannot tell the object from stars; to NCOC.
8 Nov 75 (1105Z)—From SAC CP: E-1 reported a bright white light (site is approximately 60 nautical miles north of Lewistown). NCOC notified.

Here we have two different Air Force documents referring to the same incident. One document talks of an "UFO" being involved. The other talks of an "unknown" being involved. Could it be that the Air Force now wishes to call UFOs unknowns?

Either way, the U.S. Air Force has yet to answer satisfactorily all the mysteries surrounding these sightings.

★★★

It would not be until the mid-nineties that the American public would learn that the Soviet Union was experiencing similar phenomena around its nuclear storage areas. There was one incident, involving a missile silo, in which the missile started to launch itself while an UFO hovered overhead. The missile crew at the site of this event was powerless to prevent the missile from launching. However, as the UFO departed the site, the missile mysteriously shutdown.

Had the missile launched, it would have been the start of World War III. The missile was programmed to strike a major city in the United States, and once it was on its way to its programmed target the Soviets would have had no way to recall it.

This event generated great concern and alarm among the Soviet military leaders. So much so, that they conducted a large-scale investigation of the event. This led to the closing of the site; and no answers were ever provided by the Soviet Military to explain the incident.

In 1976, the National Military Command Center (NMCC) in the Pentagon continued to receive UFO reports from its military personnel—whether or not it wanted them. UFOs, it seemed, just would not go away, no matter how badly the military wished them too.

On January 21, 1976, the following report was received by the NMCC: (See doc. 2-2.)

Two UFOs are reported near the flight line at Cannon AFB, New Mexico. Security Police observing them reported the UFOs to be 25 yards in diameter, gold or silver in color with blue light on top, hole in the middle and red light on bottom. Air Force is checking with radar. Additionally, checking weather inversion data.

The NMCC did not have to wait long for the next UFO report from the field. On January 31,1976, they received the following report from Eglin Air Force Base, Florida: (See doc. 2-3.)

At 310805 received phoncon from AFOC: MG Lane, Armament and Development Test Center, Eglin AFB, Florida called and reported an UFO sighting from 0430 EST to 0600 EST. Security Policemen spotted lights from what they called an UFO near an Eglin Radar site.

Photographs of the lights were taken. The Eglin Office of Information has made a press release on the UFO.

An interesting side note to this case is that the Air Force in its news release stated that the UFO was nothing more then lights from a nearby building. However, the Air Force has to this day never released the photographs taken by the Security Police.

The United States Army was also having its share of UFO sightings. On July 30, 1976, the NMCC received the following report from Fort Ritchie: (See doc. 2-4.)

0255 - Two separate patrols from Site R reported sighting 3 oblong objects with a reddish tint, moving east to west. Personnel were located at separate locations on top of the mountain at Site R. 0300 - Desk Sergeant at Site R went to the top of the Site R mountain and observed an UFO over the ammo storage area at 100-200 yards altitude. 0345 - An Army Police Sergeant on the way to work at Site R reported sighting an UFO in the vicinity of Site R.

The United States Navy had its problems with UFOs, too. On the night of May 14, 1978, the Navy's Pinecastle Electronic Warfare Range had an UFO Incident. In this case the UFO was both visually sighted and tracked by radar. It was reported as displaying red, green, and white lights. Also, the UFO apparently took evasive action when there was an attempt to lock radar on the object.

The Public Affairs Officer, in the cover letter to the information that was sent to me by the Jacksonville Naval Air Station, had this to say about the incident: (See doc. 2-5.)

I have never been a believer in "UFOs," but I assure you I am convinced that a number of people witnessed an unexplainable event that night. The speed of the object ruled out a helicopter and the reported maneuverability ruled out any aircraft including VSTOLs that we are aware of.

What was seen by the people at Pinecastle that night? We may never know.

With the Air Force maintaining that it no longer has any interest in UFOs, it is interesting to note that in July and August 1980, the Air Force Office of Special Investigations (AFOSI) found it necessary to become involved in events happening around Kirtland Air Force Base, New Mexico. (See docs. 2-6 and 2-7.)

On August 8, 1980, three Security Policemen on duty inside the Manzano Weapons Storage Area sighted an unidentified light in the air that traveled from north to south over the Coyote Canyon area of the Department of Defense Restricted Test Range of Kirtland Air Force Base. The light traveled "at great speed," and would make sudden stops. In addition, the three observers saw the object land in the Coyote Canyon area.

On August 9, 1980, a Sandia Security Guard reported observing a round, disk-shaped object that had landed near an alarmed structure. As the Security Guard approached the object on foot, the object, he said, "took off in a vertical direction at a high rate of speed."

On October 24, 1980, a Dr. Paul F. Bennewitz reported to the Kirtland Office of Special Investigations that he had knowledge and evidence of a threat against Manzano Weapons Storage area. According to the OSI report: "The threat was from Aerial Phenomena over Manzano." Dr. Bennewitz's evidence consisted of "photographs and over 2600 feet of 8mm motion film depicting unidentified aerial objects flying over and around Manzano Weapons Storage Area and Coyote Canyon Test Area." Bennewitz's data was analyzed by Jerry Miller, Chief, Scientific Advisor for the Air Force Test and Evaluation Center.

After analyzing Dr. Bennewitz's data, Miller informed the Kirtland OSI Office:

> ... the evidence clearly shows that some type of unidentified aerial objects were caught on film. However, no conclusions could be made whether these objects pose a threat to Manzano/Coyote Canyon areas.

On November 10, 1980, Dr. Bennewitz presented a briefing of his data to the Air Force brass at Kirtland Air Force Base. According to the OSI report, "[the] AFOSI would not become involved in the investigation of these objects."

This same response was given to Senator Domenici when his office contacted the Kirtland AFOSI Office. Here, again, we have unusual objects being reported and photographed in restricted areas vital to our nation's defense and the Air Force would have us believe they are not interested. Should we ignore all this? Can we afford to?

During the period between December 27–29, 1980, a chain of unusual events occurred at the Royal Air Force Base in Woodbridge, England. These events were witnessed by U.S. Air Force Security Police Personnel, as well as by the Deputy Base Commander, LTC. Charles I. Halt. (See docs. 2-8 and 2-9.)

Strange lights were reported being seen outside the back gate at RAF Woodbridge, early in the morning of December 27, 1980. The security police patrolmen who were sent to investigate the strange lights reported seeing an object. The object was described as metallic in appearance and triangular in shape, approximately two to three meters across the base and approximately two meters high. The object itself had a pulsating red light on top and banks of blue lights underneath. The object was either hovering or on legs. The next day, three depressions were found in the area where the object had apparently landed. Also, the background radiation readings were above normal in the landing area with peak readings in the three depressions.

Later on, in the early morning hours of December 29, 1980, a red sun-like object was seen through the trees near the base. The object moved about and pulsed. At one time it appeared to throw off glowing particles, then broke into five separate white objects, and then disappeared. Immediately thereafter, three star-like objects were seen in the sky—two objects to the north and one to the south. The objects to the north appeared to be elliptical through an 8–12-power lens. They then turned to full circles. These objects remained in the sky for an hour or more. The object to the south was visible for two or three hours and beamed down a stream of light from time to time.

The official explanation for these sightings was a lighthouse. If the sightings were in fact caused by a lighthouse, why were they not seen before or since? What kind of lighthouse moves around and flies? That would have to be some very special lighthouse!

The thirty or so military personnel who witnessed these events have no idea what they saw. They do know it was not a lighthouse, meteor, or anything else they can identify with. To them, the events they were involved in and witnessed those nights in December 1980 still remain unexplained and unsolved.

The next incident we will discuss is taken from a U.S. Defense Intelligence Agency (DIA) Report concerning UFOs sighted over Brazil. The text of the report reads as follows: (See doc. 2-10.)

> 1. [censored]... according to sources, at least 20 unidentified objects were observed by several aircrews and on radar the night of 19 May 86. The objects were first seen by a pilot of a Xingu aircraft, transporting Ozires Silva, former President of Embraer between São Paulo and Rio de Janeiro. Fighters were launched from Santa Cruz AB (Air Base) [censored]... at approximately 2100 hours (9:00 P.M.). Although all three made radar

> contact, only one of the three pilots managed to see what he described as red, white and green lights. Shortly afterward, radar contact was made with similar objects near Brasilia and three Mirages (jet fighters) were launched from Annapolis AB [censored]... . All made radar and visual contact at 20,000 feet. They reported that they were escorted by thirteen of these disks with red, green, and white lights at a distance of one to three miles. The objects then rapidly disappeared from both ground and airborne radars.

> 2. [censored]... the Air Minister is quoted by the press as saying there were three groups of targets on the ground radar and that the scopes of the airborne radars were saturated.

> Comment: [censored]... while RO does not believe in UFOs or all the hoopla that surrounds previous reporting, there is too much here to be ignored. Three visual sightings and positive radar contact from three different types of radar systems, leads one to believe that something arrived over Brazil the night of 19 May.

The subject of this report was entitled, "BAF [Brazilian Air Force] Has a Close Encounter of the First Kind." The report also carried the following warning: "This is an info report, not finally evaluated intel [intelligence]."

In addition, the DIA released six pages of a larger document, dealing with the sightings of UFOs over Belgium in 1990. It is interesting to note that, according to the DIA, there is no requirement for that agency to collect information on UFOs and, as a result, no analysis was done on these sightings. However, the DIA still felt it necessary to consider some of the information pertaining to these sightings as classified in the interest of national security.

The cover letter from the DIA states: "The information withheld is exempt from release pursuant to (Title) 5 U.S.C. (Section) 552 (b) (1) and (b) (2), Freedom of Information Act. Subsection (b) (1) applies to information properly classified under the criteria provided by Executive Order 12356."

Then, in the next paragraph, the DIA states: "This Agency has no requirements for the collection of information pertaining to the subject of UFOs, therefore this Agency does not analyze information relating to that subject."

I asked the DIA why did they have classified information on UFOs if they are not required to collect such material and analyze it; and since this information is classified in the interest of national security, should it not be analyzed?

To date, the DIA has been unable or unwilling to answer those questions.

★★★

I feel that the cases we have discussed in this chapter clearly show that some type of unknown object or objects is operating in our airspace and has the ability to come and go as "they" wish. It would also appear that our military is powerless to do anything about "them."

This does represent a potential threat to our national security, as well as to our ability to defend ourselves should we ever find it necessary to do so.

On December 7, 1941, radar was still relatively new to the American Military. However, a radar unit was operational on the morning of December 7, 1941, in the Hawaiian Islands when they picked up many targets heading toward the islands. The duty officer (OD) was notified of these targets by the radar operators. The OD chose to disregard the report, dismissing them for the B-17s (bombers) known to be coming in from the mainland. Had this officer been more alert and properly carried out his duties, the outcome of the attack on Pearl Harbor would have been very different.

All the information concerning the incidents that we have discussed in this chapter is raw intelligence data. None of the in-

telligence assessments of the raw data has ever been released via the Freedom of Information Act (FOIA). The U.S. Government would have us believe that no such reports or assessments exist.

Could it really be that the military has forgotten the lesson learned at Pearl Harbor? Are the people in our government who are in charge of these matters alert, and are they correctly carrying out their duties? From a military viewpoint, I cannot accept that, given the evidence presented in this book, they are properly doing their jobs.

DEPARTMENT OF THE AIR FORCE
HEADQUARTERS AEROSPACE DEFENSE COMMAND
PETERSON AIR FORCE BASE, COLORADO 80914

REPLY TO
ATTN OF: DAD

11 AUG 1978

SUBJECT: Freedom of Information Request

TO: SP5 Clifford E. Stone
HQ Det, Hanau Mil Comm
APO New York 09165

1. Your letter of 23 July 1978 has been forwarded to this headquarters for a reply. After reviewing your letter and considering the type of information you are requesting, I presume you are referring to the article recently published in the 27 June 1978 edition of the National Enquirer pertinent to UFOs. I believe the following documents are applicable to your request.

    a. CIRVIS Reporting Instructions. I am not at liberty to release this document, therefore your request is being forwarded to the Director of Freedom of Information and Security Review, Office of Assistant Secretary of Defense, Washington DC 20301 for a decision on its release.

    b. UFO Checklist. The National Enquirer pictured a copy of a letter from the 21st Air division forwarding a UFO checklist to a requester. Actually, the letter was from the 26th Air Division, Luke Air Force Base, Arizona. The use of the term "UFO" on the checklist was inappropriate. The person who drew up that unofficial checklist should have used the expression "unknown aircraft." Therefore, to avoid any misconception that the Air Force still investigates and maintains files on UFO reports, the UFO checklist no longer exists. The enclosed UFO Fact Sheet (Atch 1) should help you understand why such investigations have been discontinued by the Air Force.

    c. In response to paragraph 3 of your letter, the attached extracts are releasable (Atch #2). The name, address and telephone number of persons reporting the incidents have been deleted because this information is exempt from mandatory disclosure under 5 U.S.C. 552b(6). Such disclosure is considered an unwarranted invasion of privacy.

2. The decision to withhold release of this information may be appealed in writing to the Secretary of the Air Force within 45 days from the date of this letter. If you appeal, include any reason for reconsideration you wish to present, and attach a copy of this letter. Address your letter as follows: Secretary of the Air Force, thru HQ ADCOM/DAD, Peterson AFB, CO 80914.

Terrence C James

TERRENCE C. JAMES, Colonel, USAF
Director of Administration

2 Atch
1. UFO Fact Sheet
2. Log entry extracts

Cy to: HQ USAF/DAD

UFO FACT SHEET

The Air Force investigation of UFO's began in 1948 and was known as Project Sign. Later the name was changed to Project Grudge, and in 1953, it became Project Blue Book. Between 1948 and 1969 we investigated 12,618 reported sightings.

The following is a statistical listing of reported UFO sightings during the Air Force investigation:

TOTAL UFO SIGHTINGS, 1947 - 1969

YEAR	TOTAL SIGHTINGS	UNIDENTIFIED
1947	122	12
1948	156	7
1949	186	22
1950	210	27
1951	169	22
1952	1,501	303
1953	509	42
1954	487	46
1955	545	24
1956	670	14
1957	1,006	14
1958	627	10
1959	390	12
1960	557	14
1961	591	13
1962	474	15
1963	399	14
1964	562	19
1965	887	16
1966	1,112	32
1967	937	19
1968	375	3
1969	146	1
TOTAL	12,618	701

Of these total sightings, 11,917 were found to have been caused by material objects (such as balloons, satellites, and aircraft), immaterial objects (such as lightning, reflections and other natural phenomena), astronomical objects (such as stars, planets, the sun and the moon), weather conditions and hoaxes. As indicated only 701 reported sightings remain unexplained.

On December 17, 1969 the Secretary of the Air Force announced the termination of Project Blue Book.

The decision to discontinue UFO investigations was based on an evaluation of a report prepared by the University of Colorado entitled, "Scientific Study of Unidentified Flying Objects;" a review of the University of Colorado's report by the National Academy of Sciences; past UFO studies; and Air Force experience investigating UFO reports for two decades.

As a result of these investigations and studies, and experience gained from investigating UFO reports since 1948, the conclusions of Project Blue Book were: (1) no UFO reported, investigated, and evaluated by the Air Force has ever given any indication of threat to our national security; (2) there has been no evidence submitted to or discovered by the Air Force that sightings categorized as "unidentified" represent technological developments or principles beyond the range of present day scientific knowledge; and (3) there has been no evidence indicating that sightings categorized as "unidentified" are extraterrestrial vehicles.

With the termination of Project Blue Book, the Air Force regulation establishing and controlling the program for investigating and analyzing UFOs was rescinded. All documentation regarding the former Blue Book investigation was permanently transferred to the Modern Military Branch, National Archives and Records Service, 8th and Pennsylvania Avenue, Washington, D.C. 20408, and is available for public review and analysis.

In 1977, President Carter asked the National Aeronautics and Space Administration (NASA) to look into the possibility of resuming UFO investigations. After studying all the facts available, they decided that nothing would be gained by further investigation. The Air Force agrees with that decision. If, however, firm evidence is found justifying further investigation, an appropriate agency will be directed to undertake the effort.

There are a number of universities and professional scientific organizations such as the American Association for the Advancement of Science, which have considered UFO phenomena during periodic meetings and seminars. In addition, a list of private organizations interested in aerial phenomena may be found in Gale's Encyclopedia of Associations (Edition 8, Vol I, pp. 432-3). Such timely review of the situation by private groups insures that sound evidence will not be overlooked by the scientific community.

For further reference material, two documents are available from the National Technical Information Service, U.S. Department of Commerce, Springfield, VA 22151:

Scientific Study of Unidentified Flying Objects. Study conducted by the University of Colorado under contract F44620-76-C-0035. Three volumes, 1,465 p. 68 plates. Photoduplicated hard copies of the official report may be ordered for $6 per volume, $18 the set of three, as AD 680:975, AD 680:976, and AD 680:977.

Review of University of Colorado Report on Unidentified Flying Objects. Review of report by a panel of the National Academy of Sciences. National Academy of Sciences, 1969, 6p. Photoduplicated hard copies may be ordered for $3 as AD 688:541.

EXTRACTS

NORAD COMMAND DIRECTOR'S LOG (1975)

29 Oct 75/0630Z: Command Director called by Air Force Operations
                    Center concerning an unknown helicopter landing
                    in the munitions storage area at Loring AFB, Maine.
                    Apparently this was second night in a row for this
                    occurrence. There was also an indication, but not
                    confirmed, that Canadian bases had been overflown
                    by a helicopter.

31 Oct 75/0445Z: Report from Wurtsmith AFB through Air Force Ops
                    Center - incident at 0355Z. Helicopter hovered over
                    SAC weapons storage area then departed area. Tanker
                    flying at 2700 feet made both visual sighting and
                    radar skin paint. Tracked object 25NM SE over
                    Lake Huron where contact was lost.

1 Nov 75/0920Z: Received, as info, message from Loring AFB, Maine,
                    citing probable helicopter overflight of base.

8 Nov 75/0753Z: 24th NORAD Region unknown track J330, heading SSW,
                    12000 feet. 1 to 7 objects, 46.46^{0}N x 109.23W. Two
                    F-106 scrambled out of Great Falls at 0754Z. SAC
                    reported visual sighting from Sabotage Alert Teams (SAT)
                    K1, K3, L1 and L6 (lights and set sounds). Weather
                    section states no anomolous propagation or northern
                    lights. 0835Z SAC SAT Teams K3 and L4 report visual,
                    K3 reports target at 300 feet altitude and L4 reports
                    target at 5 miles. Contact lost at 0820Z. F-106's
                    returned to base at 0850Z with negative results.
                    0905Z Great Falls radar search and height had inter-
                    mittent contact. 0910Z SAC teams agains had visual
                    (Site C-1, 10 miles SE Stanford, Montana). 0920Z SAC
                    CP reported that when F-106's were in area, targets
                    would turn out lights, and when F-106's left, targets
                    would turn lights on. F-106's never gained visual
                    or radar contact at anytime due to terrain clearance.
                    This same type of activity has been reported in the
                    Malmstrom area for several days although previous to
                    tonight no unknowns were declared. The track will
                    be carried as a remaining unknown.

10 Nov 75   Apparently Minot AFB was reportedly "buzzed" by a
                    bright object. The object's size seemed to be that
                    of an automobile. It was flying at an altitude of
                    1000 to 2000 feet and was noiseless. No further
                    information or description has been received by this
                    organization.

12 Nov 75/0715Z: Falconbridge Canadian Forces station relayed a report from Mr. ▓▓▓▓▓▓▓▓▓▓▓▓▓▓▓▓▓▓▓, Sudbury, Ontario. He saw two objects with what appeared to be artificial light fading on and off with a jerky motion.

14 Nov 75/0530Z: An unidentified civilian, located two miles from Falconbridge Canadian Forces station, saw a dot-like object for 1 and 1/4 hours. It was rotating - going back and forth at a high altitude and had white, blue and red lights.

15 Nov 75/0742Z: A Mr. ▓▓▓▓▓▓▓▓▓▓▓▓▓▓▓▓▓▓▓▓▓▓▓▓, Sudbury, Ontario, was facing south. He observed one bright yellow object going up and back, leaving a tail. It was very high, but did not change position in relation to other stars.

15 Nov 75/1229Z: A Mr. ▓▓▓▓▓▓▓▓▓▓▓▓▓▓▓▓, married student residence, Laurentian University, Sudbury, Ontario, reported he had been looking east. In a partly cloudy sky, he saw one bright object about 70° elevation, like a cup in a bowl. He was looking at it through binoculars. It climbed high out of range of his binoculars. He observed it for 20 minutes and was witnessed by his wife.

17 Nov 75/1705Z: An unidentified caller reported a large orange ball was seen on an azimuth of 45° from River Court, Ontario. It had two red lights and was stationary.

23 Nov 75/1700Z: A Ms ▓▓▓▓▓▓▓▓▓▓▓▓▓▓▓▓▓▓▓, Chelmsford, reported she and friends were travelling by car from Sudbury to Chelmsford. They were followed by a huge oval-shaped object with white blinking lights. It remained below the clouds all the while and kept up with the car.

16 Nov 75/0644Z: The Command Post received a report from a ▓▓▓▓▓▓ ▓▓▓▓▓▓▓▓▓▓▓▓▓▓▓▓▓▓▓, Cloquet, MN (phone ▓▓▓▓ ▓▓▓▓). At 0430Z, while driving toward home, he passed through the town of Esko. He saw a cigar shaped objective with red, green and white flashing lights, going up and down and making sharp turns. He observed this for two hours. Sky conditions were clear.

18 Nov 75/1255Z: The Command Post was told that sightings of fire balls, vicinity of Mendicino County, California, had taken place. No further information, e.g., time, location, duration, etc., was available.

25 Nov 75/1245Z: ▓▓▓▓▓▓▓▓▓▓▓▓▓▓▓▓▓▓▓▓▓▓ Petersburg, Virginia, reported that at about 0600 EST, she saw an object hovering at tree-top level in a clearing near power lines one-half mile distant. It had 4 red lights in diamond shape and 2 white flashing lights. She heard no noise, saw no movement and could not distinguish any color. She was in her car at the time, and slowed to 10 mph but did not stop. At 1340, the Command Post was informed that she had been reinterviewed by local authorities. She stated that the object was diamond-shaped with one red light at each point and that she did not see any wings. The location was reported to be one mile WSW of Petersburg, in a wooded area where power lines were being installed.

EXTRACTS

24 NORAD REGION SENIOR DIRECTOR LOG

7 Nov 75 (1035Z) - Received a call from the 341st Strategic Air Command Post (SAC CP), saying that the following missile locations reported seeing a large red to orange to yellow object: M-1, L-3, LIMA and L-6. The general object location would be 10 miles south of Moore, Montana, and 20 miles east of Buffalo, Montana. Commander and Deputy for Operations (DO) informed.

7 Nov 75 (1203Z) - SAC advised that the LCF at Harlowton, Montana observed an object which emitted a light which illuminated the site driveway.

7 Nov 75 (1319Z) - SAC advised K-1 says very bright object to their east is now southeast of them and they are looking at it with 10 x 50 binoculars. Object seems to have lights (several) on it, but no distinct pattern. The orange/gold object overhead also has small lights on it. SAC also advises female civilian reports having seen an object bearing south from her position six miles west of Lewistown.

7 Nov 75 (1327Z) - L-1 reports that the object to their northeast seems to be issuing a black object from it, tubular in shape. In all this time, surveillance has not been able to detect any sort of track except for known traffic.

7 Nov 75 (1355Z) - K-1 and L-1 report that as the sun rises, so do the objects they have visual.

7 Nov 75 (1429Z) - From SAC CP: As the sun rose, the UFOs disappeared. Commander and DO notified.

8 Nov 75 (0635Z) - A security camper team at K-4 reported UFO with white lights, one red light 50 yards behind white light. Personnel at K-1 seeing same object.

8 Nov 75 (0645Z) - Height personnel picked up objects 10-13,000 feet, Track J330, EKLB 0648, 18 knots, 9,500 feet. Objects as many as seven, as few as two A/C.

8 Nov 75 (0745Z)- Conversation about the UFOs; Advised to go ahead and scramble; but to be sure and brief pilots, FAA. Go easy and the fighters will not descend below 12,000 ft.

8 Nov 75 (0753Z) - J330 unknown 0753. Stationary/seven knots/ 12,000. One (varies to seven) object. None, no possibility, EK LB 3746, two F-106, GTF, SCR 0754. NCOC notified.

8 Nov 75 (0820Z) - Lost radar contact, fighters broken off at 0825, looking in area of J331 (another height finder contact).

8 Nov 75 (0850Z) - Directed ftrs to RTB (return to base).

8 Nov 75 (0905Z) - From SAC CP; L-sites had fighters and objects; fighters did not get down to objects.

8 Nov 75 (0915Z) - From SAC CP: From four different points: Observed objects and fighters; when fighters arrived in the area, the lights went out; when fighters departed, the lights came back on; to NCOC.

8 Nov 75 (0953Z) - From SAC CP: L-5 reported object increased in speed - high velocity, raised in altitude and now cannot tell the object from stars. To NCOC.

8 Nov 75 (1105Z) - From SAC CP: E-1 reported a bright white light (site is approximately 60 nautical miles north of Lewistown). NCOC notified.

9 Nov 75 (0305Z) - SAC CP called and advised SAC crews at Sites L-1, L-6, and M-1 observing UFO. Object yellowish bright round light 20 miles north of Harlowton, 2 to 4,000 feet.

9 Nov 75 (0320Z) - SAC CP reports UFO 20 miles southeast of Lewistown, orange white disc object. 24th NORAD Region surveillance checking area. Surveillance unable to get height check.

9 Nov 75 (0320Z) - FAA Watch Supervisor reported he had five air carriers vicinity of UFO, United Flight 157 reported seeing meteor, "arc welders blue" in color. SAC CP advised, sites still report seeing object stationary.

9 Nov 75 (0348Z) - SAC CP confirms L-1, sees object, a mobile security team has been directed to get closer and report.

9 Nov 75 (0629Z) - SAC CP advises UFO sighting reported around 0305Z. Cancelled the flight security team from site L-1, checked area and all secure, no more sightings.

2

10 Nov 75 (0125Z) - Received a call from SAC CP. Report UFO sighting from site K-1 around Harlowton area. Surveillance checking area with height finder.

10 Nov 75 (0153Z) - Surveillance report unable to locate track that would correlate with UFO sighted by K-1.

10 Nov 75 (1125Z) - UFO sighting reported by Minot Air Force Station, a bright star-like object in the west, moving east, about the size of a car. First seen approximately 1015Z. Approximately 1120Z, the object passed over the radar station, 1,000 feet to 2,000 feet high, no noise heard. Three people from the site or local area saw the object. NCOC notified.

12 Nov 75 (0230Z) - UFO reported from K01. They say the object is over Big Snowy mtn with a red light on it at high altitude. Attempting to get radar on it from Opheim. Opheim searching from 120° to 140°.

12 Nov 75 (0248Z) - Second UFO in same area reported. Appeared to be sending a beam of light to the ground intermittently. At 0250Z object disappeared.

12 Nov 75 (0251Z) - Reported that both objects have disappeared. Never had any joy (contact) on radar.

13 Nov 75 (0951Z) - SAC CP with UFO report. P-SAT team enroute from R-3 to R-4 saw a white lite, moving from east to west. In sight approx 1 minute. No determination of height, moving towards Brady. No contact on radar.

19 Nov 75 (1327Z) - SAC command post report UFO observed by FSC & a cook, observed object travelling NE between M-8 and M-1 at a fast rate of speed. Object bright white light seen 45 to 50 sec following terrain 200 ft off ground. The light was two to three times brighter than landing lights on a jet.
------------LAST ENTRY PERTAINING TO THESE INCIDENTS------

3

N.M.C.C

THE NATIONAL MILITARY COMMAND CENTER
WASHINGTON, D.C. 20301

THE JOINT STAFF

21 January 1976
0630 EST

MEMORANDUM FOR RECORD

Subject: Report of UFO - Cannon AFB NM

Reference: AFOC Phonecon 21055 EST Jan 76

The following information was received from the Air Force
Operations Center at 0555 EST:

"Two UFOs are reported near the flight line at Cannon AFB,
New Mexico. Security Police observing them reported the UFOs
to be 25 yards in diameter, gold or silver in color with blue
light on top, hole in the middle and red light on bottom. Air
Force is checking with radar. Additionally, checking weather
inversion data."

J.B. MORIN
Rear Admiral, USN
Deputy Director for
Operations, NMCC

N M C C

THE NATIONAL MILITARY COMMAND CENTER
WASHINGTON. D.C. 20301

THE JOINT STAFF

31 January 1976
1900 EST

MEMORANDUM FOR THE RECORD

Subject: Unidentified Flying Object Sighting

1. At 310805 received phoncon from AFOC: MG Lane, CG, Armament
and Development Test Center, Eglin AFB, Florida called and reported
a UFO sighting from 0430 EST to 0600 EST. Security Policemen
spotted lights from what they called a UFO near an Eglin radar
site.

2.   ographs of the lights were taken. The Eglin Office of
In...mation has made a press release on the UFO.

3. The temperature inversion analysis indicated no significant
temperature inversion at Eglin AFB at that time. The only
inversion present was due to radiation from the surface to 2500
feet. The Eglin surface conditions were clear skies, visibility
10-14 miles, calm winds, shallow ground fog on the runway, and
a surface temperature of 44 degree F.

FRED A. TREY
Brigadier General, USAF
Deputy Director for
Operations (NMCC)

DISTRIBUTION:
DDO
ADDO
CCOC
West Hem
PA
AFOC
J-30
J-32

NMCC

THE NATIONAL MILITARY COMMAND CENTER
WASHINGTON, D.C. 20301

THE JOINT STAFF

30 July 1976
0345 EDT

MEMORANDUM FOR RECORD

Subject: Reports of Unidentified Flying Objects (UFOs)

1.   At approximately 0345 EDT, the ANMCC called to indicate
they had received several reports of UFO's in the vicinity
of Fort Ritchie. The following events summarize the reports
(times are approximate).

    a.   0130 - Civilians reported a UFO sighting near
Mt. Airy, Md. This information was obtained via a call
from the National Aeronautics Board (?) to the Fort
Ritchie Military Police.

    b.   0255 - Two separate patrols from Site R reported
sighting 3 oblong objects with a reddish tint, moving
east to west. Personnel were located at separate locations
on top of the mountain at Site R.

    c.   0300 - Desk Sgt at Site R went to the top of the
Site R mountain and observed a UFO over the ammo storage
area at 100-200 yards altitude.

    d.   0345 - An Army Police Sgt on the way to work at
Site R reported sighting a UFO in the vicinity of Site R.

2.   ANMCC was requested to have each individual write a
statement on the sightings. One individual stated the object
was about the size of a 2 1/2 ton truck.

3.   Based on a JCS memorandum, subject: Temperature Inversion
Analysis, dated 13 November 1975, the NMCC contacted the Air
Force Global Weather Central. The Duty Officer, LTC OVERBY,
reported that the Dulles International Airport observations
showed two temperature inversions existed at the time of the

Subject: Reports of Unidentified Flying Objects (UFOs)

alleged sightings. The first extended from the surface to
1,000 feet absolute and the second existed between 27,000
and 30,000 feet, absolute. He also said the atmosphere
between 12,000 and 20,000 feet was heavily saturated with
moisture. A hard copy message will follow.

L. J. Le Blanc Jr.

L. J. LEBLANC, Jr.
Brigadier General, USMC
Deputy Director for
Operations, NMCC

DISTRIBUTION:
J-30
J-31
J-32
J-33
DDO
ADDO
CCOC
WHEM Desk
ASD/PA Rep

2

DEPARTMENT OF THE NAVY
COMMANDER SEA BASED ASW WINGS ATLANTIC
BOX 102, NAVAL AIR STATION
JACKSONVILLE, FLORIDA 32212

1 August 1979

Staff Sergeant Clifford E. Stone
301-50-0182
HQ Det, Hanau MilCom
APO New York, New York 09165

Dear Sergeant Stone:

Records in the Naval Air Station, Jacksonville, Public Affairs Office
indicate that a reply to your request for information on the Pinecastle
Electronic Warfare Range UFO sighting was mailed to you at the above
address on 30 September 1978. I regret that you did not receive it.

Enclosed are duplicates of the information mailed. As you will notice,
the handwritten log entry is quite sketchy and really provides little
information on the incident. Naval Air Station, Jacksonville did release an advisory message on the subject to the Chief of Naval Operations, but it only provided a summary of the same information contained
in the Ocala Star-Banner article that is enclosed. The only addition
was a statement verifying the reliability of Petty Officers Clark and
Collins.

No formal investigation or informal investigation was made into the
reported sightings. It was considered by command that some unexplained
object was in the air as reported and there was no way to reenact the
situation. Once the command certified the reliability of the individuals involved, there was nothing that could be accomplished.

I worked very closely with the incident, fielding requests from media
throughout the nation and arranging interviews with Clark and Collins.
I have never been a believer in "UFOs," but I assure you I am convinced that a number of people witnessed an unexplainable event at
Pinecastle that night. The speed of the object ruled out a helicopter
and the reported maneuverability ruled out any aircraft including
VSTOLs that we are aware of.

Again, I regret you did not receive the first package and assure you
there was no intent to deny you the information whether or not the
request was filed under the Freedom of Information Act.

I realize that the information furnished is at best sketchy, but there
was little to be documented and actually little command concern. As
I recall, the incident was not reported to command until the story
broke in the Star-Banner. At that time the message, a condensation
from the Star-Banner, was released and other than handling media requests, no further command action was taken.

Sincerely,

N. P. YOUNG
Public Affairs Officer

Encls.

OTTCZYUW RUCLEKA0462 1371718-CCCC--RUCBSAA RUENAAA RUEOALL RUCITNA.
ZNY CCCCC
O 171824Z MAY 78
FM NAS JACKSONVILLE FL
TO RUCBSAA/CINCLANTFLT NORFOLK VA

INFO RUENAAA/CNO WASHINGTON DC
RUEOALL/COMNAVAIRLANT NORFOLK VA
RUCITNA/COMSIX CHARLESTON SC
ZEN/COMSEABASEDASWWINGSLANT JACKSONVILLE FL
BT
C O N F I D E N T I A L
NAS JACKSONVILLE /OPREP-3 NAVY BLUE 171800Z MAY 78/006
A. REPORTS OF UFO DISPLAYING RED, GREEN AND WHITE LIGHTS
A1. SITUATION UNDER CONTROL
H1. INITIAL REPORTED UFO SIGHTING BY TWO UNIDENTIFIED CIVILIANS.
H2. NA
H3. 142200L MAY 78 TO 150020L MAY78
H4. NA
H5. AT 2200 LOCAL, 14 MAY 1978, PINECASTLE RANGE DUTY OFFICER, SK1
CLARK, RECEIVED A TELEPHONE CALL FROM AN UNIDENTIFIED FEMALE. SAID
SHE LIVED NEAR SILVER GLEN SPRINGS AND WANTED TO KNOW IF RANGE WAS
OPEN AND WHETHER NAVY WAS DROPPING PARACHUTE FLARES OVER LAKE GEORGE

PAGE 2 RUCLEKA0462 C O N F I D E N T I A L
(SHE HAD OBSERVED NUMEROUS PARACHUTE DROPS IN THE PAST).
WHEN TOLD THE RANGE WAS CLOSED, SHE TOLD CLARK SHE WAS LOOKING
(AT THAT TIME) AT STRANGE RED, GREEN AND WHITE LIGHTS ABOVE THE
TREES OVER THE WEST BANK OF LAKE GEORGE NEAR AN AREA CALLED THE "SINK-
HOLE." CALLER IMMEDIATEL HUNG UP WITHOUT IDENTIFYING HERSELF.
     AT 2210 LOCAL, CLARK RECEIVED A TELEPHONE CALL FROM AN
UNIDENTIFIED MALE, WHO ALSO WANTED TO KNOW IF RANGE WAS IN OPER-
ATION. WHEN TOLD IT WAS NOT, CALLER SAID HE AND EIGHT OTHER PEOPLE
--LOCATED ON STATE HIGHWAY 19-- HAD OBSERVED AND OBJECT, ABOUT
50-60 FEET IN DIAMETER, PASS OVER THEM AT TREE--TOP LEVEL. IT WAS
DISPLAYING "MULTI-COLORED" LIGHTS. CALLLER IMMEDIATELY HUNG UP
WITHOUT IDENTIFYING HIMSELF.
     CLARK THEN NOTIFIED THE CONTROL TOWER WATCHSTANDER TO SEARCH
THE AREA TOWARDSILVER GLEN SPRINGS WITH BINOCULARS. THE WATCH-
STANDER OBSERVED STATIONARY LIGHTS AT AN ESTIMATED ALTITUDE OF
OF 1600 FEET IN THE AREA REPORTED BY THETELEPHONE CALLERS.
CLARK THEN CHECKED WITH JACKSONVILLE CENTER FOR THE POSSIBLITY
OF COMMERICAL/MILITARY AIRCRAFT OPERATIONS IN THE AREA. CENTER
HAD NO INFORMATION ON KNOWN FLIGHT OPERATIONS IN THE LAKE GEORGE AREA.

PAGE 3 RUCLEKA0462 C O N F I D E N T I A L
     CLARK THEN SUMMONED TD2 COLLINGS FROM THE BARRACKS TO ACTIVATE
THE MSO-102 RADAR. AFTER A 20 MINUTE WARMUP, COLLINS LOCKED ON TO
A KNOWN TARGET IN THE AREA-- THE CIVIL DEFENSE TOWER-- IN AUTOMATIC

     DY/3   3/3   13   173824Z MAY 78
          ****
     IMMEDIATE   * C O N F I D E N T I A L *
          ****

Doc. 2-5d Navy Dept. letter with Encls., Aug 1, 1979

00757   137 210231   00210408   B137

TRACK MODE. HIS "ALPHA" SCAN INDICATED ONE STATIONARY TARGET
(THE CD TOWER) AND ONE UNIDENTIFIED BLIP "FLUTTERING" OVER THE
TOWER. COLLINS PUT THE TRACKING COMPUTER ON THE UNIDENTIFIED
TARGET, AND IT WAS NOT REGISTERING ANY SIGNIFICANT GROUND VELOCITY.
BEARING TO THE C/D TOWER WAS 291 DEGREES MAGNETIC, BUT COLLINS WAS
UNABLE TO LOCK ON THE UNIDENTIFIED TARGET IN THE SAME VICINITY AND
STATED THERE SEEMED TO BE SOME CONFUSION AT THIS TIME AS TO THE EXACT
BEARING OF THE OBJECTS FROM HIM. HE HAD OBSERVED THE TARGET FOR PERHAPS
  WHN IT BEGAN MOVING ACROSS THE RADAR SCOPE, FROM
NORTHWEST TO SOUTH, AT ABOUT 400-500 KNOTS, COLLINGS SAID HE TRIED TO
"TRAIN" THE RADAR ON THE OBJECT, BUT IT ACCELERATED RAPIDLY,
EVADING HIS EFFORTS TO LOCK AND TRACK IT ON THE COMPUTER. WHEN HE
CAUGHT UP WITH THE OBJECT, IT REVERSED DIRECTION AND STARTED BACK
TOWARD PINECASTLE. COLLINS FINALLY LOCKED ON THE OBJECT AFTER IT HAD
PRACTICALLY STOPPPED MOVING. THE COMPUTER THEN INDICATED 2 KNOTS
GROUND VELOCITY. SHORTLY AFTER, THE TARGET BROKE RADAR LOCK, AND
COLLINGS SECURED THE RADAR. AT THIS TIME, IT WAS 0020L ON 15 MAY.
COLLINS HAS BEEN OPERATING RADAR FOR MOST OF HIS EIGHT YEARS OF

PAGE 4 RUCLEKA0462 C O N F I D E N T I A L
SERVCE.

    A TOTAL OF EIGHT NAVAL PERSONNEL VISUALLY OBSERVED THE RED, GREEN
AND WHITE LIGHTS OF THE OBJECT FROM THE CONTROL TOWER FOR OVER AN
HOUR. TOWARD THE END OF THIS PERIOD, THE LIGHTS WERE OBSERVED TO MOVE
SOUTH FOR ABOUT 20 MILES AND THEN RETURN TO THE VICINITY OF THE
PINECASTLE RANGE.
H. WEST SOUTHWEST BANK OF LAKE GEORGE NEAR SETTLEMENT OF SILVER
GLEN SPRINGS ON STATE HIGHWAY 19 APPROX 5 MILES NORTH OF THE
NAVY'S PINECASTLE ELECTRONIC WARFARE RANGE.
K. NONE
Z. INITIAL REPORTS BY PEWR MILITARY PERSONNEL WERE NOT CONSIDERED TO
BE PARTICULARLY UNUSUAL OR POSITIVE BUT RATHER INFLUENCED BY TWO
UNIDENTIFIED CIVILIAN CALLERS AND ACTIVE CURIOSITY. UNOFFICIAL
CONTACT BETWEEN MEDIA AND SERVICEMEN RESULTED IN MEDIA PRESENTING
SERVICEMEN'S REMARKS AS AN OFFICIAL NAVY NEWS RELEASE PRIOR TO COMMAND
EVEN HAVING DISCUSSED SEQUENCE OF EVENTS WITH SERVICEMEN. OINC
PEWR STATES HIS QUOTED STATEMENT WAS INACCURATE AS PRINTED. OPREP
NOT SUBMITTED EARLIER AS INITIAL REPORT CONSIDERED HOAX AND WOULD
NOT GENERATE SIGNIFICANT PRESS INTEREST IF APPROACHED IN A FACTUAL

PAGE 5 RUCLEKA0462 C O N F I D E N T I A LL
MANNER. PERRY OFFICERS CLARK AND COLLINS ON NORMAL LIBERTY 15 MAY
AS A RESULT OF WATCH STANDING. STATEMENTS OF CLARK AND COLLINS
TAKEN AFTERNOON OF 16 MAY AT PEWR BUT NOT AVAILABLE TO NAS JAX UNTIL
MORNING OF THE 17 MAY DUE TO COMMUNICATION LINE PROBLEM.
ABNORMAL AMOUNT OF PRESS AND TV INTEREST PRESENTLY BEING SHOWN.
Z1. LAST OPREP-3 REPORT THIS INCIDENT.
ADS-17 JUN 1978
BT

                            2/2   11

DEPARTMENT OF THE AIR FORCE
HEADQUARTERS UNITED STATES AIR FORCE
WASHINGTON, D.C. 20330

30 June 1983

SSG Clifford E. Stone
HQ Det, Hnu Mil Comm
APO New York 09165

Dear Sergeant Stone

This responds to your Freedom of Information Act letter dated
13 June 1983. We received it 16 June 1983.

We were unable to locate any records at this headquarters
responsive to your request.

We also checked with the Freedom of Information Act office at
Kirtland AFB New Mexico and they have no records of any UFO
sightings over Kirtland AFB during August 1980.

Sincerely

ANNE W. TURNER
HQ USAF Freedom of
    Information Manager

83-442

DEPARTMENT OF THE AIR FORCE
HEADQUARTERS AIR FORCE OFFICE OF SPECIAL INVESTIGATIONS
BOLLING AIR FORCE BASE, DC 20332-6001

9 DEC 1985

SFC Clifford E. Stone
Department of Military Science
New Mexico Military Institute
Roswell NM 88201-2173

Dear SFC Stone

This is in response to your request for information of 19
November 1985.

The Defense Central Index of Investigations (DCII) was searched
using the data that you provided. The search revealed that AFOSI
is not maintaining any information pertaining to "an alleged UFO
incident....in the Fort Dix-McGuire AFB area." The DCII is a
consolidated index of investigative files held by Department of
Defense components.

If you would like to correspond directly with McGuire Air Force
Base concerning the alleged incident, their address is:

    438ABG/DADF
    McGuire AFB NJ 08641-6337

Portions of AFOSI file 8017D93-0/29 are exempt from disclosure to
you. Notations were added to identify the portions deleted and
the reasons therefore. The notations are explained as follows:
"b7C" pertains to information that, if disclosed to the public,
would result in a clearly unwarranted invasion of personal
privacy. The authority for this exemption may be found in the
United States Code, Title 5, Section 552(b)(7)(C) and Air Force
Regulation 12-30, paragraph 10g(1)(c).

Should you decide that an appeal to this decision is necessary,
you must write to the Secretary of the Air Force within 45 days
from the date of this letter. Include in the appeal your reasons
for reconsideration and attach a copy of this letter. Address
your letter as follows:

    Secretary of the Air Force
    Thru: HQ AFOSI/DADF
    Bolling AFB DC 20332-6001

"HELPING TO PROTECT A GREAT WAY OF LIFE"

On 19 December 1975, AFOSI transferred Project BLUE BOOK files and other AFOSI investigations regarding UFO sightings to the National Archives and Records Service (NARS). The documents included all files pertaining to unidentified flying objects (UFOs) that AFOSI had been maintaining, and consisted of classified as well as unclassified documents. At the time of the transfer, NARS planned to incorporate AFOSI documents with other similar documents into Accession No. NN-375-209. The documents transferred to NARS included data recorded from 1948 to 1968 concerning Air Force investigations of UFOs, and policy on investigating such matters.

Subsequent to the transfer of the aforementioned documents to NARS, alleged UFO sighting reported to AFOSI were and continue to be, referred to the commander of the Air Force installation where the report was received. No investigation is conducted by AFOSI. Additionally, we are unaware of what action, if any, is taken by the concerned commander when such a report is referred. Such referrals by AFOSI are not indexed in the DCII.

If you wish to receive information regarding a particular sighting which was reported to Air Force officials, you should write to the commander of the installation where the report was received.

Sincerely,

CECIL W. Fry, SA
Chief, Information Release Division
Directorate of Administration

1 Atch
Cy of AFOSI File
8017D93-0/29, Less
Exemptions

COMPLAINT FORM

ADMINISTRATIVE DATA

TITLE KIRTLAND AFB, NM, 8 Aug - 3 Sep 80, Alleged Sigthings of Unidentified Aerial Lights in Restricted Test Range.	**DATE** 2 - 9 Sept 80 **TIME** 1200

Doc. 2-7c U.S.A.F. Letter with Encls., Dec 9, 1985

PLACE AFOSI Det 1700, Kirtland AFB, NM

HOW RECEIVED:

X IN PERSON	TELEPHONICALLY	IN WRITING

SOURCE AND EVALUATION
MAJOR ERNEST E. EDWARDS.

RESIDENCE OR BUSINESS ADDRESS
Commander, 1608 SPS, Manzano
Kirtland AFB, NM

PHONE 4-7516

CR 44 APPLIES

SUMMARY OF INFORMATION

REMARKS

1. On 2 Sept 80, SOURCE related on 8 Aug 80, three Security Policemen assigned to 1608 SPS, KAFB, NM, on duty inside the Manzano Weapons Storage Area sighted an unidentified light in the air that traveled from North to South over the Coyote Canyon area of the Department of Defense Restricted Test Range on KAFB, NM. The Security Policemen identified as: SSGT STEPHEN FERENZ, Area Supervisor, AIC MARTIN W. RIST and AMN ANTHONY D. FRAZIER, were later interviewed separately by SOURCE. and all three related the same statement; At approximately 2350hrs., while on duty in Charlie Sector, East Side of Manzano, the three observed a very bright light in the sky approximately 3 miles North-North East of their position. The light traveled with great speed and stopped suddenly in the sky over Coyote Canyon. The three first thought the object was a helicopter, however, after observing the strange aerial maneuvers (stop and go), they felt a helicopter couldn't have performed such skills. The light landed in the Coyote Canyon area. Sometime later, three witnessed the light take off and leave proceeding straight up at a hight speed and disappear.

2. Central Security Control (CSC) inside Manzano, contacted Sandia Security, who conducts frequent building checks on two alarmed structures in the area. They advised that a patrol was already in the area and would investigate.

3. On 11 Aug 80, RUSS CURTIS, Sandia Security, advised that on 9 Aug 80, a Sandia Security Guard, (who wishes his name not be divulged for fear of harassment), related the following: At approximately 0020hrs., he was driving East on the Coyote Canyon access road on a routine building check of an alarmed structure. As he approached the structure he observed a bright light near the ground behind the structure. He also observed an object he first thought was a helicopter. But after driving closer, he observed a round disk shaped object. He attempted to radio for a back up patrol but his radio would not work. As he approached the object on foot armed with a shotgun, the object took off in a vertical direction at a high rate of speed. The guard was a former helicopter mechanic in the U.S. Army and stated the object he observed was not a helicopter.

4. SOURCE advised on 22 Aug 80, three other security policemen observed the same

DATE FORWARDED HQ AFOSI HQ IVOS 10 Aug 80	**AFOSI FORM 80 ATTACHED** ☐ YES ☐ NO	
DATE 9 Sept 80	**TYPED OR PRINTED NAME OF SPECIAL AGENT** RICHARD C. DOTY, SA	**SIGNATURE** *Richard C. Doty*
DISTRICT FILE NO. 8017 8 93-0/29		**DCII RESULTS** ☐ NEGATIVE ☐ POSITIVE (See Attached)

AFOSI FORM 1   PREVIOUS EDITION WILL BE USED.

CONTINUED FROM COMPLAINT FORM 1, DTD 9 Sept 80

aerial phenomena described by the first three. Again the object landed in Coyote Canyon. They did not see the object take off.

5. Coyote Canyon is part of a large restricted test range used by the Air Force Weapons Laboratory, Sandia Laboratories, Defense Nuclear Agency and the Department of Energy. The range was formerly patrolled by Sandia Security, however, they only conduct building checks there now.

6. On 10 Aug 80, a New Mexico State Patrolman sighted an aerial object land in the Manzano's between Belen and Albuquerque, NM. The Patrolman reported the sighting to the Kirtland AFB Command Post, who later referred the patrolman to the AFOSI Dist 17. AFOSI Dist 17 advised the patrolman to make a report through his own agency. On 11 Aug 80, the Kirtland Public Information office advised the patrolman the USAF no longer investigates such sightings unless they occur on an USAF base.

7. WRITER contacted all the agencies who utilized the test range and it was learned no aerial tests are conducted in the Coyote Canyon area. Only ground tests are conducted.

8. On 8 Sept 80, WRITER learned from Sandia Security that another Security Guard observed a object land near an alarmed structure sometime during the first week of August, but did not report it until just recently for fear of harassment.

9. The two alarmed structures located within the area contains HQ CR 44 material.

ऽ└८-

IN REPLY TO	AFOSI COMMUNICATION	DATE OF TRANSMITTAL 30 July 1981

TO:

AFOSI/CC

SUBJECT

Dr. PAUL FREDRICK BENNEWITZ
Congressional Inquiry

FROM:

AFOSI District 17/CC
Kirtland AFB, NM 87117

REFERENCE

8017D93-0/29

ITEMS CHECKED ARE APPLICABLE TO ABOVE SUBJECT

- INVESTIGATION HAS BEEN INITIATED AND REPORTS WILL BE FORWARDED AS SOON AS POSSIBLE.
- THIS MATTER IS ☐ PENDING ☐ CLOSED.
- REQUEST REPORT OF ACTION TAKEN (AFR 124-4).
- NOTE RESTRICTIVE LEGENDS ON FRONT OF THE ATTACHMENT(S).
- REQUEST INSTRUCTIONS AS TO DISPOSITION OF EVIDENCE LISTED BELOW.
- ATTACHED IS AN INTELLIGENCE INFORMATION REPORT (IIR) TRANSMITTED ELECTRICALLY IN THE INTERESTS OF TIMELINESS. NUMERICAL DESIGNATORS IN THE IIR ARE AS FOLLOWS: 1. COUNTRY; 2. REPORT NUMBER; 3. TITLE; 4. PROJECT NUMBER; 5. DATE OF INFORMATION; 6. DATE OF REPORT; 7. DATE AND PLACE OF ACQUISITION; 8. REFERENCES; 9. ASSESSMENT; 10. ORIGINATOR; 11. REQUEST EVALUATION; 12. PREPARING OFFICER; 13. APPROVING AUTHORITY; 12. SOURCE.
- ATTACHED IS AN INFORMATION COLLECTION REPORT (ICR) WHICH CONTAINS INFORMATION CONCERNING AN INDIVIDUAL UNDER YOUR COMMAND. THE ICR IS FURNISHED FOR YOUR INFORMATION ONLY AND IT DOES NOT CONSTITUTE A FORMAL OR COMPLETE INVESTIGATION OF THE INDIVIDUAL. IF A FORMAL INVESTIGATION IS WARRANTED, IT SHOULD BE REQUESTED IN ACCORDANCE WITH AFR 124-4.
- THE ATTACHED REPORT HAS BEEN LOANED TO THE USAF BY ANOTHER AGENCY. DISSEMINATION OF THAT REPORT TO ANOTHER AGENCY OR ITS PERMANENT INCORPORATION INTO ANY USAF RECORDS SYSTEM WILL NOT BE MADE WITHOUT PRIOR APPROVAL OF THE ORIGINATING AGENCY. WHEN THIS REPORT HAS SERVED ITS PURPOSE, IT WILL BE DESTROYED; NO RECORD OF THE REPORT IS BEING MAINTAINED BY AFOSI.
- WHEN ATTACHMENT(S) IS/ARE REMOVED. THE CLASSIFICATION OF THIS CORRESPONDENCE WILL BE ☐ RETAINED ☐ DOWNGRADED TO ___ ☐ CANCELED ☐ MARKED "FOR OFFICIAL USE ONLY"

OTHER/REMARKS:

On 30 Jul 81, the 1606th ABW IG contacted DO 17/BID and advised that Senator PETER DOMENICI desired to talk to SA RICK DOTY regarding the matter involving BENNEWITZ. After checking with Col HARVELL, Acting AFOSI/CC, it was agreed SA DOTY and DO 17/CC would meet with Senator DOMENICI. Senator DOMENICI was present in the IG's Office but departed immediately to meet with BENNEWITZ. A subsequent check with Mr. TIJEROS, Senator DOMENICI's Aide, in an effort to determine the Senator's specific questions, determined his sole interest was to know whether AFOSI had conducted a formal investigation of SUBJECT. Mr. TIJEROS was informed that no formal investigation of BENNEWITZ was conducted by AFOSI. Mr. TIJEROS stated that he assumed if any information were available, and was to be requested from AFOSI, it would have to be requested from our Headquarters. He was provided Col BEYEA's name and the Bolling AFB address of our HQ AFOSI in event he desired any further information. Mr. TIJEROS thanked us and indicated no further inquiries from the Senator regarding this matter are anticipated.

8017D93-0/29.X

NAME, GRADE, TITLE, SIGNATURE	ATTACHMENTS	COPIES TO
FRANK M. HUEY, Colonel, USAF Commander		HQ AFOSI/IVOS File

AFOSI FORM ___ JUL 77 ___ PREVIOUS EDITION IS OBSOLETE.

MULTI PURPOSE INTER. OSI FORM
(Complete only applic.. 's)

O NO.(S) 17/180	SUBJECT
ET NO.(S)	KIRTLAND AFB, NM, 8 Aug - 3 Sep 80
EADQUARTERS	Alleged Sightings of Unidentified Aerial
O NO. 17/BID	Lights in Restricted Test Range
ET NO.	
EADQUARTERS	

FILE NO.
8017093-0/29

TRANSMITTAL DATE
28 Oct 80

SUSPENSE DATE

RENCE

AFOSI Fm 1, 8 Sep 80; Same Title.

INOR DISCREPANCIES NOTED ARE LISTED BELOW.

OUR DISTRICT IS DESIGNATED OFFICE OF ORIGIN.

TTACHED REQUIRES INVESTIGATION IN YOUR AREA.

ETERMINE SUBJECTS ACCESS TO CLASSIFIED INFORMATION AS REQUIRED BY OSIS 124-1, PARA 2-6-1.

ORWARD RESULTS DIRECTLY TO OFFICE OF ORIGIN, OR TO:

O FURTHER INVESTIGATION CONTEMPLATED.

UR FILES REFLECT PRIOR INVESTIGATION BY _____, DTD _____, FILE _____ (By copy of this form _____ is requested to furnish _____ copies of prior investigation/letter summary, if applicable, to _____)

EPORT OF PRIOR INVESTIGATION/SUMMARY ATTACHED.

VESTIGATION CONTINUING AND YOU WILL BE FURNISHED FURTHER REPORTS.

ISCONTINUE INVESTIGATION. FORWARD RESULTS OF ANY INVESTIGATION ACCOMPLISHED.

ISCREPANCIES BETWEEN LEAD REQUEST AND DEVELOPED INFORMATION ARE SET FORTH.

EPORT OF COMMAND ACTION HAS NOT BEEN RECEIVED.

EQUEST STATUS OF THIS MATTER AND/OR DATE REPORT MAY BE EXPECTED. *(Requestor, forward 2 copies of this form.) (Recipient, use one received copy for answer with proper signature in remarks section unless OSI directives state reply not required.)*

EFER ATTACHED TO INTERESTED COMMANDER FOR INFORMATION OR ACTION IF NOT PREVIOUSLY REPORTED.

HECK WORLD-WIDE LOCATOR FOR BELOW LISTED PERSON OR SUBJECT

TTACHED IS FORWARDED FOR INFORMATION AND/OR ACTION.

PON REMOVAL OF ATTACHMENT(S) _____ THE CLASSIFICATION ON THIS CORRESPONDENCE WILL BE

☐ RETAINED. ☐ DOWNGRADED TO _____ ☐ CANCELED. ☐ MARKED "FOR OFFICIAL USE ONLY."

(If classification is retained, with or without attachments, indicate reason for security classification and grouping per AFR 205-1.)

ARKS

On 24 Oct 80, Dr PAUL FREDRICK BENNEWITZ, Male Born 30 Sep 27, KS, Civ, SSAN: [b7C]
[b7C] Albuquerque, NM, contacted SA RICHARD C. DOTY through Major
TEST E. EDWARDS, Commander, 1608 SPS, Kirtland AFB, NM and related he had knowledge and
idence of threats against Manzano Weapons Storage area. The threat was from Aerial
enomena over Manzano.

On 26 Oct 80, SA DOTY, with the assistance of JERRY MILLER, GS-15, Chief, Scientific
visor for Air Force Test and Evaluation Center, KAFB, interviewed Dr. BENNEWITZ at his
me in the Four Hills Section of Albuquerque, which is adjacent to the northern boundary
Manzano Base. (NOTE: MILLER is a former Project Blue Book USAF investigator who was
signed to Wright-Patterson AFB (W-PAFB, OH, with FTD. Mr. MILLER in one of the most know
dgeable and impartial investigators of Aerial Objects in the southwest). Dr. BENNEWITZ
oduced photographs and over 2600 feet of 8mm motion picture film depicting unidentified
rial objects flying over and around Manzano Weapons Storage Area and Coyote Canyon Test
ea. Dr. BENNEWITZ has been conducting independent research into Aerial Phenomena for
e last 15 months. Dr. BENNEWITZ also produced several electronic recording tapes,

IES TO	ATTACHMENTS	FILE STAMP AND/OR OTHER
AFOSI/IVQS; File		90 1717193-0/2941
AL GRADE TITLE SIGNATURE		
HOMAS A. CSEH, Major, USAF		
ommander		
ise Investigative Detachment	FOR OFFICIAL USE ONLY	

SI FORM 96
JAN 76

'allegedly' showing high periods of electrical magnetism being emitted from Manzano/Coyote Canyon area.' Dr. BENNEWITZ also produced several photographs of flying objects taken over the general Albuquerque area. He has several pieces of electronic surveillance equipment pointed at Manzano and is attempting to record high frequency electrical beam pulses. Dr. BENNEWITZ claims these Aerial Objects produce these pulses.

3. After analyzing the data collected by Dr. BENNEWITZ, Mr MILLER related the evidence clearly shows that some type of unidentified aerial objects were caught on film; however no conclusions could be made whether these objects pose a threat to Manzano/Coyote Canyon areas. Mr MILLER felt the electronical recording tapes were inconclusive and could have been gathered from several conventional sources. No sightings, other than these, have been reported in the area.

4. Mr MILLER has contacted FTD personnel at W-P AFB, OH, who expressed an interest and are scheduled to inspect Dr. BENNEWITZ' data.

5. Request a DCII check be made on Dr BENNEWITZ.

6. This is responsive to HQ CR 44.

7. Command was briefed but did not request an investigation at this time.

BEST COPY AVAILABLE

2

LT. JRPOSE INTERNAL OSI
(Complete only applicable items)

		SUBJECT	FILE NO.
	DO NO.(S)	KIRTLAND AFB, NM, 8 Aug – 3 Sep 80,	8017D93-0/29
	DET NO.(S)	Alleged Sightings of Unidentified Aerial	TRANSMITTAL DATE
	HEADQUARTERS IVOS	Lights In Restricted Test Range	26 Nov 80
	DO NO.		SUSPENSE DATE
	DET NO.		
	HEADQUARTERS		

REFERENCE

AFOSI Form 96, 28 Oct 80, Same Title

MINOR DISCREPANCIES NOTED ARE LISTED BELOW.

YOUR DISTRICT IS DESIGNATED OFFICE OF ORIGIN.

ATTACHED REQUIRES INVESTIGATION IN YOUR AREA.

DETERMINE SUBJECT'S ACCESS TO CLASSIFIED INFORMATION AS REQUIRED BY OSIM 124-1, PARA 2-6-1

FORWARD RESULTS DIRECTLY TO OFFICE OF ORIGIN, OR TO:

NO FURTHER INVESTIGATION CONTEMPLATED.

OUR FILES REFLECT PRIOR INVESTIGATION BY _____ OTD _____ FILE _____ (By copy of this form _____ is requested in /which _____ copies of prior investigation/letter summary, if applicable, to _____

REPORT OF PRIOR INVESTIGATION/SUMMARY ATTACHED.

INVESTIGATION CONTINUING AND YOU WILL BE FURNISHED FURTHER REPORTS.

DISCONTINUE INVESTIGATION. FORWARD RESULTS OF ANY INVESTIGATION ACCOMPLISHED.

DISCREPANCIES BETWEEN LEAD REQUEST AND DEVELOPED INFORMATION ARE SET FORTH.

REPORT OF COMMAND ACTION HAS NOT BEEN RECEIVED.

REQUEST STATUS OF THIS MATTER AND/OR DATE REPORT MAY BE EXPECTED.   (Requester, forward 2 copies of this form.) (Recipient, use one received copy /or answer with proper signature in remarks section unless OSI directives state reply not required.)

REFER ATTACHED TO INTERESTED COMMANDER FOR INFORMATION OR ACTION IF NOT PREVIOUSLY REPORTED.

CHECK WORLD-WIDE LOCATOR FOR BELOW LISTED PERSON OR SUBJECT

ATTACHED IS FORWARDED FOR INFORMATION AND/OR ACTION.

UPON REMOVAL OF ATTACHMENT(S) _____ THE CLASSIFICATION ON THIS CORRESPONDENCE WILL BE
☐ RETAINED. ☐ DOWNGRADED TO _____ ☐ CANCELED. ☐ MARKED "FOR OFFICIAL USE ONLY."
(If classification is retained, with or without attachments, indicate reason for security classification and grouping per AFR 205-1 .)

REMARKS

1. On 10 Nov 80, a meeting took place in 1606 ABW/CC Conference Room attended by the following individuals: BGen WILLIAM BROOKSHER, AFOSP/CC, COL JACK W. SHEPPARD, 1606 ABW/CC, COL THOMAS SIMMONS, 1606 ABW/CV, COL CRES BACA, 1606 SPGp/CC, COL FRANK M. HUEY, AFOSI Dist 17/CC, LTC JOE R. LAMPORT, 1606 ABW/SJ, MAJ THOMAS A. CSEH, AFOSI Det 1700/CC, Dr. LEHMAN, Director, AFWL, ED BREEN, AFWL Instrumentations Specialist and Dr. PAUL F. BENNEWITZ, President Thunder Scientific Laboratory, Albuquerque. Dr. BENNEWITZ presented film and photographs of alleged unidentified Aerial Objects photographed over KAFB, NM during the last 15 months. Dr. BENNEWITZ also related he had documented proof that he was in contact with the aliens flying the objects. At the conclusion of the presentation, Dr. BENNEWITZ expressed an interest in obtaining financial assistance from the USAF in furthering his investigation regarding these objects. DR. LEHMAN advised DR. BENNEWITZ to request a USAF grant for research. DR. LEHMAN advised DR. BENNEWITZ he would assist him in filling out the proper documents.

2. On 17 Nov 80, SA RICHARD C. DOTY, advised DR. BENNEWITZ that AFOSI would not become involved in the investigation of these objects. DR. BENNEWITZ was advised

COPIES TO	ATTACHMENTS	FILE STAMP AND/OR OTHER
Dist 17 IVO, File		8017D93-0/29.x 2
NAME-GRADE-TITLE-SIGNATURE		
THOMAS A. CSEH, Major, USAF		
Commander		
Base Investigative Detachment	FOR OFFICIAL USE ONLY	

AFOSI FORM 96   REPLACES OSI FORM ~ JUN 71 WHICH WILL BE USED

that AFOSI was not in a position to evaluate the information and photographs he has collected, to date or technically investigate such matters.

3. On 26 Nov 80, SA DOTY received a phone call from an individual who identified himself as U.S. Senator HARRISON SCHMIDT, of New Mexico. SEN SCHMIDT inquired about AFOSI'S role in investigating the aerial phenomena reported by Dr. BENNEWITZ. SA DOTY advised SEN SCHMIDT that AFOSI was not investigating the phenomena. SA DOTY then politely referred SEN SCHMIDT to AFOSI Dist 17/CC. SEN SCHMIDT declined to speak with 17/CC and informed SA DOTY he would request that SAF look into the matter and determine what USAF agency should investigate the phenomena.

4. It should be noted that DR. BENNEWITZ has had a number of conversations with SEN SCHMIDT during the last few months regarding BENNEWITZ'S private research. SEN SCHMIDT has made telephone calls to BGEN BROOKSHER, AFOSP/CC regarding the matter since Security Police are responsible for the security of Manzano Storage Area.

OFFICE OF THE ASSISTANT SECRETARY OF DEFENSE

WASHINGTON, D.C. 20301

19 JAN 1984

PUBLIC AFFAIRS

Ref: 84-FOI-11

Mr. Clifford E. Stone
683 Atwood Drive
Biloxi, MS 39532

Dear Mr. Stone:

Your 27 December 1983 Freedom of Information Act for a report by LtColonel Charles Halt concerning a UFO incident at the Royal Air Force Base in Woodbridge, England has been transferred to the Department of the Air Force as a matter under their cognizance for direct response to you.

Sincerely,

Charles W. Hinkle
Director, Freedom of Information
and Security Review

DEPARTMENT OF THE AIR FORCE
HEADQUARTERS UNITED STATES AIR FORCES IN EUROPE
APO NEW YORK 09012

.13 JAN 1984

Mr Clifford E. Stone
683 Atwood Drive
Biloxi MS 39532

Dear Mr Stone

This is in response to your 27 December 1983 Freedom of Information Act request concerning alleged UFO sightings in England during December 1980. We are furnishing you with a copy of the only records in the possession of the United States Air Forces in Europe documenting this incident. Search and copy fees have been waived.

Sincerely

Albert S. Stewart
ALBERT G. STEWART, Colonel, USAF
Director of Administration

1 Atch
81 CSG/CD Ltr, 13 Jan 81

COPY

DEPARTMENT OF THE AIR FORCE
HEADQUARTERS 81ST COMBAT SUPPORT GROUP (USAFE)
APO NEW YORK 09755

REPLY TO
ATTN OF: CD

13 Jan 81

SUBJECT: Unexplained Lights

TO: RAF/CC

1. Early in the morning of 27 Dec 80 (approximately 0300L), two USAF
security police patrolmen saw unusual lights outside the back gate at
RAF Woodbridge. Thinking an aircraft might have crashed or been forced
down, they called for permission to go outside the gate to investigate.
The on-duty flight chief responded and allowed three patrolmen to proceed on foot. The individuals reported seeing a strange glowing object
in the forest. The object was described as being metalic in appearance
and triangular in shape, approximately two to three meters across the
base and approximately two meters high. It illuminated the entire fores
with a white light. The object itself had a pulsating red light on top
a bank(s) of blue lights underneath. The object was hovering or on leg
As the patrolmen approached the object, it maneuvered through the trees
and disappeared. At this time the animals on a nearby farm went into a
frenzy. The object was briefly sighted approximately an hour later near
the back gate.

2. The next day, three depressions 1 1/2" deep and 7" in diameter were
found where the object had been sighted on the ground. The following
night (29 Dec 80) the area was checked for radiation. Beta/gamma readi
of 0.1 milliroentgens were recorded with peak readings in the three depressions and near the center of the triangle formed by the depressions.
A nearby tree had moderate (.05-.07) readings on the side of the tree
toward the depressions.

3. Later in the night a red sun-like light was seen through the trees.
It moved about and pulsed. At one point it appeared to throw off glowin
particles and then broke into five separate white objects and then disappeared. Immediately thereafter, three star-like objects were noticed
in the sky, two objects to the north and one to the south, all of which
were about 10° off the horizon. The objects moved rapidly in sharp angu
movements and displayed red, green and blue lights. The objects to the
north appeared to be elliptical through an 8-12 power lens. They then
turned to full circles. The objects to the north remained in the sky fo
an hour or more. The object to the south was visible for two or three
hours and beamed down a stream of light from time to time. Numerous ind
duals, including the undersigned, witnessed the activities in paragraphs
2 and 3.

        (SIGNED)
CHARLES I. HALT, Lt Col, USAF
Deputy Base Commander

DEPARTMENT OF DEFENSE
JCS MESSAGE CENTER

ROUTINE:
P 272000Z MAY 86
FR USDAO BRASILIA BP
TO DIA WASHDC//DC-4A/AT-5//
INFO USDAO RIO DE JANEIRO   HQUSAF WASHDC//XOXXD/CVAI//
    AFIS WASHDC
    USCINCSO QUARRY HEIGHTS//SCJ2-3/BIOS//

ZYUW RUEHBRAS781 1472007

FROM THREE DIFFERENT TYPES OF RADAR SYSTEMS, LEADS
ONE TO BELIEVE THAT SOMETHING ARRIVED OVER BRAZIL
THE NIGHT OF 19 MAY.

//JPSP: PG1300//
//COMSOBJ: 11//
PROJ: (U) NONE
INSTR: (U) US BF

_____ BRASILIA BP 05781

SERIAL: (U) IIR 6 809 0179 86

PASS: DIA PASS TO AIG 11881

COUNTRY: (U) BRAZIL (BR)

SUBJECT: IIR 6 809 0179 86/BAF HAS A CLOSE
         ENCOUNTER OF THE FIRST KIND (U)

WARNING: (U) THIS IS AN INFO REPORT, NOT
FINALLY EVALUATED INTEL

DOI: (U) 860521

REQS: (U) INITIATIVE

SOURCE: (U) VARIOUS BAF SOURCES/OPEN SOURCES

SUMMARY: (U) NUMEROUS UNIDENTIFIED OBJECTS WERE
SIGHTED IN THE SKIES OVER BRAZIL, BUT BAF FIGHTERS
WERE UNABLE TO INTERCEPT THEM.

TEXT: 1. _____ ACCORDING TO SOURCES, AT
LEAST 20 UNIDENTIFIED OBJECTS WERE OBSERVED BY
SEVERAL AIRCREWS AND ON RADAR THE NIGHT OF
19 MAY 86. THE OBJECTS WERE FIRST SEEN BY THE
PILOT OF A XINGU AIRCRAFT, TRANSPORTING OZIRES
SILVA, FORMER PRESIDENT OF EMBRAER, BETWEEN SAO
PAULO AND RIO DE JANEIRO. FIGHTERS WERE LAUNCHED
FROM SANTA CRUZ AB_____AT APPROXIMATELY
2100 HOURS. ALTHOUGH ALL THREE MADE RADAR CONTACT,
ONLY ONE OF THE THREE PILOTS MANAGED TO SEE WHAT HE
DESCRIBED AS RED, WHITE AND GREEN LIGHTS. SHORTLY
AFTERWARD, RADAR CONTACT WAS MADE WITH SIMILAR
OBJECTS NEAR BRASILIA AND THREE MIRAGES WERE
LAUNCHED FROM ANAPOLIS AB_____ ALL MADE
RADAR AND VISUAL CONTACT AT 20,000 FEET. THEY
REPORTED THAT THEY WERE ESCORTED BY THIRTEEN OF
THESE DISKS WITH RED, GREEN, AND WHITE LIGHTS AT A
DISTANCE OF ONE TO THREE MILES. THE OBJECTS THEN
RAPIDLY DISAPPEARED FROM BOTH GROUND AND AIRBORNE
RADARS.

2. _____ THE AIR MINISTER IS QUOTED BY
THE PRESS AS SAYING THERE WERE THREE GROUPS OF
TARGETS ON THE GROUND RADAR AND THAT THE SCOPES
OF THE AIRBORNE RADARS WERE SATURATED.

COMMENT: _____ WHILE RO DOES NOT BELIEVE
IN UFO'S OR ALL THE HOOPLA THAT SURROUNDS PREVIOUS
REPORTING, THERE IS TOO MUCH HERE TO BE IGNORED.
THREE VISUAL SIGHTINGS AND POSITIVE RADAR CONTACT

ACTION DC-4A(1)   (U,6,7,8,F)
INFO CJCS(4) NIDS(1) J5(2) SECDEF(9) USDP(11) ASD:PA&E(1)
      DI-1(1) NMIC(1) NTS-2B(1) JS1-4B(1) DIC-3A(1)
      AT-5(1) DIO(1) DE-3(1) DB-3C(2) DB-3C2(1) DJ-4B2(1)
      DI-SD2(1) DT-1(1) DIA(1) DT-5(1) DC-4AS(1)
      +NPIC WASHINGTON DC//IEG//
      +SAFE
      +AIG 11881

MCN=86147/05259   TOR=86147/2010Z   TAD=86147/2010Z   CDSN=MIA339

272006Z MAY 86

CHAPTER THREE

UFOs and Advanced Technology

In the last chapter we discussed cases involving the military in UFO sightings. It was my desire to show the reader that the U.S. Government does, in fact, have documentation reflecting that some UFOs present a potential threat to our national security by their actions. This is evident by the interest shown them by the military.

The official documents that were used to illustrate these points were initially classified by the U.S. Government, in the interests of national security. Also, those cases of UFO sightings were incidents that happened after the closure of the official U.S. Government involvement in UFO research.

In this chapter we will discuss some cases, once again involving the military, which I feel best illustrate that in some UFO incidents the object or objects involved clearly demonstrated the existence of advanced technology.

I would ask the reader to keep in mind the terms defined in Chapter Two. These definitions are important, for they show that Top Secret is the highest security classification. They also show that, with Secret and Top Secret classifications, information can, and often does, become compartmented and requires a special access clearance—thus leading to the misconception that there exist classifications *higher* than Top Secret.

The documents that will be used to discuss the incidents in this chapter were, at one time, classified as at least Confidential, in the interest of national security. It is my belief that the information the U.S. Government has on the very first incident we will discuss in this chapter is classified Top Secret Umbra (TSU). To view Top Secret Umbra information, you need to be cleared for Top Secret information, possess a special access clearance, and have a strict need-to-know (Umbra is the code word to identify compartmentalized information gathered from signal intelligence intercepts—intelligence gathered from monitoring military radio traffic). Although the information was obtained by the U.S. Air Force Security Service (OLA "A," 6947th Security Squadron), for some unknown reason it is being maintained and controlled by the National Security Agency.

One day in March, 1967, Cuban radar installations reported a bogey approaching the Cuban landmass from the northeast. Two Cuban MIG-21 interceptors were scrambled when the bogey crossed Cuban air space at an altitude of approximately 10,000 meters and at a speed approaching Mach (the speed of sound). The interceptors were directed to the bogey by Cuban Ground Control Intercept and were guided to within 5 kilometers of the object. According to U.S. intelligence reports, the wing leader reported that the object was a bright metallic sphere with no visible markings or appendages.

After a futile attempt to contact the object for identification, Cuban Air Defense Headquarters ordered the wing leader to arm his weapons and destroy the object. The wing leader reported his missiles armed and his radar locked-on. Seconds later, the wing man began screaming to the ground controller that the wing leader's aircraft had exploded. After regaining his composure,

19

he further reported that there was neither smoke nor flame: the aircraft had disintegrated. U.S. intelligence also detected that Cuban radar reported that the object quickly accelerated and climbed beyond 30,000 meters. At last report it was heading south-southwest toward South America.

A spot report was sent to the National Security Agency (NSA) Headquarters, which is standard operating procedure (SOP) in any case involving aircraft loss by a hostile country. The NSA was—and still is—required to acknowledge receipt of such a report. However, the NSA for some unexplained reason did *not* acknowledge receipt of this report. Therefore, a follow-up spot report was submitted by the U.S. Air Force Security Service. Within hours of the retransmission of the spot report, the 6947th received orders to ship all tapes and pertinent intelligence to the Agency (NSA) and was told to list the incident in the squadron files as aircraft loss due to equipment malfunction.

We are indebted to author and researcher Stanton T. Friedman, who initially broke news of the above incident to the public after being told the story by a former Air Force Intelligence Specialist. However, did this incident really happen? Is this story true?

I wrote to the National Security Agency and asked them, under the Freedom of Information Act, for any information they might have on the incident. They never answered my request.

Next, I wrote to the Office of the Secretary of Defense. I also asked for the aid of Senator Richard Stone's office to insure that I received a reply. On November 15, 1979, an interim response from the Air Force's Electronic Security Command was forwarded to me in which I was informed that a time extension was necessary for the proper processing of my request for the following reason: "The need for consultation, which shall be conducted with all practicable speed, with another agency having a substantial interest in the determination of the request." That other agency was in fact the National Security Agency, which still does not wish for the public to know the truth about this most unusual incident. (See doc. 3-1.)

On November 27, 1979, I was forwarded the agency's decision, which read in part as follows: (See doc. 3-2.)

> The type of information necessary to respond to your request is classified in accordance with DOD security directives and is therefore exempt from release under authority of (Title) 5 U.S.C. 552(b). This information is properly and currently classified in the interest of national defense as specifically authorized under criteria established by Executive Order 12056 and implemented by regulation.

Here we have an admission of the existence of some type of information dealing with the March 1967 Cuban Incident. Armed with this admission, I decided to appeal the Air Force's decision to withhold this information.

The Office of the Secretary, Department of the Air Force, responded to my appeal in a letter dated February 21, 1980. The letter read in part: (See doc. 3-3.)

> We may neither confirm nor deny the occurrence of the incident you described, or the existence of any records on the subject.

Also, they corrected an error that appeared in every piece of my correspondence with the Intelligence Community concerning the incident. I was asking for information on the loss of a MIG-23. In the Air Force's response to me on February 21, 1980, they correctly called the lost aircraft a MIG-21. How could they have known it was a MIG-21, when I was asking for information pertaining to a MIG-23? Unless, of course, they had documentation concerning the loss of a MIG-21, which I had described to them in my correspondence. Also, the Air Force apparently had upgraded the security classification of these documents.

If an agency acknowledges the existence of classified information on an incident, as the U.S. Air Force did in its response of November 27, 1979, this clearly indicates the existence of some sort of information. If that same agency then chooses to respond that they may neither deny nor confirm the existence or nonexistence of information concerning this same incident upon appeal, this once again clearly shows that the information has gone from Secret or Top Secret under the regular classification system to Secret or Top Secret under the Special Access Program, as outlined under the authority of Executive Order 12356. In other words, the agency is stating, in effect, that, using the authority of Executive Order (EO) 12356, Section 3.4 (f)(1), it may neither confirm nor deny the existence or nonexistence of information at the direction of the President of the United States.

After the final appeal action was taken on my request, all information and tapes pertaining to the incident were returned to the National Security Agency for safekeeping, where it remains, still classified Top Secret Umbra, to this day. (See doc. 3-4.)

If the U.S.S.R. or the United States does not have a weapons system that can disintegrate a fighter aircraft in flight, then exactly who or what had this advanced technology in March 1967?

★★★

In our next case we will see that in many incidents members of the Intelligence Community do not communicate with one another, leading some agencies to believe documents are still classified after they have been downgraded and released to the public. We will also find the Department of Defense stating, as in this case, that no other documentation exists—only to find out later that more documentation does exist at a higher classification!

At about 12:30 A.M. on the morning of September 19, 1976, the Imperial Iranian Air Force's (IIAF) command post in the Tehran area received four calls from one of the city's suburbs reporting a series of strange airborne objects. Some reported seeing a bird-like object while others reported a helicopter with bright lights. However, there was no helicopter activity in the area of the reports at that time. The senior officer on duty at the command post attempted to convince the callers that they were only seeing stars. The officer, unable to convince the callers that they were just seeing stars, decided to have a look for himself.

Stepping outside the command post and looking to the north, he observed a star-like object. Only the object was larger and brighter then a star or planet. In addition, the object appeared to be moving! Knowing that there was no aircraft activity in the area of his observation, he immediately had an IIAF F-4 scrambled to investigate and attempt to identify the unknown.

As the F-4 approached the city of Tehran, the pilot reported seeing a brilliantly lit object that could be seen easily from 70 miles away. When the F-4 was approximately 25 miles from the object, the F-4 lost all instrumentation and UHF/VHF communications. Upon breaking off the intercept and turning toward his home base, all systems returned to normal. As one U.S. Air Force Intelligence Officer involved in the case commented, "[It was] as if the strange object no longer regarded the aircraft as a threat."

At 1:40 A.M. a second F-4 was scrambled. As this second F-4 approached the UFO the backseater (weapons officer) reported a radar-lock on the UFO at 27 NM (nautical miles) in a 12 o'clock high position with a rate of closure (VC) of 150 knots. When the F-4 reached the 25 NM point, the object began to move away maintaining a constant separation distance while still visible on the radar scope. The size of radar return was comparable to that of a KC-135 military tanker (a 707 airliner used by the military for refueling other aircraft in flight). The brilliance of the light from the object made it impossible to estimate the actual size of object. However, visually, according the U.S. intelligence reports on the incident, it resembled flashing strobe lights arranged in a rectangular pattern and alternating blue, green, red, and orange. The sequence of the lights was so fast that all the colors could be seen at once.

As the second F-4 pursued the object south of Tehran, a second brightly lit giant object (appearing to be about one-half to one-third the size of the full moon) detached itself from the original UFO and headed straight for the F-4 at a high rate of speed. The pilot attempted to fire an AIM-9 missile at the object, but at that instant his weapons control panel went off and he lost all UHF/VHF communications. At this point the pilot initiated a turn and negative G dive to get away from the oncoming object. However, as he turned the object fell in behind his aircraft at what appeared to be about a 3- to 4-NM distance. As the pilot continued to turn away from the primary object, the second object went to the inside of his turn, then returned to the primary object for a perfect rendezvous.

Shortly after the second object joined with the primary object, another object appeared to come out of the other side of the primary one, going straight down at a great rate of speed. Having regained control of their weapons and communication systems, the F-4 crew watched the third object, anticipating a large explosion when it struck the ground. However, it landed gently and cast a bright light over a two- to three-kilometer area. The pilot flew his aircraft as low over the area as possible, fixing the exact location where the object landed.

Upon returning to their base, both crewmen had difficulty in adjusting their night vision devices for landing. There was also a lot of interference on the UHF, and each time they passed through a magnetic bearing of 150 degrees from Fhrabad they lost their communications and the INS fluctuated from 30 to 50 degrees. A civilian airliner that was approaching Mehrabad during this same time experienced communications failure in the same vicinity but did not report seeing anything unusual.

While the F-4 was on a long final approach, the crew noticed another cylinder-shaped object (about the size of a T-bird at 10 meters) with bright, steady lights on each end and a flasher in the middle. When the pilot queried the tower, the tower stated there was no other known traffic in the area. During the time that the object passed over the F-4, the tower did not have a visual on the object but picked it up after the pilot told them to look between the mountains and the refinery.

During daylight, the F-4 crew was taken out to the area in a helicopter where the object apparently had landed. Nothing was noticed at this spot (a dry lake bed), but as they circled off to the west of the area, they picked up a very noticeable beeper signal. At the point where the return was the loudest was a small house with a garden. They landed and asked the people within whether they had noticed anything strange the night before. The people talked about a loud noise and a very bright light, like lighting. The aircraft and area where the object was believed to have landed were to be checked for possible radiation. However, the results of the radiation tests and other various tests conducted were never made public.

When I first heard of this case, I wrote to the Office of the Secretary of Defense (DOD), the National Security Agency (NSA), and the Department of the Air Force (HQ, USAF) for any information that they might have on this incident. DOD responded by sending a three-page report said to be the only known existing document concerning the incident. This document was at once classified: Confidential. The NSA responded by asking for $250 to do a search and suggested that any information they might have on the incident would not be releasable due to national security.

The response from the Department of the Air Force was most interesting as it shows there is sometimes a breakdown in communications within the Intelligence Community itself. The Air Force stated that it did not have any information on the incident. However, it did have a classified document belonging to the Joint Chiefs of Staff dealing with the incident, which they were not at liberty to release. This turned out be the document that was released to me earlier by DOD. Apparently the Department of the Air Force was not aware that the document had been downgraded, declassified, and released to the public. Also, the Air Force apparently did not wish to mention the existence of a "Secret" document dealing with the incident that had been written by one of its own officers. (See docs. 3-5 and 3-6.)

In the U.S. Air Force Security Service publication, *MIJI Quarterly*, MQ 3-78, there appeared an article entitled, "Now You See It, Now You Don't," written by a Captain Henry S. Shields, HQ USAFE/INOMP. (See doc. 3-7.) The article dealt with the Iranian incident and it was classified Secret. Captain Shields' very first paragraph in the article is most interesting and I would like to quote it to the reader.

> Sometime in his career, each pilot can expect to encounter strange, unusual happenings which will never be adequately or entirely explained by logic or subsequent investigation. The following article recounts just such an episode as reported by two F-4 Phantom crews of the Imperial Iranian Air Force during late 1976. No additional information or explanation of the strange events has been forthcoming; the story will be filed away and probably forgotten, but it makes interesting, and possibly disturbing, reading.

Is this another example in which the information concerning what our Intelligence Community knows about UFOs is classified Top Secret, compartmented, and to be viewed only by those with a strict need-to-know? Maybe. But only time will tell.

In addition to this incident, a State Department cable tells of interesting UFO sightings taking place in Kuwait during the months of November and December, 1978. According to the cable, the Government of Kuwait was so concerned by these sightings that it appointed an investigatory committee of "experts" from the Kuwait Institute for Scientific Research (KISR) to look into the cases. The cable states: "The KISR Committee rejected the notion that the 'UFOS' were espionage devices but remained equivocal about whether they were of extraterrestrial origin." The KISR Committee recommended, "The government take all possible measures to protect Kuwait's air space and territory as well as the country's oil resources." (See doc. 3-8.)

The cable tells of an interesting event which is a clear demonstration of some highly advanced technology. The cable states:

> The "UFO" which first appeared over the northern oil fields seemingly did strange things to KOC's [Kuwait Oil Company] automatic pumping equipment. This equipment is designed to shut itself down when there is some failure which may seriously damage the petroleum gathering and transmission system and it can only be restarted manually. At the time of the "UFOs" appearance the pumping system automatically shut itself down and when the "UFOs" vanished the system started up again.

What could cause this to happen? Did the equipment truly shut down or was it merely suspended in time and space for the duration of the UFO's appearance? I will leave it to the reader to ponder this one.

★★★

The last case we will discuss in this chapter is taken from a Defense Intelligence Agency document. (See doc. 3-9.) It was originally classified Confidential. The Peruvian Air Force officer who observed and reported the events was a party to the conversation concerning the events and had proven reliable in the past.

An UFO was spotted on two different occasions near the Peruvian Air Force Base in southern Peru. The Peruvian Air Force tried to intercept and destroy the UFO, but without success.

On May 9, 1980, a group of Peruvian Air Force officers were in formation at Mariano Malgar when they spotted an UFO hovering near the airfield. The UFO was reported to have a round shape. The air field commander scrambled an SU-22 aircraft to make an intercept. The pilot intercepted the UFO and fired upon it at very close range without causing any apparent damage. The pilot attempted to make another pass at the UFO, but the UFO outran the fighter aircraft.

The second sighting was during the night of May 10, 1980. This UFO was displaying lights. Again an SU-22 was scrambled, but the UFO outran the aircraft. The document further commented, "Apparently some vehicle was spotted, but its origin remains unknown."

Here we have three, officially documented incidents involving UFOs that clearly demonstrated advanced technology. I know of no weapons system that can disintegrate a fighter aircraft in flight; or knock out the on-board weapons and communication systems of a fighter aircraft in flight; or any aircraft currently flying that can withstand point-blank cannon fire. If we already have this type of technology, then we are spending entirely too much on defense. The question is, Do we have this type of technology? And if we don't, then who or what does?

Once again, I would remind the reader that the incidents discussed in this chapter are raw intelligence data. The assessments and evaluations of this data, in this writer's opinion, remain classified, we are told, in the interest of national security—or could it be national *in*security?

I find it too incredible to believe that these incidents would not have created some concern within the Intelligence Community. Surely some evaluation would have been made of all this shocking data. The security of our nation may well be at stake.

DEPARTMENT OF THE AIR FORCE
HEADQUARTERS ELECTRONIC SECURITY COMMAND
SAN ANTONIO, TEXAS 78243

REPLY TO
ATTN OF: DAD

15 Nov 1979

SUBJECT: Request for Information on UFO Incident

TO: SSG Clifford E. Stone
Hq Det, Hanou Mil Comm
APO New York 09165

1. Your letter of 29 October was received on 2 November. A time extension has been found necessary for the proper processing of the request under the Freedom of Information Act, 5 U.S.C., for the following reason:

   a. The need for consultation, which shall be conducted with all practicable speed, with another agency having a substantial interest in the determination of the request.

2. A determination is expected to be made regarding your request by 30 November.

FOR THE COMMANDER

JOHN R. JACOBS, Capt, USAF
Chief, Documentation Sys Div

DEPARTMENT OF THE AIR FORCE
HEADQUARTERS ELECTRONIC SECURITY COMMAND
SAN ANTONIO, TEXAS 78243

27 NOV 1979

REPLY TO
ATTN OF: DAD

SUBJECT:

TO: SSG Clifford E. Stone
Hq Det, Hanou Mil Comm
APO New York 09165

Dear SSG Stone

Reference your Freedom of Information Act request of 29 October and our letter dated 15 November.

The type of information necessary to respond to your request is classified in accordance with DOD security directives and is therefore exempt from release under authority of 5 U.S.C. 552(b). This information is properly and currently classified in the interest of national defense as specifically authorized under criteria established by Executive Order 12065 and implemented by regulation.

The decision to withhold release of classified information may be appealed in writing to the Secretary of the Air Force within 45 days of the date of this letter. Include in your appeal any reasons for reconsideration you wish to present. Attach a copy of this letter. Address your letter as follows: Secretary of the Air Force, thru HQ ESC/DAD, San Antonio, Texas 78243.

Sincerely

BOBBY J. BERRY, Colonel, USAF
Chief of Staff

DEPARTMENT OF THE AIR FORCE
WASHINGTON, D.C. 20330

OFFICE OF THE SECRETARY

2 1 FEB 1980

Staff Sergeant Clifford E. Stone
Headquarters Detachment
Hanau Military Command
APO New York 09165

Dear Sergeant Stone:

This is in response to your letter of 5 December 1979, appealing, under the Freedom of Information Act, the denial of your request for information concerning the loss of a Cuban MIG-21 aircraft.

The Office of the Secretary of the Air Force has considered your appeal, and I have determined that it must be denied.

We may neither confirm nor deny the occurrence of the incident you described, or the existence of any records on the subject. To do so would compromise intelligence interests, and intelligence gathering policies, practices, and techniques, which are currently and properly classified in the interest of the national defense, pursuant to Executive Order 12065, as implemented by Department of Defense Directives 5200.1-R and 5200.7. This action is taken under the authority of 5 U.S.C. 552(b)(1). Confirmation of the existence or the nonexistence of any records on this subject would cause identifiable damage to the national security.

This letter constitutes the final Air Force action on your appeal. The Freedom of Information Act, 5 U.S.C. 552, provides for judicial review of this determination.

Sincerely,

ROBERT W. CRITTENDEN
Administrative Assistant (Acting)

DEPARTMENT OF THE AIR FORCE
HEADQUARTERS 31ST COMBAT SUPPORT GROUP (TAC)
HOMESTEAD AIR FORCE BASE, FLORIDA 33039

REPLY TO
ATTN OF: DADF

5 JUN 1980

SUBJECT: Freedom of Information Act Request

TO: SSgt Clifford E. Stone
Hq Det, Hanau Mil Comm
APO New York 09165

1. Your letter of 19 May 1980 was referred to this installation by Hq USAF/DADF, Washington, D.C. on 29 May 1980 and received on 3 June 1980.

2. The 6947th Electronic Security Squadron (formerly OLA "A", 6947th Security Squadron) was contacted in regards to your request. We have been advised that a thorough search of all records was made, with negative results.

3. May we suggest that you contact the Albert Simpson Research Center, AU, Maxwell AFB, AL 36112 and request they research your request.

CURTIS W. LEDGERWOOD, Captain, USAF
Chief, Central Base Administration

Doc. 3-5 U.S.A.F. Letter, Apr 16, 1979   APR 16 1979

DADF

SP5 Clifford E. Stone
HQ Det, Hanau Mil Comm
APO New York 09165

Dear SP5 Stone

Your Freedom of Information Act request of February 21,
1979, addressed to the Director, Defense Investigative
Service, was received in this office for Air Force action on
March 30, 1979.

We checked with offices within the organization of the
Assistant Chief of Staff for Intelligence. They did not
locate any Air Force records pertinent to your request.
However, they did find a copy of a classified Joint Chiefs
of Staff (JCS) message, DTG 230810Z Sep 76 concerning
information on an incident in Iran in September 1976. The
Air Force does not have disclosure authority for this
report. Therefore, we suggest you write directly to the
Office of the Assistant Secretary of Defense (Public
Affairs), Directorate for Freedom of Information and
Security Review, Washington DC 20301, concerning the
releasability of the message.

No records were located with regard to paragraph 2 of your
request. The Modern Military Branch of the National
Archives, Washington, DC, may have records responsive to
this paragraph. However, your request is not specific
enough to locate any records with the information given.

We believe that your request in paragraph 3 does not
reasonably describe the records you seek, as required under
the Freedom of Information Act. If you can be more
specific, we will try to assist you further.

Sincerely

(Ms) M. K. WARD
HQ USAF Freedom of
  Information Manager

Doc. 3-6a DOD Letter, Aug 1, 1979

OFFICE OF THE ASSISTANT SECRETARY OF DEFENSE
WASHINGTON, D. C. 20301

1 AUG 1979

PUBLIC AFFAIRS

Ref: 79-DFOI-717

SSG Clifford E. Stone
Hq Det Hanau Mil Comm
APO New York 09165

Dear Sergeant Stone:

This responds to your Freedom of Information request for a
copy of JCS Message 230810Z September 1976. A copy has been
provided to you previously. This date-time group identifies
a retransmission by the JCS Communications Center of the
USDAO Tehran Message 230630Z September 1976. Both identifying date-time groups and originators are in the address section of the message.

Sincerely,

Charles W. Hinkle
Director, Freedom of Information
  and Security Review

Enclosure

UNCLASSIFIED

PRIORITY

DCT1   MSG654   PAGE   04 267   NR 13

ACTION: NONE-00

INFO:

PATC7YIN RUFKJCS9717 7608I0 MTMS-CCCC — RJFFHOA

7NY CCCCC

P 2308107 SEP 76

FM JCS

INFO RUEHC/SECSTATE WASH DC

RUFAIIF/C I A

RUFOTAH/NPA WASH DC

RUFADWW/WHITE HOUSE WASH DC

RUFFHOA/CSAF WASH DC

RUFNAAA/CNO WASH DC

RUFADWD/CSA WASH DC

P 2306302 SEP 76

FM USDAO TEHRAN

TO RUFKJCS/DIA WASHDC

INFO RUFKJCS/SECDEF DEPSECDEF WASHDC

RUFRBAA/COMIDEASTFOR

RUDOECA/CINCUSAFE LINDSEY AS GE/INCF

RHFRAAB/CINCUSAFE RAMSTEIN AB GE/INOCN

RUSNAAA/EUDAC VAIHINGEN GER

RUSNAAA/USCINCEUR VAIHINGEN GER/ECJ-2

BT

CONFIDENTIAL 1735 SEP 76

THIS IS IR 6 866 0139 76

1. (U) IRAN

2. REPORTED UFO SIGHTING (U)

3. (U) NA

4. (U) 19 & 20 SEP 76

5. (U) TEHRAN, IRAN: 20 SEP 76

6. (U) F-5

7. (U) 6 846 0008 (NOTE RO COMMENTS)

8. (U) 6 846 0139 76

9. (U) 22SEP 76

10. (U) NA

11. (U) "INITIATE" IPSP PT-1640

12. (U) USDAO TEHRAN, IRAN

13. (U) FRANK B. MCKENZIE, COL, USAF, DATT

14. (U) NA

15. (C) THIS REPORT FORWARDS INFORMATION CONCERNING THE
SIGHTING OF AN UFO IN IRAN ON 19 SEPTEMBER 1976.

A. AT ABOUT 1230 AM ON 19 SEP 76 THE
                    RECEIVED FOUR TELEPHONE CALLS
FROM CITIZENS LIVING IN THE SHEMIRAN AREA OF TEHRAN SAYING

UNCLASSIFIED

PRIORITY

Doc. 3-6c DOD Letter, Aug 1, 1979

THAT THEY HAD SEEN STRANGE OBJECTS IN THE SKY. SOME REPORTED
A KIND OF BIRD-LIKE OBJECT WHILE OTHERS REPORTED A HELICOPTER
WITH A LIGHT ON. THERE WERE NO HELICOPTERS AIRBORNE AT THAT
TIME.

                    AFTER HE TOLD THE CITIZEN IT WAS ONLY
STARS AND HAD TALKED TO MEHRABAD TOWER HE DECIDED TO LOOK FOR
HIMSELF. HE NOTICED AN OBJECT IN THE SKY SIMILAR TO A STAR
BIGGER AND BRIGHTER. HE DECIDED TO SCRAMBLE AN F-4 FROM
SHAHROKHI AFB TO INVESTIGATE.
   B. AT 0130 HRS ON THE 19TH THE F-4 TOOK OFF AND PROCEEDED
TO A POINT ABOUT 40 NM NORTH OF TEHRAN. DUE TO ITS BRILLIANCE
THE OBJECT WAS EASILY VISIBLE FROM 70 MILES AWAY.
AS THE F-4 APPROACHED A RANGE OF 25 NM HE LOST ALL INSTRUMENTATION
AND COMMUNICATIONS (UHF AND INTERCOM). HE BROKE OFF THE
INTERCEPT AND HEADED BACK TO SHAHROKHI. WHEN THE F-4 TURNED
AWAY FROM THE OBJECT AND APPARENTLY WAS NO LONGER A THREAT
TO IT THE AIRCRAFT REGAINED ALL INSTRUMENTATION AND COM-
MUNICATIONS. AT 0140 HRS A SECOND F-4 WAS LAUNCHED. THE
BACKSEATER ACQUIRED A RADAR LOCK ON AT 27 NM, 12 O'CLOCK
HIGH POSITION WITH THE VC (RATE OF CLOSURE) AT 150 NMPH.
AS THE RANGE DECREASED TO 25 NM THE OBJECT MOVED AWAY AT A
SPEED THAT WAS VISIBLE ON THE RADAR SCOPE AND STAYED AT 25NM.
   C. THE SIZE OF THE RADAR RETURN WAS COMPARABLE TO THAT OF
A 707 TANKER. THE VISUAL SIZE OF THE OBJECT WAS DIFFICULT
TO DISCERN BECAUSE OF ITS INTENSE BRILLIANCE. THE
LIGHT THAT IT GAVE OFF WAS THAT OF FLASHING STROBE LIGHTS
ARRANGED IN A RECTANGULAR PATTERN AND ALTERNATING BLUE, GREEN,
RED AND ORANGE IN COLOR. THE SEQUENCE OF THE LIGHTS WAS SO
FAST THAT ALL THE COLORS COULD BE SEEN AT ONCE. THE OBJECT
AND THE PURSUING F-4 CONTINUED ON A COURSE TO THE SOUTH OF
TEHRAN WHEN ANOTHER BRIGHTLY LIGHTED OBJECT, ESTIMATED TO BE
ONE HALF TO ONE THIRD THE APPARENT SIZE OF THE MOON, CAME
OUT OF THE ORIGINAL OBJECT. THIS SECOND OBJECT HEADED STRAIGHT
TOWARD THE F-4 AT A VERY FAST RATE OF SPEED. THE PILOT
ATTEMPTED TO FIRE AN AIM-9 MISSILE AT THE OBJECT BUT AT THAT
INSTANT HIS WEAPONS CONTROL PANEL WENT OFF AND HE LOST ALL
COMMUNICATIONS (UHF AND INTERPHONE). AT THIS POINT THE PILOT
INITIATED A TURN AND NEGATIVE G DIVE TO GET AWAY. AS HE
TURNED THE OBJECT FELL IN TRAIL AT WHAT APPEARED TO BE ABOUT
3-4 NM. AS HE CONTINUED IN HIS TURN AWAY FROM THE PRIMARY
OBJECT THE SECOND OBJECT WENT TO THE INSIDE OF HIS TURN THEN
RETURNED TO THE PRIMARY OBJECT FOR A PERFECT REJOIN.
   D. SHORTLY AFTER THE SECOND OBJECT JOINED UP WITH THE
PRIMARY OBJECT ANOTHER OBJECT APPEARED TO COME OUT OF THE

150

Doc. 3-6d DOD Letter, Aug 1, 1979

OTHER SIDE OF THE PRIMARY OBJECT GOING STRAIGHT DOWN AT A
GREAT RATE OF SPEED. THE F-4 CREW HAD REGAINED COMMUNICATIONS
AND THE WEAPONS CONTROL PANEL AND WATCHED THE OBJECT APPROACH
THE GROUND ANTICIPATING A LARGE EXPLOSION. THIS OBJECT APPEARED
TO COME TO REST GENTLY ON THE EARTH AND CAST A VERY BRIGHT
LIGHT OVER AN AREA OF ABOUT 2-3 KILOMETERS.
THE CREW DESCENDED FROM THEIR ALTITUDE OF 26M TO 15M AND
CONTINUED TO OBSERVE AND MARK THE OBJECT'S POSITION. THEY
HAD SOME DIFFICULTY IN ADJUSTING THEIR NIGHT VISIBILITY FOR
LANDING SO AFTER ORBITING MEHRABAD A FEW TIMES THEY WENT OUT
FOR A STRAIGHT IN LANDING. THERE WAS A LOT OF INTERFERENCE
ON THE UHF AND EACH TIME THEY PASSED THROUGH A MAG. BEARING
OF 150 DEGREE FROM EHRABAD THEY LOST THEIR COMMUNICATIONS (UHF
AND INTERPHONE) AND THE INS FLUCTUATED FROM 30 DEGREES - 50 DEGREES
THE ONE CIVIL AIRLINER THAT WAS APPROACHING MEHRABAD DURING THIS
SAME TIME EXPERIENCED COMMUNICATIONS FAILURE IN THE SAME
VICINITY (KILO ZULU) BUT DID NOT REPORT SEEING ANYTHING.
WHILE THE F-4 WAS ON A LONG FINAL APPROACH THE CREW NOTICED
ANOTHER CYLINDER SHAPED OBJECT (ABOUT THE SIZE OF A T-BIRD
AT 10M) WITH BRIGHT STEADY LIGHTS ON EACH END AND A FLASHER
IN THE MIDDLE. WHEN QUERIED THE TOWER STATED THERE WAS NO
OTHER KNOWN TRAFFIC IN THE AREA. DURING THE TIME THAT THE
OBJECT PASSED OVER THE F-4 THE TOWER DID NOT HAVE A VISUAL
ON IT BUT PICKED IT UP AFTER THE PILOT TOLD THEM TO LOOK
BETWEEN THE MOUNTAINS AND THE REFINERY.
   E. DURING DAYLIGHT THE F-4 CREW WAS TAKEN OUT TO THE
AREA IN A HELICOPTER WHERE THE OBJECT APPARENTLY HAD LANDED.
NOTHING WAS NOTICED AT THE SPOT WHERE THEY THOUGHT THE OBJECT
LANDED (A DRY LAKE BED) BUT AS THEY CIRCLED OFF TO THE
WEST OF THE AREA THEY PICKED UP A VERY NOTICEABLE BEEPER
SIGNAL. AT THE POINT WHERE THE RETURN WAS THE LOUDEST WAS
A SMALL HOUSE WITH A GARDEN. THEY LANDED AND ASKED THE PEOPLE
WITHIN IF THEY HAD NOTICED ANYTHING STRANGE LAST NIGHT. THE
PEOPLE TALKED ABOUT A LOUD NOISE AND A VERY BRIGHT LIGHT
LIKE LIGHTENING. THE AIRCRAFT AND AREA WHERE THE OBJECT IS
BELIEVED TO HAVE LANDED ARE BEING CHECKED FOR POSSIBLE RADIATION.

                              MORE INFORMATION WILL BE
FORWARDED WHEN IT BECOMES AVAILABLE.
XGDS 2-31DEC2000.
BT
#9717
PTCCZYUW RUFKJCS9717 2670810 0130-CCCC   2670814

UNCLASSIFIED

~~SECRET~~

UNITED STATES AIR FORCE SECURITY SERVICE

Doc. 3-7a MIJI Quarterly, Oct 1978

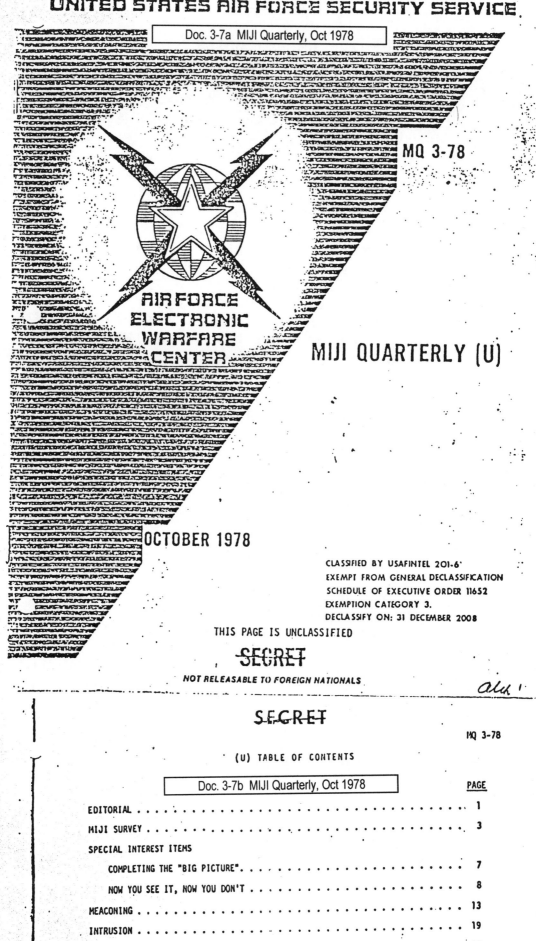

MQ 3-78

AIR FORCE
ELECTRONIC
WARFARE
CENTER

MIJI QUARTERLY (U)

OCTOBER 1978

CLASSIFIED BY USAFINTEL 201-6
EXEMPT FROM GENERAL DECLASSIFICATION
SCHEDULE OF EXECUTIVE ORDER 11652
EXEMPTION CATEGORY 3.
DECLASSIFY ON: 31 DECEMBER 2008

THIS PAGE IS UNCLASSIFIED

~~SECRET~~

NOT RELEASABLE TO FOREIGN NATIONALS

~~SECRET~~

MQ 3-78

(U) TABLE OF CONTENTS

Doc. 3-7b MIJI Quarterly, Oct 1978

NOW YOU SEE IT, NOW YOU DON'T! (U)

Captain Henry S. Shields, HQ USAFE/INOMP

Sometime in his career, each pilot can expect to encounter strange, unusual happenings which will never be adequately or entirely explained by logic or subsequent investigation. The following article recounts just such an episode as reported by two F-4 Phantom crews of the Imperial Iranian Air Force during late 1976. No additional information or explanation of the strange events has been forthcoming; the story will be filed away and probably forgotten, but it makes interesting, and possibly disturbing, reading.

* * * * *

Until 0030 on a clear autumn morning, it had been an entirely routine night watch for the Imperial Iranian Air Force's command post in the Tehran area. In quick succession, four calls arrived from one of the city's suburbs reporting a series of strange airborne objects. These Unidentified Flying Objects (UFOs) were described as 'bird-like', or as brightly-lit helicopters (although none were airborne at the time). Unable to convince the callers that they were only seeing stars, a senior officer went outside to see for himself. Observing an object to the north like a star, only larger and brighter, he immediately scrambled an IIAF F-4 to investigate.

Approaching the city, the F-4 pilot reported that the brilliant object was easily visible 70 miles away. When approximately 25 NM distant, the interceptor lost all instrumentation and UHF/Intercom communications. Upon breaking off the intercept and turning towards his home base, all systems returned to normal, as if the strange object no longer regarded the aircraft as a threat.

DECLASSIFY ON: 4 Dec 81
by: ALS/I HQUSAF

~~CONFIDENTIAL~~

A second F-4 was scrambled ten minutes after the first.
The backseater reported radar-lock on the UFO at 27 NM/12 o'clock
igh position, and a rate of closure of 150 knots. Upon reaching the
25 NM point, the object began rapidly moving away to maintain a
constant separation distance while still visible on the radar scope.
While the size of the radar return was comparable to that of a KC-
135, its intense brilliance made estimation of actual size impossible.
Visually, it resembled flashing strobe lights arranged in a rectangular pattern and alternating blue, green, red, and orange. Their
sequence was so fast that all colors could be seen at once.

As the F-4 continued pursuit south of Tehran, a second
brightly-lit object (about one-half to one-third the size of the moon)
detached from the original UFO and headed straight for the F-4 at a
high rate of speed. The pilot attempted to fire an AIM-9 missile at
the new object but was prevented by a sudden power loss in his
weapons control panel. UHF and internal communications were
simultaneously lost. The pilot promptly initiated a turn and negative-
G dive to escape, but the object fell in behind the F-4 at 3-4 NM
distance. Continuing the turn, the pilot observed the second object
turn inside of him and then away, subsequently returning to the primary UFO for a perfect rendezvous.

The two UFOs had hardly rejoined when a second object
detached and headed straight down toward the ground at high speed.
Having regained weapons and communications systems, the aircrew
watched the third object, anticipating a large explosion when it struck
the ground. However, it landed gently and cast a bright light over a
two-three kilometer area. The pilot flew as low over the area as
possible, fixing the object's exact location.

Upon return to home base, both crewmen had difficulty in

DECLASSIFY ON: 4 Dec 81
by: ACS/I, HQ US AF

33

~~CONFIDENTIAL~~

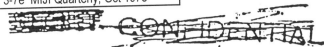

~~CONFIDENTIAL~~

adjusting their night vision devices for landing. The landing was further complicated by excessive interference on UHF and a further complete loss of all communications when passing through a 150 degree magnetic bearing from the home base. The inertial navigation system simultaneously fluctuated from 30 to 50 degrees. A civil airliner approaching the area also experienced a similar communications failure, but reported no unusual sightings.

While on a long final approach, the F-4 crew noted a further UFO. This was described as a cylinder-shaped object (about the size of a T-33 trainer) with bright steady lights on each end and a flasher in the middle. It quickly approached and passed directly over the F-4. In answer to the pilot's query, the control tower reported no other air traffic in the area, although they subsequently obtained a visual sighting of the object when specifically directed where to look.

The following day, the F-4 crew was flown by helicopter to the location where they believed the object had landed. This turned out to be a dry lake bed, but nothing unusual was noticed. As the helicopter circled off to the west, however, a very noticeable beeper signal was received, and eventually traced to a nearby house. They immediately landed and asked the inhabitants if anything strange or unusual had occurred the previous night. Yes, they replied, there had been loud noises and a very bright light, like lightning. The helicopter returned to base and arrangements were made to conduct various tests, such as radiation checks, in the vicinity of the house. Unfortunately, the results of such tests have not been reported.

DECLASSIFY ON: 4 Dec 81
by: ACS/I, HQ USAF

34

WHITE JOYCE A   03-05/80 123634   PRINTER· LI
79 KUWAIT 486
                        UNCLASSIFIED
UNCLASSIFIED
PAGE 01   KUWAIT 00486 290820Z
ACTION NEA-07
INFO   OCT 01 EUR 12 ISO 00 OES 09 NASA 02 NSF 02 DOE 15
       SOE-02 CIAE-00 PM-05 H 02 INR 10 L 03 NSAE 00
       NSC-05 PA-02 SP-02 SS-15 NAS-01 /095 W
       --------------------102479 290900Z /11
R 290600Z JAN 79
FM AMEMBASSY KUWAIT
TO SECSTATE WASHDC 2864
INFO·AMEMBASSY ABU DHABI
AMEMBASSY DOHA
AMEMBASSY LONDON
AMEMBASSY MANAMA
AMEMBASSY MUSCAT
SECDEF WASHDC
USCINCEUR
USICA WASHDC
UNCLAS KUWAIT 0486
CINCEUR ALSO FOR POLAD
E.O. 12065: N/A
TAGS: MPOL, PINS, MASS, SOPN, TGEN, KU
SUBJECT: 'UFO' SIGHTINGS CAUSE SECURITY CONCERN IN KUWAIT
1. A SERIES OF "UFO" SIGHTINGS ON NOVEMBER 9 CAUSED THE
GOK TO APPOINT AN INVESTIGATORY COMMITTEE OF EXPERTS FROM
THE KUWAIT INSTITUTE FOR SCIENTIFIC RESEARCH (KISR)
THE COMMITTEE'S REPORT WHICH WAS RELEASED JANUARY 20 DESCRIBED
EIGHT SIGHTINGS FROM NOVEMBER TO DECEMBER 14. A NUMBER OF
THE EARLY SIGHTINGS TOOK PLACE NEAR A KUWAIT OIL COMPANY
GATHERING CENTER NORTH OF KUWAIT CITY. RELEASE OF THE
COMMITTEE'S REPORT WAS SOMETHING OF A MEDIA EVENT AS IT
COINCIDED WITH JAN 21 FRONT PAGE STORIES OF YET ANOTHER 'UFO'
SIGHTING OVER KUWAIT CITY, WHICH INCLUDED PHOTOGRAPHS IN
LOCAL NEWSPAPERS.
UNCLASSIFIED

UNCLASSIFIED
PAGE 02   KUWAIT 00486 290820Z
2. THE KISR COMMITTEE REJECTED THE NOTION THAT THE
"UFO'S" WERE ESPIONAGE DEVICES BUT REMAINED EQUIVOCAL
ABOUT WHETHER THEY WERE OF EXTRATERRESTRIAL ORIGIN
THE KISR COMMITTEE REPRESENTATIVE RATIB ABU ID TOLD
EMBOFF THAT THE SCIENTISTS DID NOT KNOW ENOUGH ABOUT THE
PHENOMENA TO SAY WITH CERTAINTY THAT THEY WEREN'T
"SPACESHIPS." THE REPORT WENT
ON TO RECOMMEND THAT THE GOVERNMENT TAKE ALL POSSIBLE
MEASURES TO PROTECT KUWAIT'S AIR SPACE AND TERRITORY AS
WELL AS THE COUNTRY'S OIL RESOURCES.
3. SOME LOCAL WAGS HAVE MADE LIGHT OF THE FIRST UFO
SIGHTINGS WHICH CAME NEAR THE END OF THE LONG AND
TRADITIONALLY EXUBERANT HOLIDAY CELEBRATIONS OF ID-AL-
ADHA. HOWEVER WE HAVE LEARNED RECENTLY OF AN EVENT
                UNCLASSIFIED

PAGE   1

WHITE JOYCE A   03/05/80 123635   PRINTER. LI
79 KUWAIT 496
                          UNCLASSIFIED
COINCIDENT WITH ONE OF THE UFO SIGHTINGS WHICH HAS
CONFOUNDED SOME OF OUR MOST LEVEL-HEADED KUWAITI FRIENDS.
AND MAY HAVE BEEN WHAT PERSUADED THE GOK TO MAKE A SERIOUS
INVESTIGATION OF THE MATTER. A SENIOR KUWAIT OIL COMPANY
(KOC) OFFICIAL TOLD US THE THE "UFO" WHICH FIRST
APPEARED OVER THE NORTHERN OIL FIELDS SEEMINGLY DID
STRANGE THINGS TO KOC'S AUTOMATIC PUMPING EQUIPMENT
THIS EQUIPMENT IS DESIGNED TO SHUT ITSELF DOWN
WHEN THERE IS SOME FAILURE WHICH MAY SERIOUSLY DAMAGE
THE PETROLEUM GATHERING AND TRANSMISSION SYSTEM AND
IT CAN ONLY BERESTARTED MANUALLY. AT THE TIME OF THE
UFO'S APPEARANCE THE PUMPING SYSTEM AUTOMATICALLY
SHUT ITSELF DOWN AND WHEN THE "UFO" VANISHED THE
SYSTEM STARTED ITSELF UP AGAIN. THIS EVENT WAS NOT
ADDRESSED BY THE KISR COMMITTEE REPORT.
4. EVEN THOSE WHO ARE NOT INCLINED TO BELIEVE IN
UNCLASSIFIED
UNCLASSIFIED
PAGE 03   KUWAIT 00496 290820Z
VISITORS FROM OUTER SPACE DO TEND TO THINK SOMETHING
STRANGE HAS BEEN GOING ON IN KUWAITI AIRSPACE
THERE HAS BEEN SPECULATION. FOR EXAMPLE. ABOUT
HELICOPTERS OR HOVERCRAFT BRINGING REFUGEES OR
MONEY OUT OF BELEAGUERED IRAN. AT THE LEAST. THE
PHENOMENA HAVE STIMULATED A NEW DEGREE OF INTEREST
AMONG TOP KUWAITI OFFICIALS IN THE COUNTRY'S AIR
DEFENSE SYSTEM, WHICH DID NOT REACT IN ANY WAY TO THE
"EVENTS" IN THE KOC NORTH FIELD BECAUSE IT WAS CLOSED DOWN
FOR THE NIGHT (SEPTEL).
MAESTRONE
UNCLASSIFIED

DEPARTMENT OF DEFENSE
JOINT CHIEFS OF STAFF
MESSAGE CENTER

RECEIVED

JUN -3 1980

VZCZCMLT565
MULT
ACTION
        DIAI
DISTR
        IADR(A1) J5(A2) JSINMCC NIDS SECDEF(07) SECDEFI USDP(15)
        ATSDIAE(81) ASDIPABE(A1) IIDIA(20) NMIC
-       CMC CC WASHINGTON DC
-       CSAF WASHINGTON DC
:   CNO WASHINGTON DC
-       CSA WASHINGTON DC
-       CIA WASHINGTON DC
:   SECSTATE WASHINGTON DC
:   NSA WASH DC
        FILE
(847)

TRANSIT/1542115/1542207/A8A152TOR1542264
DE RUESLMA #4888 1542115
7NY CCCCC
R A220527 JUN 80
FM USDAO LIMA PERU
TO RUEKJCS/DIA WASHDC
INFO RULPALJ/USCINCSO QUARRY HTS PN
RULPAFA/USAFSO HOWARD AFB PN
BT

SUBJI IR 6 876 0146 80 (U)
THIS IS AN INFO REPORT, NOT FINALLY EVAL INTEL
1. (U) CTRYI PERU (PE)
2. TITLE (U) UFO SIGHTED IN PERU (U)
3. (U) DATE OF INFOI 800510
4. (U)   ORIGI USDAO AIR LIMA PERU
5. (U) REQ REFSI Z-D13-PE030
6. (U) SOURCEI 6 876 013B. OFFICER IN THE PERUVIAN AIR FORCE
WHO OBSERVED THE EVENT AND IS IN A POSITION TO BE PARTY
TO CONVERSATION CONCERNING THE EVENT. SOURCE HAS REPORTED
RELIABLY IN THE PAST.

7.   SUMMARYI SOURCE REPORTED THAT A UFO WAS SPOTTED
ON TWO DIFFERENT OCCASIONS NEAR PERUVIAN AIR FORCE (FAP) BASE
IN SOUTHERN PERU. THE FAP TRIED TO INTERCEPT AND DESTROY THE
UFO, BUT WITHOUT SUCCESS.

PAGE 1

DEPARTMENT OF DEFENSE
JOINT CHIEFS OF STAFF
MESSAGE CENTER

PAGE 2   18134
8A.   DETAILS: SOURCE TOLD RO ABOUT THE SPOTTING OF AN
UNIDENTIFIED FLYING OBJECT IN THE VICINITY OF MARIANO MELGAR AIR
BASE, LA JOYA, PERU (168A5S, 87153A6W). SOURCE STATED THAT THE
VEHICLE WAS SPOTTED ON TWO DIFFERENT OCCASIONS. THE FIRST WAS
DURING THE MORNING HOURS OF 9 MAY 80, AND THE SECOND DURING
THE EARLY EVENING HOURS OF 10 MAY 80.
              SOURCE STATED THAT ON 9 MAY, WHILE A GROUP OF FAP
OFFICERS WERE IN FORMATION AT MARIANO MALGAR, THEY SPOTTED A
UFO THAT WAS ROUND IN SHAPE, HOVERING NEAR THE AIRFIELD. THE
AIR COMMANDER SCRAMBLED AN SU-22 AIRCRAFT TO MAKE AN
INTERCEPT. THE PILOT, ACCORDING TO A THIRD PARTY, INTERCEPTED
THE VEHICLE AND FIRED UPON IT AT VERY CLOSE RANGE WITHOUT
CAUSING ANY APPARENT DAMAGE. THE PILOT TRIED TO MAKE A
SECOND PASS ON THE VEHICLE, BUT THE UFO OUT-RAN THE SU-22.
              THE SECOND SIGHTING WAS DURING HOURS OF DARKNESS.
THE VEHICLE WAS LIGHTED. AGAIN AN SU-22 WAS SCRAMBLED, BUT THE
VEHICLE OUT-RAN THE AIRCRAFT.
8B.   ORIG CMTS: RO HAS HEARD DISCUSSION ABOUT THE
SIGHTING FROM OTHER SOURCES. APPARENTLY SOME VEHICLE WAS
SPOTTED, BUT ITS ORIGIN REMAINS UNKNOWN.
9. (U) PROJ NO: N/A
10. (U) COLL MGMT CODES: AB
11. (U) SPEC INST: NONE. DIRC: NO.
12. (U) PREP BY: NORMAN H. RUNGE, COL, AIRA
13. (U) APP BY: VAUGHN E. WILSON, CAPT, DATT, ALUSNA
14. (U) REQ EVAL: NO   REL TO: NONE
15. (U) ENCL: N/A
16. (U) DIST BY ORIG: N/A

BT
#4888
ANNOTES
JAL 117

CHAPTER FOUR

Government Disinformation—Or Fraud?

In recent years the UFO field has been flooded with purported "official" documents, allegedly "leaked" by persons unknown within the American Intelligence Community. These documents have been very difficult to confirm or repudiate. The reason? When U.S. Government agencies have been queried, they have either been unwilling to answer inquiries or have not known what they were supposed to do under Federal Law established for just such inquiries.

In June 1987, the UFO research community tried very hard to confirm or repudiate what has become known as the "MJ-12 Briefing Document." (See doc. 4-1.) This document is allegedly a briefing paper that was prepared on November 18, 1952, by Admiral Roscoe H. Hillenkoetter for presentation to then-President-Elect Dwight D. Eisenhower. The document is said to be classified as Top Secret, and it dealt with American recovery operations of crashed UFOs. Every effort to validate this document by the UFO Community has been unsuccessful.

The FBI became aware of the document on September 15, 1988, when a Special Agent of the Air Force, Office of Special Investigations (OSI), gave a copy of it to an FBI agent in Dallas, Texas. (See doc. 4-2.) The FBI agent requested that the Bureau "discern if the document is still classified."

It is interesting to note that in response to this request, FBI Headquarters answered, in a cable dated December 2, 1988: (See docs. 4-3, 4-4, and 4-5.)

The Office of Special Investigations, U.S. Air Force, advised on November 30, 1988, that the document was fabricated. Copies of that document have been distributed to various parts of the United States. The document is completely bogus.

The document having been declared bogus, one might believe that the FBI would have no further interest in it. However, in a letter dated November 15, 1991, FBI Headquarters informed the U.S. Air Force, Office of Special Investigations: (See doc. 4-6.)

It is noted that although this document may represent some type of hoax, it is our responsibility to insure that all incidents involving the mishandling of classified data receive adequate investigative attention. Therefore, we request that your agency attempt to ascertain the originator and/or the current classification of the enclosed document.

To date, no one has been charged with any involvement of wrongdoing; that is, fabrication or hoaxing this document. Moreover, in the military it is illegal to falsify a document and pass it as a classified document.

In 1983, an alleged "Secret" document surfaced. This document dealt with the alleged photo-imagery interpretation of the film evidence taken by Paul Bennewitz during the Kirtland Air Force Base sightings of August 1980 (see Chapter Two). In this case the Air Force Intelligence Service and the Air Force Office of Special Investigations did exactly what they were suppose to do in such cases.

The U.S. Air Force believed the document was a hoax from the every first time they received it, because of the following reasons:

a. There never has been an office within AFSAC (or 7602nd) with the symbol INS, INSR, or IT.
b. There has never been a "Capt Grace" (or anyone with the surname Grace) assigned to AFSAC.
c. The purported imagery interpretation that was done is outside AFSAC's and AFOSI's mission. Further, AFSAC has no individuals who are photo interpreters.
d. The term WNINTEL is spelled phonetically on each occurrence. OSI should certainly be familiar with the correct spelling. Further, the document is replete with grammatical errors, typing errors, and in general makes no sense.
e. The document is not in the standard, accepted format for classified messages.

We can see from the above that the Air Force clearly thought the document was a hoax. However, until a determination was made as to the status of the document, the Air Force considered it to be classified Secret. This was correct procedure in accordance with existing regulations and an Executive Order.

I, too, felt that the document was a hoax. However, I still have questions about some of the information appearing in the document. The document mentioned a "Project Aquarius," and that this project was classified Top Secret. Also, the document mentioned this project was under the control of NASA. I later heard that the correct term should have been NSA and that it was changed to read NASA for some reason.

In a letter dated April 15, 1986, to an UFO researcher, the National Security Agency (NSA) finally admitted to the existence of a Project Aquarius and stated that it was classified Top Secret. (See doc. 4-7.) The NSA has never stated what the mission of Project Aquarius is.

How could the perpetrator(s) of the hoaxed document that surfaced in 1983 have known of the existence of a Top Secret project named Aquarius under the NSA when that information was not made public until April 15, 1986? As a matter of fact, the NSA even considered the project's name sensitive. Therefore, it would appear that either the perpetrator was damned good at guessing or had inside information.

★★★

The next document to be examined is known, within the UFO Community, as the "Snowbird Document." (See doc. 4-8.) It came to the attention of UFO researchers in 1985. I felt certain that the agencies I wrote to, requesting their assessment of the document, would expose the document within weeks as a hoax. However, my efforts to get to the truth of this document almost forced my retirement from the U.S. Army and led the NSA to consider my request for congressional assistance as a matter of "National Security Policy."

A copy of the Snowbird Document came into my possession in April 1985. Believing it to be just another fake, I filed it away. In June 1985, I started to hear stories concerning an alleged underground "alien" base in the area of Dulce, New Mexico. One of these stories dealt with an alleged recovered alien aircraft that crashed during a test flight by the U.S. Government. This raised my interest and I began to look at the Snowbird Document in a new light.

I spent over 700 hours checking the document very carefully, to insure that it conformed to existing Department of Defense (DOD) Directives and Regulations for a classified document. To my amazement, it did. Furthermore, the document seemed to make sense as written. However, this did not make it the valid document of some American governmental agency. I needed more proof before I could accept the document as genuine.

Knowing that Senator Pete Domenici's office had been involved with the alleged crash of the alien aircraft, I decided to call his office and ask what information they had on the alleged incident. I contacted the Senator's Washington office on February 6, 1986, and talked to a Mr. Paul Gilman there. I was informed that the only involvement the Senator's office had with the case was to inform the individual who contacted the Senator's office what government agency he should notify concerning the alleged crash. I then asked Mr. Gilman if he had any knowledge of an alleged Top Secret document dealing with a Project Snowbird. He stated that he believed the individual who had earlier contacted the Senator had sent such a document. However, all the information sent by that individual had been returned to him. Also, Gilman appeared to want to cut our conversation short.

My brief conversation with Paul Gilman still did not convince me that the document was genuine. After all, the Senator's office apparently had taken no action regarding the alleged incident.

My next step was to write to every government agency that I felt might have knowledge of, or an interest in, the document. At least I felt these agencies would do the same thing the Air Force did with the 1983 document: either confirm the document as genuine or expose it as a hoax. While these agencies did not confirm the Snowbird Document as genuine, they did not deny or expose it as a hoax. (See docs. 4-9, 4-10, 4-11, 4-12, 4-13, 4-14, and 4-15.)

On November 6, 1986, I decided to write Senator Domenici's office for assistance in once and for all getting an answer to whether or not the Snowbird Document was genuine. In a letter dated February 10, 1987, the Senator sent, in reply to my letter, the response his office received from the National Security Agency. The NSA replied, in part: (See doc. 4-16.)

… his [my] letter asks for NSA analysis of the document he attached. It appears to be an Air Force document. The project names which are referenced, Sigma and Snowbird, are not NSA projects. We have no knowledge of the information contained in the document.

The NSA's response to the Senator shocked me. I felt that the NSA should have realized the document appeared to be a Top Secret document, and that if it was in fact genuine, someone had a security leak since the document does not appear to have been released under the Freedom of Information Act. Furthermore, Executive Order 12356 and DOD Directives and Regulations were apparently not being followed. Executive Order 12356, Part 1, Section 1.2, paragraph e, states:

When an employee, contractor, licensee, or grantee of an agency that does not have original classification authority originates information believed by that person to require classification, the information shall be protected in a manner consistent with this Order and its implementing directives. The information shall be transmitted promptly as provided under this Order or its implementing directives to the agency that has appropriate subject matter interest and classification authority with respect to this information. That agency shall decide within thirty (30) days whether to classify this information. If it is not clear which agency has classification responsibility for this information, it shall be sent to the Director of the Information Security Oversight Office. The Director shall determine the agency having primary subject matter interest and forward the information, with appropriate recommendations, to that agency for a classification determination.

So, under the above-cited Executive Order, if the NSA could not determine whether the document was genuine, they should have sent it to the Director of the Information Security Oversight Office for a determination. It would appear, however, that the NSA had failed to do this.

On April 8, 1987, I delivered to Senator Domenici's Roswell (New Mexico) office another letter, once again requesting his assistance in getting to the bottom of this document. However, this time the NSA phoned the Senator's office and stated that my letter dealt with "National Security Policy" as written and that they would like me to rewrite my letter. I informed the Senator's office that I would be more than happy to rewrite the letter just as soon as the NSA informed me, in writing, what they wanted me to take out. I never got a response or any acknowledgment from either the Senator's office or the NSA.

On June 21, 1987, an article was run in the *Roswell Daily Record* concerning my contacts with Senator Domenici's office over the Snowbird Document. This article was the result of efforts from my executive officer and adjutant to force my retirement from the U.S. Army after twenty years' service. For the next twelve months, my life was to become a living hell. But that's another story and, hopefully, another book.

I called Senator Domenici's office on August 5, 1987, and asked for the status of my April 8 letter. I was informed by a Mr. Marco Caceras that the NSA really did not want response to my letter. However, Mr. Caceras stated that he would check into the matter. In a letter from the Senator's office dated August 24, 1987 (see docs. 4-17 and 4-18), I received a copy of the interim response from the NSA. According to that response, the NSA had only received my letter on August 5, 1987. On October 9, Senator Domenici's office sent me a copy of the response they had received from the NSA. In the NSA's response, that agency refused to answer any of my questions concerning the validity of the Snowbird Document.

On January 4, 1988, once again I wrote the Senator's office requesting his assistance in getting someone to either confirm as genuine, or repudiate as a hoax, the Snowbird Document. To date, I have not received a response from either the Senator's office or the NSA. On January 17, 1989, I called Senator Domenici's office for the last time concerning my January 4 letter. I was informed that the NSA was not going to respond to my letter because my request involved "a matter of National Security Policy."

If classified information is "leaked" to the public, it becomes "compromised." When this happens, the following action is to be taken, as outlined in AR 380-5, paragraph 2-210a:

a. The original classifying authority, upon learning that a loss or possible compromise of specific classified information has occurred, shall prepare a written damage assessment and:
1. Reevaluate the information involved and determine whether (a) its classification should be continued without change; (b) the specific information, or parts thereof, should be modified to minimize or nullify the effects of the reported compromise and the classification retained; (c) declassification, downgrading, or upgrading is warranted; and (d) countermeasures are appropriate and feasible to negate or minimize the effect of the compromise.
2. Give prompt notice to all holders of such information when the determination is within categories (b), (c), or (d) of subparagraph 1, above.

In addition, paragraph 2-207b of AR 380-5 states:

...If mere knowledge of the existence of the item of equipment or object would compromise or nullify its national security advantage, its existence would warrant classification.

Could it be that the U.S. Government is test-flying recovered "alien" aircraft? If not, why not simply tell me that the Snowbird Document is a hoax and put an end to my questioning? Why does the NSA consider my letters to Senator Domenici's office a matter of "National Security Policy"? But remember, validation of the Snowbird Document by the U.S. Government would be an admission that we have recovered "alien" aircraft!

Could it be that the Snowbird document is genuine and that the government does not wish to acknowledge it as such due to the National Security reasons stated above? Is it possible that the document is disinformation by some government agency?

The answers to those questions can only be provided by the U.S. Government. The agencies of the government to which I have written continue to remain noncommittal.

Doc. 4-1a Alleged MJ-12 Briefing Document,
Nov 18, 1952

COPY ONE OF ONE.

BRIEFING DOCUMENT: OPERATION MAJESTIC 12

PREPARED FOR PRESIDENT-ELECT DWIGHT D. EISENHOWER: (EYES ONLY)

18 NOVEMBER, 1952

WARNING! This is a TOP SECRET – EYES ONLY document containing

compartmentalized information essential to the national security

of the United States. EYES ONLY ACCESS to the material herein

is strictly limited to those possessing Majestic-12 clearance

level. Reproduction in any form or the taking of written or

mechanically transcribed notes is strictly forbidden.

EYES ONLY

Doc. 4-1b Alleged MJ-12 Briefing Document, Nov 18, 1952

COPY ONE OF ONE.

SUBJECT: OPERATION MAJESTIC-12 PRELIMINARY BRIEFING FOR
    PRESIDENT-ELECT EISENHOWER.

DOCUMENT PREPARED 18 NOVEMBER, 1952.

BRIEFING OFFICER: ADM. ROSCOE H. HILLENKOETTER (MJ-1)

NOTE: This document has been prepared as a preliminary briefing
only. It should be regarded as introductory to a full operations
briefing intended to follow.

    • • • • • •

OPERATION MAJESTIC-12 is a TOP SECRET Research and Development/
Intelligence operation responsible directly and only to the
President of the United States. Operations of the project are
carried out under control of the Majestic-12 (Majic-12) Group
which was established by special classified executive order of
President Truman on 24 September, 1947, upon recommendation by
Dr. Vannevar Bush and Secretary James Forrestal. (See Attachment
"A".) Members of the Majestic-12 Group were designated as follow

                    Adm. Roscoe H. Hillenkoetter
                    Dr. Vannevar Bush
                    Secy. James V. Forrestal*
                    Gen. Nathan F. Twining
                    Gen. Hoyt S. Vandenberg
                    Dr. Detlev Bronk
                    Dr. Jerome Hunsaker
                    Mr. Sidney W. Souers
                    Mr. Gordon Gray
                    Dr. Donald Menzel
                    Gen. Robert M. Montague
                    Dr. Lloyd V. Berkner

The death of Secretary Forrestal on 22 May, 1949, created
a vacancy which remained unfilled until 01 August, 1950, upon
which date Gen. Walter B. Smith was designated as permanent
replacement.

EYES..ONLY
• TOP SECRET •
• • • • • • • • • • •

EYES ONLY

Doc. 4-1c Alleged MJ-12 Briefing Document,
Nov 18, 1952

COPY ONE OF ONE.

On 24 June, 1947, a civilian pilot flying over the Cascade
Mountains in the State of Washington observed nine flying
disc-shaped aircraft traveling in formation at a high rate
of speed. Although this was not the first known sighting
of such objects, it was the first to gain widespread attention
in the public media. Hundreds of reports of sightings of
similar objects followed. Many of these came from highly
credible military and civilian sources. These reports resulted in independent efforts by several different elements
of the military to ascertain the nature and purpose of these
objects in the interests of national defense. A number of
witnesses were interviewed and there were several unsuccessful
attempts to utilize aircraft in efforts to pursue reported
discs in flight. Public reaction bordered on near hysteria
at times.

In spite of these efforts, little of substance was learned
about the objects until a local rancher reported that one
had crashed in a remote region of New Mexico located approximately seventy-five miles northwest of Roswell Army Air
Base (now Walker Field).

On 07 July, 1947, a secret operation was begun to assure
recovery of the wreckage of this object for scientific study.
During the course of this operation, aerial reconnaissance
discovered that four small human-like beings had apparently
ejected from the craft at some point before it exploded.
These had fallen to earth about two miles east of the wreckage
site. All four were dead and badly decomposed due to action
by predators and exposure to the elements during the approximately one week time period which had elapsed before their
discovery. A special scientific team took charge of removing
these bodies for study. (See Attachment "C".) The wreckage
of the craft was also removed to several different locations.
(See Attachment "B".) Civilian and military witnesses in
the area were debriefed, and news reporters were given the
effective cover story that the object had been a misguided
weather research balloon.

EYES ONLY

· · · · · · · · · · · · · ·
· TOP SECRET ·
· · · · · · · · · · · · · ·

EYES ONLY

Doc. 4-1d Alleged MJ-12 Briefing Document,
Nov 18, 1952

COPY ONE OF ONE

A need for as much additional information as possible about these craft, their performance characteristics and their purpose led to the undertaking known as U.S. Air Force Project SIGN in December, 1947. In order to preserve security, liason between SIGN and Majestic-12 was limited to two individuals within the Intelligence Division of Air Materiel Command whose role was to pass along certain types of information through channels. SIGN evolved into Project GRUDGE in December, 1948. The operation is currently being conducted under the code name BLUE BOOK, with liason maintained through the Air Force officer who is head of the project.

On 06 December, 1950, a second object, probably of similar origin, impacted the earth at high speed in the El Indio - Guerrero area of the Texas - Mexican boder after following a long trajectory through the atmosphere. By the time a search team arrived, what remained of the object had been almost totally incinerated. Such material as could be recovered was transported to the A.E.C. facility at Sandia, New Mexico, for study.

Implications for the National Security are of continuing importance in that the motives and ultimate intentions of these visitors remain completely unknown. In addition, a significant upsurge in the surveillance activity of these craft beginning in May and continuing through the autumn of this year has caused considerable concern that new developments may be imminent. It is for these reasons, as well as the obvious international and technological considerations and the ultimate need to avoid a public panic at all costs, that the Majestic-12 Group remains of the unanimous opinion that imposition of the strictest security precautions should continue without interruption into the new administration. At the same time, contingency plan MJ-1949-04P/78 (Top Secret - Eyes Only) should be held in continued readiness should the need to make a public announcement present itself. (See Attachment "G".)

TOP SECRET / MAJIC

EYES ONLY
. . . .
* TOP SECRET *
. . . .

EYES ONLY

COPY ONE OF ONE.

Doc. 4-1e Alleged MJ-12 Briefing Document,
Nov 18, 1952

A covert analytical effort organized by Gen. Twining and
Dr. Bush acting on the direct orders of the President, resulted in a preliminary concensus (19 September, 1947) that
the disc was most likely a short range reconnaissance craft.
This conclusion was based for the most part on the craft's
size and the apparent lack of any identifiable provisioning.
(See Attachment "D".) A similar analysis of the four dead
occupants was arranged by Dr. Bronk. It was the tentative
conclusion of this group (30 November, 1947) that although
these creatures are human-like in appearance, the biological
and evolutionary processes responsible for their development
has apparently been quite different from those observed or
postulated in homo-sapiens. Dr. Bronk's team has suggested
the term "Extra-terrestrial Biological Entities", or "EBEs",
be adopted as the standard term of reference for these
creatures until such time as a more definitive designation
can be agreed upon.

Since it is virtually certain that these craft do not originate in any country on earth, considerable speculation has
centered around what their point of origin might be and how
they get here. Mars was and remains a possibility, although
some scientists, most notably Dr. Menzel, consider it more
likely that we are dealing with beings from another solar
system entirely.   -

Numerous examples of what appear to be a form of writing.
were found in the wreckage. Efforts to decipher these have
remained largely unsuccessful. (See Attachment "E".)
Equally unsuccessful have been efforts to determine the
method of propulsion or the nature or method of transmission
of the power source involved. Research along these lines
has been complicated by the complete absence of identifiable
wings, propellers, jets, or other conventional methods of
propulsion and guidance, as well as a total lack of metallic
wiring, vacuum tubes, or similar recognizable electronic
components. (See Attachment "F".) It is assumed that the
propulsion unit was completely destroyed by the explosion
which caused the crash.

TOP SECRET / MAJIC

EYES ONLY
. . . .
* TOP SECRET *
. . . .

EYES ONLY

COPY ONE OF ONE.

Doc. 4-1f Alleged MJ-12 Briefing Document, Nov 18, 1952

ENUMERATION OF ATTACHMENTS:

*ATTACHMENT "A".........Special Classified Executive
                        Order #092447. (TS/EO)

*ATTACHMENT "B".........Operation Majestic-12 Status
                        Report #1, Part A. 30 NOV '47.
                        (TS-MAJIC/EO)

*ATTACHMENT "C".........Operation Majestic-12 Status
                        Report #1, Part B. 30 NOV '47.
                        (TS-MAJIC/EO)

*ATTACHMENT "D".........Operation Majestic-12 Preliminary
                        Analytical Report. 19 SEP '47.
                        (TS-MAJIC/EO)

*ATTACHMENT "E".........Operation Majestic-12 Blue Team
                        Report #5. 30 JUN '52.
                        (TS-MAJIC/EO)

*ATTACHMENT "F".........Operation Majestic-12 Status
                        Report #2. 31 JAN '48.
                        (TS-MAJIC/EO)

*ATTACHMENT "G".........Operation Majestic-12 Contingency
                        Plan MJ-1949-04P/78: 31 JAN '49.
                        (TS-MAJIC/EO)

*ATTACHMENT "H".........Operation Majestic-12, Maps and
                        Photographs Folio (Extractions).
                        (TS-MAJIC/EO)

. . . .
* TOP SECRET *
TOP SECRET / MAJIC

EYES ONLY

EYES ONLY

T52-EXEMPT (E)

170

U C

ATTACHMENT "A"

THE WHITE HOUSE
WASHINGTON

September 24, 1947.

MEMORANDUM FOR THE SECRETARY OF DEFENSE

Dear Secretary Forrestal:

As per our recent conversation on this matter, you are hereby authorized to proceed with all due speed and caution upon your undertaking. Hereafter this matter shall be referred to only as Operation Majestic Twelve.

It continues to be my feeling that any future considerations relative to the ultimate disposition of this matter should rest solely with the Office of the President following appropriate discussions with yourself, Dr. Bush and the Director of Central Intelligence.

[signature: Harry Truman]

F3 171

July 14, 1954

~~TOP SECRET RESTRICTED
SECURITY INFORMATION~~

MEMORANDUM FOR GENERAL TWINING

SUBJECT: NSC/MJ-12 Special Studies Project

The President has decided that the MJ-12 SSP briefing should take place during the already scheduled White House meeting of July 16, rather than following it as previously intended. More precise arrangements will be explained to you upon arrival. Please alter your plans accordingly.

Your concurrence in the above change of arrangements is assumed.

ROBERT CUTLER
Special Assistant
to the President

DECLASSIFIED
Authority NND 857013
By SD/TH NARA Date 1/12/87

L.W.r.

TRANSMIT VIA:
☐ Teletype
☐ Facsimile .
☒ **Airtel**

PRECEDENCE:
☐ Immediate
☐ Priority
☐ Routine

C'ASSIFICATION:
L☐ TOP SECRET
☐ SECRET
☐ CONFIDENTIAL
☐ UNCLAS E F T O
☐ UNCLAS

Doc. 4-2a FBI Airtel Message, Oct 25, 1988

S E C R E T

Date ___ 10/25/88

---

1   TO: DIRECTOR, FBI

2   FROM: . SAC, DALLAS (65C-) (P)

DECLASSIFIED BY 980
ON 8/28/91
FOIA 348,033   b2

(SECRET MATERIAL
ATTACHED)

3   SUBJECT: UNSUB(S);
4   POSSIBLE DISCLOSURE OF
             CLASSIFIED INFORMATION REGARDING
             OPERATION MAJESTIC-12;
5   ESP-X
             OO: DALLAS

7   This communication is classified "SECRET" in i
entirety.

    Enclosed for the Bureau is an envelope which contai
9   a possible classified document.

10 On September 15, 1988, UNITED STATES AIR FORCE, OFFI
OF SPECIAL INVESTIGATIONS (OSI), Special Agent
contacted the Dallas FBI with the enclosed document.
received the document from

claims that an individual at the scho
whom he refused to name, gave it to him, claiming he rece
it in the mail.

N65-81170-1 b2

Classified by: G-3
Declassify on: OADR

NOV 3 19

2 - Bureau (Enc. 1)
2 - Dallas
(4)

ENCLOSURE
contained by C12D

b7C

b2

S E C R E T

Approved: BR___   Transmitted _____   Per _____
                    (Number)   (Time)

S E C R E T

DL 65C-

Dallas notes that within the last six weeks, there has been local publicity regarding "OPERATION MAJESTIC-12" with at least two appearances on a local radio talk show, discussing the MAJESTIC-12 OPERATION, the individuals involved, and the Government's attempt to keep it all secret. It is unknown if this is all part of a publicity campaign.

from OSI, advises that "OPERATION BLUE BOOK," mentioned in the document on page 4 did exist.

Dallas realizes that the purported document is over 35 years old, but does not know if it has been properly declassified.

REQUEST OF THE BUREAU

The Bureau is requested to discern if the document is still classified. Dallas will hold any investigation in abeyance until further direction from FBIHQ.

S E C R E T

2*

Doc. 4-3 FBI Teletype Message, Dec 2, 1.988

12/2/88 | SECRET | ROUTINE

FM DIRECTOR FBI

TO FBI DALLAS (65C-NEW) ROUTINE

BT

S E C R E T

DECLASSIFIED BY 9803 ___ 67C
ON 8/28/91
FOIA # 348,053

UNSUB(S)& POSSIBLE DISCLOSURE OF CLASSIFIED INFORMATION

REGARDING OPERATION MAJESTIC-12& ESPIONAGE-X& OO: DALLAS.

THIS COMMUNICATION IS CLASSIFIED "SECRET" IN ITS ENTIRETY.

REFERENCE DALLAS AIRTEL DATED OCTOBER 25, 1988.

REFERENCED AIRTEL REQUESTED THAT FBIHQ DETERMINE IF THE

DOCUMENT ENCLOSED BY REFERENCED AIRTEL WAS CLASSIFIED OR NOT.

THE OFFICE OF SPECIAL INVESTIGATIONS, U. S. AIR FORCE,

ADVISED ON NOVEMBER 30, 1988, THAT THE DOCUMENT WAS FABRICATED.

COPIES OF THAT DOCUMENT HAVE BEEN DISTRIBUTED TO VARIOUS PARTS

OF THE UNITED STATES. THE DOCUMENT IS COMPLETELY BOGUS. 67C

DALLAS IS TO CLOSE CAPTIONED INVESTIGATION.

4808, D OADR

BT

65-81170-2

67C

SEE NOTE PAGE THREE

2 DEC 9 1988

2010ZC

FBI

358

TRANSMIT VIA:	PRECEDENCE:	CLASSIFICATION:
☐ Teletype	☐ Immediate	☐ TOP SECRET
☐ Facsimile	☐ Priority	☐ SECRET
☒ AIRTEL	☐ Routine	☐ CONFIDENTIAL
		☐ UNCLAS E F T O
		☐ UNCLAS

Date __10/31/91__

TO   : DIRECTOR, FBI
          (ATTN: INTD: CI-2 SC ▮▮▮▮▮▮▮▮▮▮▮▮)

FROM   : SAC, SALT LAKE CITY (65-0)

SUBJECT : MAJESTIC-12;
          ESP-X

     This communication is classified "CONFIDENTIAL" in its entirety.

     Re Secure telcalls between SSA ▮▮▮▮▮▮▮▮▮▮▮▮▮▮ Salt Lake City, and SSA ▮▮▮▮▮▮▮▮▮▮ FBIHQ, on 10/25/91, and 10/30/91.

     Enclosed for FBIHQ is the below mentioned 9-page document dated 11/18/52.

     <u>Request of the Bureau:</u>

     Pursuant to instructions relayed from DAD H.B. BRANDON III via referenced secure telcall on 10/30/91, INTD, Section CI-2 should attempt to determine any DOD interest in the enclosed document.

               CONFIDENTIAL

             Classified By: 2335
             Declassify On: OADR

65-81170-3

② - Bureau (Enc. 1)
1 - SU (65-0)
▮▮▮▮▮▮▮▮
(3)

#379,923

CONFIDENTIAL

b7c

Approved: _____ Transmitted _____ Per _____
                               (Number)   (Time)

At 12:10 p.m. on 10/18/91, an individual identifying himself as ███████████ telephonically contacted the Salt Lake City Division and spoke with the duty Agent, SA ██████████████████ identified himself as an employee of ██ Utah, telephone number ██████████, extension ████████ advised SA ██████ that while walking through the lobby of his place of employment on the morning of 10/18/91, he found the enclosed document lying on the lobby floor. ████████ stated that he read the document and due to the nature of the contents thereof, decided to contact the FBI. During the early afternoon of 10/18/91, ██████ delivered the enclosed document to the receptionist in the Salt Lake City Field Office.

Salt Lake City indices are negative on ██████████ ██████ A review of public source records revealed the following information:

Based upon the contents of the document and the manner in which it was recovered, Salt Lake City initially dismissed the document and its classification markings as a hoax. In an effort to determine possible DOD interest in the unusual document, via referenced secure telcall on 10/25/91, SSA ██████████ was provided with a synopsis of the contents of the enclosed document, with a request for him to determine through his DOD contacts any DOD interest in "OPERATION MAJESTIC-12", U.S. AIR FORCE "PROJECT SIGN" or "PROJECT GRUDGE".

b7C

b7c

65-0

CONFIDENTIAL

Based upon DOD representations made to SSA ████████ which, incredibly, tended to buttress a portion of the document, he discussed this matter with DAD BRANDON on 10/30/91. Based upon those DOD comments and DAD BRANDON's instructions, Salt Lake City is submitting the enclosed document to FBIHQ in order for the latter to further determine any DOD interest in the enclosed document which discusses the three above-mentioned code name operations.

(Editorial comment: The fact that this airtel is dated on Halloween day is purely coincidental; it could have been worse, and dated on the first of April.)

Doc. 4-5 FBI Letter to U.S.A.F. OSI, Nov 15, 1991

1

Date: November 15, 1991

To: Commander
Office of Special Investigations
Department of the Air Force
Bolling Air Force Base
Washington, D.C.

From: Harry B. Brandon, III, Acting Assistant Director
Intelligence Division

Subject: POSSIBLE UNAUTHORIZED DISCLOSURE OF CLASSIFIED
INFORMATION RELATING TO "OPERATION MAJESTIC 12"

For your information, our Bureau recently recovered what may
possibly be a classified document, dated November 18, 1952, relating
to "OPERATION MAJESTIC 12." The document indicates that this project
related to sightings/recovery of extra-terrestrial aircraft.

It is noted that although this document may represent some
type of hoax, it is our responsibility to insure that all incidents
involving the mishandling of classified data receive adequate
investigative attention. Therefore, we request that your agency
attempt to ascertain the originator and/or the current classification
of the enclosed document. Your cooperation in this matter is
appreciated.

The Point of Contact for this matter is, Supervisory Special
Agent ████████████████████████ Intelligence Division,
Federal Bureau of Investigation Headquarters, STU III ████████████

NOTE:

Instant requests assistance from the OSI in this
matter.

Enclosure

Delivered by Liaison

Classified by: 8381
Declassify on: OADR
SECRET

DEPARTMENT OF THE AIR FORCE
HEADQUARTERS AIR FORCE INTELLIGENCE SERVICE
FORT BELVOIR VIRGINIA 22060

n: TO   DAD
TN OF   25 January 1983

 maci   Possible Unauthorized Release of Classified Material

TO   INSA (MSgt Heldman)
        DA

1. Per our telephone conversation today, I am forwarding Mr Robert Todd's FOIA request along with the AFOSI message for determination as to classification level. As you can see, Mr Todd retyped the message "for easier reading." I have talked to AFOSI/DADF, Nadine Dulacki. According to her, they did not release the message to Mr Todd nor does she know how it came into his possession. Maj Kilikauskas (AFSAC/INOB, 664-4488) has looked at the message and he feels that it is a fake for several reasons:

   a. There never has been an office within AFSAC (or 7602nd) with the symbol INS, INSR; or IT.

   b. There has never been a "Capt Grace" (or anyone with the surname Grace) assigned to AFSAC.

   c. The purported imagery interpretation done is outside AFSAC's and AFOSI's mission. Further, AFSAC has no individuals who are photo interpreters.

   d. The term WNINTEL is spelled phonetically on each occurrence. OSI should certainly be familiar with the correct spelling. Further, the document is replete with grammatical errors, typing errors, and in general, makes no sense.

   e. The document is not in the standard, accepted format for classified messages.

Neither Maj Kilikauskas nor Mr Nehlig (who has worked in AFSAC many years) remember hearing of a "Project Aquarius." Further, Maj Kilikauskas had no idea if the information purportedly supplied by this Capt Grace is, in fact, classified at the Secret/WNINTEL level. He suggests that both NASA and Coast and Geodetic Survey be contacted to see if they have an interest in the message.

2. Finally, I have talked to Mr Earl Middaugh (AFOSI/IVOE, 767-5144). He remembers a FOIA request that his office staffed which involved an AFOSI message similar to this one. However, they were unable to identify it as OSI originated. He thinks perhaps this might be the same message. I have forwarded a copy of the Todd request to the AFOSI Freedom of Information Office (Bob Walker, 767-5262). Upon receipt both Mr Walker and Mr Middaugh will be better able to determine if this is a legitimate AFOSI document.

3. Until a determination is made, we will regard the document as classified.

/s/

SUSAN COOKSEY
Documentation Management Branch

2 Atch
1. Todd Request
2. Message, 2 cys (S/WNINTEL)

(THIS FORM IS SUBJECT TO THE PRIVACY ACT OF 1974)

...about any individual unless the person is informed
...this inquiry.

...IS VOLUNTARY: The SSN when used will be used for positive identification of the individual. It will not be used for any
...pose.

QUERY INFORMATION

RECEIVED		RESPONSE ACTION OFFICER	SUSPENSE DATE
DATE 05 AUG 82	TIME 1335	TSGT BAHLER AFIS/PA	N/A

RECEIVED FROM

(also known as KPIX-TV ch. 5 415-362-

Mr BOB Peters/ KPIX Radio/ San Francisco/(415) 765-8968

DESCRIPTION OF QUERY

1. Location of a Capt Grace of the 7602nd now known as AFSAC. (first name unknown)

2. AFSAC's involvement in UFO's. (investigations, etc)

3. Was a research center in Rockville, Md actually a cover for AFSAC's UFO studies, as indicated by Capt. Grace?

4. AFSAC's involvement in a Project Aquarius.

RESPONSE

1. Location unknown(he was not part of any organizational chart) plus I could not ju... release that information over the phone.

2. Stated the official Air Force position on UFO's and to the best of my knowledge, denied AFSAC's participation in any UFO studies.

3. Restated #2.

4. Stated I had never heard of the Project.

Mr Peters was not satisfied with all replys and asked for a superior that he might ta... with, I refered him to Capt Malesich, AFSAC/CE # 664-6341. I then went to brief the Ca... and Col Bale, AFSAC/CV. Col Bale made appropriate response and then contacted OSI, due to the fact Mr. Peters had a possibly classified message in his hands from "Capt Grace". The msg was sent from Bolling AFOSI, DTG 292039z NOV 80 - 7602nd was an info address. Mr Peters was satisfied with Col Bale's response and appeared to be very cooperative(at least to a point).

SOURCE OF RESPONSE		COORDINATION			
PHONE NO.	OFFICE SYMBOL	OFFICE SYMBOL	NAME	PHONE NO.	DATE
664-2228	AFIS/PA	AFSAC/CE	CAPT Malesich	664-6341	06 AUG 82
		AFSAC/CV	COL Bale	664-6341	06 Aug 82
NAME OF SOURCE		AFIS/CV	COL Jack Morris	695-4738	06 Aug 82
		AFOSI	COL		06 Aug 82
DATE	TIME				

REMARKS

RTTEZYVW RUFLOJA9136

ZNY ~~SECRET~~

GT

Doc. 4-6c U.S.A.F. Intelligence Service Letter
with Encls., Jan 25, 1983

17 NOV 1980

SECRET   FOR AFOSI ONLY

R 171130Z NOV 80

FM HQ AFOSI BOLLING AFB DC//IVOE

TO RUWTFBA AFOSI DIST 17 KIRTLAND AFB NM//BID

INFO 7602 AINTELG FT BELVOIR VA//INSR

~~SECRET~~   FOR AFOSI ONLY

REF: REQUEST FOR PHOTO IMAGERY INTERPRETATION YOUR MSG 292030Z OCT 80.

SUBJECT CASE NR: 8017D93-126 HQ CR 44

1. SUBJECT NEGATIVES/FILM WERE ANALYZED BY HQ IVT AND 7602 AINTELG, IT AND THE FOLLOWING RESULTS WERE FOUND:

A. NEGATIVE #1: DEPLICTING C-5A AIRCRAFT ON APPROACH AND STREAKING UNIDENTIFIED AERIAL OBJECT IN LOWER RIGHT PORTION OF FILM. FILM FOUND TO BE UNALTERED. SIZE DIFFERENTIAL WAS NOT CONSISTENT WITH SIZE OF AIRCRAFT. CONCLUSION: INCONCLUSIVE

B. NEGATIVE #2: DEPLICTING CYLINDER SHAPED UNIDENTIFIED AERIAL OBJECT IN UPPER LEFT PORTION OF PHOTO. FILM FOUND TO BE UNALTERED. FILM SHOWED OBJECT TO BE CONSISTENT WITH FIELD DEPTH AND CONSISTENT WITH RELATIVE SIZE OF FIXED OBJECTS. CONCLUSION: LEGITIMATE NEGATIVE OF UNIDENTIFIED AERIAL OBJECT. BOLTON/REINFELD METHOD DID NOT REVEAL VISIBLE MARKINGS ON OBJECT.

C. NEGATIVE #3: DEPLICTING IRREGULAR SHAPED UNIDENTIFIED AERIAL OBJECT IN SEVEN FRAMES OF 8MM FILM. BECAUSE OF THE SIZE AND APPARENT SPEED OF OBJECT NO FURTHER CLASSIFICATION OR CONCLUSION COULD BE DRAWN. FILM SHOWN TO BE UNALTERED.

D. 34 INCHES OF 8MM FILM: DEPLICTING APPARENT COLORED OBJECT MOVING IN FRONT OF STILL CAMERA. FILM FOUND TO BE UNALTERED. SPECTROGRAPHY REVEALED COLORES TO BE BASIC PRISM FEATURES. DEPTH ANALYSIS REVEALED OBJECT TO BE WITHIN 152MM OF CAMERA. OBJECT WAS NOT CONSISTENT WITH RELATIVE SIZE OF FIXED OBJECTS OBSERVED FOR SEVERAL SECONDS IN FILM. CONCLUSION: INCONCLUSIVE.

E. ORIGINAL NEGATIVE DEPLICTING UNIDENTIFIED OBJECT. FILM FOUND TO BE UNALTERED. BECAUSE OF A LACK OF FIXED OBJECTS IN THE FILM, NO DEPTH ANALYSIS COULD BE PERFORMED. BOLTON, REINFELD METHOD REVEALED OBJECT TO BE SAUCER SHAPED, APPROXIMATE DIAMETER 37 FEET. OBJECT CONTAINED A TRILATERAL INSIGNIA ON THE LOWER PORTION OF OBJECT. CONCLUSION: LEGITIMATE NEGATIVE OF UNIDENTIFIED AERIAL OBJECT.

2. REF YOUR REQUEST FOR FURTHER INFORMATION REGARDING HQ CR 44, THE FOLLOWING IS PROVIDED: CAPT GRACE 7602 AINTELG, INS CONTACTED AND RELATED FOLLOWING: (S/WINTEL) USAF NO LONGER PUBLICLY ACTIVE IN UFO RESEARCH, HOWEVER USAF STILL HAS INTEREST IN ALL UFO SIGHTINGS OVER USAF INSTALLATION/TEST RANGES. SEVERAL OTHER GOVERNMENT AGENCIES, LEAD BY NASA, ACTIVELY INVESTIGATES LEGITIMATE SIGHTINGS THROUGH COVERT COVER. (S/WINTEL/FSA) ONE SUCH COVER IS UFO REPORTING CENTER, US COAST AND GEODETIC SURVEY, ROCKVILLE, MD 20852. NASA FILTERS RESULTS OF SIGHTINGS TO APPROPRIATE MILITARY DEPARTMENTS WITH INTEREST IN THAT PARTICULAR SIGHTING. THE OFFICIAL US GOVERNMENT POLICY AND RESULTS OF PROJECT AQUARIUS IS STILL CLASSIFIED TOP SECRET WITH NO DISSEMINATION OUTSIDE OFFICIAL INTELLIGENCE CHANNELS AND WITH RESTRICTED ACCESS TO "MJ TWELVE". CASE ON BENNEWITZ IS BEING MONITORED BY NASA INS, WHO REQUEST ALL FUTURE EVIDENCE BE FORWARDED TO THEM THRU AFOSI, IVOE.

4. REF YOUR REQUEST FOR TECHNICAL ASSISTANCE. BECAUSE OF A CHANCE OF PUBLIC DISCLOSURE, NO KNOWLEDGEABLE PERSONNEL WITH SPA WILL BE PROVIDED. CONTINUE TO RECEIVE ASSISTANCE FROM INDIVIDUALS MENTIONED IN YOUR MESSAGE, MILLER, FUGATE. BECAUSE OF THE SENSITIVITY OF CASE, REQUEST THEY BE THOROUGHLY DEBRIEFED AT REGULAR INTERVALS.

BTS

IDIS

DOWNGRADE 17NOV2020

NATIONAL SECURITY AGENCY
CENTRAL SECURITY SERVICE
FORT GEORGE G. MEADE, MARYLAND 20755-6000

Serial: J9014C

15 APR 1986

This responds to your letter of 7 March 1986 in which you further narrowed your Freedom of Information Act (FOIA) request for records pertaining to Project Aquarius.

The document located in response to your request as stated in your 7 March letter has been reviewed by this Agency as required by the FOIA and has been found to be currently and properly classified in accordance with Executive Order 12356. This document meets the criteria for classification as set forth in subparagraphs 2, 4, and 8 of section 1.3 and remains classified TOP SECRET as provided in section 1.1 of Executive Order 12356. The document is classified because its disclosure could reasonably be expected to cause exceptionally grave damage to the national security. Because the document is currently and properly classified, it is exempt from disclosure pursuant to the first exemption of the FOIA (5 U.S.C. section 552(b)(1)).

In addition, this Agency is authorized by various statutes to protect certain information concerning its activities. We have determined that such information exists in this document. Accordingly, those portions are also exempt from disclosure pursuant to the third exemption of the FOIA which provides for the withholding of information specifically protected from disclosure by statute. The specific statutes applicable in this case are Title 18 U.S. Code 798; Title 50 U.S. Code 403(d)(3); and Section 6, Public Law 86-36 (50 U.S. Code 402 note).

No portion of the information is reasonably segregable.

Since your request has been denied, you are hereby advised of this Agency's appeal procedures.

Any person denied access to information may, within 45 days after notification of the denial, file an appeal to the NSA/CSS Freedom of Information Act Appeal Authority. The appeal shall be in writing addressed to the NSA/CSS FOIA Appeal Authority, National Security Agency, Fort George G. Meade, MD 20755-6000.

Serial: J9014C

The appeal shall reference the initial denial of access and shall contain, in sufficient detail and particularity, the grounds upon which the requester believes release of the information is required. The NSA/CSS Appeal Authority shall respond to the appeal within 20 working days after receipt.

In your letter, you take exception to the amount requested by this Agency for manpower and computer search fees to process your original request for all information on Project Aquarius. Please be advised that NSA search and duplication fees are computed in accordance with guidance promulgated in sections 6-201 and 6-202 of DoD Directive 5400.7-R.

Sincerely,

JULIA B. WETZEL
Director of Policy

TOP SECRET

UNCLASSIFIED

SUB PROJECTS UNDER PROJECT

2. (TS/ORCON)   PROJECT SIGMA: (PROWORD: ~~████~~). Originally established as part of Project ~~████~~ in 1954. Became a separate project in 1976. Its mission was to establish communication with Aliens. This Project met with positive success when in 1959, the United States established primitive communications with the Aliens. On April 25, 1964, a USAF intelligence Officer, met two Aliens at a pre-arranged location in the desert of New Mexico. The contact lasted for approximately three hours. ~~████████████~~ the Air Force officer managed to exchange basic information with the two Aliens (Atch 7). This project is continuing at an Air Force base in New Mexico. (TOP: ~~████~~

TOP SECRET   UNCLASSIFIED

DEPARTMENT OF THE AIR FORCE
HEADQUARTERS UNITED STATES AIR FORCE
WASHINGTON, D.C.   20330-5025

11 February 1986

Mr. Clifford E. Stone
1421 E. Tilden
Roswell NM 88201

Dear Mr. Stone

We are in receipt of your letter dated 7 February 1986.

We cannot render an opinion on the record you enclosed. We can tell you it was not released from this office as a result of a Freedom of Information Act request.

We have no records relating to the projects listed in your letter.

Sincerely

ANNE W. TURNER
HQ USAF Freedom of
    Information Manager

NASA

National Aeronautics and
Space Administration

Washington, D.C.
20546

Reply to Attn of: LB

February 18, 1986

Mr. Clifford E. Stone
1421 E. Tilden
Roswell, NM 88201

Dear Mr. Stone:

This is in response to your letter of February 7, 1986, pursuant
to the Freedom of Information Act, requesting NASA's "opinion as
to the validity of the attached document marked TOP SECRET." You
also requested any information NASA might have on the following:

> "1.   PROJECT SIGMA

> "2.   PROJECT SNOWBIRD

> "3.   PROJECT ORCON"

The document that was attached to your letter does not contain
sufficient identification to permit any opinion of its
authenticity.

A search of the NASA Security Office files has revealed no
information on Projects SIGMA, SNOWBIRD, or ORCON.

Sincerely,

Lillian R. Levy
Freedom of Information
  Act Officer

DEPARTMENT OF THE AIR FORCE
HEADQUARTERS AIR FORCE OFFICE OF SPECIAL INVESTIGATIONS
BOLLING AIR FORCE BASE, DC 20332-6001

FEB 2 7 1986

Mr Clifford E. Stone
1421 E. Tilden
Roswell NM 88201

Dear Mr Stone

This is in response to your Freedom of Information Act request of 7 February 1986.

Access to files within the Air Force Office of Special Investigations (AFOSI) is through a computerized index maintained by the Defense Investigative Service. This index known as the Defense Central Index of Investigations (DCII) identifies investigative records held by any Department of Defense component and is not restricted to AFOSI files. A search of the DCII disclosed no record of AFOSI maintaining any files identifiable with "PROJECT SIGMA, PROJECT SNOWBIRD, AND PROJECT ORCON".

AFOSI cannot attest to the validity of the document which was provided with your letter dated 7 February 1986.

Sincerely

CECIL W. FRY, SA
Chief, Information Release Division
Directorate of Administration

DEFENSE INTELLIGENCE AGENCY
WASHINGTON, D.C. 20301

U-3,355/RTS-1   27 February 1986

Mr. Clifford E. Stone
1421 E. Tilden
Roswell, New Mexico 88201

Dear Requester:

This is to inform you that we are in receipt of your FOIA/PA request dated 7 February 1986.

As a result of the large number of FOIA/PA requests received by the Defense Intelligence Agency some delay may be encountered in processing your request. We solicit your patience and understanding and assure you that your request will be processed as soon as possible.

Your request has been assigned case number 0109-86. Please refer to this case number in all future correspondence to us.

Sincerely,

ROBERT C. HARDZOG
Freedom of Information Act

DEFENSE LOGISTICS AGENCY
DEFENSE TECHNICAL INFORMATION CENTER
CAMERON STATION
ALEXANDRIA, VIRGINIA 22304-6145

IN REPLY
REFER TO DTIC-L

4 MAR 1986

Mr. Clifford E. Stone
1421 E. Tilden
Roswell, NM 88201

Dear Mr. Stone:

Reference your letter of 7 Feb 86 requesting information under the Freedom of Information Act (FOIA).

In response to your question concerning the classification of the document from which you forwarded a copy of a page, the Defense Technical Information Center (DTIC) cannot make this classification determination. You will have to return the document to the originator in order to obtain a classification evaluation.

The enclosed bibliography identifies documents in the DTIC technical report collection related to projects Orcon, Orion, and Snowbird. You may obtain these reports from:

> National Technical Information Service (NTIS)
> Department of Commerce
> 5285 Port Royal Road
> Springfield, VA 22161

NTIS provides such reports to members of the general public.

Sincerely,

Jean Wiley

JEAN WILEY
DTIC Freedom of Information
Act Focal Point

1 Encl

OFFICE OF THE ASSISTANT SECRETARY OF DEFENSE

WASHINGTON D.C. 20301-1400

6 MAR 1986

Ref: 86-FOI-307

PUBLIC AFFAIRS

Mr. Clifford E. Stone
1421 E. Tilden
Roswell, NM 88201

Dear Mr. Stone:

This is an interim response to your February 7, 1986,
Freedom of Information Act request, received in this
Directorate on February 18, 1986.

Your request has been forwarded to the cognizant Component
within the Office of the Secretary of Defense/Organization
of the Joint Chiefs of Staff (OSD/OJCS) and is being processed
as expeditiously as possible. As soon as all OSD/OJCS processing
is complete, you will be provided a more substantive response.

Even though your letter did not indicate a willingness to
pay search and reproduction costs as required, your request is
being processed as the costs are expected to be minimal.

Should you have questions pertaining to your request,
please call one of my action officers at (202) 697-4026 and
refer to the above "Ref" number.

Sincerely,

W. M. McDonald
Director, Freedom of Information
and Security Review

OFFICE OF THE ASSISTANT SECRETARY OF DEFENSE

WASHINGTON D.C. 20301-1400

19 MAR 1986
Ref: 86-FOI-307

PUBLIC AFFAIRS

Mr. Clifford E. Stone
1421 E. Tilden
Roswell, NM 88201

Dear Mr. Stone:

This replies to your February 7, 1986, Freedom of
Information Act request which was received in this office on
February 18, 1986.

The Defense Advanced Research Projects Agency (DARPA) has
reviewed your request. Regarding Projects Orcon and Snowbird,
the DARPA reports that they have no records concerning the two
projects, therefore they are unable to provide an opinion as
to the validity of the document attached to your request. The
DARPA further reports that they have no Project Sigma records,
however, the final reports for the project are available at
the National Technical Information Service. The address is:

National Technical Information Service
5285 Port Royal Road
Springfield, VA 22161

Due to the minimal costs incurred, all fees are waived in
this instance.

Sincerely,

W. M. McDonald
Director, Freedom of Information
and Security Review

United States Senate

WASHINGTON, D.C. 20510

February 10, 1987

Mr. Clifford E. Stone
1421 East Tilden
Roswell, New Mexico 88201

Dear Clifford:

Enclosed please find a copy of the response which I
have received from the National Security Agency regarding
your inquiries about UFO's.

My staff mentioned that you have been in contact
with them. I also understand that you did not receive
my first letter to you in December. For that, I
apologize - perhaps it was lost in the mail.

I hope the response from the National Security Agency
is satisfactory. If I can be of any further assistance,
please let me know.

My warmest personal regards.

Sincerely,

Pete V. Domenici
United States Senator

PVD/mc
Enclosure

NATIONAL SECURITY AGENCY
CENTRAL SECURITY SERVICE
FORT GEORGE G. MEADE, MARYLAND 20755-6000

Serial: Q4-112-87

0 4 FEB 1987

The Honorable Pete V. Domenici
United States Senate
ATTN: Marco Caceras
Room 430 Dirksen Senate Office Building
Washington, DC 20510

Dear Senator Domenici:

This responds to your letter to the Office of the
Secretary, Department of Defense dated 19 December 1986 on
behalf of your constituent, Mr. Clifford E. Stone (Enclosure
1). Your letter has been directed to this Agency for response
to you.

The National Security Agency (NSA) has received numerous
Freedom of Information Act (FOIA) requests for information
pertaining to UFO incidents. Our records show that Mr. Stone
has submitted six such requests over the past 7 years. One of
those requests was for the information mentioned in paragraph 2
of his letter to you, the UFO incident at RAF Woodbridge Base.
In our 1 February 1984 response to Mr. Stone (Enclosure 2), we
notified him that the estimated manpower and computer search
costs involved in locating records responsive to his request
were $250.00. We advised him that, upon receipt of half that
amount, a search would be made. Mr. Stone did not respond to
our letter.

Regarding the information in paragraph 1 of Mr. Stone's
letter, we have no record of receiving an FOIA request for
documents dealing with a UFO destruction of a Cuban MiG-23.

Paragraph 3 of his letter asks for NSA analysis of the
document he attached. It appears to be an Air Force document.
The project names which are referenced, Sigma and Snowbird, are
not NSA projects. We have no knowledge of the information
contained in the document.

The subject of paragraph 4, project Aquarius, has been the
subject of numerous FOIA requests. Apparently there is or was
an Air Force project by that name which dealt with UFOs.
Coincidentally, there is also an NSA project by that name. The
NSA project does not deal with UFOs. We believe that the
confusion on this issue results from an FOIA request submitted
by another person with interest in UFOs, Mr. Christian Lambright.

Serial: Q4-112-87

Mr. Lambright requested all information on the NSA project Aquarius, apparently believing that the project pertains to UFOs. We advised Mr. Lambright that our project does not deal with UFOs. He then requested records revealing the "goal" of Aquarius, and we withheld the document because it is classified. We have reason to believe that our final response to Mr. Lambright, denying him access to the records, has been disseminated within a circle of those interested in UFOs and that subsequently a misunderstanding has developed regarding NSA, Aquarius and UFOs.

In responding to general FOIA requests for UFO information, certain documents have been withheld from the public pursuant to the first and third exemptions of the FOIA. The first exemption provides for the protection of information which is currently and properly classified in accordance with the provisions of Executive Order 12356. The third exemption protects information from disclosure by statute. The statutes applicable in this case are 50 U.S.C. 402 note (Public Law 86-36, Section 6), 50 U.S.C. 403(d)(3) and 18 U.S.C. 798. This Agency's decision to protect those records has been upheld by the United States Court of Appeals for the District of Columbia.

We hope that the information being provided to you will be of help to Mr. Stone.

Sincerely,

JULIA B. WETZEL
Director of Policy

PETE V. DOMENICI
NEW MEXICO

United States Senate
WASHINGTON, DC 20510

COMMITTEES:
BUDGET
APPROPRIATIONS
ENERGY AND NATURAL RESOURCES
AGING

August 24, 1987

Clifford E. Stone
1421 E. Tilden
Roswell, New Mexico 88201

Dear Clifford:

I am forwarding to you an interim response from the National Security Agency. I hope we can obtain answers to the questions you've raised. I will surely keep you advised of any correspondence I receive from NSA.

With warmest personal regards.

Sincerely,

Pete V. Domenici
United States Senator

PVD/mc

ENCLOSURE

NATIONAL SECURITY AGENCY
CENTRAL SECURITY SERVICE
FORT GEORGE G. MEADE, MARYLAND 20755-6000

Serial: J1-072-87
7 August 1987

The Honorable Pete V. Domenici
United States Senate
ATTN: Mr. Marco Caceras
430 Dirksen Senate Office Building
Washington, DC 20510

Dear Senator Domenici:

The National Security Agency received your letter dated
August 5, 1987 on behalf of your consitutent; Mr. Clifford E. Stone.

The appropriate organization has been tasked to handle your
request and upon completion, your office will be notified of the
action taken.

I welcome the opportunity to assist you with any future
inquiry relating to the National Security Agency.

Sincerely,

RALPH W. ADAMS
Chief
Legislative Affairs

PETE V. DOMENICI
NEW MEXICO

United States Senate
WASHINGTON, DC 20510

COMMITTEES:
BUDGET
APPROPRIATIONS
ENERGY AND NATURAL RESOURCES
AGING

October 9, 1987

Clifford E. Stone
1421 E. Tilden
Roswell, New Mexico 88201

Dear Clifford:

Enclosed is the response I recently received from the
National Security Agency regarding your request for information
on UFO incidents. I regret the answers are not as substantive, as
you would like.

I'm glad to be of service to you.

With my personal regards.

Sincerely,

Pete V. Domenici
United States Senator

PVD/mc

NATIONAL SECURITY AGENCY
CENTRAL SECURITY SERVICE
FORT GEORGE G. MEADE, MARYLAND 20755-6000

Serial: Q4-1085-87

3 0 SEP 1987

The Honorable Pete V. Domenici
United States Senate
ATTN: Mr. Marco Caceras
430 Dirksen Senate Office Building
Washington, DC 20510

Dear Senator Domenici:

This responds to your letter of 5 August 1987 on behalf of your constituent, Clifford E. Stone. Enclosed is Mr. Stone's latest correspondence which raises the same questions as his November 1986 correspondence to you. Our response is keyed to the exceptions he has taken to our previous reply.

Item 1. Mr. Stone takes exception to our request for $250.00 to conduct an Agency-wide search for the information. As you know, the FOIA provides for fees to be waived but only under certain carefully defined circumstances. He also reiterates his request for information on the RAF Woodbridge Base incident. Given that NSA's primary missions include communications security, computer security and the production of foreign intelligence information, the probability of our having information on this incident would be unlikely. It is possible, however, that the general term "unidentified flying object" may appear in certain Agency material and therefore would be considered a responsive record if located during a search. The Agency material in which those words may appear is currently and properly classified according to Executive Order and is not segregable. The FOIA specifically exempts classified information from disclosure. Additionally, unidentified flying object is a general term and is not exclusively used to refer to extraterrestrial spacecraft.

Item 2. We cannot determine whether we were the "agency" referred to in the 15 November 1979 USAF letter. If the Agency did have any records on the March 1967 UFO destruction of a Cuban MiG, they would not be available for release since they would be currently and properly classified.

Item 3. NSA has no information on a Project Aquarius dealing with UFOs. Since Mr. Stone refers to an Air Force project of that name, we recommend he query them on the matter.

Serial: Q4-1085-87

As for the issues raised in items 4 and 5, we have no knowledge of Snowbird and therefore would not have undertaken any action regarding the points Mr. Stone raises.

With respect to the classification issue raised in items 6 and 7, we can only reiterate what has been said before. We make every effort to interpret any FOIA request as broadly as possible in order to comply with the spirit of the law. An agency may not have individual records dealing solely with UFOs but could have records containing a reference of some type to UFOs which are either currently and properly classified under Executive Order 12356 or protected by statute. If this is the case and the reference to UFOs is not easily segregable from the classified information, the record would be withheld. The withholding of this information has been upheld by the United States Court of Appeals for the District of Columbia.

As for Mr. Stone's allegation in item 4.(4), classified information is not withheld from Congress during Congressional inquiries as long as arrangements are made to protect the information.

Please assure Mr. Stone that we have responded as completely as possible. We have no information on Aquarius or Snowbird and documents even remotely responsive to requests for records on UFOs are properly classified. We hope that this information will assist you in your response to Mr. Stone.

Sincerely,

JULIA B. WETZEL
Director of Policy

Encls:
a/s

CHAPTER FIVE

UFOs and Other Government Agencies

Prior to 1974, very little information concerning UFOs had come out of the Intelligence Community, other than comments by the Air Force. For the most part, the Intelligence Community was denying any knowledge of UFO activity. However, with the passing of the "Freedom of Information Act" by Congress in 1974, it was soon learned that other government agencies were more involved than they wished the public to know.

On July 16, 1978, I wrote the NSA requesting any information they might have on UFOs. I did not receive a response to this first letter, so I wrote them again on February 21, 1979. Finally the NSA responded to my requests under a cover letter dated January 10, 1980. (See doc. 5-1.)

The NSA denied me the release of all their records concerning UFOs, with the exception of two documents; the agency stated that the information was classified in the interests of National Security and to avoid unwarranted invasion of personal privacy. However, they did forward other records they were holding to the agencies that originated them, for these agencies' review and release to me. In addition, the NSA wanted me to understand that the two documents they did release to me were not "NSA reports per se, and they in no way reflect an official NSA position concerning UFOs."

The first NSA document was entitled "UFO Hypothesis and Survival Questions." (See doc. 5-2.) Its purpose was, as stated, to "consider briefly some of the human survival implications suggested by the various principal hypothesis concerning the nature of the phenomena loosely categorized as UFO."

Under the Extra-Terrestrial Hypothesis, the report had this to say:

If "they" discover you, it is an old but hardly invalid rule of thumb, "they" are your technological superiors. Human history has shown us time and again the tragic results of a confrontation between a technologically superior civilization and a technologically inferior people. The "inferior" is usually subject to physical conquest.

The report gave some excellent examples of how an inferior people might survive and maintain their identity. These were:

(1) Full and honest acceptance of the nature of the inferiorities separating you from the advantages of the other people, (2) complete national solidarity in all positions taken in dealing with the other culture, (3) highly controlled and limited intercourse with the other side—doing only those actions advantageous to the foreigner which you are absolutely forced to do by circumstances, (4) a correct but friendly attitude toward the other people, (5) a national eagerness to learn everything possible about the other culture—its technological and cultural strengths and weaknesses. This often involves sending selected groups and individuals to the other's country to

become one of his kind, or even to help him in his wars against other adversaries, (6) adopting as many of the advantages of the opposing people as you can, and doing it as fast as possible—while still protecting your own identity by molding each new knowledge increment into your own cultural cast.

While the NSA states this is not a official report, it is clear that the writer, an NSA employee, thought the question of survival was an important issue to be addressed seriously in any study of UFOs.

The title of the second document released to me by the NSA is still classified as at least Secret in the interest of National Security—with the exception of the term "UFOs." (See doc. 5-3.) This document deals with the human response to an event of high strangeness such as the sighting of an UFO. The document stated, in part:

> Whether the person's psychological structure is being assaulted by the unusual and shocking brutality of a murder or the strangeness of an UFO sighting, the effect is the same.

The document goes on to list those effects.

It is interesting to note that the writer of this document listed in an appendix what he called "Other Examples of Blindness to Surprise Material Causing Defeat." It would appear that the author of this document not only believed in UFOs, but felt that the matter should be taken seriously.

It seems that some government agency was interested in what type of unclassified information the Defense Technical Information Center (DTIC) had on UFOs in the mid to late 1970s. A government employee requested a bibliography report on "Unidentified Flying Saucers" from the DTIC sometime in the late '70s. (See doc. 5-4.) We have no way of knowing the exact date, as the report is undated. It is interesting to note that the report considered such subject titles as "An Approach to

Understanding Psychotronics" and "A Case of 'Autostasis' or Reverse Autokinesis" as having something to do with UFOs.

★★★

The Central Intelligence Agency is the next governmental agency that I wish to discuss. However, before we begin, let me state that, according to the CIA, its only official involvement in the government UFO investigations was via a Scientific Advisory Panel—known as the Robertson Committee—which met at the direction of the CIA in January 1953. (I also want the reader to know that given the Agency's well-known past history of deception, I have never trusted the CIA to tell the truth about anything.) (See doc. 5-5.)

A CIA document dated January 29, 1976, talks about the physical effect of magnetic fields on astronauts, the possible propulsion system of UFOs, and even recovered fragments of a possible UFO in Brazil. The document, which is greatly censored in the interest of National Security, states: (See doc. 5-6.)

> U.S. scientists believe that low magnetic fields do not have a serious effect on astronauts, but high magnetic fields, oscillating magnetic fields, and electromagnetic fields can or do have considerable effect. There is a theory that such fields are closely associated with superconductivity at very low temperatures, such as in space. This in turn is related to the possible propulsion system of UFOs. There is a rumor that fragments of a possible UFO found in Brazil bore a relationship to superconductors and magnetohydrodynamics.

A series of documents that surfaced from the CIA dating from April through July 1976 deals with a so-called "UFO Study." (See docs. 5-7, 5-8, 5-9, 5-10, 5-11, 5-12, 5-13, 5-14, and 5-15.) This study apparently was compiled by an individual outside the CIA. Nevertheless, the documents clearly indicate that high-ranking scientists, working within the CIA, had more than a passive interest in this individual's UFO research. One of the documents had this to say, in part:

> At the present time, there are offices and personnel within the agency who are monitoring the UFO phenomena, but again, this is not currently on an official basis, Dr. [censored]... feels that the best approach would be to keep in touch with and in fact develop reporting channels in this area to keep the agency/community informed of any new developments. In particular, any information which might indicate a threat potential would be of interest, as would specific indications of foreign developments or application of UFO related research.

Another document in the series had this to say:

> At a recent meeting to evaluate some material from [censored]... you mentioned a personal interest in the UFO phenomena. As you may recall, I mentioned my own interest in the subject as well as the fact that DCD had been receiving UFO related material from many of our S&T sources who are presently conducting related research. These scientists include some who have been associated with the Agency for years and whose credentials remove them from the "nut" variety.

These documents, released by the CIA, give the impression that many of the scientific personnel employed by the CIA are very concerned about the phenomena—and about the government's apparent *lack* of concern. One can deduce this by the fact that these scientific personnel are doing "related research" without official sanction.

Many of the related documents dealing with this UFO study, as well as the study itself, have never been declassified and re-leased to the public. These papers and documents remain classified in the interests of National Security.

Under a letter dated October 16, 1980, the State Department was kind enough to release five documents to me, and then two other documents a little less than a year later. (See docs. 5-16 and 5-17.) These documents proved to be most interesting in that they discussed, for the most part, an attempt by the Grenadian Delegation to the United Nations to create a organization within the UN for the gathering and exchanging of information on UFO investigations and sightings among the member nations. The documents also showed that the United States' delegation, at the direction of the State Department, was working very hard to insure that this resolution was never passed!

One document dated November 18, 1978, had this to say, among other things: "Please provide instructions on U.S. position to be taken on this matter as well as desired level of visibility. Last year Grenada requested our support and Misoff had to scramble hard behind the scenes to water down the resolution and, in effect, delay a vote for one year. Another consideration is whether to issue a disclaimer on statements made by U.S. Nationals on the Grenadian Delegation." (See docs. 5-18, 5-19, 5-20, 5-21, 5-22, and 5-23.)

The United States was able to get the matter referred to the Outerspace Committee, thereby avoiding a vote on the matter. As a document dated December 2, 1978, states:

> A draft decision (datafaxed) to be taken by the Special Political Committee [SPC] has been agreed upon by the participants in the informal negotiations, subject to concurrence of their respective capitals. We think referral of the matter to the Outerspace Committee [OSC] without a preordained mandate as to what action is to be taken, provides the flexibility the OSC needs to take whatever action it deems

appropriate. It will also obviate the need to vote on a resolution (and gamble on the results).

I wonder what could have been the reasoning behind the United States' interest in blocking a vote? Could it be the U.S. has something to fear or hide?

To be sure, there exist many other U.S. Government agencies—as well as agencies of other countries—that maintain highly classified records on the subject of UFOs. But why?

Are we citizens just too unsophisticated to handle the true facts as to what is really going on?

Will ordinary Americans panic if they were told the truth about unexplained flying objects that have been observed by the U.S. Military?

Doc. 5-1a NSA Letter, Jan 10, 1980

NATIONAL SECURITY AGENCY
CENTRAL SECURITY SERVICE
FORT GEORGE G. MEADE, MARYLAND 20755

Serial: N9094
1 0 JAN 1980

SP5 Clifford E. Stone
301-50-0182
HQ Det, Hanau Mil Comm
APO NY   09165

Dear Specialist Stone:

This replies to your Freedom of Information Act (FOIA) requests of July 16, 1978 and February 21, 1979 in which you request any information that this Agency may have concerning Unidentified Flying Objects (UFOs).

Your request has been processed in accordance with 5 U.S.C. 552, the Freedom of Information Act. Two documents that are within the scope of your request are enclosed.

These documents were released pursuant to an administrative appeal under the FOIA. The documents were written in 1968 by an NSA employee with an interest in UFOs. One of the documents was originally classified because portions of it tangentially discussed protected activities pertaining to the NSA. Most of the remaining portions of the documents reflected open-source information on UFOs. We wish to emphasize that these draft documents were never published, formally issued, acted upon, or responded to by any government official or agency. Moreover, they are not "NSA reports" per se, and they in no way reflect an official NSA position concerning UFOs. They are subject to the provisions of the FOIA only because they have been retained by this Agency for historical reference purposes.

Deletions have been made to these two documents pursuant to the following provisions of Title 5 U.S.C. 552, the FOIA:

1. Title 5 U.S.C. 552(b)(1), which provides that the FOIA does not apply to matters that are specifically authorized under criteria established by an Executive Order to be kept secret in the interest of national defense or foreign policy and are in fact properly classified pursuant to such Executive Order. The classified information that has been deleted from the enclosed records is currently and properly classified in accordance with the criteria for classification in Section 1-3 of Executive Order 12065, and paragraph 2-202 of Department of Defense (DoD) Regulation 5200.1-R. The information has been reviewed for possible declassification or downgrading according to the provisions of Sections 3-3, 3-4, and 3-6 of Executive Order 12065 and Chapter III of DoD Regulation 5200.1-R and found to be properly excluded from declassification or downgrading.

Serial: N9094

2. Title 5 U.S.C. 552(b)(3), which provides that the FOIA does not apply to matters that are specifically exempted from disclosure by statute. The applicable statutes in this case are Title 18 U.S.C. 798, Title 50 U.S.C. 403(d)(3), and Public Law 86-36.

Other records that fall within the scope of your request are being withheld in their entirety. These records are exempt from disclosure pursuant to the following provisions of the FOIA:

1. Title 5 U.S.C. 552(b)(1);

2. Title 5 U.S.C. 552(b)(3), in conjunction with Title 18 U.S.C. 798, Title 50 U.S.C. 403(d)(3), and Public Law 86-36;

3. Title 5 U.S.C. 552(b)(5); which exempts inter-agency or intra-agency memorandums or letters which would not be available by law to a party other than an agency in litigation with this Agency;

4. Title 5 U.S.C. 552(b)(6), which provides that the FOIA does not apply to personnel and similar files the disclosure of which would constitute a clearly unwarranted invasion of personal privacy.

No portion of the information being withheld in its entirety is reasonably segregable.

Certain other information, which originated with other Federal agencies and components, is also being withheld. Department of Defense (DoD) Directive 5400.7, which implements the FOIA for all DoD agencies, provides that when records requested under the FOIA originate with another agency or component, the request shall be referred to that agency or component for disposition. The agencies to which we have referred records will correspond directly with you concerning those records.

Since your requests have been denied in part, you are hereby advised of this Agency's appeal procedures.

Any person denied access to records may, within 30 days after notification of such denial, file an appeal to the NSA/CSS Freedom of Information Act Appeal Authority, National Security Agency, Fort George G. Meade, MD 20755. The appeal shall reference the initial denial of access and shall contain, in sufficient detail and particularity, the grounds upon which the requester believes release of the information is required. The NSA/CSS Appeal Authority shall respond to the appeal within 20 working days after receipt.

Sincerely,

ROY R. BANNER
Chief, Policy Staff

2 Encls:
a/s

1968

DRAFT

U F O HYPOTHESIS AND SURVIVAL QUESTIONS

It is the purpose of this monograph to consider briefly some of the

human survival implications suggested by the various principal hypothesis

concerning the nature of the phenomena loosely categorized as U F O [1].

1. ALL UFO's ARE HOAXES: From the time when hoaxes were first

noted in history, they were characterized by infrequency of occurrence

and usually by a considerable restriction of their geographical extent.

Rarely have men of science, while acting within their professional

capacities, perpetrated hoaxes. The fact that UFO phenomenon have been

witnessed all over the world from ancient times, and by considerable

numbers of reputable scientists in recent times, indicates rather .

strongly that UFO's are not all hoaxes. [2] rather than diminishing, If anything, the modern trend

is toward increased reports, from all sources. In one three month per-

iod in 1953 (June, July, and August) Air Force records show 35 sightings

whose nature could not be determined [3]. If UFO's, contrary to all

---

(1) All flying, sailing or maneuvering aerial objects whether glowing,
pulsating, or of a constant metalic hue, whose shape is somewhat circular
or cigarish.

(2) Anatomy of a Phenomenon, Jacques Vallee, Henry Regnery Co. Chicago,
1965. p 9-17. (Vallee has degrees in Astronomy and Physics and is
currently consultant to NASA's MARS MAP STUDY.)

(3) United States Air Force Projects Grudge and Bluebook Reports 1-12
(1951-1953) National Investigation Committee on Aerial Phenomena.
Washington June 1968. p 216.

(4) Visitors from Outer Space, Sputnik, (condensed from the almanac on
Land and Sea) Vladeslav Zaitsev, p 164-181.

DRAFT

implications and expectations, are indeed hoaxes - hoaxes of a world-wide dimension - hoaxes of increasing frequency, then a human mental aberration of alarming proportions would appear to be developing. Such an aberration would seem to have serious implications for nations equipped with nuclear toys - and should require immediate and careful study by scientists.

2. ALL UFO's ARE HALLUCINATIONS: People, of course, do hallucinate. Although groups of people hallucinating is rare, it has been known to happen. Machines have their own form of hallucination; the radar, in particular, "sees" temperature inversions. But a considerable number of instances exist in which there are groups of people and a radar or radars seeing the same thing at the same time; sometimes a person and a guncamera confirm each other's testimony[4]. On occasion, physical evidence of a circumstantial nature was reported to have been found to support witnessed sightings [5]. A continuing high percentage of reports of unusual aerial objects are being reported by people in responsible positions in science, government, and industry.[6]. The sum of such evidence seems to argue strongly against all UFO's being hallucinations. In spite of all the evidence to the contrary, if UFO's did turn out to be largely illusionary, the psychological implications for man would

---

(4) ibid., p 208, 192, 149, 146

(5) op. cit., Vallee, p. 70, 71, 74.

(6) The Report on Unidentified Flying Objects, Edward J. Ruppelt, Doubleday, New York 1956. p 242. (Ruppelt was Chief of the Bluebook Study at one time.)

certainly bring into strong question his ability to distinguish reality
from fantasy. The negative effect on man's ability to survive in an
increasingly complex world would be considerable - making it imperative
that such a growing impairment of the human capacity for rational judgment
be subjected to immediate and thorough scientific study - so that the
illness could be controlled before it reaches epidemic proportions (7).
(For comments on mass hysteria and UFO's see source 8 below which contains a statement by Dr. Robert L. Hall, a social psychologist formerly
with the AF Personnel and Training Research Center and the Program
Director, Sociology and Psychology, National Science Foundation.)

3. ALL UFO's ARE NATURAL PHENOMENA: If this hypothesis is correct
the capability of air warning systems to correctly diagnose an attack
situation is open to serious question.

a. Many UFO's have been reported by trained military observers
to behave like high speed, high performance, high altitude rockets or
aircraft. The apparent solidity and craft-like shape of the objects
have often been subject to radar confirmation (9). If such objects can
appear to trained military men as rockets or air craft and if such objects

---

(7) op. cit., Ruppelt p 237 (Dutch Liner, Rome, Italy)

(8) Symposium on Unidentified Flying Objects (Second Session).
July 29, 1968 nr 7 (House Committee on Science and Astronautics).

(9) op. cit., Project Grudge, pp.192, 149, 146.

should come over the Artic from the direction of Russia on the United
States, they could trigger "false reports of missile attacks". (10)

b. Many responsible military officers have developed a mental
"blind spot" to objects which appear to have the characteristics of
UFO's. (10) Such an attitude is an open invitation to the enemy to build
a replica of the phenomena in order to penetrate the "hole" in his
adversaries' defenses - Was this the purpose of the lens-shaped reentry
vehicle tested by the U.S. Air Force in 1960 and recently featured in
the Washington, D.C. Evening Star, dated 24 September 1968, page A4?

c. Sometimes the phenomena appear to defy radar detection and
to cause massive electromagnetic interference. Surely it is very important
to discover the nature of these objects or plasmas before any prospective
enemy can use their properties to build a device or system to circumvent
or jam our air and space detection systems - Any nation certainly could
use a system or device to penetrate enemy defenses. (11)

4. SOME UFO's ARE SECRET EARTH PROJECTS: The above referenced
U.S. Air Force reentry vehicle and an often publicized Canadian "saucer"
project (9) leave little doubt as to the validity of this hypothesis.
Undoubtedly, all UFO's should be carefully scrutinized to ferret out such
enemy (or "friendly") projects. Otherwise a nation faces the very strong

---

(10) Firing Phenomena, Sovietskaya Latviya, No. 287, 10 December 1967,
p 3, Col 1-3, by R. Vitolniyek (Director of the Station for the Radio
Observation of the Ionosphere and Artificial Earth Satellites).

(11) ibid., Project Grudge.

UFO's and the Colorado Project, Encyclopedia Brittanica Book of the Year
1968, p 133.

DRAFT

possibility of being intimidated by a new secret "doomsday" weapon.

5.   SOME UFO's ARE RELATED TO EXTRA-TERRESTRIAL INTELLIGENCE: *According to several scientists closely associated with the study of this phenomenon, this hypothesis cannot be disregarded.* 12 *(The use of nuclear weapons over Hiroshima in 1952 may verify current theories).*
This hypothesis has a number of far-reaching human survival implications:

a.   If "they" discover you, it is an old but hardly invalid rule of thumb, "they" are your technological superiors. Human history has shown us time and again the tragic results of a confrontation between a technologically superior civilization and a technologically inferior people. The "inferior" is usually subject to physical conquest.

b.   Often in the past, a technologically superior people are also possessors of a more virile or aggressive culture. In a confrontation between two peoples of significantly different cultural levels, those having the inferior or less virile culture, most often suffer a tragic loss of identity and are usually absorbed by the other people.

c.   Some peoples who were technologically and/or culturally inferior to other nations have survived - have maintained their identity - have equalized the differences between them and their adversaries. The Japanese people have given us an excellent example of the methods required to achieve such a survival:

(1) full and honest acceptance of the nature of the inferiorities separating you from the advantages of the other peoples,

(2) complete national solidarity in all positions taken in dealing with the other culture,

(3) highly controlled and limited intercourse with the other side - doing only those actions advantageous to the foreigner which you are absolutely forced to do by circumstances,

(4) a correct but friendly attitude toward the other people,

12. *Professor James E. McDonald, Astronomer, Professor Allen J. Hynek, Astrophysicist, Jacques Vallee, Astronomer, Eugene Hess, Astronomer. Belief that some of these objects are probably EXTRA-TERRESTRIAL in origin is also supported by a 1952 report by a committee of scientific investigators.*

DRAFT

(5) A national eagerness to learn everything possible about the other culture - its technological and cultural strengths and weaknesses. This often involves sending selected groups and individuals to the other's country to become one of his kind, or even to help him in his wars against other adversaries.

(6) Adopting as many of the advantages of the opposing people as you can, and doing it as fast as possible - while still protecting your own identity by molding each new knowledge increment into your own cultural cast.

6. COMMENT: Although this paper has hardly exhausted the possible hypotheses related to the UFO phenomena, those mentioned above are the principal ones presently put forward. All of them have serious survival implications. The final answer to this mystery will probably include more than one of the above hypotheses.

Up until this time, the leisurely scientific approach has too often taken precedence in dealing with UFO questions. If you are walking along a forest path and someone yells, "rattler" your reaction would be immediate and defensive. You would not take time to speculate before you act. You would have to treat the alarm as if it were a real and immediate threat to your survival. Investigation would become an intensive emergency action to isolate the threat and to determine it's precise nature - It would be geared to developing adequate defensive measures in a minimum amount of time.

It would seem a little more of this survival attitude is called for in dealing with the UFO problem.

Observations of chimpanzees while in a captive environment have
shown that the animals tend to become confused and disoriented. Since
they do not usually have adult chimps to teach them how to be good apes,
they are not even sure of their behavior. Often their actions are patterned
after human behavior and would have virtually no survival value in the
wild. Lacking the challenge of environmental adaptation, the bodies of the
animals atrophy and become subject to many diseases - mostly unknown in
their wild counterparts. Reactions to stimulis usually become less responsive and suitable. Sex often becomes a year-long preoccupation
instead of a seasonal madness.

Do the captivity characteristics of modern civilization cause a
similar lessening of man's adaptive capability, of his health, of his
ability to recognize reality, of his ability to survive?

Perhaps the UFO question might even make man undertake studies which
could enable him to construct a society which is most conducive to
developing a completely human being, healthy in all aspects of mind and
body - and most important able to recognize and adapt to real environmental situations.

λ 2307
2143

205

SUBJECT: UFO's

2. Scientific Findings: Dr. Jacques Vallee* famed communications science expert has studied thousands of cases where human beings have observed unusual phenomena. He has found that the human response to such observation is predictable and graphically depictable. Whether the person's psychological structure is being assaulted by the unusual and shocking brutality of a murder or the strangeness of a UFO sighting, the effect is the same:

a. Initially as by a kind of psychological inertia, the mind records fairly objectively what the eye is reporting.*

b. But when it has realized the strange nature of the phenomena it goes into shock. The mind likes to live in a comfortable world where it feels it knows what to expect, and that, is not too threatening either physically or psychologically. The unusual dispells the comfortable illusion the mind has created. This shock tears at the very mooring of the human psychological structure.*

c. To protect itself against such an intrusive and threatening reality the mind will begin to add imagination and interpretation to the incoming data to make it more acceptable. Since the mind is doing all this in haste some of the hurridly added details and suggestions tumble over one another and contradict one another in a bizzare fashion (as any police officer interrogating murder witnesses will tell you*) (See Chart A).

d. Once the mind has constructed a "safe" framework for the new information it may again peek out and collect some more objective data. If the data is still threatening it will again go into shock and the process starts all over again.*

e. If the data is at the highest strangness level where it brings terror either:

(1) The mind will pass out and go into amnesia burying the events perhaps permanently in the unconscious.*

(2) The personal psychological structure will collapse and the mind will reach down into its deepest place where "that which cannot be destroyed" is and it will abandon itself to this entity for survival protection. Encounter with this changeless indestructable entity is usually referred to as a religious experience. In the confusion and the shock, this experience is often attributed to the shocking event or object and that is why primative peoples worship such bizzare things as airplanes or cigarette lighters.

f. The degree of strangness of the phenomena dictates how many people the mind is willing and able to tell the event to. A mildly unusual or shocking event will be told to many people. A very shocking event of high strangness will be told to few people or practically none at all. Occasionally the event is so shockingly unusual that it isn't even reported to the person's conscious mind but is buried in the unconscious of the person* where it is only accessible to hypnosis or careful level six communication sharing with another person. (See Chart B.)

DEFENSE LOGISTICS AGENCY
DEFENSE TECHNICAL INFORMATION CENTER
CAMERON STATION
ALEXANDRIA, VIRGINIA 22314

1 1 MAR 1980

Staff Sergeant Clifford E. Stone
Headquarters Detachment
  Hanau Military Command
APO New York 09165

Dear Sergeant Stone:

In response to your letter of 29 Jan 80, enclosed is the report bibliography identifying reports in the DTIC technical report collection relating to UFOs.

Receipt of your check in the amount of $21 for the enclosed report is acknowledged.

Sincerely,

HUBERT E. SAUTER
Administrator

1 Encl

REPORT BIBLIOGRAPHY

DEFENSE TECHNICAL INFORMATION CENTER
DEFENSE LOGISTICS AGENCY
Cameron Station, Alexandria, Virginia 22314

This Report Bibliography has been prepared by the Defense Documentation Center as a mission assignment in accordance with the provisions of DoD Instruction 5100.38.

HUBERT E. SAUTER
Administrator
Defense Technical Information Center

UNCLASSIFIED

SEARCH CONTROL NO. 031643

UNIDENTIFIED FLYING SAUCERS(U)

025643
TO: DEF TECHNICAL INF CTR
      CAMERON STA   BG 5
      ALEXANDRIA, VA   22314

REQUESTED BY: RICHARD HUNTER

PREPARED
BY

DEFENSE TECHNICAL INFORMATION CENTER
DEFENSE LOGISTICS AGENCY
CAMERON STATION, ALEXANDRIA, VIRGINIA 22314

THIS REPORT (COMPILATION) IS MARKED TO REFLECT THE HIGHEST CLASSIFICATION OF ANY COMPONENT PART THEREOF. IT SHOULD BE DESTROYED WITHIN 12 MONTHS AS THESE RECORDS ARE UPDATED AT LEAST ANNUALLY.

UNCLASSIFIED

(THIS PAGE IS UNCLASSIFIED)

Doc. 5-4e Defense Logistics Agency with Encl.,
Mar 11, 1980

An Approach to Understanding
   Psychotronics.
   AD-A027 866

A CASE OF 'AUTOSTASIS' OR REVERSE
   AUTOKINESIS,
   AD- 687 960

The One Human Problem, Its
   Solution, and Its Relation to UFO
   Phenomena.
   AD-A034 236

PROJECT BLUE BOOK
   AD- 069 180

PROJECT BLUE BOOK
   AD- 069 211

PROJECT GRUDGE
   AD- 128 982

REVIEW OF THE UNIVERSITY OF
   COLORADO REPORT ON UNIDENTIFIED
   FLYING OBJECTS BY A PANEL OF THE
   NATIONAL ACADEMY OF SCIENCES.
   AD- 688 541

SCIENTIFIC STUDY OF UNIDENTIFIED
   FLYING OBJECTS, VOLUME 1.
   AD- 680 975

SCIENTIFIC STUDY OF UNIDENTIFIED
   FLYING OBJECTS, VOLUME 2.
   AD- 680 976

SCIENTIFIC STUDY OF UNIDENTIFIED
   FLYING OBJECTS, VOLUME 3.
   AD- 680 977

UFOs AND RELATED SUBJECTS: AN
   ANNOTATED BIBLIOGRAPHY,
   AD- 688 332

UNIDENTIFIED AERIAL OBJECTS PROJECT
   'SIGN',
   AD- 311 102

Writing the Observer back into the
   Equation.
   AD-A027 867

DDC REPORT BIBLIOGRAPHY   SEARCH CONTROL NO. 091643

AD-A027 867   5/10
SYSTEM DEVELOPMENT CORP HUNTSVILLE ALA

Writing the Observer back into the Equation.

DESCRIPTIVE NOTE: Technical address,
   MAR 76   90P   Bearden,Thomas E. ;

UNCLASSIFIED REPORT

SUPPLEMENTARY NOTE: Presented at Princeton Center for Alternative Futures, 5 Mar 76, Princeton, N. J.

DESCRIPTORS: *Parapsychology, *Logic, *Perception(Psychology), *Brain, *Observers, *Detection, *Equations, Consciousness, Death, Models, Biological systems, Life(Biology).

IDENTIFIERS: *Psychotronics, *Fourth law of logic, *Mind/Body problem, Metaphysics, Ego, Anaenergy, UFO's, Two-slit experiment

The speaker advances a fourth law of logic which contains the negation of each of Aristotle's three laws of logic. Thus the four-law system is closed. It contains and resolves all present paradoxes since a paradox by definition is a violation of one or more of the first three laws, and hence is a statement of, or included in, the fourth law. The four-law logic encloses everything which can be thought - physics and metaphysics - in one logical system. By the author's perception approach to perception, the fourth law (identify of opposites on their common boundary) can at last be comprehended. The fourth law resolves, e.g., the two-slit experiment, the Hieronymus device, the mind/body problem, the nature of mind, the nature of nothing, and the difficulties in the logical basis of probability. Using the fourth law and the author's perception approach to perception, a fundamental particle becomes an Einsteinian closure of the universe, in the manner of Einstein's spherical model of the cosmos. Based on a time-clustered set of orthogonal 4-spaces selected from Everett's many-worlds interpretation of quantum mechanics, a model of both mind and matter can be constructed. Einstein's postulates of special relativity are derived. A new defining equation for mass is given.

AD-A027 867   UNCLASSIFIED

PAGE 1

091643   (U)

DDC REPORT BIBLIOGRAPHY   SEARCH CONTROL NO. 091643

AD-A034 236   20/10   5/10
SYSTEM DEVELOPMENT CORP HUNTSVILLE ALA

The One Human Problem, Its Solution, and Its Relation to UFO Phenomena.

DESCRIPTIVE NOTE: Technical summary,
   JAN 77   25P   Bearden,Thomas E. ;

UNCLASSIFIED REPORT

DESCRIPTORS: *Intelligence, *Philosophy, Quantum theory, Brain

IDENTIFIERS: Psychotronics, Unidentified flying objects

The author divides development of life in a biosphere into seven stages: (1) development of planet, primordial atmosphere and ocean; (2) appearance of amino acids; (3) appearance of self-replicating supermolecules; (4) formation of one-celled organisms; (5) formation of multicellular organisms; (6) brain linkage of an intelligent technological species; (7) the omega or oilness stage. The sixth stage consists of linkage of all individual brains in the species into one single superbrain. The author presents a quantitative argument for the existence of sixth-stage beings. Granted the existence of one, the existence of others follows. A calculation, given which indicates that linkage results in exponential increase of such effects as psychokinesis (literally) of inception of intent onto ordinary spacetime) so that the superbeing gains absolute mastery over spacetime and physical dimensionality. A brief sketch of how to develop a psychotronic brain link is given, and the automatic establishment of a hyperchannel link when sufficient brains are psychotronically linked is pointed out.

AD-A034 236   UNCLASSIFIED

UNCLASSIFIED

DDC REPORT BIBLIOGRAPHY   SEARCH CONTROL NO. 091643

AD-688 541   1/2   22/1
NATIONAL ACADEMY OF SCIENCES WASHINGTON D C

REVIEW OF THE UNIVERSITY OF COLORADO REPORT ON
UNIDENTIFIED FLYING OBJECTS BY A PANEL OF THE
NATIONAL ACADEMY OF SCIENCES.   (U)

DESCRIPTIVE NOTE: Special rept.,
JAN 69   10P   Clemence,Gerald M. ;
CONTRACT: F18600-67-C-0071
PROJ: AF-9730
MONITOR: AFOSR 69-1276TR

UNCLASSIFIED REPORT

PORTIONS OF THIS DOCUMENT ARE ILLEGIBLE. SEE
INTRODUCTION SECTION OF THIS ANNOUNCEMENT JOURNAL FOR CFSTI
ORDERING INSTRUCTIONS.
DESCRIPTORS: (*OPTICAL PHENOMENA, REVIEWS), VISUAL
PERCEPTION, REPORTS   (U)
IDENTIFIERS: *UNIDENTIFIED FLYING OBJECTS   (U)

The ad hoc committee concurs with the findings of
the report of the University of Colorado entitled
'Scientific Study of Unidentified Flying
Objects.' Dr. Edward U. Condon,
Scientific Director (see AD-680 975, AD-680
976, and AD-680 977). Panel agrees that a
study of UFOs in general is not a promising way to
expand scientific understanding of the phenomena, and
adds: 'On the basis of present knowledge the
least likely explanation of UFOs is the hypothesis
of extraterrestrial visitations by intelligent
beings.' (Author)   (U)

AD-688 541   UNCLASSIFIED

PAGE   2   091643

UNCLASSIFIED

DDC REPORT BIBLIOGRAPHY   SEARCH CONTROL NO. 091643

AD-A027 866   5/6   5/10
SYSTEM DEVELOPMENT CORP HUNTSVILLE ALA

An Approach to Understanding
Psychotronics.   (U)

DESCRIPTIVE NOTE: Technical briefing.
JUN 76   87P   Bearden,Thomas E. ;

UNCLASSIFIED REPORT

DESCRIPTORS: *Parapsychology. *Logic.
*Perception(Psychology). *Brain. *Observers.
*Detection. *Equations. Charged particles,
Models, Holograms, Mass, Time,
Life(Biology), Cosmology, Photons, Four
dimensional, Quantum theory, Interactions,
Physics
IDENTIFIERS: *Psychotronics, Metaphysics. Fourth
law of logic, Identity of opposites, Aristotlean
laws of logic, Many worlds interpretation,
Biofields, Orthogonal problem, Metaphysics,
Mind, Body problem, Orthogonal, Orthogonal
three dimensional spatial frames, Debroglie waves,
Antigravity, UFO's, Tulpas, Two slit
experiment   (U)

Psychotronics refers to the interaction of mind and
matter, and so to a union of physics and metaphysics.
The author advances a fourth law of logic together
with the first three Aristotlean laws of logic form
a complete, closed metalogic encompassing both
physics and metaphysics. A cluster of an infinite
number of orthogonal 3-dimensional spatial frames,
all containing the same single fourth dimension, or
time axis, provides a framework onto which mind,
matter, fields, being, life, and both physical and
metaphysical phenomena can be fitted and precisely
modelled. Thus metaphysics can be precisely
modelled by, and related to, physics. A mind
becomes a complete 3-dimensional physical world.
From the model, constructs that model life, death,
a biological system, psi, consciousness, inception,
telepathy, psychokinesis, UFO's, God, and the
collective unconscious can be taken.
Materialization, dematerialization, and mind
linkage also exist, as does a specific mechanism for
tulpas (materialized thought forms). The two-
slit experiment and the Hieronymus device are shown
to involve the fourth law of logic. Feynman's   (U)

AD-A027 866   UNCLASSIFIED

UNCLASSIFIED

DDC REPORT BIBLIOGRAPHY   SEARCH CONTROL NO. 091643

AD- 687 960   6/5
COLORADO UNIV BOULDER

A CASE OF 'AUTOSTASIS' OR REVERSE AUTOKINESIS.   (U)

            FEB 68   3P   Wertheimer,Michael ;
CONTRACT: F44620-67-C-0035
PROJ: AF-9730
MONITOR: AFOSR 69-1150TR

UNCLASSIFIED REPORT

Availability: Pub. in Perceptual and Motor
Skills, v26 p417-418 1968.
DESCRIPTORS: (*VISUAL PERCEPTION, ILLUSIONS),
(*ILLUSIONS, *OPTICAL PHENOMENA), PHYSIOLOGY. VISION.   (U)
HUMANS
IDENTIFIERS: AUTOKINESIS. UNIDENTIFIED FLYING   (U;
OBJECTS

Three of five observers of a light in the night sky
that was actually moving continuously along a linear
course reported it as stationary as long as the light
was on. This phenomenon, 'autostasis,' seems to be
opposite to the well-known phenomenon of autokinesis,
or apparent motion of an actually stationary light in
an undifferentiated field. (Author)   (U)

UNCLASSIFIED

DDC REPORT BIBLIOGRAPHY   SEARCH CONTROL NO. 091643

AD- 688 332   1/2   22/1
COLORADO UNIV BOULDER

UFOs AND RELATED SUBJECTS: AN ANNOTATED   (U)
BIBLIOGRAPHY,

DESCRIPTIVE NOTE: Special rept.,
    JUL 69   415P   Catoe,Lynn E. ;
CONTRACT: F44620-67-C-0035
PROJ: AF-9730
MONITOR: AFOSR 68-1656

UNCLASSIFIED REPORT

SUPPLEMENTARY NOTE: Prepared in cooperation with Library
of Congress, Washington,D. C. Science and
Technology Div. LC-68-62196.
DESCRIPTORS: (*OPTICAL PHENOMENA, *BIBLIOGRAPHIES),
BIOLOGY, SOLAR SYSTEM. LIGHTNING, AIRCRAFT, DISKS,
RELIGION, GRAVITY, ILLUSIONS, THEORY, ABSTRACTS   (U)
IDENTIFIERS: *UNIDENTIFIED FLYING OBJECTS   (U)

The report is an annotated bibliography of books,
journal articles, pamphlets, conference proceedings,
tapes, original manuscripts, books of photographs,
cartoons, motion picture films and other such
material on the subject of unidentified flying
objects (UFOs), totaling more than 1,600 separate
items, with author index. Major categories
include: UFOs, origin of life, mankind, solar
system, extraterrestrial life, e.t. visitors, ball
lightning and fireballs, disc-like aircraft,
unidentified submarine objects, Fortean phenomena,
UFOs and religion. UFOs and time, gravity and
ant-gravity, hollow earth theory, disappearances,
cartoons, mirages, and related subjects.   (U)
(Author)

AD- 683 332   UNCLASSIFIED

AD- 687 960

PAGE   3   UNCLASSIFIED   091643

UNCLASSIFIED

DDC REPORT BIBLIOGRAPHY   SEARCH CONTROL NO. 091643

AD- 680 977   1/2   22/1   5/10.
COLORADO UNIV BOULDER.

SCIENTIFIC STUDY OF UNIDENTIFIED FLYING OBJECTS,
VOLUME 3.   (U)

DESCRIPTIVE NOTE: Final rept.,
    JAN 69   527P   Condon,Edward U. ;
CONTRACT: F44620-67-C-0035
PROJ: AF-9730
MONITOR: AFOSR 69-0027TR-3

         UNCLASSIFIED REPORT

SUPPLEMENTARY NOTE: See also Volume 2, AD-680 976.
DESCRIPTORS: (*OPTICAL PHENOMENA, AIR FORCE RESEARCH).
VISUAL PERCEPTION, PSYCHOLOGY, RADAR, SONIC BOOM,
ATMOSPHERIC ELECTRICITY, PLASMA MEDIUM, BALLOONS,
STATISTICAL ANALYSIS, PUBLIC OPINION, ILLUSIONS   (U)
IDENTIFIERS: CASE STUDIES, *UNIDENTIFIED FLYING
OBJECTS   (U)

The report contains the results of a scientific
inquiry into the phenomena of Unidentified Flying
Objects. This volume contains: (1) The
scientific context, (2) Appendices A-X, and
(3) The index. (Author)   (U)

AD- 680 977   UNCLASSIFIED

UNCLASSIFIED

DDC REPORT BIBLIOGRAPHY   SEARCH CONTROL NO. 091643

AD- 680 976   1/2   22/1   5/10
COLORADO UNIV BOULDER.

SCIENTIFIC STUDY OF UNIDENTIFIED FLYING OBJECTS.
VOLUME 2.   (U)

DESCRIPTIVE NOTE: Final rept.,
    JAN 69   419P   Condon,Edward U. ;
CONTRACT: F44620-67-C-0035
PROJ: AF-9730
MONITOR: AFOSR 69-0026TR

         UNCLASSIFIED REPORT

SUPPLEMENTARY NOTE: See also Volume 1, AD-680 975 and
Volume 3, AD-680 977.
DESCRIPTORS: (*OPTICAL PHENOMENA, AIR FORCE RESEARCH).
PHOTOGRAPHIC ANALYSIS, OPTICAL ANALYSIS, HISTORY, VISUAL
PERCEPTION   (U)
IDENTIFIERS: CASE STUDIES, *UNIDENTIFIED FLYING
OBJECTS   (U)

The report contains the results of a scientific
inquiry into the phenomena of Unidentified Flying
Objects. This volume contains: (1) Case
studies during the term of the contract, (2)
Photographic case studies, and (3) Historical
aspects of UFO phenomena. (Author)   (U)

PAGE   4   AD- 680 976   UNCLASSIFIED

091643

091643

UNCLASSIFIED

DDC REPORT BIBLIOGRAPHY   SEARCH CONTROL NO. 091643

AD- 680 975   1/2   22/1   5/10
COLORADO UNIV BOULDER

SCIENTIFIC STUDY OF UNIDENTIFIED FLYING OBJECTS. VOLUME 1.   (U)

DESCRIPTIVE NOTE: Final rept.,
JAN 69   443P   Condon,Edward U. ;
CONTRACT: F44620-67-C-0035
PROJ: AF-9730
MONITOR: AFOSR 69-0025TR

UNCLASSIFIED REPORT

SUPPLEMENTARY NOTE: See also Volume 2, AD-680 976.
DESCRIPTORS: (*OPTICAL PHENOMENA. AIR FORCE RESEARCH).
PHOTOGRAPHIC ANALYSIS, OPTICAL ANALYSIS, RADAR,
ASTRONAUTS, ATTITUDES(PSYCHOLOGY), HISTORY, VISUAL
PERCEPTION, SONIC BOOM, ATMOSPHERIC ELECTRICITY, PLASMA
MEDIUM, BALLOONS, STATISTICAL ANALYSIS, PUBLIC OPINION,
ILLUSIONS   (U)
IDENTIFIERS: CASE STUDIES, *UNIDENTIFIED FLYING
OBJECTS   (U)

The report contains the results of a scientific
inquiry into the phenomena of Unidentified Flying
Objects. This volume contains: (1)
Conclusions and recommendations, (2) Summary
of the study, and (3) Case studies predating
the term of the project. (Author)   (U)

AD- 680 975   UNCLASSIFIED

UNCLASSIFIED

DDC REPORT BIBLIOGRAPHY   SEARCH CONTROL NO. 091643

AD- 311 102
AIR MATERIEL COMMAND WRIGHT-PATTERSON AFB OHIO

UNIDENTIFIED AERIAL OBJECTS PROJECT "SIGN".   (U)

FEB 49   35P   Truettner,L. H. ;Deyarmond,A.
B. ;
PROJ: XS304
MONITOR: FTD   F TR2274IA

UNCLASSIFIED REPORT

SUPPLEMENTARY NOTE:
DESCRIPTORS: (*AIR INTELLIGENCE, IDENTIFICATION).
CLASSIFICATION, MOTION, ANALYSIS, PSYCHOLOGY, ILLUSIONS,
CONFIGURATION, SPACECRAFT, AIRCRAFT, PILOTS   (U)
IDENTIFIERS: UNIDENTIFIED FLYING OBJECTS UFO)   (U)

A descriptive and analytical study of the
unidentified aerial objects that have been reported
both in the United States and from foreign
countries is presented. Individual cases are
described in brief form as an appendix. The
analytical treatment of the subject is largely of a
qualitative and generalized nature. However,
detailed analyses and detailed results are presented
where this procedure is possible, and will assist in
establishing the validity or tenability of an overall
hypothesis. Project 'Sign' is still largely
characterized by the collection of data, without
sufficient information to permit definite, specific
conclusions to be made. No definite evidence is yet
available to confirm or disprove the actual existence
of unidentified flying objects as new and unknown
types or aircraft. A limited number of the
incidents have been identified as known objects.
(Author)   (U)

PAGE 5   UNCLASSIFIED   AD- 311 102   091643

UNCLASSIFIED

DDC REPORT BIBLIOGRAPHY   SEARCH CONTROL NO. 091643

AD- 69 211
FOREIGN TECHNOLOGY DIV WRIGHT-PATTERSON AFB OHIO

PROJECT BLUE BOOK   (U)

DESCRIPTIVE NOTE: Monthly status rept. no. 9, 1-30 Nov
52.
      JAN 53   44P

            UNCLASSIFIED REPORT

DESCRIPTORS: *AIR INTELLIGENCE, *AIRCRAFT, DETECTION.   (M)
IDENTIFICATION   (M)
IDENTIFIERS: BLUE BOOK PROJECT

UNCLASSIFIED

DDC REPORT BIBLIOGRAPHY   SEARCH CONTROL NO. 091643

AD- 69 180
FOREIGN TECHNOLOGY DIV WRIGHT-PATTERSON AFB OHIO

PROJECT BLUE BOOK   (U)

DESCRIPTIVE NOTE: Monthly status rept. no. 10, Dec 52-
Feb 53,
      FEB 53   80P
REPT. NO. T53 3695

            UNCLASSIFIED REPORT

DESCRIPTORS: *AIR INTELLIGENCE, *AIRCRAFT, DETECTION,   (M)
IDENTIFICATION   (M)
IDENTIFIERS: BLUE BOOK PROJECT

UNCLASSIFIED

DDC REPORT BIBLIOGRAPHY   SEARCH CONTROL NO. 091643

AD- 128 982
FOREIGN TECHNOLOGY DIV WRIGHT-PATTERSON AFB OHIO

PROJECT GRUDGE   (U)

DESCRIPTIVE NOTE: Status rept. no. 2.
      DEC 51   22P

            UNCLASSIFIED REPORT

DESCRIPTORS: *AIR INTELLIGENCE, AIRCRAFT, DETECTION,   (M)
IDENTIFICATION   (M)
IDENTIFIERS: BLUE BOOK PROJECT

AD- 128 982   UNCLASSIFIED

Central Intelligence Agency

Washington D.C. 20505

3 1 AUG 1987

Clifford E. Stone
1421 E. Tilden
Roswell, NM 88201

Reference: F87-1027

Dear Mr. Stone:

    This is in response to your undated letter postmarked 15 August
1987 in which you requested, under the Freedom of Information Act
(FOIA), copies of what appears to be an Air Force document ("Air
Intelligence Report No. 100-203-79, dated 10 December 1948"), an
unidentifiable document vintage 1948, and all documents concerning
UFOs. For identification purposes, we have assigned our reference
number F87-1027 to this request.

    There is no organized Central Intelligence Agency effort to do
research in connection with the UFO phenomena, nor has there been
an organized effort to study or collect intelligence on UFOs since
the 1950s. At that time, the Air Force, specifically the Air
Technical Intelligence Center at Wright Patterson Air Force Base,
had the primary responsibility for the investigation of all reports
of UFO sightings. The CIA's role was in connection with a
Scientific Advisory Panel, established to investigate and evaluate
reports of UFOs. The panel was concerned only with any aspect of
the UFO phenomena which might present a potential threat to the
United States national security. The panel later issued a report
of its findings, the Report of the Scientific Panel on Unidentified
Flying Objects-17 January 1953, also known as the Robertson
Report. The report was released by the Air Force Office of Public
Information on 9 April 1958. The Air Force investigation, called
Project Bluebook, was terminated in 1969. We understand that the
Air Force turned its records on this subject over to the National
Archives and Records Administration (NARA), where they are
available for inspection and purchase. There is currently no CIA
program to actively collect information on UFOs, although, since
the time of the Robertson Report, there have been sporadic
instances of correspondence dealing with the subject, and we
occasionally receive various kinds of unsolicited reports of
sightings of objects in the UFO category.

    As of this date, the Agency has released to numerous previous
requesters 819 pages of UFO-related documents under the Freedom of
Information Act. These documents are not indexed, and most of the

material deals with matters related to the report by the Scientific
Advisory Panel. We should advise you that most of the reports
dealing with the UFO sightings considered by the Panel originated
with other government agencies such as the Air Force, and that much
of the later CIA-originated reports concern sightings as reported
in the foreign news media. We also must advise you that, at the
time this released material was first located, in response to
inquiries under the Freedom of Information Act, many of the
original documents had already been destroyed in accordance with
routine records destruction schedules and, as a consequence, many
of the copies available in our microfiche archives are of poor
quality. If you want copies of these documents, the cost is ten
cents per page for reproduction charges (less the first hundred
pages at no charge, or $10.00). Please send us your check or money
order in the amount of $71.90, made payable to the Treasurer of the
United States, and cite our F87-0957 to ensure proper credit to
your account.

    This concludes action on your request. If you will send us
your check or money order for copying costs, we will reopen your
FOIA case file and send you copies.

                                        Sincerely,

                                        Lee S. Strickland
                          Information and Privacy Coordinator

Domestic Collection Division

Foreign Intelligence Information Report

TORATE CP
LATIONS

TRY	Mexico	DCD REPORT NO.	OO-B-321/00943-76
CT	International Congress of Space Medicine	DATE DISTR.	29 January 1976
		NO. PAGES	2
		REFERENCES	

OF INFO   September 1975

THIS IS UNEVALUATED INFORMATION

4.

US scientists
believe that low magnetic fields do not have a serious effect on astronauts,   5
but high magnetic fields, oscillating magnetic fields, and electromagnetic   4
fields can or do have considerable effect. There is a theory that such   3
fields are closely associated with superconductivity at very low temperatures,   3
such as in space. This in turn is related to the possible propulsion   2
system of UFOs. There is a rumor that fragments of a possible UFO found

in Brazil bore a relationship to superconductors and magnetohydrodynamics.

D-

#66

PRIORITY

.3 APRIL 1976   1030   1   1

14596

: DCD/████████

ATTN   : ████████

FROM   : DCD/████████████████████████████

SUBJECT : NEW DCD CASE ████████ - UFO RESEARCH

REFERENCE: FORM 610 DATED 9 APRIL 1976 TRANSMITTING UFO STUDY

1. WE ARE ATTEMPTING TO PROVIDE SOME SORT OF
ANALYTICAL GUIDANCE ON THE REFERENCE. IN THE MEANTIME,
PLEASE FORWARD BY TWX THE FULL NAME OF THE SOURCE OF THE
REFERENCE AS WELL AS HIS AFFILIATION. IN ADDITION, PLEASE
ADVISE WHETHER THE MATERIAL WAS CLASSIFIED CONFIDENTIAL
AT THE REQUEST OF THE SOURCE.-

2. IN VIEW OF THE UNIQUE QUALITY OF THIS INFORMATION
██ WE
REQUEST THAT YOU PROVIDE THIS INFORMATION ASAP.

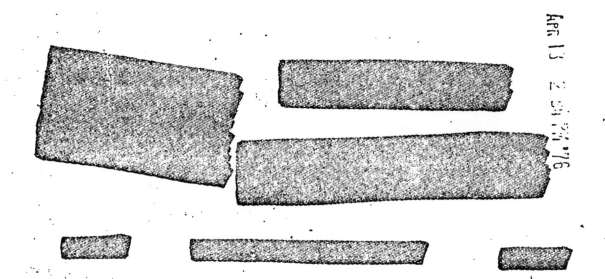

Carry— other foreign gov. obtaining

C O N F I D E N T I A L 141445Z APR 76 STAFF

CITE DCD/▓▓▓▓▓▓▓▓

TO: PRIORITY DCD/HEADQUARTERS.

ATTN: ▓▓▓▓▓▓▓▓▓▓▓▓

FROM: DCD/▓▓▓▓▓▓▓▓▓

SUBJECT: CASE ▓▓▓▓▓ — UFO RESEARCH

REF (A): DCD/HEADQUARTERS 14596

(?): FORM 610 DATED 9 APRIL 1976, UFO STUDY.

1. SOURCE'S FULL NAME IS ▓▓▓▓▓▓▓▓▓▓▓▓▓▓▓
HE IS EMPLOYED AS ▓▓▓▓▓▓▓▓▓▓▓▓▓▓▓▓▓▓▓▓▓▓▓

2. REFERENT B MATERIAL CLASSIFIED CONFIDENTIAL AT HIS
REQUEST. SOURCE SEEKS GUIDANCE FROM CIA UFO EXPERTS AS TO
MATERIAL IN HIS REPORT THAT SHOULD REMAIN CLASSIFIED. ▓▓▓▓
▓▓

15 April 1976

study

The UFO ▓▓▓▓▓▓▓▓▓▓ was turned over to Dr. ▓▓▓▓▓▓▓▓▓▓ (ADDS&T)

who was also briefed on the developments to date. Dr. ▓▓▓▓ said he

would show the study to a few people to determine possible implications of

the ~~infxxix~~ information and would be back to us soon on this matter.

ROUTINE

14755

26 APRIL 1976   1000   1   APR 26 1 31 PM '76

        :   DCD/▒▒▒▒▒

ATTN   :   ▒▒▒▒▒

FROM   :   DCD/▒▒▒▒▒▒▒▒▒▒▒▒▒▒▒▒▒▒▒▒▒▒▒▒▒▒

SUBJECT   :   DCD CASE ▒▒▒▒ - UFO RESEARCH/▒▒▒▒▒▒▒▒▒▒▒
              ▒▒▒▒▒▒▒▒▒▒▒▒▒▒▒▒▒▒▒▒▒▒▒▒▒▒▒▒▒▒

REFERENCES: A) ▒▒▒▒▒▒▒▒ TELECON, 22 APRIL 1976

              B) ▒▒▒▒▒▒▒▒

1. PER THE REQUEST IN REFERENCE (B), WE ATTEMPTED TO OBTAIN
ANALYTICAL GUIDANCE ON THE UFO ▒▒▒▒▒▒▒▒▒▒▒▒ SUBJECT.

2. WE CONTACTED THE A/DDS&T (DR ▒▒▒▒▒▒▒▒▒ TO SEE IF HE
KNEW OF ANY OFFICIAL UFO PROGRAM AND ALSO TO ATTEMPT TO ANSWER
SOME OF THE QUESTIONS POSED BY ▒▒▒▒▒▒ DR ▒▒▒▒▒ EXHIBITED INTERES
IN ▒▒▒▒▒ WHICH WAS HANDCARRIED TO HIS OFFICE. AFTER A SHORT
EXAMINATION OF ITS CONTENTS DR ▒▒▒▒▒ ADVISED US THAT HE WOULD
PERSONALLY LOOK INTO THE MATTER AND GET BACK TO US. AS WE DISCUSSED
IN REFERENCE (A) DR ▒▒▒▒▒ HAS SINCE CONTACTED US AND RELAYED THE
FOLLOWING INFORMATION.

3. IT WOULD APPEAR TO BE BEST IF YOU ADVISED ▒▒▒▒▒ THAT HE
SHOULD ▒▒

 IT DOES NOT ~~APPEAR~~ _{SEEM} THAT THE GOVERNMENT HAS ANY ~~APPARENT~~ ^{FORMAL} PROGRAM IN

PROGRESS FOR THE IDENTIFICATION/SOLUTION OF THE UFO PHENOMENA. DR

████ FEELS THAT THE EFFORTS OF INDEPENDENT RESEARCHERS, ████

████████████████████████████████████, ARE VITAL

FOR FURTHER PROGRESS IN THIS AREA. AT THE PRESENT TIME, THERE ARE

OFFICES AND PERSONNEL WITHIN THE AGENCY WHO ARE MONITORING THE UFO

PHENOMENA, BUT AGAIN, THIS IS NOT CURRENTLY ON AN OFFICIAL BASIS.

DR ████ FEELS THAT THE BEST APPROACH WOULD BE TO KEEP IN TOUCH

WITH ~~AND IN FACT DEVELOP~~ REPORTING CHANNELS IN THIS AREA TO KEEP

THE AGENCY/COMMUNITY INFORMED OF ANY NEW DEVELOPMENTS. IN PARTICULAR,

ANY INFORMATION WHICH MIGHT INDICATE A THREAT POTENTIAL WOULD BE OF

INTEREST, AS WOULD SPECIFIC INDICATIONS OF FOREIGN DEVELOPMENTS OR

APPLICATIONS OF UFO RELATED RESEARCH.

   4. DR ████ HAS ADVISED US THAT HE WOULD EVALUATE ANY

ADDITIONAL INFORMATION WE MIGHT RECEIVE AS WELL AS DISSEMINATE

SIGNIFICANT DEVELOPMENTS THROUGH APPROPRIATE CHANNELS SHOULD IT BE

WARRANTED.

   5. WE WISH TO STRESS AGAIN, THAT THERE DOES NOT NOW APPEAR TO

BE ANY SPECIAL PROGRAM ON UFOS WITHIN THE INTELLIGENCE COMMUNITY AND

THIS SHOULD BE RELAYED TO ████████

   6. IN VIEW OF DR ████ WILLINGNESS TO REVIEW ADDITIONAL

INFORMATION RECEIVED ON THE UFO PHENOMENA WE WILL KEEP SUBJECT

CASE OPEN TO YOUR OFFICE FOR THE PRESENT.

   7. PLEASE KEEP US ADVISED OF ANY NEW DEVELOPMENTS.

Doc. 5-11a CIA Document, May 27, 1976

DATE

27 May 1976

TO: (Officer designation, room number, and building)	DATE		OFFICER'S INITIALS	COMMENTS (Number each comment to show from whom to whom. Draw a line across column after each comment)
	RECEIVED	FORWARDED		
1. Dr.				Dr.
2.				Regarding our recent discussion
3.				▓▓▓▓▓▓, attached is some material in which you may be interested.
4.				In particular, please note attachment A. Our source obtained it
5.				
6.				
7.				
8.				
9.				Our source felt that ▓▓▓▓ work might be of interest to the US Government and that it should be evaluated by the Agency. The source also felt that it could be analyzed outside the context of its UFO connection if necessary to remove it from a controversial subject.
0.				
				As before we are faced with the problem of having UFO related data which is deemed potentially important for the US by our S&T sources, evaluated. As you are aware, at this time there is no channel or working group to which we can turn for this type of analysis and dissemination. Thus, if it is acceptable to you we will continue to periodically advise you or your designee of any new or potentially important FI

developments which might arise from current independent scientific research on the UFO phenomena.

If you feel that ▓▓▓▓▓▓▓▓▓▓▓▓ ▓▓▓▓ offers some potential we can obtain more detailed report through our source.

MEMO FOR THE FILE

On 25 June 1976, ▓▓▓▓▓▓ xxxx met with ▓▓▓▓▓▓▓▓ of ORD(▓▓▓▓ ▓▓▓▓▓▓▓▓▓) regarding possible interest by that office in the UFO case. ▓▓▓▓▓▓▓ was provided copies of the ▓▓▓▓▓▓ and the later ▓▓▓▓ memo as well as the original ▓▓▓▓▓▓▓▓. These items were provided at his request.

▓▓▓▓▓▓ felt that there may be some ongoing ORD interest, ~~dependent~~ depending on the evaluation by that office of the material provided.

▓▓▓▓▓ asked that we ~~attempt to~~ obtain additional info on the ▓▓▓ ▓▓▓▓▓▓▓ system which we agreed to do. (a TWX was sent ~~to this effect~~ requesting additional info) to the ▓▓▓▓ Office on 25 June 1976).

~~Nxxinfxxxxix~~

▓▓▓▓▓▓ asked that the ORD interest be kept at a low profile until some evaluation could be made, but at the same time indicated that he would be in touch with me on a fairly ~~regular~~ regular basis.

25 June 1976

MULTIPLE ADDRESS MESSAGE		BOOK MESSAGE	CHECK NO.(S)
DATE	TIME		
25 June 1976	1425	PAGE 1 OF 1	

TO DCD/▮▮▮▮▮   INFO

<u>1567</u>

NUMBER

SUBJECT: CASE ▮▮▮▮ - UFO RESEARCH/ORD REQUEST FOR ADDITIONAL INFORMATION ▮▮▮▮▮

REFERENCE: A. ▮▮▮▮▮
            B. ▮▮▮▮▮

1. ORD HAS EXHIBITED SOME INTEREST IN THE WORK OF ▮▮▮▮▮ A QUALIFIED ANALYST IS CURRENTLY ATTEMPTING TO EVALUATE ▮▮▮▮▮ SYSTEM AND HAS REQUESTED ADDITIONAL INFORMATION.

2. WE NOTE THAT IN SOME OF THE EARLIER CORRESPONDENCE FROM YOUR OFFICE (REFERENCE B) MENTION WAS MADE OF THE POSSIBILITY OF OBTAINING A MORE COMPLETE DESCRIPTION OF ▮▮▮ ▮▮▮▮ SYSTEM. IF THIS POSSIBILITY STILL EXISTS, ORD WOULD APPRECIATE SEEING WHATEVER IS AVAILABLE.

3. PLEASE KEEP US ADVISED OF ANY NEW DEVELOPMENTS.

AUTHENTICATING OFFICER   COORDINATING OFFICERS   RELEASING OFFICER

CLASSIFICATION

FORM 172 USE PREVIOUS EDITIONS
9-63

Read instructions on reverse side before typing

DATE   14 July 1976

COMMENTS (Number each comment to show from whom to whom. Draw a line across column after each comment.)

Mr. ▓▓▓▓▓▓

At a recent meeting to evaluate some material from ▓▓▓▓▓▓▓▓▓ you mentioned a personal interest in the UFO phenomena. As you may recall, I mentioned my own interest in the subject as well as the fact that DCD had been receiving UFO related material from many of our S&T sources who are presently conducting related research. These scientists include some who have been associated with the Agency for years and whose credentials remove them from the "nut" variety.

The attached material came to my attention through these sources and it appears to have some legitimate FI or community interest potential.

The ▓▓▓▓▓▓▓▓▓ work being carried out by Dr. ▓▓▓▓▓▓▓▓▓▓▓▓ should, in the view of our S&T sources, be evaluated by the Agency or community.

In view of the expertise associated with your office, as well as your own interest in the subject, I felt you might like to see the material.

[If you need additional information, or if you feel there is some potential, I would be glad to discuss this with you. If not, please feel free to destroy the material.]

▓▓▓▓▓▓▓

☒ CONFIDENTIAL ☐ UNCLASSIFIED

Doc. 5-14 CIA Document, Jul 14, 1976

Doc. 5-15 CIA Document, Sept 24, 1976

T 232104   E14339 _ | PAGE 01

TCR124'17453 SEP 76

▓▓▓▓▓▓▓   241716Z SEP 76 STAFF

CITE ▓▓▓▓▓▓

TO: IMMEDIATE DIRECTOR, ▓▓▓▓▓▓

▓▓▓▓▓▓▓▓

REF: ▓▓▓▓▓▓▓▓▓▓

1. ▓▓▓▓▓▓▓▓▓▓▓▓▓▓▓▓▓▓▓
▓▓▓▓▓▓▓▓▓▓▓▓▓▓

2. ▓▓▓▓▓▓▓▓▓▓▓▓▓▓▓▓▓▓
▓▓▓▓▓▓▓▓▓▓▓▓▓▓▓▓▓▓▓▓▓
▓▓▓▓▓▓▓▓▓▓▓▓▓▓▓▓▓▓▓▓▓

3. 23 SEPT ▓▓▓▓▓▓▓▓▓▓▓▓▓▓▓

WITH PERSONAL REQUEST TO INVESTIGATE UFO SIGHTED MOROCCO,

DEPARTMENT OF STATE

Washington, D.C. 20520

FOI Case No. 8000085

Doc. 5-16 State Dept. Letter, Oct 16, 1980

SSG Clifford E. Stone
Hq, Det,. Hanau Military Community
APO New York 09165

OCT 16 1980

Dear Sargeant Stone:

I refer to your letter of January 10, 1980 requesting the release of certain Department of State documents under the Freedom of Information Act (Title 5 USC Section 552).

A search of files under the Department's control has resulted in the retrieval of nine documents which appear relevant to your request. After careful review, we have determined that three of these documents can be released. Two more can be released subject to excisions. Two must be withheld from release.

All the denied and excised material (unless otherwise specified below) has been determined to be properly exempt from release under Paragraph (b) (1) or Section 552 as currently and properly classified under Executive Order 12065 and authorized by that Order to remain protected in the interest of national defense or foreign policy. All non-exempt material in the excised documents that is reasonably segregable from the exempt material is released herewith.

The decision whether an additionaltwo documents can be released requires coordination with another government agency. We will write to you again concerning that decision.

With respect to material denied or excised, you have the right to appeal this determination within sixty days. Appeals should be addressed to the Assistant Secretary for Public Affairs, Department of State, Washington, D.C. 20520. A letter of appeal should refer to the Freedom of Information case number shown above.

Sincerely,

For the Deputy Assistant Secretary
for Classification/Declassification

Thomas W. Ainsworth
Director, Mandatory Review
Bureau of Administration

DEPARTMENT OF STATE

Washington, D.C. 20520

JUN 1 5 1981

FOI No. 8000085

SSG. Clifford E. Stone
Hg. Det. Hanau Military Community
APO New York 09165

Dear Sgt. Stone:

We have received replies from the two U.S. Government agencies to whom we referred two documents mentioned in our response of October 16, 1980 to your letter of January 10, 1980 requesting the release of certain Department of State documents.

In view of the concurrence of those agencies, the two documents may be released to you in their entirety.

Sincerely,

For the Deputy Assistant Secretary
for Classification/Declassification

Thomas W. Ainsworth
Director, Mandatory Review
Bureau of Administration

Department of State **TELE(**

Doc. 5-18a State Dept. Teletype, Sept 26, 1973

CONFIDENTIAL

AN: D730070-0403

PAGE 01   BERLIN 01662   261620Z

45
ACTION EUR-25

INFO OCT-01 ISO-00 SS-15 PM-07 NSC-10 CIAE-00 INR-10 L-03

NEA-10 NSAE-00 PA-03 RSC-01 PRS-01 SPC-03 USIA-15

TRSE-00 MBFR-04 SAJ-01 DODE-00 EB-11 FAA-00 DRC-01

·/121 W
-------------------------- 068561
R 261446Z SEP 73
FM USMISSION BERLIN
TO SECSTATE WASHDC 2450
INFO AMEMBASSY BONN
CINCEUR FOR POLAD AND OPS
CINCUSAFE FOR POLAD AND OPS
:CINCUSAREUR FOR POLAD, OPS AEAGG OCO AND AEAGB C
USELMO

C O N F I D E N T I A L BERLIN 1662

E.O. 16652: GDS
TAGS: PGOV, PBOR, WB, UR, GE
SUBJECT: FLIGHT OF UNIDENTIFIED AIRCRAFT IN SOUTH CORRIDOR
1. AT 1230 Z 22 SEPTEMBER, AN UNIDENTIFIED AIRCRAFT
ENTERED SOUTH CORRIDOR AND AFTER FLYING 30 MILES UPP
CORRIDOR ON OR NEAR CENTER LINE BEGAN TO DEVIATE TO
NORTH. AT 1245, IT WAS REPORTED 40 MILES NORTHEAST
OF MANSBACH AND 6 MILES NORTH OF CORRIDOR CENTER LINE,
STILL WITHIN CORRIDOR. ALTITUDE WAS ESTIMATED AT
10,000 FEET OR POSSIBLY HIGHER. WE WERE UNABLE TO
ESTABLISH RADIO CONTACT, LOCATE A FLIGHT PLAN OR
RECEIVE IFF TRANSMISSION, AND, ACCORDINGLY, WERE
UNABLE TO RESPOND TO SOVIET CONTROLLER.S REQUEST
IN BASC FOR FURTHER INFORMATION.

2. RADAR CONTACT WAS LOST AT 1256, WHEN AIRCRAFT WAS
ESTIMATED TO BE 35 MILES ON 026 DEGREE RADIAL FROM
MANSBACH (OUTSIDE CORRIDOR BUT STILL OVER GDR).
PAGE 02   BERLIN 01662   261620Z

CONFIDENTIAL

Doc. 5-18b State Dept. Teletype, Sept 26, 1973

CONFIDENTIAL

PREVIOUSLY, RADAR INDICATED AIRCRAFT HAD APPARENTLY
BEEN INTERCEPTED BY POSSIBLY TWO OTHER AIRCRAFT.
SOVIETS IN BASC, IN RESPONSE TO OUR REQUEST, WERE UNABLE
TO PROVIDE ADDTIONAL INFORMATION.

3. USAFE AT 1607 INFORMED US CHIEF CONTROLLER THAT
AN AIRCRAFT HAD REENTERED WEST GERMAN AIRSPACE AT
1306 AND HAD BEEN IDENTIFIED AS FOUR-SEATER CIVILIAN
PLANE. USAFE INDICATED CONTACT WAS SUBSEQUENTLY LOST
AGAIN, AND NEITHER WE NOR BRITISH AND FRENCH HAVE
RECEIVED ANY FURTHER INFORMATION (OR PROTEST) IN REGARD
TO INCIDENT.

4. USCOB CONCURS.KLEIN

DECLASSIFIED

NPR

(R) cl

WHITE JOYCE A   03-05/80 075628   PRINTER: LI
78 BRIDGETOWN 2864
                          LIMITED OFFICIAL USE
LIMITED OFFICIAL USE
PAGE 01   BRIDGE 02864 082237Z
ACTION IO 15
INFO OCT-01 ARA-11 ISO-00 SS-15 NSCE-00 CPR-02 PA-01
      SY-05 USSS-00 FBIE 00 CIAE 00 INR-10 NSAE-00
      OES-09 SSO-00 INRE-00 /069 W
                  --------------081803 091552Z /53
R 061832Z OCT 78
FM AMEMBASSY BRIDGETOWN
TO SECSTATE WASHDC 6384
INFO USMISSION USUN NEW YORK
LIMITED OFFICIAL USE BRIDGETOWN 2864
E.O. 11652: N/A
TAGS: OVIP, PPDC, TGEN, UNGA. GJ
SUBJ: REQUEST BY PRIMIN GAIRY OF GRENADA FOR MEETING WITH
PRESIDENT CARTER ON UNIDENTIFIED FLYING OBJECTS 'UFO'S'
REF: BRIDGETOWN 2839
1. AT INSTRUCTION OF AMBASSADOR WHO IS IN ST. LUCIA ON OFFICIAL
VISIT, DCM CARRIED OUT PROTOCOLARY COURTESY OF MEETING PRIME
MINISTER SIR ERIC GAIRY AT AIRPORT THIS MORNING WHEN GAIRY
TRANSITED BARBADOS ON WAY TO UNGA. GAIRY REPEATED REQUEST
WHICH HE SAID HE HAD ALREADY MADE PREVIOUSLY THROUGH UNNAMED
"SCIENTIFIC GROUP" IN USA THAT PRESIDENT CARTER MEET WITH HIM
AND OTHER MEMBERS OF GROUP IN NEW YORK, SHOULD PRESIDENT BE
ABLE ALLOCATE 5 MINUTES WHILE AT UNGA TO DISCUSS UFO'S.
2. GAIRY DID NOT SEEM REALLY BELIEVE SUCH A MEETING WOULD
BE POSSIBLE IN VIEW OF PRESIDENT'S HEAVY COMMITMENTS, NOR DID
WE GIVE HIM SLIGHTEST ENCOURAGEMENT. BUT HE WISHED HIS REQUEST RE
CORDED ANYWAY. GAIRY'S CONTACT ON UFO'S IS DR. JOHN
HYNECK. ADVISOR TO GRENADIAN DELEGATION, UNITED NATIONS
LIMITED OFFICIAL USE
LIMITED OFFICIAL USE
PAGE 02   BRIDGE 02864 082237Z
NEW YORK. GAIRY WILL BE AT NEW YORK HILTON UNTIL OCTOBER 17.
ORTIZ
LIMITED OFFICIAL USE

DEPARTMENT OF STATE A/CDC/MR

REVIEWED BY [signature] WJ DATE 6/3/81

RDS[] or XDS[]EXT. DATE _____
TS AUTH. _____ REASON(S) _____
ENDORSE EXISTING MARKINGS []
DECLASSIFIED[X] RELEASABLE[]
RELEASE DENIED[]
PA or FOI EXEMPTIONS _____

EXCISE

WILLIAMS JESSIE M   03/04/80 164755   PRINTER: LI
78 USUN NEW YORK 5165
                    CONFIDENTIAL
CONFIDENTIAL
PAGE 01   USUN N 05165   180251Z
ACTION IO-15
INFO   OCT-01   ARA-11   ISO-00   DOE-15   ACDA-12   CIAE-00
       DODE-00   PM-05   INR-10   L-03   NSAE-00   NASA-01   NSC-05
       SOE-02   SS-15   OES-09   AF-10   EA-10   EUR-12   NEA-11
       SP-02   SVC-00   /149 W
                    ------------------076211   180256Z /14
P 180251Z NOV 78
FM USMISSION USUN NEW YORK
TO SECSTATE WASHDC PRIORITY 5565
INFO AMEMBASSY BRIDGETOWN
C O N F I D E N T I A L USUN NEW YORK 05165
E.O. 11652:GDS
TAGS: UNGA, GJ, TSPA
SUBJECT: GRENADIAN UFO CRUSADE:DEJA VU

DEPARTMENT OF STATE A/CDC/MR
REVIEWED BY W EJ DATE 10/13/?
PORTIONS DENIED AS INDICATED

1. ESTABLISHMENT OF AN AGENCY OR A DEPARTMENT OF THE
UNITED NATIONS FOR UNDERTAKING, COORDINATING AND DIS-
SEMINATING THE RESULTS OF RESEARCH INTO UNIDENTIFIED
FLYING OBJECTS AND RELATED PHENOMENA (UNGA ITEM 126) IS
SCHEDULED TO BE TAKEN UP BY THE SPECIAL POLITICAL COM-
MITTEE (SPC) ON 27 NOVEMBER. UNDAUNTED BY A LACK OF
RESPONSE TO THE ITEM DURING AND SINCE THE 32ND UNGA,
PRIME MINISTER GAIRY HAS APPARENTLY LAID THE GROUND-
WORK FOR A BLITZKRIEG SALES PITCH WHICH WILL INCLUDE
A CAST OF SUPPORTERS RANGING FROM SCIENTISTS TO ASTRO-
NAUTS. SUPPLEMENTED BY A HOLLYWOOD FILM PRODUCTION.

2. [REDACTED]

B-1) ED

CONFIDENTIAL
CONFIDENTIAL
PAGE 02   USUN N 05165   180251Z

[REDACTED]

3. TWO MEETINGS HAVE BEEN ALLOCATED FOR THIS ITEM
BY THE CHAIRMAN OF THE SPC. PRESUMABLY DELEGATES WILL
BE GIVEN A DAY OR SO TO DIGEST THE INFORMATION PRE-
SENTED AND THEN RETURN TO ACT ON THE RESOLUTION.
4. THUS FAR ONLY TWO COUNTRIES HAVE GONE ON RECORD
WITH A POSITION ON THE GENERAL PROPOSAL. SEYCHELLES
SUPPORTED THE IDEA WHILE INDIA REJECTED THE ESTABLISH-
                    CONFIDENTIAL   /

PAGE   1

WILLIAMS JESSIE M   03/04/80 164756   PRINTER: LI
78 USUN NEW YORK 5165
                          CONFIDENTIAL
MENT OF A SEPARATE UN AGENCY OR COMMITTEE BUT SUG-
GESTED THAT SOME DISCUSSION OF UFO'S COULD BE INCLUDED
WITHIN THE BROADER CONTEXT OF THE "EXTRATERRESTRIAL
LIFE/INTELLIGENCE" ITEM UNDER CONSIDERATION BY THE
OUTERSPACE COMMITTEE. THERE APPEARS TO BE VERY LITTLE
INTEREST ON THE PART OF MOST DELEGATES TO PURSUE THIS
MATTER. NEVERTHELESS GRENADA WILL PRESS FORWARD
UNDER INSTRUCTIONS FROM GAIRY WHO SEES HIS COUNTRY AS
HOST OF A CENTER FOR UFO RESEARCH.
5. ACTION REQUESTED: PLEASE PROVIDE INSTRUCTIONS ON
U.S. POSITION TO BE TAKEN IN THIS MATTER AS WELL AS
DESIRED LEVEL OF VISIBILITY. LAST YEAR GRENADA REQUESTED
OUR SUPPORT AND MISOFF HAD TO SCRAMBLE HARD BEHIND THE
SCENES TO WATER DOWN THE RESOLUTION AND, IN EFFECT,
DELAY A VOTE FOR ONE YEAR. ANOTHER CONSIDERATION IS
WHETHER TO ISSUE A DISCLAIMER ON STATEMENTS MADE BY U.S.
CONFIDENTIAL
CONFIDENTIAL
PAGE 03   USUN N 05165 180251Z
NATIONALS ON THE GRENADIAN DELEGATION. IF LAST YEAR'S
INSTRUCTIONS STILL OBTAIN, IT WOULD APPEAR THAT THE
INDIAN SUGGESTION WOULD BE ABOUT AS FAR AS WE WOULD BE
WILLING TO GO ON THE ISSUE. LEONARD
CONFIDENTIAL

EXCISE

ETHERIDGE CAROLYN R   03/04/80 165630   PRINTER: LI
78 USUN NEW YORK 5425
                              CONFIDENTIAL

CONFIDENTIAL
PAGE 01   USUN N 05425 01 OF 02 2821002
ACTION IO-15
INFO OCT-01 AF-10 ARA-11 EA-10 EUR-12 NEA-11 ISO-00
      DOE-15 ACDA-12 CIAE-00 DODE-00 PM-05 INR-10 L-03
      NSAE-00 NASA-01 SOE-02 SS-15 OES-09 TRSE-00 OMB-01
      INRE-00 NSCE-00 SSO-00 /143 W
                              ---------116199 2821292 /23

C 2820542 NOV 78
FM USMISSION USUN NEW YORK
TO SECSTATE WASHDC IMMEDIATE 5996
INFO AMEMBASSY BRIDGETOWN
C O N F I D E N T I A L SECTION 01 OF 02 USUN NEW YORK 05425
E.O. 11652:GDS
TAGS: UNGA, GJ, TSPA
SUBJECT: GRENADIAN UFO RESOLUTION
REF: USUN 5323 AND PREVIOUS
BEGIN UNCLASSIFIED.

DEPARTMENT OF STATE A/CDC/MR
REVIEWED BY W EJ   DATE 4 16/80
PORTIONS DENIED AS INDICATED

1. SUMMARY: AS ANTICIPATED, GRENADIAN PM SIR ERIC GAIRY
ADDRESSED THE SPECIAL POLITICAL COMMITTEE (SPC) ON
AGENDA ITEM 126 AND INTRODUCED A RESOLUTION (DATAFAXED)
WHICH WOULD ESTABLISH AN EXPERT GROUP TO SET GUIDELINES
FOR A UN STUDY OF UFOS. HE WAS FOLLOWED BY DR. FRIDAY
(MINISTER OF EDUCATION) AND FOUR OTHER SPEAKERS, ALL OF
WHOM ARGUED IN FAVOR OF A "UN CLEARINGHOUSE" FOR THE
EXCHANGE OF DATA AND COORDINATION OF RESEARCH ON UFOS.
THE SPEAKERS WERE SUPPLEMENTED BY A SHORT FILM WHICH
CONSISTED OF STILL AND MOTION PICTURES SPLICED TOGETHER
PURPORTING TO DEPICT ACTUAL SIGHTINGS OF UFOS. CONSIDERA-
TION OF THE ITEM WAS SUSPENDED TO PERMIT DELEGATES TO
CONSIDER THE RESOLUTION. END SUMMARY.
2. GAIRY, IN HIS STATEMENT TO THE COMMITTEE ON 27 NOV.
CONFIDENTIAL
CONFIDENTIAL
PAGE 02   USUN N 05425 01 OF 02 2821002
SAID HE HAD COME TO NEW YORK TO PRESENT THE ITEM BECAUSE
OF HIS "DEEP PERSONAL CONVICTION" THAT THE SUBJECT OF UFOS
WAS ONE OF "WORLD-WIDE IMPORTANCE AND SIGNIFICANCE" AND
INDEED, ONE WHICH WARRANTED VERY SERIOUS CONSIDERATION
BY THE UNITED NATIONS.
     THE RECENT REPORT OF THE ABDUCTION OF A CESSNA AIRCRAFT
IN AUSTRALIA SEEMED TO HIM TO BE A COMPELLING REASON FOR
THE UNITED NATIONS TO "COME ALIVE TO ITS RESPONSIBILITIES
AND TAKE A SERIOUS LOOK AT THE U.F.O. PHENOMENON TO WHICH
PLANET EARTH HAS BEEN CONSPICUOUSLY EXPOSED SINCE 1947."
3. MR. FRIDAY READ OUT THE TEXT OF A RESOLUTION ADOPTED IN
APRIL 1977, AT ACAPULCO, MEXICO, AT THE FIRST INTERNATIONAL
CONGRESS ON UFO PHENOMENON, WHICH HAD ENDORSED GRENADA'S
INITIATIVE TO BRING THIS MATTER TO THE ATTENTION OF THE
UNITED NATIONS. IT WAS AGAINST THIS BACKGROUND, HE SAID,
THAT THE GRENADA DELEGATION HAD INVITED SOME OF THE
                  CONFIDENTIAL   /

PAGE   1

ETHERIDGE CAROLYN R   03/04/80 165631   PRINTER: LI
78 USUN NEW YORK 5425
                    CONFIDENTIAL
SCIENTISTS WHO HAD PARTICIPATED IN THE CONGRESS TO JOIN
HIS DELEGATION TODAY IN ORDER TO SPEAK ON THE SUBJECT.
4. DR. J. ALLEN HYNEK (PROFESSOR OF ASTRONOMY AT NORTH-
WESTERN) COMPLEMENTED GRENADA FOR HAVING THE COURAGE TO
INTRODUCE THE SUBJECT AND THUS "TROD WHERE MIGHTIER
NATIONS FEARED TO TREAD." HE WENT ON TO DEFINE THE
PHENOMENON OF UFO'S SIMPLY AS "ANY AERIAL OR SURFACE
SIGHTING, OR INSTRUMENTAL RECORDING (E.G. RADAR,
PHOTOGRAPHY, ETC.) WHICH REMAINS UNEXPLAINED BY CON-
VENTIONAL METHODS EVEN AFTER COMPETENT EXAMINATION
BY QUALIFIED PERSONS." A CARDINAL MISTAKE, AND A SOURCE
OF GREAT CONFUSION, HE REMARKED, HAD BEEN THE ALMOST
UNIVERSAL SUBSTITUTION OF AN INTERPRETATION OF THE UFO
PHENOMENON FOR THE PHENOMENON ITSELF. HYNEK SAID THAT UFO
CONFIDENTIAL
CONFIDENTIAL
PAGE 03   USUN N 05425 01 OF 02 282100Z
REPORTS HAD BEEN ASSEMBLED FROM 133 COUNTRIES. IN SIGNIFI-
CANT NUMBERS, THESE REPORTS HAD BEEN MADE BY HIGHLY
RESPONSIBLE PERSONS -- ASTRONAUTS, RADAR EXPERTS, MILITARY
AND COMMERCIAL PILOTS, OFFICIALS OF GOVERNMENTS AND
SCIENTISTS, INCLUDING ASTRONOMERS. HYNEK CONCLUDED BY
POINTING OUT THAT THERE ARE MANY SCIENTISTS AND SPECIALISTS
AROUND THE WORLD WHO ARE STUDYING THE UFO PHENOMENON BUT
THEY HAD NO MEANS, EITHER GOVERNMENTAL OR PRIVATE, BY
WHICH THEY COULD SHARE THE RESULTS OF THEIR WORK. HE
SUGGESTED THAT THE UN CREATE THE NECESSARY FRAMEWORK TO
PROVIDE THIS CAPABILITY FOR SCIENTISTS.
5. DR. JACQUES VALLEE (CURRENTLY AN AUTHOR OF SCIENCE
FICTION) WAS THE NEXT SPEAKER INTRODUCED BY DR. FRIDAY.
HE HAS SPENT FIFTEEN YEARS ANALYZING UFO REPORTS ON A
COMPUTER AND CONCLUDED THAT DESPITE THE LACK OF CONCLUSIVE
PROOF, THE UFO PHENOMENON IS REAL BECAUSE PEOPLE BELIEVE
IT IS REAL.
     HIS CONCLUSION WAS THAT THIS PHENOMENON HAD THREE
ASPECTS: FIRST, PHYSICAL MANIFESTATION THAT COULD AND
SHOULD BE INVESTIGATED THROUGH AVAILABLE SCIENTIFIC
EQUIPMENT; SECOND, A PSYCHO-PHYSIOLOGICAL ASPECT. WITNESSES
AT THE SCENE EXHIBITED DISORIENTATION SYMPTOMS, A LOSS OF
THE SENSE OF TIME. PARTIAL PARALYSIS OR LOSS OF VOLUNTARY
MUSCLE CONTROL, AUDITORY AND VISUAL HALLUCINATIONS, EYE
COMPLAINTS RANGING FROM CONJUNCTIVITIS TO TEMPORARY
BLINDNESS, MASSIVE PSYCHIC REACTIONS AND LONGER-TERM
EFFECTS SUCH AS DISTURBANCE OF SLEEP AND DREAM PATTERNS
AND RADICAL BEHAVIOR CHANGES. HE DID NOT BELIEVE IT WAS
WITHIN THE PROVINCE OR THE BUDGET OF THE UNITED NATIONS
TO ADDRESS SUCH EFFECTS DIRECTLY, EXCEPT WHERE THE UNITED
NATIONS COULD SERVE ITS TRADITIONAL ROLE IN DISSEMINATING
SCIENTIFIC INFORMATION AND FACILITATING EXCHANGES AMONG
SCHOLARS.
CONFIDENTIAL

                CONFIDENTIAL   /   PAGE   2

ETHERIDGE CAROLYN R   03/04/80 165632   PRINTER: LI
78 USUN NEW YORK 5425
                           CONFIDENTIAL
CONFIDENTIAL
PAGE 01   USUN N 05425 02 OF 02 282101Z
ACTION IO-15
INFO OCT-01 AF-10 ARA-11 EA-10 EUR-12 NEA-11 ISO-00
      DOE-15 ACDA-12 CIAE-00 DODE-00 PM-05 INR-10 L-03
      NSAE-00 NASA-01 NSC-05 SOE-02 SS-15 OES-09 TRSE-00
      OMB-01 NSCE-00 SSO-00 ICAE-00 INRE-00 DOEE-00
      /148 W
                              ─────────116218 282132Z /23
O 282054Z NOV 78
FM USMISSION USUN NEW YORK
TO SECSTATE WASHDC IMMEDIATE 5997
INFO AMEMBASSY BRIDGETOWN
C O N F I D E N T I A L SECTION 02 OF 02 USUN NEW YORK 05425
6. DR. FRIDAY THEN INTRODUCED LT.COL. LARRY COYNE, U.S.ARMY,
WHO APPEARED IN A PRIVATE CAPACITY. COYNE DESCRIBED
TO THE SPC A PERSONAL ENCOUNTER WITH A UFO NEAR COLUMBUS,
OHIO IN 1973 WHEN HIS ARMY HELICOPTER ALMOST COLLIDED IN
MID-AIR WITH A UFO. HE ACKNOWLEDGED THAT HE WAS PREPARING
A MANUSCRIPT ABOUT HIS EXPERIENCE FOR A BOOK.
7. THE CHAIR RECESSED THE SPC SO THAT THE FILM ON UFO'S
COULD BE SHOWN. DR. HYNEK INDICATED THAT EACH OF THE
SIGHTINGS DEPICTED IN THE FILM HAD BEEN THOROUGHLY
INVESTIGATED AND SEVERAL OF THEM WERE HIGHLY SUSPECT.
8. WHEN THE AFTERNOON SESSION OPENED, DR. FRIDAY ANNOUNCED
THAT EX-U.S. ASTRONAUT L. GORDON COOPER WAS UNABLE TO
ATTEND THE MEETING AS SCHEDULED. HE DID, HOWEVER, READ
A LETTER FROM COOPER WHICH STATED HIS BELIEF THAT EXTRA-
TERRESTRIAL VEHICLES AND THEIR CREWS ARE VISITING THIS
PLANET FROM MORE TECHNICALLY ADVANCED CIVILIZATIONS.
COOPER HAD OBSERVED FORMATIONS OF UFO'S IN 1951, BUT
INDICATED MOST ASTRONAUTS WERE RELUCTANT TO DISCUSS THE
SUBJECT BECAUSE OF THE CHICANERY WHICH HAS BEEN ASSOCIATED
WITH IT. HE CLAIMED THAT IF THE UN PURSUES THE GRENADIAN
CONFIDENTIAL
CONFIDENTIAL
PAGE 02   USUN N 05425 02 OF 02 282101Z
PROJECT, MORE QUALIFIED PEOPLE WILL STEP FORWARD TO
PROVIDE HELP AND INFORMATION.
9. DR. FRIDAY THEN INTRODUCED HIS FINAL SPEAKER WHO
WAS STANTON FRIEDMAN, A FULL TIME UFOLOGIST AND LECTURER.
FRIEDMAN AGREED WITH COOPER THAT EARTH HAS BEEN
VISITED BY VEHICLES FROM EXTRA-TERRESTRIAL SOURCES AND
OPINED THAT SINCE WE WILL HAVE THE CAPABILITY OF
VISITING OTHER STAR SYSTEMS IN THE NEXT CENTURY, THEY
WANT TO KEEP TABS ON US. SINCE THERE IS NO SINGLE LEADER
TO BE TAKEN TO, THE ALIENS HAVE NOT INITIATED CONTACT
WITH ANY RECOGNIZED AUTHORITY.
10. FRIDAY CLOSED BY SOLICITING THE COMMENTS AND OR
SUGGESTIONS REGARDING THE RESOLUTION FROM OTHER DELEGATES.
THERE WERE NO OTHER INTERVENTIONS MADE AT THAT TIME
                    CONFIDENTIAL   /

234

C
R

ILLIAMS JESSIE M   23/04/80 164820   PRINTER: LI
E USUN NEW YORK 5603
                         UNCLASSIFIED

NCLASSIFIED
AGE 01   USUN N 05603 040739Z
CTION IO-15
NFC OCT-01 ARA-15 ISO-00 AF-10 EA-12 EUR-12 NEA-06
     CIAE-00 DODE-00 PM-05 H-02 INR-10 L-03 NSAE-00
     NSC-05 PA-02 SP-02 SS-15 ICA-20 DOE-15 ACDA-12
     NASA-00 SOE-00 OES-09 TRSY-02 OMB-01 /RB N 44
     ----------------------------226440 041252Z

0202162 DEC 78
M USMISSION USUN NEW YORK
C SECSTATE WASHDC 6246
NFO AMEMBASSY BRIDGETOWN
NCLAS USUN NEW YORK 05603
.O. 12065: N/A
AGS: UNGA, GJ, TSPA
UBJECT: GRENADIAN UFO RESOLUTION
EF: USUN 5425 AND PREVIOUS
. SUBSEQUENT TO THE INTRODUCTION OF THE GRENADIAN
FO RESOLUTION, MISOFF HAS ENGAGED IN TWO SEPARATE
NFORMAL NEGOTIATING SESSIONS, WHICH INCLUDED REPRESENTA
ION FROM AUSTRIA, USSR, AND GRENADA. IN AN ATTEMPT
O ARRIVE AT A MUTUALLY ACCEPTABLE COMPROMISE SOLUTION
C THE PROBLEM. INDIA AND FRG (REPRESENTING EC-9)
AVE BEEN KEPT APPRISED OF OUR DISCUSSIONS
. A DRAFT DECISION (DATAFAXED) TO BE TAKEN BY THE SPECIAL
OLITICAL COMMITTEE (SPC) HAS BEEN AGREED UPON BY THE
ARTICIPANTS IN THE INFORMAL NEGOTIATIONS, SUBJECT
C CONCURRENCE OF THEIR RESPECTIVE CAPITALS. WE THINK
EFERRAL OF THE MATTER TO THE OUTERSPACE COMMITTEE (OSC)
ITHOUT A PREORDAINED MANDATE AS TO WHAT ACTION IS TO
E TAKEN, PROVIDES THE FLEXIBILITY THE OSC NEEDS TO TAKE
HATEVER ACTION IT DEEMS APPROPRIATE. IT WILL ALSO
EVIATE THE NEED TO VOTE ON A RESOLUTION (AND GAVELE
NCLASSIFIED
NCLASSIFIED
AGE 02   USUN N 05603 040739Z
N THE RESULTS).
. IF THE PARTICIPANTS ARE ABLE TO CONFIRM AGREEMENT ON
HE DRAFT DECISION, THE SPC WILL BRING THE MATTER UP FOR
CTION DURING THE WEEK OF 4 DECEMBER.
. ACTION REQUESTED: THAT THE DEPARTMENT APPROVE THE
RAFT DECISION AND/OR PROVIDE THE MISSION WITH APPROPRIATE
NSTRUCTIONS. LEONARD
NCLASSIFIED

DEPARTMENT OF STATE A/CDC/MR
REVIEWED BY WES DATE 19 15
RDS ☐
TS AUTH. ☐ or XDS ☐ EXT. DATE ____ REASON(S) ____
ENDORSE EXISTING MARKINGS ☐
DECLASSIFIED ☐ RELEASABLE ☒
RELEASE DENIED ☐
PA or FOI EXEMPTIONS ☐

8
K

WHITE JOYCE A   03/25/80 123820   PRINTER: LI
78 STATE 312955
                          LIMITED OFFICIAL USE
LIMITED OFFICIAL USE
PAGE 01   STATE 310955
ORIGIN IO 15
INFO   OCT-01 ARA-11 ISO-00 DOE-15 ACDA-12 CIAE-00
       DODE-20 PM-05 INR-10 L-03 NSAE-00 NASA-01 NSC-05
       SOE-02 SS-15 OES-09 H-01 PA-01 SP-02 ICA-11
       TRSY-02 CMB-01 AF-10 EA-10 EUR-12 NEA-06   160 R
DRAFTED BY IO/UNP JKWARD:LW
APPROVED BY IO/UNP:PSBRIDGES
OES:IPIKUS
L/UNA:SBOND
NASA:NMCNEIL
ARA/CAR:DPIERCE
                    ---------------279579   091922Z /45
R 091653Z DEC 78
FM SECSTATE WASHDC
TO USMISSION USUN NEW YORK
INFO AMEMBASSY BRIDGETOWN
LIMITED OFFICIAL USE STATE 310955
E.O. 12065: N/A
TAGS: UNGA, TSPA, GJ
SUBJECT: GRENADIAN UFO RESOLUTION
REF: USUN 5603 AND PREVIOUS
DEPARTMENT APPROVES DRAFT DECISION CALLING FOR REFERRAL
OF UFO ITEM TO OUTER SPACE COMMITTEE WITHOUT SPECIFIC
MANDATE TO ENGAGE IN A STUDY. THE ONLY AMENDMENT WE
WOULD LIKE IS TO CHANGE RATHER ABRUPT PHRASE "WILL PERMIT"
IN FINAL PARA TO "IS REQUESTED TO PERMIT."
CHRISTOPHER
LIMITED OFFICIAL USE
LIMITED OFFICIAL USE
PAGE 02   STATE 310955
LIMITED OFFICIAL USE

DEPARTMENT OF STATE A/CDC/MR
REVIEWED BY W E J   DATE 10/15/80
RDS ☐ or XDS ☐ EXT. DATE _____
TS AUTH. _____
ENDORSE EXISTING MARKINGS ☐
DECLASSIFIED ☐ RELEASABLE ☒
RELEASE DENIED ☐
PA or FOI EXEMPTIONS _____

CHAPTER SIX

Recovery Operations

On July 2, 1947, something crashed or landed on a ranch about 75 miles northwest of Roswell, New Mexico. At first, the Army Air Force stated to the media that they had recovered a flying disk. However, within hours the military was to change its story and announce that the object was nothing more than a weather balloon.

The testimonies of eyewitnesses, however, clearly indicate that whatever the object was, it definitely was not a weather balloon. We may never know for sure what the object truely was because the military classified the entire incident and has never permitted the files to be opened to the American public.

But this does not prove that the military established a recovery program. So, the question remained "open," for many years—because of lack of proof—as to the existence of any type of formal UFO recovery program.

In 1977 and 1978, many UFO researchers requested that the U.S. Government release whatever information it might have on a "Project Moon Dust." Most of the documents, released under the Freedom of Information Act, dealt with alleged fallen space debris—mainly fallen space debris belonging to the United States. However, one document from the Office of Air Force Intelligence raised more questions than that agency was willing to answer. Also, this document made it clear the neither Project Moon Dust nor "Operation Blue Fly" (see below) dealt with the recovery of U.S. fallen space debris. This project and operation dealt with the recovery of only two items.

These were debris of descended foreign space vehicles and objects of unknown origin. (See doc. 6-1.)

Later, in a 1973 document, the Department of State would require their embassies to use the code word "Moon Dust" when making reports of alleged fallen space debris of unknown origin. (See doc. 6-2.) The document was released to me in April 1982. On page 3 it reads: "The designator 'MOONDUST' is used in cases involving the examination of non-U.S. space objects or objects of unknown origin." As of March 1991, the State Department apparently has reclassified this document as Secret. In the documents released to me that March by the State Department, the 1973 document was identified as a classified document and not releasable.

According to the U.S. Air Force document, Project Moon Dust is a specialized aspect of the Air Force's overall material exploitation program to locate, recover, and deliver descended foreign space vehicles. We shall see, later, that this was to include "objects of unknown origin."

This same document also made mention of "Operation Blue Fly." Operation Blue Fly was established to facilitate expeditious delivery to the Foreign Technological Division (FTD) of Moon Dust other items of great technical intelligence interest. The document makes it clear that UFOs were to be considered for Blue Fly Operations. Furthermore, the document states: "These... peacetime projects all involve a potential for employment of qualified field intelligence personnel on a quick reaction basis to recover or perform field exploitation of unidentified flying objects, or known Soviet/Bloc aerospace vehicles, weapons systems, and/or residual components of such equipment."

Wanting to know more about Operation Blue Fly, I wrote to several agencies for whatever information they might have on the subject. The responses I received were interesting, to say the least. Many of the agencies stated that they did not have any information responsive to my request—only to reverse themselves, once documents were released to me by the State Department. Other agencies stated they had information, but that it was classified in the interests of national security and not releasable.

The question remained, however: Were any objects of unknown origin ever recovered? If so, was either Project Moon Dust or Operation Blue Fly involved?

The Department of State released 280 documents to me concerning Project Moon Dust on March 12, 1991. Once again, these documents dealt primarily with the recovery of U.S. space objects and several Soviet space objects. However, as a result of my request to the State Department, they uncovered 38 documents belonging to other agencies. These required the respective agencies' approval prior to their release. Some of the documents clearly showed that objects of unknown origin were recovered.

In March 1968, the Government of Nepal recovered four objects believed to have fallen from space. One of these was a nose-cone-shaped object. The American Embassy was made aware of these objects, and was requested to assist in the efforts of the Nepalese Government in identifying the launching state so that these objects could be returned to the country or countries that had originally launched them into space.

The State Department documents dealing with this case were classified at a low level. However, we find that the Defense Intelligence Agency (DIA) documents were classified at the higher level of at least Secret. (See docs. 6-3 and 6-4.) Furthermore, the DIA did not wish to give out any information on this case. A memorandum for record on one of the DIA documents states:

> M/R: By ref a, [censored]... advised sequence [censored]... in obtaining MOON DUST specimens, advised film of nose cone photographed by DATT on 19 July forwarded unprocessed to DIACO-2B, and requested copies of prints of film for [censored]... as well as guidance as to what DATT can tell [censored]... as to identity of object photographed. By ref b, [censored]... requested permission to retransmit ref a [censored]... . By ref c, FTD requested FTD team [censored]... see items in possession [censored]... or to courier these items back to [censored]... and further requested [censored]... to attempt to obtain results of [censored]... . By ref e, [censored]... stresses need to protect our knowledge of [censored]... this matter, and state we cannot approach [censored]... on any of the objects which [censored]... had in their possession. MSG above coordinated with DIACO-D in draft. (See docs. 6-5, 6-6, 6-7, and 6-8.)

If these objects were of American origin, does it not stand to reason that NASA would have been more involved than the DIA or the Air Force's "FTD team"?

As we can see from the above example, the documents released by the DIA are heavily censored. Neither the Department of State nor the DIA has ever informed the Government of Nepal what these objects were. In fact, that bit of information remains classified in the interests of national security to this very day, as do several other such cases.

What could be so sensitive about space junk that it must remain protected after twenty-three years of classification? What is the American Intelligence Community trying to hide in cases such as the one above?

Another item of interest among the DIA documents was one dealing with an alleged satellite recovered in Sudan on August 3, 1967. According to this document:

> A satellite, cube shaped, weighing approximately three tons discovered 3 August, 50 miles from Kutum 1425N 2460E. Satellite described as made of soft metal presumably light aluminium in oblong cubes measuring two inches by one inch tightly fastened together and covered by a silky material. Nationality not identified as no inscriptions evident on outer surface. Local authorities in El Fasher have photographs and with difficulty cut samples. (See docs. 6-9 and 6-10.)

Once again, the DIA would not or could not identify the nationality of this object, for it too is classified in the interests of national security. This case is over twenty-four years old.

★★★

The documents mentioned above were documents released by the DIA after they were discovered within the Department of State files. The DIA considers the documents within their own files— concerning Project Moon Dust and Operation Blue Fly—to be a matter of national security and not releasable. They remain classified, at least Secret, to this very day.

It should be noted here that since my initial request to the State Department for Moon Dust and Blue Fly information, the State Department seems to have misplaced my request and has no record of it. Therefore, other documents that required coordination between agencies are bogged down in this frustrating lengthy process and, as you have seen, are usually not released or even acknowledged.

In December 1989, I asked the U.S. Air Force for any information they might have on Project Moon Dust and Operation Blue Fly. Both the offices of the Secretary of the Air Force and the Air Force Intelligence Agency responded in January 1990 that they did not have any information responsive to my request. (See docs. 6-11 and 6-12.) However, in a letter dated May 3, 1990, the Air Force Intelligence Agency confirmed they had two such documents. They also stated that these documents were classified in the interests of national security and not releasable.

I appealed the Air Force's decision not to release these documents on May 18, 1990. (See doc. 6-13.) Then, in a letter from the Air Force's Litigation Division dated July 2, 1990, I was informed:

> Because of the requirement of conducting a classification review in your case, it will necessarily take more time to complete the appeal review process. (See doc. 6-14.)

Based on this letter from the Litigation Division, I felt sure it would take the Air Force at least another two months to respond to my appeal action. This, strangely enough, was not to be the case.

The Air Force advised me, in a letter dated July 25, 1990, that my appeal had been denied because

> The information responsive to your request that is being withheld is properly classified pursuant to Executive Order and is exempt from disclosure under the Freedom of Information Act, 5 U.S.C. 552(b)(1), and Air Force Regulation 12-30, paragraph 10a. (See doc. 6-15.)

Although I did not know it at that time, the Air Force would later upgrade the classification of these documents, as well as others uncovered by the State Department, to insure that they would not be released. As a matter of fact, it was after the State Department had sent the documents that were in their possession to the Air Force for review that my FOIA file at the State Department came up missing. To be sure, the U.S. Air Force Intelligence Agency does not wish the general public to even know of the existence of Project Moon Dust and Operation Blue Fly, as we shall see later on in this chapter. Perhaps this book, along with readers' indignation, will create enough pressure so they are forced to reveal whatever it is they are hiding.

On April 3, 1991, the Air Force received my letter from the State Department along with the documents that department had that belonged to the Air Force and required Air Force review prior to release. The Air Force found it necessary to extend the time on this request twice, in order to "search for, collect, and examine those records responsive to my request." In the final analysis, the Air Force had uncovered ten documents responsive to the items I had requested. However, the Air Force was no longer calling this information classified. They had, in fact, upgraded the classification to insure that it would not become known to the general public. (See docs. 6-16 and 6-17.)

In its response, dated June 5, 1991, the Air Force was to state:

> We can neither confirm nor deny the existence or nonexistence of records responsive to your request...as any other response could reveal classified information concerning military plans, weapons, or operations under section 1.3(a)(1) of Executive Order 12356 "National Security Information." (See doc. 6-18.)

In other words, the U.S. Air Force was now stating that the President of the United States had declared this information so sensitive that the existence or nonexistence of Project Moon Dust and Operation Blue Fly could be neither confirmed nor denied. These documents, regardless of their classification, were now protected under the Special Access Program.

Actually, the Air Force misquoted the wrong section of the Executive Order. They quoted section 1.3(a)(1), which states: "Information shall be considered for classification if it concerns: (a) military plans, weapons, or operations... ." While this section would allow for the admission that the information is classified and not releasable, it does not allow for use of the neither-confirm-nor-deny statement. The only section of Executive Order 12356 that allows the use of that statement is section 3.4(f)(1), which states: "An agency shall refuse to confirm or deny the existence or nonexistence of requested information whenever the fact of its existence or nonexistence is itself classifiable under this Order."

On June 10, 1991, I appealed the Air Force's decision in their letter of June 5. The basis of my appeal was the existence of information, already in the public domain, confirming the existence of both Project Moon Dust and Operation Blue Fly. I felt this should overrule their denial because confirmation had already been made. Apparently this made sense to the Air Force, too. After more than two months of trying to decide just how to respond to my appeal letter, the Air Force decided it did not have to respond because it had already responded to my request in its July 25, 1990, response, and told me so in a letter dated August 27, 1991: "No further action is required and this matter is considered closed." (See doc. 6-19.)

This response is so laughable and absurd that it becomes an embarrassment to the Air Force when considered with the following facts:

> FACT: The Air Force Intelligence Agency did rightly consider this action separate from my FOIA Request to them on the basis of the documentation forwarded to them by the State Department, as required by Executive Order 12356, section 3.4(f)(2).

FACT: The Air Force Intelligence Agency attempted to respond to the appeal action. However, the Air Force's Litigation Division would not accept any of their responses. I was told by Major Heinz at the Litigation Office that the Air Force Intelligence Agency's response to me was returned for correction after the Litigation's review of that response.

FACT: Based upon the response of the June 5, 1991, letter, the Air Force violated Executive Order 12356, section 3.4(f)(2), which states, "When an agency receives any request for documents in its custody that were classified by another agency, it shall refer copies of the request and requested documents to the originating agency for processing and may, after consultation with the originating agency, inform the requester of the referral. In cases in which the originating agency determines in writing that a response under section 3.4(f)(1) is required, the referring agency shall respond to the requester in accordance with that section."

In short, the Air Force was not to respond to me at all based on its decision to deny my request under Executive Order 12356, section 3.4(f)(1). The referring agency in this case was the State Department, and the Air Force's denial was in fact Executive Order 12356, section 3.4(f)(1). Therefore, it should have been the Department of State that responded and not the Air Force.

I have discovered through various documents uncovered in my numerous Freedom Of Information Act requests that prior to November 1961, the United States Air Force was definitely involved in both Project Moon Dust and Operation Blue Fly. Through reviewing a letter from Air Force intelligence known as the Betz memo, I had learned that the missions of Operation Blue Fly and Project Moon Dust involved a

potential for employment of qualified field intelligence personnel on a quick reaction basis to recover or perform field exploitation of unidentified flying objects or known Soviet/Bloc aerospace vehicles, weapons systems, and/or residual components of such equipment.

If we have in fact, recovered space vehicles belonging to the then-Soviet Government, we are required by law to return them to the launching state. I do not believe we would violate that law. However, the fact remains that the U.S. Government has recovered what appears to be space vehicles, and even refuses to let the countries in which the recoveries have taken place know what these objects were or even the nationality of the objects.

Now, if we are to believe the Air Force letter to me of June 5, 1991 rebuffing my request for information, it would appear that Project Moon Dust and Operation Blue Fly are considered so sensitive that, by direction of the President of the United States, the U.S. Air Force may neither confirm nor deny their existence or nonexistence.

What could be so sensitive about these programs that the President of the United States wishes their cover-up? Has the U.S. Government violated international law and are some members of the government now trying to cover this up, or have we really recovered space vehicles from some other planet that exists in some other solar system?

Only the censors know for sure. And, of course, the President of the United States.

DEPARTMENT OF THE AIR FO E
HEADQUARTERS UNITED STATES AIR FORCE
WASHINGTON 25, D.C.

AFCIN-1E-0/Colonel Betz

(U) AFCIN Intelligence Team Personnel　　　　1 3 NOV 1961

TO   AFCIN-1E
      AFCIN-1
      IN TURN

PROBLEM:

1. (U) To provide qualified personnel for AFCIN intelligence teams.

FACTORS BEARING ON THE PROBLEM:

2.

c. In addition to their staff duty assignments, intelligence team personnel have peacetime duty functions in support of such Air Force projects as Moondust, Bluefly, and UFO, and other AFCIN directed quick reaction projects which require intelligence team operational capabilities (see Definitions).

d. Normal personnel attrition, through PCS, discharge, retirement, etc., has reduced the number of intelligence team qualified personnel below a minimum requirement, and programmed personnel losses within the next ten months will halve the current manning.

e. Personnel actions within the authority of AFRO, AFCIN and AFCIN-1E can be taken to reverse the trend toward diminishment of the intelligence team capability.

3.

4. ☁ Criteria.

a. Intelligence team personnel can perform effectively only with
an adequate background of training and experience. Inadequately
qualified personnel in such assignment would be a liability rather
than an asset to successful accomplishment of the mission.

5. ☁ Definitions.

a. Linguist: Personnel who can develop intelligence information
through interrogation and translation from Russian and/or Bloc country
languages to English.

b. Tech Man: Personnel qualified to develop intelligence information through field examination and analysis of foreign materiel,
with emphasis on the Markings Program and technical photography.

c. Ops Man: Intelligence team chief. Qualified to direct intelligence teams in gaining access to target, in exploitation of enemy
personnel and materiel, and in use of field communications equipment
for rapid reporting of intelligence information.

d. Airborne Personnel: Military trained and rated parachutists.

e. Unidentified Flying Objects (UFO): Headquarters USAF has
established a program for investigation of reliably reported unidentified flying objects within the United States. AFR 200-2 delineates
1127th collection responsibilities.

f. Blue Fly: Operation Blue Fly has been established to facilitate
expeditious delivery to FTD of Moon Dust or other items of great technical intelligence interest. AFCIN SOP for Blue Fly operations,
February 1960, provides for 1127th participation.

g. Moon Dust: As a specialized aspect of its over-all materiel
exploitation program, Headquarters USAF has established Project Moon
Dust to locate, recover and deliver descended foreign space vehicles.
ICGL #4, 25 April 1961, delineates collection responsibilities.

DISCUSSION:

6. ☁

a. Headquarters USAF (AFCIN) maintains intelligence teams as a
function of AFCIN-1E (1127th USAF Field Activities Group). Personnel
comprising such teams have normal AFCIN-1E staff duties, and their
maintenance of qualification for intelligence team employment is in
addition to their normal staff duties. For example, the Chief of
AFCIN-1E-OD, the Domestic Operations Section, additionally participates
in approximately 16 hours of training per month for intelligence team
employment. Such training includes physical training, classroom combat
intelligence training, airborne operations, field problems, etc.

b. Intelligence teams are comprised of three men each, to include a linguist, a tech man, and an ops man. All are airborne qualified. Cross-training is provided each team member in the skills of the other team members to assure a team functional capability despite casualties which may be incurred in employment.

c. Peacetime employment of AFCIN intelligence team capability is provided for in UFO investigation (AFR 200-2) and in support of Air Force Systems Command (AFSC) Foreign Technology Division (FTD) Projects Moon Dust and Blue Fly. These three peacetime projects all involve a potential for employment of qualified field intelligence personnel on a quick reaction basis to recover or perform field exploitation of unidentified flying objects, or known Soviet/Bloc aerospace vehicles, weapons systems, and/or residual components of such equipment. The intelligence team capability to gain rapid access, regardless of location, to recover or perform field exploitation, to communicate and provide intelligence reports is the only such collection capability available to AFCIN, and is vitally necessary in view of current intelligence gaps concerning Soviet/Bloc technological capabilities.

d. Wartime employment of AFCIN intelligence team capability is currently primarily geared to the CONAD/NORAD air defense mission (Atch 1). The intelligence team concept was originally developed within the Air Defense Command (ADC). The ADC Director of Intelligence was charged in 1953 with organizing the 4602d Air Intelligence Service Squadron (AISS), with a wartime mission of exploiting downed enemy "people, paper, and hardware" for intelligence information that would contribute to the air defense of the continental US, and ADC was allocated manpower for this function (ADC Regulation 24-4, 3 Jan 53, Organization and Mission of the 4602d Air Intelligence Service Squadron).

e. As an economy move, the 201 spaces of the 4602d AISS were transferred to AFCIN in July 1957 (Hq Comd General Order 46, dtd 8 Jul 57), to provide manning for peacetime AFCIN functions, but with the contingency that AFCIN would continue to maintain a capability to support CONAD/NORAD in the wartime people, paper, and hardware mission (Atchs 2 and 3). From the 194 spaces that AFCIN allocated to the 1006th AISS, activated by Hq Comd General Order #49, 2 Jul 57, this capability was provided for (Dept of AF Ltr, dtd 16 Jul 59, subj: Mission of the 1006th AISS), and the capability has been maintained to the present time, through the redesignation of the 1006th to the 1127th USAF Field Activities Group (AFCIN Policy Ltr 205-13, 12 April 1960).

f. The maintenance of the intelligence team capability over the four year period since inactivation of the 4602d AISS has been possible largely because members of the original highly select and trained 4602d personnel remained with the organization during its subsequent designations.

In addition, a minimum number of new personnel assigned to the organization and fortuitously possessing basic requisite skills, were further trained and integrated into the intelligence team program as additional duty.

g. Manning of the intelligence teams from these sources has now reached the point of diminishing returns. Only 21 qualified intelligence team personnel are now assigned, and of these approximately half are scheduled for PCS departure from the organization during the next 12 months. There is no forecast input of previously qualified personnel. There are currently five basically qualified volunteers for further training and assignment to intelligence team additional duty.

h. In an effort to augment the diminishing capability, USAF personnel assigned to organizations other than the 1127th within the Washington area who have airborne/intelligence team qualification, and/or who are former members of this organization's intelligence teams, and who have been approved by their organization of assignment and Hq USAF (AFCIN) for wartime assignment to the 1127th, have been issued appropriate orders, and participate in the peacetime training program for wartime employment. Two such personnel are attached, with no known available additional personnel.

i. The most serious immediate and forecast intelligence team shortage is in Linguists. There are now only five Russian Linguists assigned or attached, and of these only two are of native fluency, with the other three of language school capability. Four of the five, including the two of native fluency, are forecast for PCS by November 1962. Only one gain, fortunately of native fluency, is scheduled for airborne training for intelligence team qualification and assignment. Two additional Russian Linguists are forecast for assignment to the 1127th, but neither are yet intelligence team qualified or are known to be volunteers for intelligence team assignment. All intelligence team personnel are volunteers.

j. [illegible]

Eight personnel in these categories are forecast for PCS loss within the next twelve months, with an input forecast of five personnel, four of whom are presently assigned, basically qualified volunteers for airborne training, and one of whom is a forecast gain to the 1127th.

k. A sizeable number of qualified Linguists are presently assigned to [illegible] 21 bases. Many of the Linguists are either airborne rated and/ or have had intelligence team assignments to this organization in its present or former designations. Reassignment of these individuals to AFCIN-1E upon completion of their present tours is a logical method by which the current and forecast shortage could be met. A problem that would be encountered in implementing such assignment is the lack of 1127th Linguist AFSC manpower vacancies. The 1127th has only twelve Linguist AFSC manpower spaces allocated and seven of these spaces are filled with either non-Russian/Bloc country Linguists or with non-intelligence team qualified Linguists.

1. Possible solutions to the current and forecast shortage are:

(1) Basically qualified personnel currently assigned to AFCIN-1E who volunteer for further training, to include airborne training, and assignment to intelligence teams, should be given such training and assignment as additional duty to normal staff duty employment.

(2) Assignment to the 1127th of intelligence team qualified Linguists returning from overseas or completing other ZI assignments on an authorized overage basis. Such authorized overages were previously assigned to the organization and provided not only for the intelligence team capability, but for fruitful peacetime ZI employment of Linguists. Ten such personnel could be fully and effectively utilized during peacetime in duties directly in or closely allied to their AFSC's, with the intelligence team capability being an additional duty.

(3) Qualified intelligence team personnel now assigned to the 1127th could be retained beyond their normal duty tours until a similarly qualified replacement is forecast or assigned.

x. A standard AFMP and AFCIN-P policy should be the identification to AFCIN-1E of previously qualified intelligence team personnel forecast for return to the ZI from overseas assignments for assignment against AFCIN-1E forecast personnel vacancies. Latitude may be required and should be authorized in the assignment of such personnel by grade and AFSC. For example, if a 204XX vacancy is forecast within AFCIN-1E, and an intelligence team qualified 203XX is forecast available, and the 203XX is determined able to perform the staff duties required, either from personal knowledge of the individual's capabilities, or by means of an exchange of correspondence between the losing command and AFCIN-1E, authorization for assignment of the 203XX against the 204XX vacancy should be granted. It is generally true that 203's with AISS background are normally able to perform 204 duties effectively with a minimum of experience on the job. To a lesser degree, and on a selective basis, this is also true of 203's being able to perform intelligence organization 702 duties.

n. Discussion to this point has covered the intelligence team development, composition, current peacetime and wartime missions, and personnel problems. To further establish the value of the unique Air Force capability represented by the intelligence teams, their future potential for employment should be considered.

CONCLUSION:

7. ☐ There is a valid current and continuing need for the AFCIN intelligence team capability for peacetime and wartime employment. Actions necessary to maintain the capability in "cadre" strength should be immediately implemented, and actions to expand the capability should be implemented on a sound basis of personnel acquisition, training, equipping, and employment.

ACTION RECOMMENDED:

8. ☐

    a. Basically qualified personnel currently assigned to AFCIN-1E who volunteer for further training, to include airborne training, and assignment to intelligence teams, should be given such training and assignment as additional duty to normal staff duty employment. Attachment 4 is a current request for airborne training quotas for five qualified volunteers.

    b. AFCIN-1E should prepare, and submit through appropriate channels, individual justifications for the following:

        (1) Authorized overage assignment on a selective basis of an initial ten intelligence team qualified Linguists returning to the ZI from overseas assignment, with a later additional supplement in the event of AFCIN authorized expansion of cadre strength of the intelligence team capability.

        (2) Retention beyond normal duty tours of qualified intelligence team personnel now assigned to the 1127th until similarly qualified replacements are forecast or assigned.

        (3) Request for establishment of an AFPMP and AFCIN-P practice to identify to AFCIN-1E previously qualified intelligence team personnel forecast for return to the ZI from overseas assignments. Latitude should be requested by AFCIN-1E in assignment of such personnel against actual or forecast vacancies in AFSC and grade spaces in variance with those possessed by the returnees if it is established that returnees have non-AFSC skills which can be effectively utilized in the vacant spaces.

        (4) Ninety-day TDY of AFCIN intelligence team to South Viet Nam for employment in Viet Nam/Laos against USAF intelligence requirements. Experience gained in establishing logistical support and operational employment will be invaluable in developing further plans for intelligence team utilization. The team should be attached to the Air Attache, Viet Nam, and under his operational control for the period of TDY.

                         4 Atch
                         1. Excerpt, 1127 COP 1-60, re NORAD Support
                         2. Cy ltr, Gen Taylor, 23 Jan 57
                         3. Cy ltr, Gen Lewis, 4 Mar 57
                         4. Req for Airborne Tng Quotas

DEPARTMENT OF STATE
AIRGRAM

SP 16. 3a (LO)
xR SP 40

PM 2-4

REP	AF	ARA
2	5	10
EA 8	NEA 10	CU S
E	P 10	5
FBO	AID	OCT 1
SS 10		
	SCI 6	
COM	FRB	INT
TAR	TR	XMB
ARMY 3	NAVY 10	OSD 34
NSA 3	CIA 10	
NSC 6		NASA 4

Original to be Filed in _____ Decentralized Files.

HANDLING INDICATOR   SECRET

FILE DESIGNATION
A-6343

ESTED DISTRIBUTION

M
4 extra
Copies

TO : ALL AMERICAN DIPLOMATIC AND CONSULAR POSTS

DEPARTMENT OF STATE A/CDC/MR 0281
REVIEWED BY _____ DATE 5/13/82
PORTIONS DENIED AS INDICATED

P730001 0281

NO.

E/EC

JUL 26 9 47 AM '73

FROM : Department of State   DATE:

SUBJECT : Guidance for Dealing with Space Objects Which Have Returned to Earth
REF : State 114584 (DTG 132148Z Feb 68)

E. O. 11652: XGDS-2
PFOR, PINR, TSPA, UN

This message supersedes previous instructions contained reftel which have been in effect for past five years and provides revised guidance to all US personnel serving abroad in an official capacity for dealing with space objects which have survived reentry and have impacted on the earth.

All posts should ensure that appropriate personnel, especially those who serve as duty officers, are aware of the guidance contained herein.

Background: The term "space object" is not clearly defined by international treaty. However, in general it may be construed to mean any object, including component parts, which has been placed in earth orbit or beyond. In addition to functioning satellites of various types, spent boosters, shrouds, fuel tanks, rocket nozzles, ballast, dummy payloads, etc., could also be considered space objects. For the purpose of this guidance, any hardware (whether intact major components or debris) from launches which were intended to achieve earth orbit but failed to do so should be

Attachment:

Extracts from Various Space Treaties and UN Resolutions Re Space

POST ROUTING

Action	Info.	Initials
	-	

CBP-FLD-IBF

n Taken:

FORM
10-64 DS-323   SECRET   For Department Use Only
□ In   ☑ Out

ed by:
M/AE.ARTurrentine/ds   Drafting Date: 7/18/73   Phone No.: 21835   Contents and Classification Approved by: PM/AE:HGHandyside

ances:SCI/SAM-Col Bastedo IO/UNP-Mr. Buffck L/UNA-Mr. Nelson
R/RSG-Mr. Lynch DOD/ISA-Mr. Anderson DOD/USAF/INY-Mr. Foley
SA/I-Mr. Mountner CIA/FMSAC-Mr. George

248

Doc. 6-2b State Dept. Airgram, Jul 26, 1973

A-6343

SECRET   2

considered as space objects. The procedures outlined
herein would not apply to debris from surface-to-surface
missile tests, even though the missiles may have passed
through "outer space" during the ballistic phase of their
flight.

EC

In general, most space objects not specifically designed
to withstand reentry burn up in the earth's atmosphere when
they decay from orbit. However, from time to time a few
space objects do survive reentry through the atmosphere and
impact on the surface of the earth.

EC

EC

When a space object impacts on the earth and is recovered,
a number of considerations and interests must be taken into
account.

EC

EC

In deciding how to proceed in
each case, a careful assessment of these sometimes competing
interests and obligations will be made by the interested
agencies in Washington and a program of action will be designed
to produce the maximum benefit to the US.

In all space object cases, it is the responsibility of the
Department of State to insure that US interests are served --

EC

SECRET

A-6343

SECRET   3

The designator "MOODUST" is used in cases involving the examination of non-US space objects or objects of unknown origin.

In the examination of an object, the following information should be obtained and reported to the extent possible:

    1.   Pre-impact observations, direction of trajectory, number of objects observed, time of impact, characteristics of impact area, and circumstances of recovery.

    2.   Description of any injury or damage caused by the object. Provide precise details to extent possible, but in making inquiries avoid stimulating claims, especially trivial or nuisance claims.

SECRET

Doc. 6-2d State Dept. Airgram, Jul 26, 1973

SECRET   4

3. Description of any identifying marks or letters.

4. Detailed description of the physical nature and condition of the object, including actual or estimated dimensions, weight, material, construction, etc.

5. If possible, photographs of the object (preferably in color) from various angles using a dimensional reference such as a ruler or pack of cigarettes.

6. Any other information which might be helpful in identifying the object or of interest to USG.

Based on the information provided by the post, the Department of State in conjunction with other interested agencies will determine subsequent action required.

The Outer Space Treaty obligates a party to return to the launching state space objects and their component parts which return to earth on its territory. The Return of Astronauts and Objects Agreement elaborates on this obligation, requiring that a party must notify a launching state and the UN Secretary General when it learns that a space object has landed on its territory. This treaty further provides that such an object must be returned if a request for return is made by the

SECRET

A-6343

Doc. 6-2e State Dept. Airgram, Jul 26, 1973

SECRET   5

launching state. The launching state may be required to
furnish identifying data prior to return of the object.
The Outer Space Liability Convention elaborates rules
and procedures concerning liability for damage caused
by space objects and payment of compensation for such
damage. Quotes of the relevant Articles of the Outer
Space Treaty and the Astronauts and Objects Agreement
are enclosed, as is the complete text of the Liability
Convention.

ROGERS

SECRET

DEFENSE INTELLIGENCE AGENCY

Doc. 6-3 DIA Letter, Jan 4, 1990

U-1,023/RTS-1   4 January 1990

Mr. Clifford E. Stone
1421 E. Tilden
Roswell, New Mexico 88201

Dear Mr. Stone:

This responds to your request under the Freedom of Information Act dated
25 December 1989. Therein you requested information pertaining to Project
"Bluefly" and Project "Moondust". A search of DIA's systems of records
located no information pertaining to Project "Bluefly".

Upon review, it has been determined that all substantive portions of the
information pertaining to Project "Moondust" are properly classified and are
not releasable. The properly classified portions withheld are exempt from
release pursuant to 5 U.S.C. 552 (b)(1), Freedom of Information Act.
Subsection (b)(1) applies to information properly classified under the
criteria provided by Executive Order 12356. There are no reasonably
segregable portions of this exempt material.

You are advised that a requester may appeal, within 60 days, an initial
decision to withhold a record or part thereof. Should you wish to exercise
this right, you may do so by referring to case #0006-90 and addressing your
appeal to:

                    Director
                    Defense Intelligence Agency
                    ATTN: RTS-1 (FOIA)
                    Washington, D.C. 20340-3299

                              Sincerely,

                              ROBERT C. HARDZOG
                              Chief, Freedom of Information and
                                Privacy Act Staff

DEFENSE INTELLIGENCE AGENCY

WASHINGTON, D.C. 20340-

U-1,802/RTS-1   26 April 1991

Mr. Clifford E. Stone
1421 E. Tilden
Roswell, NM 88201

Doc. 6-4 DIA Letter, Apr 26, 1991

Dear Mr. Stone:

This responds to your request under the Freedom of Information Act dated
25 December 1989. Therein you requested, from the Department of State
(DOS), information pertaining to "Moondust." In processing your request,
the DOS located eight documents originated by this Agency and forwarded them
for review by letter dated 12 March 1991.

Upon review, it has been determined that some portions of six documents are
not releasable. The information withheld is exempt from release pursuant to
5 U.S.C. 552 (b)(1) and (b)(2), Freedom of Information Act. Subsection
(b)(1) applies to information properly classified under the criteria
provided by Executive Order 12356. Subsection (b)(2) applies to information
which pertains solely to the internal rules and practices of the Agency.
All reasonably segregable portions of these documents are attached hereto.

All substantive portions of the remaining two documents are not releasable.
The information withheld is exempt from release pursuant to 5 U.S.C. 552
(b)(1) and (b)(2), Freedom of Information Act. There are no reasonably
segregable portions of this exempt material.

You are advised that a requester may appeal, within 60 days, an initial
decision to withhold a record or part thereof. Should you wish to exercise
this right, you may do so by referring to case #0224-91 and addressing your
appeal to:

                    Director
                    Defense Intelligence Agency
                    ATTN: RTS-1B
                    Washington, D.C. 20340-3299

                              Sincerely,

                              ROBERT C. HARDZOG
                              Chief, Freedom of Information and
                                Privacy Act Staff

6 Enclosures a/s

71 D229
BOX 12291
NEA/INC

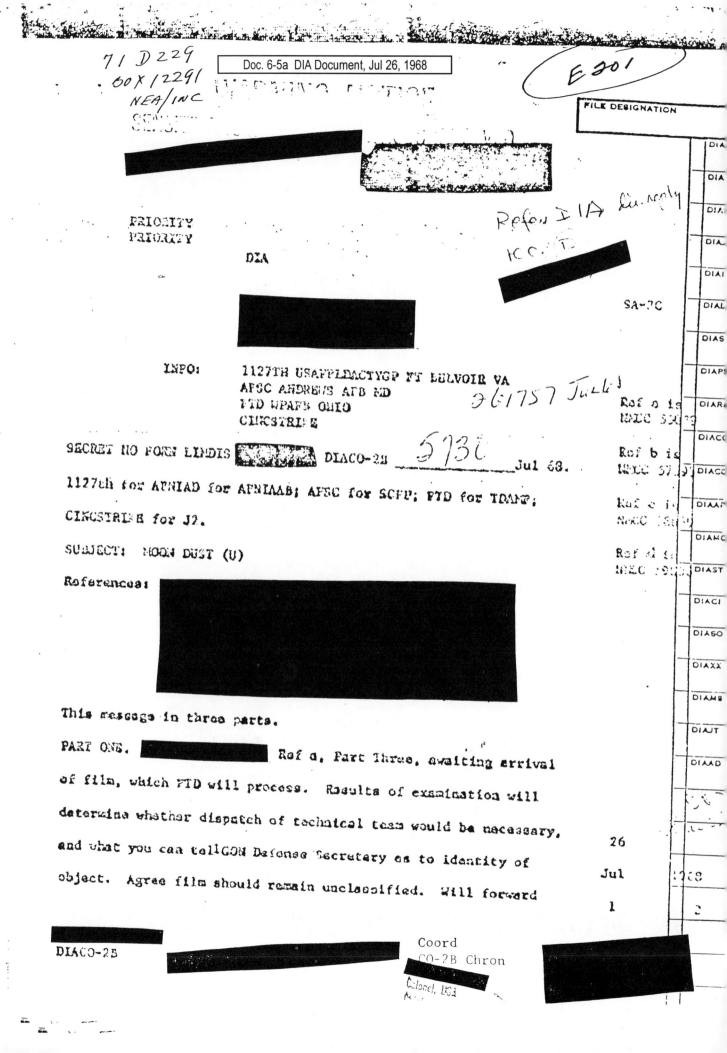

E 201

FILE DESIGNATION

PRIORITY
PRIORITY

DIA

Refer DIA direct ly
ICO/IT

INFO: 1127TH USAFFLDACTYGP FT BELVOIR VA
         AFSC ANDREWS AFB MD
         FTD WPAFB OHIO
         CINCSTRIPE   261757 Jul 68

SECRET NO FORN LIMDIS   DIACO-2B   5730   Jul 68.

1127th for AFNIAD for AFNIAAB; AFSC for SCFU; FTD for TDUNT;
CINCSTRIPE for J2.

SUBJECT: MOON DUST (U)

References:

This message in three parts.

PART ONE.   Ref a, Part Three, awaiting arrival
of film, which FTD will process. Results of examination will
determine whether dispatch of technical team would be necessary,
and what you can tellCON Defense Secretary as to identity of
object. Agree film should remain unclassified. Will forward

DIACO-2B   Coord
                                      CO-2B Chron

                                      Colonel, USA

Ref a is
DIAC 57.9
Ref b is
Ref c is
Ref d

26
Jul
1968

two copies all prints as you request.

PART TWO. ████████████████████████ Ref b, due increasing political sensitivity this case and ████████████████████ desire no retransmittal ref a and subsequent traffic at this time. Suggest ██████████ query DIACO-2B for guidance if approached by ████ in this matter.

PART THREE. ████████████████ Ref c, Part Eight, Request you take no action unless tasked by DIA. GP 1

M/R: By ref a, ██████████ advised sequence ████████████████ in obtaining MOON DUST specimens, advised film of nose cone photographed by DATT on 19 July being forwarded unprocessed to DIACO-2B, and requested copies of prints of film for ████████████████████ ██████, as well as guidance as to what DATT can tell ████ as to identity of object photographed. By ref b, ██████████████ requested permission to retransmit ref a ████████████ By ref c, FTD requested FTD team ██████████████ see items in possession ██████████ or to courier these items back to ████████ and further requested ████████ to attempt to obtain results of ████████████████ By ref e, ██████ stresses need to protect our knowledge of ████████████ this matter, and state we cannot approach ████ on any of the objects which ██████████████ had in their possession. MSG above coordinated with DIACO-D in draft.

2   2

71 D 229
BOX 12291
NEA/INC

NATIONAL MILITARY COMMAND CENTER
MESSAGE CENTER

55029

(E 20-

Doc. 6-6a DIA Teletype, Jul 23, 1968

CALL 53337
FOR NMCC/HC
SERVICE

723 0G 472

VZCZCJCS343
PP RUEOJFA
DE RUSBHT 300 2050520
ZNY SSSSS
P 230519Z JUL 68
FM USDAO AMEMBASSY KATHMANDU
TO RUEOJFA/DIA WASH DC
INFO RUEFHQA/1127TH USAF FAG FT BELVOIR VA
RUEDFIF/FTD WPAFB OHIO
RUEBRAA/AFSC ANDREWS AFB MD
RUEBREA/CINCSTRIKE MACDILL AFB FLA
DA GRNC
BT

FOR AFNIAD FOR AFNIAABJ AFSC FOR SDFPJ FTD FOR TDAHFJ CINCSTRIKE   DAO 0215 JUL 68. 1127TH
FOR J2. DIA PASS TO STATE.
SUBJECT: MOON DUST (U)
REF: DAO NEPAL SECRET MSG 0212 JUL 68.
THIS MSG IN THREE PARTS.
PART I.

(. FULL COORDINATION JUST EFFECTED ▮▮▮▮▮▮▮▮▮▮▮▮▮▮▮▮▮▮▮▮ REVEALS
HISTORY GON MAJOR ACTIONS REGARD SPCE OBJECTS AS FOLLOWS:
    A. 23 APR, RNA SHOWS TWO OBJECTS TO DATT.
    B. 20 MAY, RNA GIVES PHOTOS OF TWO OBJECTS TO DATT.
    C. 27 MAY, RNA SHOWS THREE OBJECTS TO ▮▮▮▮▮▮▮▮▮▮▮▮▮▮▮ OBJECT
NOT SHOWN TO DATT WAS OVAL SHAPE, 10 X 15 INCHES AND 2 INCHES
THICK (THIRD OBJECT).
    D. 29 MAY, RNA GIVES THREE OBJECTS TO ▮▮▮▮▮▮▮▮▮▮▮▮▮▮
AND TELLS ▮▮▮▮▮▮▮ THAT A COMPLETE NOSE CONE (FOURTH OBJECT)
EXISTS BUT CANNOT BE SEEN.
    E. 17 JUNE, RNA TELLS DATT THERE IS A COMPLETE NOSE
CONE BUT IMPOSSIBLE TO SEE.
    F. 19 JULY, DATT INVITED TO SEE FOURTH OBJECT. RNA
CINC ASKS ▮▮▮▮▮▮▮▮▮▮▮▮▮▮▮▮▮▮▮▮ THREE OBJECTS BACK ASAP.
OBJECTS NOW EXPECTED BACK IN NEPAL OA 28 JULY ▮▮▮▮▮▮▮▮
    G. 22 JULY, ▮▮▮▮▮▮▮▮▮▮▮▮▮▮ STILL HASN'T BEEN ABLE TO
SEE FOURTH OBJECT BUT RECEIVES SMALL PHOTO OF SAME.

ACTION: DIA-5 R/FILE-1(6)DJD-SE

FILE-

REPRODUCED BY /   /

22672

B.   DEFENSE SECRETARY CHITTRA BAHADUR K.C. ASKED DATT
LAST NIGHT IF ORIGIN OF OBJECT HAD BEEN DETERMINED AND IF WE
INTENDED TO SEND EXPERTS.   ANSWER TO BOTH QUESTIONS
WAS THAT DATT DID NOT YET KNOW.   FUTURE ACCESS TO FOURTH
OBJECT SHOULD BE NO PROBLEM BUT UNKNOWN AS TO FIRST THREE.
PART II.
1. _____ OFFICER TO POKHARA 15-25 JUNE TO
INVESTIGATE FALL OF OBJECTS.   ALL FOUR OBJECTS FELL NIGHT
25-26 MARCH AT THREE LOCATIONS E8358-N2816, E8402-N2815,
AND E8334-N2751 FROM BEARING OF 020 RPT 020 DEGREES.

FELL NIGHT 25-26 MARCH.   LARGE TRIANGULAR PIECE FROM
)TOR NOZZLE. CIRCULAR METAL DISK IS ELECTRICAL CONNECTOR,
OVAL PIECE (THIRD OBJECT) IS BASE OF UHF RPT UHF
AERIAL. CONFIDENT LARGE CONE (FOURTH OBJECT) MUST BE MOTOR
NOZZLE.   METAL ANALYSIS CONTINUING.
3.   BRITISH MILATT PASSING LONDON INFO GP RNA EXCEPT FOR
FACT THAT COSMOS 208 IS PHOTO RECON SINCE RUSSIANS HAVE
STATED 208 IS SCIENTIFIC SATELLITE.
PART III.
1.   IN VIEW OF ALL OF THE ABOVE, DATT NOW FEELS THAT
TECHNICAL TEAM SHOULD NOT RPT NOT BE SENT UNLESS VISUAL
EXAMINATION OF FOURTH OBJECT IS FELT ESSENTIAL.
2.   IF TEAM IS NOT RPT NOT SENT, REQUEST GUIDANCE AS TO
WHAT DATT CAN TELL GON DEFENSE SECRETARY AS TO WHAT OUR
DETERMINATION OF OBJECTS IS IN ORDER TO CLOSE CASE.
3.   RECOMMEND PRINTS REQUESTED BY PARA 2, PART II, OF
REF MSG RETAIN UNCLASSIFIED STATUS.   FILM IN REGISTERED
PACKAGE 221-68 DEPARTED KATHMANDU 22 JULY IN EMBASSY
POUCH NUMBER 09 RPT 09.
GP-1
BT

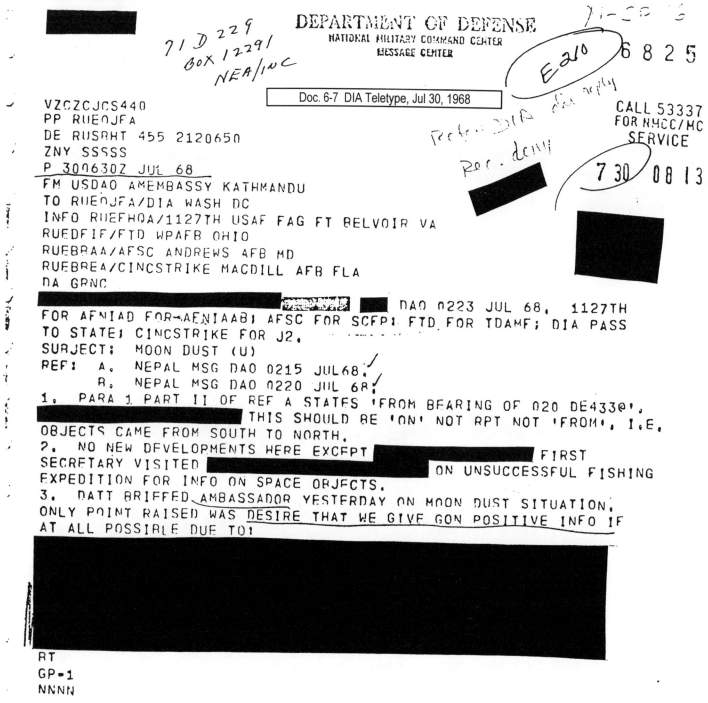

DEPARTMENT OF DEFENSE
NATIONAL MILITARY COMMAND CENTER
MESSAGE CENTER

71 D 229
BOX 1229/
NEA/INC

E210 68258

CALL 53337
FOR NMCC/MC
SERVICE

730 08132

Doc. 6-7 DIA Teletype, Jul 30, 1968

VZCZCJCS440
PP RUEOJFA
DE RUSBHT 455 2120650
ZNY SSSSS
P 300630Z JUL 68
FM USDAO AMEMBASSY KATHMANDU
TO RUEOJFA/DIA WASH DC
INFO RUEFHQA/1127TH USAF FAG FT BELVOIR VA
RUEDFIF/FTD WPAFB OHIO
RUEBRAA/AFSC ANDREWS AFB MD
RUEBREA/CINCSTRIKE MACDILL AFB FLA
DA GRNC

███████████████████████ ████ DAO 0223 JUL 68. 1127TH
FOR AFNIAD FOR AFNIAAB; AFSC FOR SCFP; FTD FOR TDAMF; DIA PASS
TO STATE; CINCSTRIKE FOR J2.
SUBJECT: MOON DUST (U)
REF: A.   NEPAL MSG DAO 0215 JUL68.
       B.   NEPAL MSG DAO 0220 JUL 68.
1.   PARA 1 PART II OF REF A STATES 'FROM BEARING OF 020 DE4330',
███████████████████ THIS SHOULD BE 'ON' NOT RPT NOT 'FROM', I.E.
OBJECTS CAME FROM SOUTH TO NORTH.
2.   NO NEW DEVELOPMENTS HERE EXCEPT ███████████████████ FIRST
SECRETARY VISITED ████████████████████████ ON UNSUCCESSFUL FISHING
EXPEDITION FOR INFO ON SPACE OBJECTS.
3.   DATT BRIEFED AMBASSADOR YESTERDAY ON MOON DUST SITUATION.
ONLY POINT RAISED WAS DESIRE THAT WE GIVE GON POSITIVE INFO IF
AT ALL POSSIBLE DUE TO:

██
██
██
██

BT
GP-1
NNNN

ACT.. DIA-5 FILE-1(6)ZIM/KS

PAGE1 OF 1

4

DEPARTMENT OF DEFENSE
NATIONAL MILITARY COMMAND CENTER
MESSAGE CENTER

71D229
BOX12291
NEA/INC

E208 59886

CALL 53337
FOR NMCC/MC
SERVICE
7 25 12 212
59886

Doc. 6-8 DIA Teletype, date unknown

VZCZCJCS789
OO RUEOJFA
DE RUSBHT 379 2071114
ZNY SSSSS
O 251112Z
FM USDAO AMEMBASSY KATHMANDU
TO RUEOJFA/DIA WASH DC
INFO RUEFHQA/1127TH USAF FAG FT B MCVOIR VA
RUEDFIF/FTD WPAFB OHIO
RUEBBAA/AFSC ANDREWS AFB MD
RUEBREA/CINCSTRIKE MACDILL AFB FLA
RUDONBA/USDAO AMEMBASSY LONDON
DA GRNC
BT
                    JHNJWEOO
L/
FMDIS/   DAO 0220 JUL 68 1127TH
FOR AFNIAN FOR AFNIAAB; AFSC FOR SCFP; FTD FOR TDAMF;
CINCSTRIKE FOR J2. DIA PASS TO STATE.
SUBJECT: MOON DUST (U)
REF: A. DAO NEPAL SECRET MSG 0215 JUL 68 (NOTAL).
      B. FTD WPAFB OHIOSDSG DTG 242020Z JUL 68.

GP-1
NNNN
ACT: DIA-5 FILE-1 (6) MAC/RP

PAGE 1 OF 1

IMMEDIATE

Department of State

TELEGRAM

E137

PAGE 0: :71:06Z

7

ACTION SCI 05

INFO AF 2:,P 04,USIA :2,CIA 04,RSC 01,NSA 02,INR 0 ,L 03,ACDA 15,

   OST 0:,NASA 04,GPM 03,NSC 10,RSR 01,/095 W

P :70915Z AUG 67
FM USDAO AMEMBASSY KHARTOUM
TO DIA WASHDC PRIORITY
INFO SECSTATE WASHDC PRIORITY

0?09 AUG 67

SUBJECT: SATELLITE FOUND IN SUDAN (U)

:. (U) LOCAL PRESS 17 AUG 67 REPORTED THAT A SATELITE, CUBE
SHAPED, WEIGHING APPROXIMATELY THREE TONS DISCOVERED 3 AUGUST
53 MILES FROM KUTUM 1425N 2460E. SATELLITE DESCRIBED AS MADE
OF SOFT METAL PRESUMABLY LIGHT ALUMINIUM IN OBLONG CUBES
MEASURING TWO INCHES BY ONE INCH TIGHTLY FASTENED TOGETHER
AND COVERED BY A SILKY MATERIAL. NATIONALITY NOT IDENTIFIED
AS NO INSCRIPTIONS EVIDENT ON OUTER SURFACE. LOCAL AUTHORITIES
IN EL FASHER HAVE PHOTOGRAPHS AND WITH DIFFICULTY CUT
SAMPLES.

2. ███ RECALL DIRECTIVE PUBLISHED ON REPORTING INFO OF THIS
NATURE BUT ALL DIRECTIVES WERE DESTROYED. REQUEST SPECIFIC
GUIDANCE OR REQIUREMENTS. ███████

(1)

SP 16

Department of State

TELEGRAM

E 276

081

PAGE 01   071744Z

43 40
ACTION INR-08

INFO   OCT-01   RSR-01   PM-05   /015 W

027641

O 071630Z OCT 70
FM USDAO/FORT LAMY
TO DIA IMMEDIATE
INFO 1127 USAF FLD ACTY GP FT BELVOIR VA IMMEDIATE
FTD WRIGHT PATTERSON AFB OHIO
CONAD ENT AFB CO
SECSTATE WASHDC

0171 OCT 70

JOINT STATE DIA MESSAGE

DIA FOR DIACO-2 AND DIAST, 1127TH FOR AFNIAAB, FTD FOR TDAMO, CONAD
FOR J2, DEPT OF STATE FOR INR AND GPM. SUBJECT: (U) MOON DUST.
DATT CALLED BY MINISTER INTERIOR TO INSPECT OBJECT FOUND NEAR LAI
(0924N-1618E) ON 1 AUGUST 1970. MINISTER SAID OBJECT FELL IN
AREA WITH THREE LOUD EXPLOSIONS AND THEN BURNED FOR FIVE DAYS.
DATT INSPECTED OBJECT WHICH IS A METAL SPHERE ABOUT 18 INCHES IN
DIAMETER WEIGHING 20-25 POUNDS. THE TWO HALVES OF THE SPHERE ARE
WELDED TOGETHER. AT EACH POLE OF SPHERE ARE PORTS WHICH HAVE
BEEN MELTED CLOSED. THE SPHERE SHOWS EVIDENCE OF BURNING AND SEVER-
AL LIGHTER STREAKS RUN THROUGH BURNED AREAS. THE OBJECT RESEM-
BLES A PRESSURIZED FUEL TANK. DATT WILL BE IN POSSESSION OF
THE OBJECT AND CAN FORWARD IF DESIRED PLEASE ADVISE.

DEPARTMENT OF THE AIR FORCE
WASHINGTON DC 20330-1000

| Doc. 6-11 U.S.A.F. Letter, Jan 11, 1990 |

OFFICE OF THE SECRETARY

Clifford E. Stone
1421 E. Tilden
Roswell, NM 88201

Dear Mr. Stone:

We are responding to your December 25, 1989 Freedom of Information Act request.

We do not have any records responsive to your request.

Sincerely,

CAROLYN W. PRICE
Assistant Freedom of
Information Manager

| Doc. 6-12 U.S.A.F. Intelligence Agency Letter, Jan 17, 1990 |

DEPARTMENT OF THE AIR FORCE
HEADQUARTERS AIR FORCE INTELLIGENCE AGENCY
FORT BELVOIR, VIRGINIA 22060-5798

1 7 JAN 1990

Mr Clifford E. Stone
1421 E. Tilden
Roswell, NM 88201

Dear Mr Stone

This is in response to your 25 December 1989 Freedom of Information request addressed to Headquarters Air Force Intelligence Service.

We have completed a thorough search of our records and found none responsive to your request.

If I can be of further assistance, please let me know.

Sincerely

JOYCE L. TRUETT
Freedom of Information Act Manager

DEPARTMENT OF THE AIR FORCE
WASHINGTON DC 20330-1000

Doc. 6-13 U.S.A.F. Letter, May 3, 1990

OFFICE OF THE SECRETARY

MAY 3 1990

Mr. Clifford E. Stone
1421 E. Tilden
Roswell, NM 88201

Dear Mr. Stone:

We are responding to your December 25, 1989 Freedom of Information Act letter.

We have two records responsive to your request. However, they are exempt from disclosure because the information contained in them is currently and properly classified.

The authority for this exemption is in the United States Code, Title 5, Section 552(b)(1) and Air Force Regulation 12-30, paragraph 10a.

The denial authority for this decision is Brigadier General Billy J. Bingham, Deputy Assistant Chief of Staff Intelligence.

Should you decide to appeal this decision, you must write to the Secretary of the Air Force within 60 calendar days from the date of this letter. You should include in the appeal your reasons for reconsideration and attach a copy of this letter. Mail it to:

    Secretary of the Air Force
    THRU: SAF/AAIS (FOIA)
    Washington, DC 20330-1000

                    Sincerely,

                    BARBARA A. CARMICHAEL
                    Freedom of Information Manager

90-0087

DEPARTMENT OF THE AIR FORCE
HEADQUARTERS UNITED STATES AIR FORCE
WASHINGTON DC 20324-1000

Doc. 6-14 U.S.A.F. Letter, Jul 2, 1990

2 JUL 1990

REPLY TO
ATTN OF: JACL

SUBJECT: Your Appeal Under the Freedom of Information Act (FOIA)

TO: Mr Clifford E. Stone
    1421 E. Tilden
    Roswell, NM 88201-7955

1. Your FOIA appeal has been received by this office. The classified nature of the subject matter of your FOIA request requires that a separate classification review be conducted in conjunction with the processing of your appeal. Such reviews are accomplished by another office within Headquarters Air Force and we have forwarded your appeal for this additional review.

2. It is the policy of our office to process FOIA appeals in the order in which they are received. Because of the requirement of conducting a classification review in your case, it will necessarily take more time to complete the appeal review process. Also, you should be aware that the office conducting this classification review has a considerable backlog of cases.

3. Once your appeal has been returned to us after its classification review, it will be completed as soon as possible. After our review, it will be sent to the Secretary of the Air Force where final action will be taken and direct notification from that office will be made to you. Thank you for your patience, and rest assured our review of your appeal will be careful and complete.

JOHN H. HEINZ, Major, USAF
Chief, FOIA/PA Branch
General Litigation Division
Office of the Judge Advocate General

DEPARTMENT OF THE AIR FORCE
WASHINGTON, D.C. 20330-1000

OFFICE OF THE SECRETARY

25 JUL 1990

Mr. Clifford E. Stone
1421 E. Tilden
Roswell, NM 88201-0920

Dear Mr. Stone:

This is in response to your letter of 18 May 1990, appealing, under the Freedom of Information Act (FOIA), the decision of the Deputy Chief of Staff Intelligence, Headquarters United States Air Force, denying your request under the Freedom of Information Act (FOIA) for information concerning projects or operations known as "Moon Dust" and "Blue Fly."

The Office of the Secretary of the Air Force has considered your appeal, and I have determined it should be denied.

The information responsive to your request that is being withheld is currently properly classified pursuant to Executive Order and is exempt from disclosure under the Freedom of Information Act, 5 U.S.C. 552(b)(1), and Air Force Regulation 12-30, paragraph 10a. Release of the information could cause identifiable damage to the national security. Thus, a significant and legitimate governmental purpose is served by its withholding, and discretionary release is not appropriate.

This letter constitutes final Air Force action on your appeal. The Freedom of Information Act, 5 U.S.C. 552, provides for judicial review of this determination.

Sincerely,

WILLIAM A. DAVIDSON
Col, USAF
Acting Deputy Administrative Assistant

DEPARTMENT OF THE AIR FORCE
WASHINGTON DC 20330-1000

OFFICE OF THE ASSISTANT SECRETARY

17 APR 1991

Mr. Clifford E. Stone
1421 E. Tilden
Roswell, NM 88201

Dear Mr. Stone:

We received your December 25, 1989, Freedom of Information Act request on April 3, 1991 from the Department of State.

To process your request properly, we find a time extension is necessary because we need to search for, collect, and examine those records you requested.

A response will be sent to you not later than May 1, 1991.

Sincerely,

CAROLYN W. PRICE
Freedom of Information Manager

DEPARTMENT OF THE AIR FORCE
WASHINGTON DC 20330-1000

1 MAY 1991

OFFICE OF THE SECRETARY

Mr. Clifford E. Stone
1421 E. Tilden
Roswell, NM 88201

Dear Mr. Stone:

This is an interim response to our letter of April 17, 1991.

We find that additional time is necessary to search for, collect, and examine those records you requested.

We assure you, your request is being processed as quickly as possible.

Sincerely,

CAROLYN W. PRICE
Freedom of Information Manager

DEPARTMENT OF THE AIR FORCE
HEADQUARTERS UNITED STATES AIR FORCE
WASHINGTON DC

Doc. 6-18 U.S.A.F. Letter, Jun 5, 1991

REPLY TO
ATTN OF   JACL   2 7 AUG 1991

SUBJECT   FOIA Appeal

TO   Mr. Clifford E. Stone
     1421 East Tilden
     Roswell NM 88201-7955

     This is in response to your Freedom of Information Act (FOIA)
Appeal, dated 10 June 1991, concerning Projects Blue Fly and Moon
Dust. The Secretary has already acted upon your 25 December 1989
FOIA Request, which is the subject of your present appeal, when he
denied your request for information pursuant to exemption (b)(1)
of the FOIA on 25 July 1990. Therefore, no further action is
required and this matter is considered closed.

Michael J. Barrett Jr.
MICHAEL J. BARRETT, JR.
Assoc. Chief, General Litigation Division
Office of The Judge Advocate General

Doc. 6-19 U.S.A.F. Letter, Aug 27, 1991

DEPARTMENT OF THE AIR FORCE
WASHINGTON DC 20330-1000

                                              0 6 JUN 1991

OFFICE OF THE SECRETARY

Mr. Clifford E. Stone
1421 E. Tilden
Roswell, NM 88201

Dear Mr. Stone:

     This is in response to your Freedom of Information Act
request of December 25, 1989. We can neither confirm nor deny the
existence or nonexistence of records responsive to your request
regarding "Projects or Operations known as BLUE FLY, MOON DUST,
AFCIN SOP, and ICGL#4," as any other response could reveal
classified information concerning military plans, weapons, or
operations under section 1.3(a)(1) of Executive Order 12356,
"National Security Information." Therefore, pursuant to Title 5,
United States Code, Section 552(b)(1), and Air Force Regulation
12-30, paragraph 10a, your request is denied.

     The denial authority is James R. Clapper, Jr., Major General,
Assistant Chief of Staff, Intelligence.

     You may appeal this decision by writing to the Secretary of
the Air Force within 60 days of the date of this letter. Include
in the appeal your reasons for reconsideration and attach a copy
of this letter. Address your appeal as follows:

               Secretary of the Air Force
               Thru: SAF/AAIS (FOIA)
               Washington, DC 20330-1000

                              Sincerely,

                              CAROLYN W. PRICE
                              Freedom of Information Manager

91-0359

CHAPTER SEVEN

The U.S. Air Force's Self-inflicted Wound

On September 8, 1994, the U.S. Air Force released a document entitled "Report of Air Force Research Regarding the 'Roswell Incident.'" The document, according to the Air Force, is meant to "serve as the final Air Force report related to the Roswell matter, for the General Accounting Office, or any other inquiries."

Actually the document is more of a whitewash than a cover-up. To be sure, the Air Force fell victim to its own officially sanctioned deception program concerning the "Roswell Incident," put in place more than fifty years ago. And, to be sure, the Air Force was willing to sacrifice its Top Secret Project Mogul Program to conceal the truth behind the events of the so-called Roswell Incident. (See docs. 7-1 and 7-2.)

But, why issue such a report at all? The Air Force gave this following justification for doing the report:

> During the in-briefing process with GAO, it was learned that this audit was, indeed, generated at the specific request of Congressman Steven Schiff of New Mexico. Earlier, Congressman Schiff had written to the Department of Defense Legislative Liaison Office for information on the "Roswell Incident" and had been advised that it was part of the former UFO "Project Bluebook" that had previously been turned over to NARA by the Air Force. Congressman Schiff subsequently learned from NARA that, although they did, indeed, have the "Bluebook" materials, the "Roswell Incident" was not part of

that report. Congressman Schiff, apparently perceiving that he had been "stonewalled" by the DOD, then generated the request for the aforementioned audit.

I have written to many members of Congress requesting their assistance in getting the release of information on this very subject. The Air Force, along with many other agencies, was less than totally responsive to the requests the various congressional offices made in my behalf. At times, the governmental agencies would totally ignore the questions I posed.

Some examples of the foolish government responses I received are:

> We have on record of receiving an FOIA request for documents. (Why do I need an FOIA request when I am asking for the release through a Congressional office?)

> These missions have never existed. (In this case, the Air Force was forced to reverse that statement when confronted with the evidence of the existence of those missions.)

> We cannot determine whether we were the "agency" referred to in the 15 November 1979 USAF letter. (Based on the information I had provided, they certainly could have determined if they were the agency—which, in fact, in this case they were, and they knew it.)

The Air Force, among other governmental agencies, has "stonewalled" other members of Congress whenever those members have asked about the same subject matter. In the case of Congressman Schiff, however, he was able to see through this, got angry, and demanded straight answers. Congressman Schiff continued to be "stonewalled," this time, by the DOD.

The Air Force Statement that "During the end briefing process with GAO, it was learned that this audit was indeed generated at the specific request of Congressman Schiff" was an effort to punish Congressman Schiff politically for asking an embarrassing question on a subject the Air Force would like to see go away. That the Air Force identified Schiff in their report was a deliberate effort on their part to discredit and harm him politically for probing into areas the Air Force preferred to keep out of the public's eye. But I have always believed that far too many political leaders dodged hard questions out of fear of this type of retribution. For this reason, I believe Congressman Schiff should be commended for his efforts in seeking out the truth.

In addition, I feel that it should be pointed out that Schiff did not ask the Air Force for documents "proving" UFOs were something extraterrestrial. All he was asking for was documents relating to the Roswell Incident, in order to ascertain what exactly the object recovered was! To be sure, Schiff's requests to the Air Force and DOD should not have even been considered to have anything to do with the UFO phenomenon.

The Air Force report concluded that, once again, the object found was "most likely" a balloon—this time, a Project Mogul balloon train. To be precise, Flight #4 of the Project Mogul balloon trains.

Let's look closely at what is wrong with this conclusion, based on the known facts of the case. The Roswell legend begins with an official news release on July 8, 1947. That release reads as follows:

> The many rumors regarding the
> flying discs became a reality yester-
> day when the intelligence office of
> the 509th Bomb Group of the
> Eighth Air Force, Roswell Army Air

Field, was fortunate enough to gain possession of a disc through the cooperation of one of the local ranchers and the Sheriff's office of Chaves County.

> The object landed on a ranch near Roswell sometime last week. Not having phone facilities, the rancher stored the disc until such time as he was able to contact the Sheriff's office, who in turn notified Major Jesse A. Marcel, of the 509th Bomb Group Intelligence office.

The Air Force report admits that they failed to "locate any documented evidence as to why that statement... was made." The Air Force report further states: "... it seems that there was over-reaction by Colonel Blanchard and Major Marcel, in originally reporting that a 'flying disc' had been recovered when, at that time, nobody for sure knew what that term meant since it had only been in use for a couple of weeks."

Also, the report makes it clear that the descriptions given by most of the witnesses, "actually described materials that sounded suspiciously like wreckage from balloons."

Furthermore, the report quoted the July 8, 1947, FBI document, which stated in the Air Force report:

> The disc is hexagonal in shape and
> was suspended from a balloon was
> approximately twenty feet in diam-
> eter...the object found resembles a
> high altitude weather balloon with
> a radar reflector...disc and balloon
> being transported.

All the above would seem to be supportive of the Air Force's report. However, if one looks at the whole picture and not just at what the Air Force wishes to reflect in its report, an entirely different conclusion emerges.

The Air Force report states:

> ...there was no physical difference
> in the radar targets and the neo-

prene balloons (other than the numbers and configuration) between Mogul balloons and normal weather balloons.

If this is the case, why would Colonel Blanchard and Major Marcel be fooled by material that made up an everyday weather balloon? Sure, in a Mogul balloon there might be much more of this material than what goes into a normal weather balloon. However, both Blanchard and Marcel were quite familiar with weather balloon devices and surely would not have been fooled by the material found, even if it appeared that there was much more of the material than what would normally go into a normal weather balloon device. What's more, there were personnel stationed at Roswell Army Air Field who could have readily identified the recovered object as some type of balloon device, even if they were not aware of the existence of Project Mogul.

They found something that, to them, was highly unusual and could not be identified as any balloon device. They believed the material recovered did, if fact, have something to do with the flying disc phenomenon being reported at that time. For this reason, they decided not to release any details concerning the recovered material until after Air Force Intelligence had had a look at the material.

I would also suggest that the Air Force had already come up with a definition of what an Unidentified Flying Object or Flying Disc was, and that the definition went something like this: any airborne object which by performance, aerodynamic characteristics, or unusual features does not conform to any presently known aircraft or missile type, or which cannot be positively identified as a familiar object.

While it is true that the witnesses have given descriptions that seem to fit a weather or Mogul balloon device, these descriptions are not what made the witnesses believe the material was mysterious. It was the strange properties of the material: It could not be bent; you could not put dents in it; it would

not tear; it could not be cut; and it would not burn. All of these characteristics are uncharacteristic of any balloon device, Project Mogul or otherwise.

The Air Force report makes the point that even the FBI teletype of July 8, 1947, stated: "The object found resembles a high altitude weather balloon with a radar reflector." However, the report omitted another key part of that teletype which states, "But that telephonic conversation between their office [Eighth Air Force Headquarters] and Wright Field HAD NOT BORNE OUT THIS BELIEF."

After the object was identified as a balloon, why wasn't the FBI officially notified, so that they could close out the case in their records? Remember, according to the July 8 teletype, they too were left with the impression that the object was something more than a balloon. We can see this confusion by reviewing the language used in the teletype stating that the object "resembles" a weather balloon and not definitively indicating that it was a weather balloon.

Furthermore, the photographs that appeared in newspapers were not of materials consistent with that of a Project Mogul balloon train. The materials that appeared in the newspaper photographs were nothing more than a weather balloon and a RAWIN target. In the Air Force report, none other than Major Irving Newton (USAF, Ret.) states this being the case. Major Newton indicates in the Air Force report: "What I know to be true, that is, the material I saw in General Ramey's office was the remains of a balloon and a RAWIN target."

In short, the object in the photographs is a complete, torn-up weather balloon with a RAWIN target device and not what one would expect to see if the material was from a downed Project Mogul balloon train or any other balloon device, being exposed to the elements of weather, that had been in a New Mexico field for several weeks, let alone several days.

Assuming that the object found was a Project Mogul balloon train, why wasn't

Professor Moore's group notified of this find at the time, so that his group could have properly identified the object as Mogul Balloon Flight #4? Remember, to this very day the official records show Flight #4 as "unrecovered." With Project Mogul being, at the time, an important and Top Secret project, why wasn't this action carried out? It was important to recover as many of the Mogul balloons as possible in order to gather the data from them so as to justify both the program's existence and its high classification. Something here doesn't make sense.

The Air Force report takes into account several news stories that appeared during the time of the alleged "Roswell Incident" to support their conclusion that the object was actually a Mogul balloon. These news stories are: the July 8, 1947, *Roswell Daily Record*'s report, "RAAF Captures Flying Saucer on Ranch in Roswell Region"; the July 9, 1947, *Roswell Daily Record*'s stories entitled "Ramey Empties Roswell Saucer" and "Harassed Rancher Who Located 'Saucer' Sorry He Told About It"; and an article published in the *Alamogordo News*, July 10, 1947, concerning multiple balloons and targets.

In the July 8 article it is made clear that the object "landed on a ranch near Roswell sometime last week." This would seem to indicate that the object was found by the rancher some time during the first week of July 1947. However, in the July 9 article the rancher states that he found the material on June 14 and picked some of it up on July 4 to take to town. In the same July 9 edition of the *Roswell Daily Record*, the story was dismissing the object as a weather balloon and radar target device.

What the Air Force report doesn't say is that the rancher was escorted by military personnel to give the story that appeared in the July 9 article. Also, the rancher stated in that article, "I am sure what I found was not any weather observation balloon." The rancher was quite familiar with weather balloons, having found two on the ranch prior to this event. Also, the description of the

object changed in this article to conform with a balloon that had been exposed to the weather for some time. The description given in this article is not indicative of the balloon photographs that appeared with the General Ramey article. Furthermore, changing the date of the find from the first week of July to June 14, 1947, would be important to support any belief that the object was a balloon—in particular, Flight #4 of the Project Mogul balloon trains. Again, something here doesn't make sense.

The Air Force report has this to say about the *Alamogordo News* article of July 10:

> However, on July 10, 1947, following the Ramey press conference, the *Alamogordo News* published an article with photographs demonstrating multiple balloons and targets at the same location as the NYU group operated from at Alamogordo AAF. Professor Moore expressed surprise at seeing this, since his was the only balloon test group in the area. He stated, "It appears that there was some type of umbrella cover story to protect our work with Mogul."

At the time this article was released, Project Mogul was a Top Secret project. Who released the story and for what reason? Why release such a story at the very location of a Top Secret government project and run the risk of drawing attention to that project? Could it be that the story was released and the Army Air Force was willing to compromise the Top Secret Mogul project in order to create some type of umbrella cover story to protect another event considered far more sensitive than Project Mogul?

★★★

After the Ramey press conference, many of the daily newspapers were not "buying" the balloon story. For this reason, I believe the Army Air Force made a conscious decision to release a story on Project Mogul so that the events in Roswell could be supported as simply a balloon. I also believe that for this reason the Army Air Force convinced the rancher to change the date of the discovery of the object from the first week of July to June 14, thereby supporting the story, even more, that the object was nothing more than Project Mogul Flight #4. By taking these actions the Army Air Force had put in place an officially sanctioned deception program to confuse and defuse any reporter who would have "gone after" the story, being convinced that the object was *not* a balloon. Sadly, I believe the Air Force fell victim to its own deception program with the release of its report some fifty years ago.

The Air Force report could not overlook the fact that many people came forth, permitting their names to be used and telling their stories, which did not support the contention that the object was a balloon of any type. The Air Force report had this to say about these witnesses: "Persons who have come forward and provided their names and made claims may have, in good faith but in the 'fog of time,' misinterpreted past events."

However, the Air Force did not even consider this a possibility when it came to their own witnesses (those supportive of the conclusion that the object was a balloon). To be sure, if one's testimony supported the Air Force position, one's thinking was intact. However, if the witness's testimony did not support the Air Force conclusion, then that person's thinking was clouded by the "fog of time," according to the Air Force report.

The Air Force, knowing that the testimony of several key witnesses would more than likely not support the balloon conclusion, chose not to question those individuals— individuals such as General Arthur Exon and Colonel Thomas DuBose, to name a few.

While I firmly believe that the Air Force set out to prove the "Roswell Incident" was merely a balloon, I cannot forget the self-serving words of an army colonel. (In this case too, it was important that a conclu-

sion be drawn that supported the U.S. Government's position and not necessarily the right conclusion.) Those convenient words were: "Witnesses sometimes make conflicting statements to different investigators. Honest men can and may reach different conclusions based on identical evidence."

As for possible classified records, the Air Force "reviewed appropriate classified records for any tie-in to this matter [the Roswell Incident]." This is what the Air Force report had to say about these records:

> With regards to highly classified records, it should be noted that any programs that employ enhanced security measures or controls are known as a Special Access Programs (SAPs). The authority for such programs comes from Executive Order 12356 and flows from the Department of Defense to the Services via DOD Directive 5205.7. These programs are implemented in the Air Force by Policy Directive 16-7, and Air Force Instruction 16-701. These directives contain detailed requirements for controlling and reporting, in very strict manner, all SAPs. This includes a report from the Secretary of the Air Force to the Secretary of Defense (and ultimately to Congress) on all SAPs submitted for approval, and a certification that there are no "SAP-like" programs being operated.

This statement is true in that this is the way SAP-like programs are supposed to work. However, I have yet to find that member of Congress who will admit full knowledge of the Iran–Contra Affair. Also, the National Security Agency (NSA), Central Intelligence Agency (CIA), and most of the other agencies that make up the intelligence network have used SAP-like programs to cover up activities they wished to conceal from Congress.

The Air Force report made no mention of the Air Force's so-called "Blue

Room," "Project Moon Dust," or "Operation Blue Fly." All of these missions, in my opinion, would play an important role in any search for the truth as to what the Roswell object really was. Yet, when I asked the Air Force office responsible for the Air Force Report about these missions, the response I received was, "I never heard of those [Blue Room, Project Moon Dust, and Operation Blue Fly] operations."

Senator Barry Goldwater once asked General Curtis LeMay if he could have a look at what was in the Blue Room located at Wright-Patterson Air Force Base. General LeMay's response was, "Not only can't you get into it, but don't you ever mention it to me again." I have letters from Senator Barry Goldwater admitting that he was, in fact, denied access to this facility.

The peacetime missions of both Project Moon Dust and Operation Blue Fly deal with the recovery of, among other things, "objects of unknown origin." The Air Force's response to me, in regard to Freedom of Information requests for information on these two missions, was to neither confirm nor deny their existence. This type of response is indicative of a SAPs-like program. Yet, according to the Air Force, the records pertaining to these missions were never checked for any possible tie-in with the recovery of "objects of unknown origin." Furthermore, documents released by agencies such as the Defense Intelligence Agency and the State Department clearly indicate that UFO reports were collected from foreign countries under the codename "Moon Dust."

I asked for and received the assistance of Senator Jeff Bingaman's office in an effort to get the Air Force's records on Project Moon Dust and Operation Blue Fly released. The Air Force's first response to the Senator's office was: "... these missions have never existed." However, I provided the Senator's office with some twenty-three documents clearly showing these "missions" did, in fact, exist. The next request from the Senator's office was provided with a watered-

down response in an effort to convince him that these missions were never used—although they did, at one time, exist.

Once again, the documents released by other agencies clearly indicate these missions were used and the watered-down statement provided to the Senator's office were nothing more than an effort on the part of the Air Force to conceal this fact.

Of course, the Air Force, realizing that people like myself would know that it did not check all its records, had this to say:

It is anticipated that detractors from this effort will complain that 'they did not search record group x, box y, or reel z, etc.; that's where the real records are!' Such complaints are unavoidable and there is no possible way that the millions of records under Air Force control could be searched page by page. The team endeavored to make logical searches in those places where records would most likely be found.

To this charge, all I can say is this: Had the Air Force been more concerned about being as fully open as possible when "detractors" such as myself asked them questions about such things as the Blue Room, Project Moon Dust, Operation Blue Fly, etc., they would not be caught in this embarassing dilemma.

Remember, the Air Force has always insisted that there was nothing classifiable about UFOs. However, when questioned about UFOs, in connection with the abovementioned missions, the Air Force response was: "... these missions have never existed"; "... the information necessary to respond to your request is properly classified"; or "... we may neither deny nor confirm the existence or nonexistence of records responsive to your request."

Such "complaints" are avoidable in our form of government. It's called being open and honest with the American people they are supposed to be serving—something the Air Force, among other governmental agencies, has yet to learn.

The Air Force report had this to say about early consideration of extraterrestrial spacecraft:

> All the records, however, indicated that the focus of concern was not on aliens, hostile or otherwise, but on the Soviet Union. Many documents from that period speak to the possibility of developmental secret Soviet aircraft overflying U.S. airspace. This, of course, was of major concern to the fledgling USAF, whose job it was to protect these same skies.

But first, where did the Air Force get the idea that Congressman Schiff was looking for "proof" of extraterrestrial spacecraft? Schiff and his staff have made it quite clear that they were looking for records (documents) as to what the Roswell object really was—nothing more, nothing less. The one thing that Congressman Schiff and his staff was *not* looking for was evidence of "extraterrestrial spacecraft." Secondly, the Air Force's statement can only be made out of its ignorance of its early history in dealing with the flying disc phenomenon.

In July or August 1948, the Air Technical Intelligence Center did a Top Secret study of the flying disc phenomenon. The study was in the form of an "Estimate of the Situation"—the situation being flying discs, and the assumption being that they, the flying discs, were interplanetary. However, the late, General Hoyt S. Vandenberg would not "buy" the possibility of interplanetary spacecraft, and he ordered that some highly unusual actions be taken with regard to this report.

General Vandenberg directed that the report be declassified and then destroyed. If a report is classified, you may order its destruction without declassifying it. However, you must complete a documented record of its destruction. If a document is declassified, then there exists no reason for its ordered destruction—it would be considered not to have any national security value. So, why did Vandenberg order this document to first be declassified and then destroyed?

Could it be that he took this action in order to insure that the American public would never see or even know of the existence of this document? If you order a classified document destroyed, there is a documented record of its existence and destruction. However, if you order a document to be declassified and then destroyed, no such record exists. I think General Vandenberg's actions speak for themself.

★★★

In conclusion, I believe the Air Force set out in advance to "prove" that the Roswell object was nothing more than a balloon device. During their research, the Air Force came across the "evidence" that was planted fifty years ago as part of an officially sanctioned deception and disinformation program to conceal the events that occurred at Roswell, New Mexico, in July 1947; and even then, the best the Air Force could come up with was that the object was "most likely" Flight #4 of Project Mogul.

Furthermore, I believe the Air Force at that time was willing to sacrifice Project Mogul to further conceal the events that had occurred in Roswell. Remember, after the release of the story that appeared in the *Alamogordo News* on July 10, 1947, the security of Project Mogul had effectively been both breached and compromised.

I believe history will record the following about the so-called "Roswell Incident": Whatever was found on that day in July 1947 will never be fully known. The object will be whatever you wish it to be. I further believe that no government on the face of this Earth will ever be honest enough to tell its people the whole truth about UFOs. Not even the United States Government, as much as I wish they would.

We now know that most world governments have highly classified records dealing with UFO sightings and that many of these sightings/incidents cannot be readily explained away, even after careful analysis. We also know that much of this information is shared among the many countries involved. So, one might ask, if this is truly the case: Who is the information being kept from—and why?

The Air Force will never be in a position of explaining away many of the reported UFO sightings/incidents, even with the many advances of modern-day science. Many incidents of Unidentified Flying Objects still continue to be reported from around the world, and science has yet to evolve to that point of perfection that might solve and answer the many questions the phenomenon invokes.

The greatest mystery of the twentieth century will, in my opinion, continue to be the greatest mystery of the twenty-first!

Doc. 7-1 U.S.A.F. Memorandum Concerning
Release of Roswell Report, Sept 8, 1994

MEMORANDUM FOR CORRESPONDENTS

No. 235-M
Sept. 8, 1994

Secretary of the Air Force Sheila E. Widnall today announced the completion of an Air Force study to locate records that would explain an alleged 1947 UFO incident. Pro-UFO researchers claim an extraterrestrial spacecraft and its alien occupants were recovered near Roswell, N.M., in July 1947 and the fact was kept from the public.

At the request of Congressman Steven H. Schiff (R-NM), the General Accounting Office in February 1994 initiated an audit to locate all records related to the Roswell incident and to determine if such records were properly handled. The GAO audit entitled "Records Management Procedures Dealing With Weather Balloon, Unknown Aircraft, and Similar Crash Incidents" is not yet complete.

The GAO audit involved a number of government agencies but focused on the Air Force. In support of the GAO effort, the Air Force initiated a systematic search of current Air Force offices as well as numerous archives and records centers that might help explain the incident. Air Force officials also interviewed a number of persons who might have had knowledge of the events. Prior to the interviews, Secretary Widnall released those persons from any previous security obligations that might have restricted their statements.

The Air Force research did not locate or develop any information that the "Roswell Incident" was a UFO event nor was there any indication of a "cover-up" by the Air Force. Information obtained through exhaustive records searches and interviews indicated the material recovered near Roswell was consistent with a balloon device of the type used in a then-classified project. No records indicated or even hinted at the recovery of "alien" bodies or extraterrestrial materials.

All documentation related to this case is now declassified and the information is in the public domain. All documentation has been turned over to the Air Force Historian. The Air Force report without attachments may be obtained by contacting Major Thurston, Air Force Public Affairs, (703) 695-0640. The report with all 33 attachments is available for review in the Pentagon Library in Room 1A518.

-END-

REPORT OF AIR FORCE RESEARCH
REGARDING THE
"ROSWELL INCIDENT"

July 1994

REPORT OF AIR FORCE RESEARCH REGARDING THE "ROSWELL INCIDENT"

EXECUTIVE SUMMARY

The "Roswell Incident" refers to an event that supposedly happened in July, 1947, wherein the Army Air Forces (AAF) allegedly recovered remains of a crashed "flying disc" near Roswell, New Mexico. In February, 1994, the General Accounting Office (GAO), acting on the request of a New Mexico Congressman, initiated an audit to attempt to locate records of such an incident and to determine if records regarding it were properly handled. Although the GAO effort was to look at a number of government agencies, the apparent focus was on the Air Force. SAF/AAZ , as the Central Point of Contact for the GAO in this matter, initiated a systematic search of current Air Force offices as well as numerous archives and records centers that might help explain this matter. Research revealed that the "Roswell Incident" was not even considered a UFO event until the 1978-1980 time frame. Prior to that, the incident was dismissed because the AAF originally identified the debris recovered as being that of a weather balloon. Subsequently, various authors wrote a number of books claiming that, not only was debris from an alien spacecraft recovered, but also the bodies of the craft's alien occupants. These claims continue to evolve today and the Air Force is now routinely accused of engaging in a "cover-up" of this supposed event.

The research located no records at existing Air Force offices that indicated any "cover-up" by the USAF or any indication of such a recovery. Consequently, efforts were intensified by Air Force researchers at numerous locations where records for the period in question were stored. The records reviewed did not reveal any increase in operations, security, or any other activity in July, 1947, that indicated any such unusual event may have occurred. Records were located and thoroughly explored concerning a then-TOP SECRET balloon project, designed to attempt to monitor Soviet nuclear tests, known as Project Mogul. Additionally, several surviving project personnel were located and interviewed, as was the only surviving person who recovered debris from the original Roswell site in 1947, and the former officer who initially identified the wreckage as a balloon. Comparison of all information developed or obtained indicated that the material recovered near Roswell was consistent with a balloon device and most likely from one of the Mogul balloons that had not been previously recovered. Air Force research efforts did not disclose any records of the recovery of any "alien" bodies or extraterrestrial materials.

INTRODUCTION

Air Force involvement in the alleged UFO-related incident popularly known as the "Roswell Incident" began as the result of a January 14, 1994, Washington Post article (Atch 1) which announced Congressman Steven Schiff's intent to initiate a General Accounting Office (GAO) effort to resolve this controversial matter. Having previously been involved in numerous Freedom of Information Act (FOIA) and Congressional requests on "unusual aircraft," to include Unidentified Flying Objects (UFOs), The Director, Security and Special Program Oversight, Office of the Secretary of the Air Force, (SAF/AAZ) believed the Air Force would become involved in any GAO effort involving this subject.

Thus, in late January, 1994, SAF/AAZ directed its research/declassification team, SAF/AAZD, to attempt to locate any official records relative to this matter. These initial research efforts focused on records at the Air Force Historical Research Agency (AFHRA), Maxwell AFB, AL, the Air Force Safety Agency (AFSA) at Kirtland AFB, NM and the National Archives and Records Administration (NARA).

On February 15, 1994, the GAO officially notified Secretary of Defense William J. Perry that, it was initiating an audit of the Department of Defense (DoD) policies and procedures for acquiring, classifying, retaining, and disposing of official government documents dealing with weather balloon, aircraft, and similar crash incidents (Atch 2). This notification was subsequently passed to the Department of Defense Inspector General who in turn officially notified the Secretaries of the Services and other affected parties of the audit in a February 23, 1994, memo (Atch 3). This memorandum indicated that the "GAO is anxious to respond to Representative Schiff's request and to dispel any concerns that the DoD is being unresponsive." These were the first official US Government documents that indicated that the purpose of the GAO was to review "crash incidents involving weather balloons and unknown aircraft, such as UFOs and foreign aircraft, and (2) the facts involving the reported crash of an UFO in 1949 (sic, 1947) at Roswell, New Mexico ... (and an) alleged DoD cover-up."

An entrance meeting of potentially concerned parties was held in the offices of the DoD Inspector General on February 28, 1994. During this meeting it was learned that, while the audit officially would be reviewing the records of a number of DoD (and possibly other Executive Branch entities), the bulk of the effort would be focused on Air Force records and systems. The audit was officially given the GAO code 701034, and entitled "Records Management Procedures Dealing With Weather Balloon, Unknown Aircraft, and Similar Crash Incidents." Although this official title appeared rather broad, there was no misunderstanding that the real purpose was to attempt to locate records and/or information on the "Roswell Incident." This incident, explained later in more detail, generally dealt with the claim that in July of 1947, the US Army Air Forces (USAAF) recovered a flying saucer and /or its alien occupants which supposedly crashed near Roswell, New Mexico. When the USAAF ultimately became the United States Air Force (USAF) in September, 1947, the USAF inherited equipment, personnel, records, policies, and procedures from the AAF. In this particular case, the Air Force also inherited the allegation that it had "covered up" the "Roswell Incident" and has continued to do so for the next 47 years.

Within the Air Force, the Office of the Administrative Assistant to the Secretary of the Air Force (SAF/AA) is responsible both for information management procedures (SAF/AAI) and security policy and oversight (SAF/AAZ). Because of this organization, SAF/AA was

2

the logical entity to assist the GAO in its audit and SAF/AAZ was officially named as the Central Point of Contact for this endeavor (Atch 4). Subsequently, the then-Administrative Assistant, Mr. Robert J. McCormick, issued a tasking memorandum dated March 1, 1994 (Atch 5), to a number of current Air Staff and Secretariat offices that might possibly have records related to such an incident if, indeed, something had actually occurred. This search for records was purposely limited to Air Force records and systems since:

(a) The Air Force had no authority to compel other agencies to review their records;

(b) The Air Force would have no way to monitor the completeness of their efforts if they did; and

(c) the overall effort was the task and responsibility of the GAO--not the Air Force.

During the in-briefing process with GAO, it was learned that this audit was, indeed, generated at the specific request of Congressman Steven Schiff of New Mexico. Earlier, Congressman Schiff had written to the Department of Defense Legislative Liaison Office for information on the "Roswell Incident" and had been advised that it was part of the former UFO "Project Bluebook" that had previously been turned over to NARA by the Air Force. Congressman Schiff subsequently learned from NARA that, although they did, indeed, have the "Bluebook" materials, the "Roswell Incident" was not part of that report. Congressman Schiff, apparently perceiving that he had been "stonewalled" by the DoD, then generated the request for the aforementioned audit.

It is within this context that the following research and assistance efforts were conducted in support of the GAO. This report is intended to stand as the final official Air Force response regarding this matter.

THE "ROSWELL INCIDENT"--WHAT WAS ORIGINALLY REPORTED IN 1947

The modern preoccupation with what ultimately came to be called Unidentified Flying Objects (UFOs) actually began in June, 1947. Although some pro-UFO researchers argue that sightings of UFOs go back to Biblical times, most researchers will not dispute that anything in UFO history can compare with the phenomenon that began in 1947. What was later characterized as "the UFO Wave of 1947" began with 16 alleged sightings that occurred between May 17 and July 12, 1947, (although some researchers claim there were as many as 800 sightings during that period). Interestingly, the "Roswell Incident" was not considered one of these 1947 events until the 1978-1980 time frame. There is no dispute, however, that something happened near Roswell in July, 1947, since it was reported in a number of contemporary newspaper articles; the most famous of which were the July 8 and July 9 editions of the Roswell Daily Record. The July 8 edition reported "RAAF Captures Flying Saucer On Ranch In Roswell Region," while the next day's edition reported, "Ramey Empties Roswell Saucer" and "Harassed Rancher Who Located 'Saucer' Sorry He Told About It."

The first story reported that the Intelligence Officer of the 509th Bomb Group, stationed at Roswell AAF, Major Jesse A. Marcel, had recovered a "flying disc" from the range lands of an unidentified rancher in the vicinity of Roswell and that the disc had been "flown to higher headquarters." That same story also reported that a Roswell couple claimed to have seen a large unidentified object fly by their home on July 2, 1947.

The July 9 edition of the paper noted that Brigadier General Roger Ramey, Commander of the Eighth Air Force at Forth Worth, Texas, stated that upon examination the debris recovered by Marcel was determined to be a weather balloon. The wreckage was described as a ."..bundle of tinfoil, broken wood beams, and rubber remnants of a balloon...." The additional story of the "harassed rancher" identified him as W.W. Brazel of Lincoln County, New Mexico. He claimed that he and his son, Vernon, found the material on June 14, 1947, when they "came upon a large area of bright wreckage made up of rubber strips, tinfoil, a rather tough paper, and sticks." He picked up some of the debris on July 4 and ."..the next day he first heard about the flying discs and wondered if what he had found might have been the remnants of one of these." Brazel subsequently went to Roswell on July 7 and contacted the Sheriff, who apparently notified Major Marcel. Major Marcel and "a man in plain clothes" then accompanied Brazel home to pick up the rest of the pieces. The article further related that Brazel thought that the material:

> ."..might have been as large as a table top. The balloon which held it up, if that is how it worked, must have been about 12 feet long, he felt, measuring the distance by the size of the room in which he sat. The rubber was smoky gray in color and scattered over an area about 200 yards in diameter. When the debris was gathered up the tinfoil, paper, tape, and sticks made a bundle about three feet long and 7 or 8 inches thick, while the rubber made a bundle about 18 or 20 inches long and about 8 inches thick. In all, he estimated, the entire lot would have weighed maybe five pounds. There was no sign of any metal in the area which might have been used for an engine and no sign of any propellers of any kind. Although at least one paper fin had been glued onto some of the tinfoil. There were no words to be found anywhere on the instrument although there were letters on some of the parts. Considerable scotch tape and some tape with flowers printed upon it had been used in the construction. No string or wire were to be found but there were some eyelets in the paper to indicate that some sort of attachment may have been used. Brazel said that he had previously found two weather balloons on the ranch, but that what he found this time did not in any way resemble either of these."

EVOLUTION OF THE EVENT FROM 1947 TO THE PRESENT

General Ramey's press conference and rancher Brazel's statement effectively ended this as a UFO-related matter until 1978, although some UFO researchers argue that there were several obtuse references to it in 1950's era literature. Roswell, for example, is not referred to in the official USAF investigation of UFOs reported in Project Bluebook or its predecessors, Project Sign and Project Grudge, which ran from 1948-1969 (which Congressman Schiff subsequently learned when he made his original inquiry).

In 1978, an article appeared in a tabloid newspaper, the National Inquirer, which reported the former intelligence officer, Marcel, claimed that he had recovered UFO debris near Roswell in 1947. Also in 1978, a UFO researcher, Stanton Friedman, met with Marcel and began investigating the claims that the material Marcel handled was from a crashed UFO. Similarly, two authors, William L. Moore and Charles Berlitz, also engaged in research which led them to publish a book, The Roswell Incident, in 1980. In this book they reported they interviewed a number of persons who claimed to have been present at Roswell in 1947 and professed to be either first or second hand witnesses to strange events that supposedly occurred. Since 1978-1980, other UFO researchers, most notably Donald Schmitt and Kevin Randle, claim to have located and interviewed even more persons with supposed knowledge of unusual happenings at Roswell. These included both civilian and former military persons.

Additionally, the Robert Stack-hosted television show "Unsolved Mysteries" devoted a large portion of one show to a "re-creation" of the supposed Roswell events. Numerous other television shows have done likewise, particularly during the last several years and a made-for-TV movie on the subject is due to be released this summer. The overall thrust of these articles, books and shows is that the "Roswell Incident" was actually the crash of a craft from another world, the US Government recovered it, and has been "covering up" this fact from the American public since 1947, using a combination of disinformation, ridicule, and threats of bodily harm, to do so. Generally, the US Air Force bears the brunt of these accusations.

From the rather benign description of the "event" and the recovery of some material as described in the original newspaper accounts, the "Roswell Incident" has since grown to mythical (if not mystical) proportions in the eyes and minds of some researchers, portions of the media and at least part of the American public. There are also now several major variations of the "Roswell story." For example, it was originally reported that there was only recovery of debris from one site. This has since grown from a minimal amount of debris recovered from a small area to airplane loads of debris from multiple huge "debris fields." Likewise, the relatively simple description of sticks, paper, tape and tinfoil has since grown to exotic metals with hieroglyphics and fiber optic-like materials. Most versions now claim that there were two crash sites where debris was recovered; and at the second site, alleged bodies of extraterrestrial aliens were supposedly retrieved. The number of these "alien bodies" recovered also varied. These claims are further complicated by the fact that UFO researchers are not in agreement among themselves as to exactly where these recovery sites were located or even the dates of the alleged crash(es).

Consistently, however, the AAF was accused of securing these sites, recovering all the material therefrom, keeping locals away, and returning the recovered wreckage (and bodies) to Roswell under extremely tight security for further processing and later exploitation.

Once back at Roswell AAF, it is generally alleged that special measures were taken to notify higher headquarters and arrangements made to have recovered materials shipped to other locations for analysis. These locations include Ft. Worth, Texas, the home of the Eighth Air Force Headquarters; possibly Sandia Base (now Kirtland AFB), New Mexico; possibly Andrews AAF, Maryland, and always to Wright Field, now known as Wright-Patterson AFB, Ohio. The latter location was the home of "T-2" which later became known as the Air Technical Intelligence Center (ATIC) and the Air Materiel Command (AMC), and would, in fact, be a logical location to study unknown materials from whatever origin. Most of the Roswell stories that contain the recovery of alien bodies also show them being shipped to Wright Field. Once the material and bodies were dispersed for further analysis and/or exploitation, the government in general, and the Army Air Forces in particular, then engaged in covering up all information relating to the alleged crash and recovery, including the use of security oaths to military persons and the use of coercion (including alleged death threats) to others. This, as theorized by some UFO researchers, has allowed the government to keep the fact that there is intelligent extraterrestrial life from the American public for 47 years. It also supposedly allowed the US Government to exploit recovered extraterrestrial materials by reverse engineering them, ultimately providing such things as fiber optic and stealth technology. The "death threats," oaths, and other forms of coercion alleged to have been meted out by the Army Air Forces personnel to keep people from talking have apparently not been very effective, as several hundred people are claimed to have come forward (without harm) with some knowledge of the "Roswell Incident" during interviews with non-government researchers and the media.

Adding some measure of credibility to the claims that have arisen since 1978 is the apparent depth of research of some of the authors and the extent of their efforts. Their claims are lessened somewhat, however, by the fact that almost all their information came from verbal reports many years after the alleged incident occurred. Many of the persons interviewed were, in fact, stationed at, or lived near Roswell during the time in question, and a number of them claim military service. Most, however, related their stories in their older years, well after the fact. In other cases, the information provided is second or third-hand, having been passed through a friend or relative after the principal had died. What is uniquely lacking in the entire exploration and exploitation of the "Roswell Incident" is official positive documentary or physical evidence of any kind that supports the claims of those who allege that something unusual happened. Conversely, there has never been any previous documentary evidence produced by those who would debunk the incident to show that something did not happen; although logic dictates that bureaucracies do not spend time documenting non-events.

SEARCH STRATEGY AND METHODOLOGY

To insure senior Air Force leadership that there were no hidden or overlooked files that might relate to the "Roswell Incident;" and to provide the GAO with the best and most complete information available, SAF/AAZ constructed a strategy based on direct tasking from the Office of the Secretary, to elicit information from those functional offices and organizations where such information might logically be contained. This included directing searches at current offices where special or unusual projects might be carried out, as well as historical organizations, archives, and records centers over which the Air Force exerted some degree of control. Researchers did not, however, go to the US Army to review historical records in areas such as missile launches from White Sands, or to the Department of Energy to determine if its forerunner, the Atomic Energy Commission, had any records of nuclear-related incidents that might have occurred at or near Roswell in 1947. To do so would have encroached on GAO's charter in this matter. What Air Force researchers did do, however, was to search for records still under Air Force control pertaining to these subject areas.

In order to determine parameters for the most productive search of records, a review was first conducted of the major works regarding the "Roswell Incident" available in the popular literature. These works included: The Roswell Incident, (1980) by William Moore and Charles Berlitz; "Crashed Saucers: Evidence in Search of Proof," (1985) by Moore; The UFO Crash at Roswell, (1991) by Kevin Randle and Donald Schmitt; The Truth About the UFO Crash at Roswell, (1994) also by Randle and Schmitt; The Roswell Report: A Historical Perspective, (1991), George M. Eberhart, Editor; "The Roswell Events," (1993) compiled by Fred Whiting; Crash at Corona (1992) by Stanton T. Friedman and Don Berliner, as well as numerous other articles written by a combination of the above and other researchers. Collectively, the above represent the "pro" UFO writers who allege that the government is engaged in a conspiracy. There are no specific books written entirely on the theme that nothing happened at Roswell. However, Curtis Peebles in Watch the Skies! (1994) discussed the development of the UFO story and growth of subsequent claims as a phenomenon. There has also been serious research as well as a number of detailed articles written by so-called "debunkers" of Roswell and other incidents, most notably Philip J. Klass who writes The Skeptical Inquirer newsletter, and Robert Todd, a private researcher. The concerns and claims of all the above authors and others were considered in conducting the USAF records search.

It was also decided, particularly after a review of the above popular literature, that no specific attempt would be made to try to refute, point by point, the numerous claims made in the various publications. Many of these claims appear to be hearsay, undocumented, taken out of context, self-serving, or otherwise dubious. Additionally, many of the above authors are not even in agreement over various claims. Most notable of the confusing and now ever-changing claims is the controversy over the date(s) of the alleged incident, the exact location(s) of the purported debris and the extent of the wreckage. Such discrepancies in claims made the search much more difficult by greatly expanding the volume of records that had to be searched.

An example of trying to deal with questionable claims is illustrated by the following example: One of the popular books mentioned that was reviewed claimed that the writers had submitted the names and serial numbers of "over two dozen" personnel stationed at Roswell in July, 1947, to the Veterans Administration and the Defense Department to confirm their military service. They then listed eleven of these persons by name and asked the question: "Why does neither the Defense Department nor the Veteran's Administration have records of any of these men when we can document that each served at Roswell Army Air Field." That claim sounded serious so SAF/AAZD was tasked to check these eleven names in the Personnel Records Center in St. Louis. Using only the names (since the authors did not list the serial numbers) the researcher quickly found records readily identifiable with eight of these persons. The other three had such common names that there could have been multiple possibilities. Interestingly, one of the listed "missing" persons had a casualty report in his records reflecting that he died in 1951, while the writers claimed to have interviewed him (or a person of the exact same name) in 1990.

While the historical document search was in progress, it was decided to attempt to locate and interview several persons identified as still living who could possibly answer questions generated by the research. This had never been officially done before, although most of the persons contacted reported that they had also been contacted in the past by some of the listed authors or other private researchers. In order to counter possible future arguments that the persons interviewed were still "covering up" material because of prior security oaths, the interviewees were provided with authorization from either the Secretary of the Air Force or the Senior Security Official of the Air Force that would officially allow discussion of classified information, if applicable, or free them from any prior restriction in discussing the matter, if such existed. Again, the focus was on interviewing persons that could address specific issues raised by research and no consideration was given to try and locate every alleged witness claimed to have been contacted by the various authors. For example, one of the interviewees thought vital to obtain an official signed, sworn statement from was Sheridan Cavitt, Lt Col, USAF (Retired) who is the last living member of the three persons universally acknowledged to have recovered material from the Foster Ranch. Others were also interviewed as information developed (discussed in detail later). Additionally, in some cases survivors of deceased persons were also contacted in an attempt to locate various records thought to have been in the custody of the deceased.

Even though Air Force research originally started in January, 1994, the first official Air Force-wide tasking was directed by the March 1, 1994, memorandum from SAF/AA, (Atch 5) and was addressed to those current Air Staff elements that would be the likely repository for any records, particularly if there was anything of an extraordinary nature involved. This meant that the search was not limited to unclassified materials, but also would include records of the highest classification and compartmentation.

The specific Air Staff/Secretariat offices queried included the following:
(a) SAF/AAI, Directorate of Information Management
(b) SAF/AQL, Directorate of Electronics and Special Programs

(c) AF/SE, Air Force Safety
(d) AF/HO, Air Force Historian
(e) AF/IN, Air Force Intelligence (including Air Force Intelligence Agency--AFIA, and the National Air Intelligence Center, NAIC)
(f) AF/XOW, Directorate of Weather
(g) (added later) The Air Force Office of Special Investigations (AFOSI)

In addition to the above Air Staff and Secretariat offices, SAF/AAZ also reviewed appropriate classified records for any tie-in to this matter. With regards to highly classified records, it should be noted that any programs that employ enhanced security measures or controls are known as a Special Access Programs (SAPs). The authority for such programs comes from Executive Order 12356 and flows from the Department of Defense to the Services via DoD Directive 5205.7. These programs are implemented in the Air Force by Policy Directive 16-7, and Air Force Instruction 16-701. These directives contain detailed requirements for controlling and reporting, in a very strict manner, all SAPs. This includes a report from the Secretary of the Air Force to the Secretary of Defense (and ultimately to Congress) on all SAPs submitted for approval, and a certification that there are no "SAP-like" programs being operated. These reporting requirements are stipulated in public law.

It followed then, that if the Air Force had recovered some type of extraterrestrial spacecraft and/or bodies and was exploiting this for scientific and technology purposes, then such a program would be operated as a SAP. SAF/AAZ, the Central Office for all Air Force SAPs, has knowledge of, and security oversight over, all SAPs. SAF/AAZ categorically stated that no such Special Access Program(s) exists that pertain to extraterrestrial spacecraft/aliens.

Likewise, the Secretary of the Air Force and the Chief of Staff, who head the Special Program Oversight Committee which oversees all sensitive programs in the Air Force, had no knowledge of the existence of any such program involving, or relating to the events at Roswell or the alleged technology that supposedly resulted therefrom. Besides the obvious irregularity and illegality of keeping such information from the most senior Air Force officials, it would also be illogical, since these officials are responsible for obtaining funding for operations, research, development, and security. Without funding such a program, operation, or organization could not exist. Even to keep such a fact "covered-up" in some sort of passive "caretaker status" would involve money. More importantly, it would involve people and create paperwork.

The aforementioned March 1, 1994, SAF/AA tasking generated negative responses (Atch 6-12) from all recipients; i.e. all offices reported that they had no information that would explain the incident. Consequently, these negative responses led to an increase in the already on-going historical research at records centers and archives.

The extensive archival and records center search was systematically carried out at by the SAF/AAZD Declassification Review Team. This team is composed entirely of Air Force

Reserve personnel who have extensive training and experience in large scale review of records. (Previous efforts include the Southeast Asia Declassification Review, declassification of POW/MIA records, and the review of the Gulf War Air Power Survey records). The team members all had the requisite security clearances for classified information and had the authority of the Secretary of the Air Force to declassify any classified record they found that might be related to Roswell. SAF/AAZD conducted reviews at a number of locations, including: the National Archives in Washington, DC; the National Personnel Records Center, St. Louis, MO; the National Archives, Suitland MD; the National Records Center, Suitland, MD; Naval Research Laboratory, Washington, DC; Federal Records Center, Ft Worth, TX; the INSCOM Archives, Ft. Meade, MD; National Air and Space Museum, Washington, DC; Air Force Historical Research Agency, Maxwell AFB, AL; Center for Air Force History, Bolling AFB, DC; Phillips Laboratory, Hanscom AFB, MA and Kirtland AFB, NM; Rome Laboratory, Griffiss AFB, NY; and the Library of Congress, Washington, DC.

A listing of the specific record areas searched is appended as Atch 13. The areas included all those subject areas logically believed to possibly contain any reference to activities at Roswell AAF during the period of time in question. It is anticipated that detractors from this effort will complain that "they did not search record group x , box y, or reel z, etc.; that's where the real records are!" Such complaints are unavoidable and there is no possible way that the millions of records under Air Force control could be searched page by page. The team endeavored to make logical searches in those places where records would likely be found. They were assisted in this task by archivists, historians, and records management specialists, including experienced persons who have continually worked in Army and Air Force records systems since 1943. The team also searched some record areas that were recommended by serious private researchers such as Robert Todd, who had independently obtained almost encyclopedic knowledge of the complexities of Air Force records systems, particularly as related to this subject area.

Not surprisingly, the research team found the usual number of problems in many of the records centers (particularly St. Louis) with misfiling, lost or misplaced documents, mismarking of documents, or the breaking up of record groups over the years and refiling in different systems. This included, for example, a small amount of missing "decimal files" from the 509th Bomb Group at Roswell that covered the years 1945-1949, that were marked on the index as "destroyed." The researchers noted that there was no pattern to any anomalies found and that most discrepancies were minor and consistent with what they had found in the past on similar projects.

WHAT THE ROSWELL INCIDENT WAS NOT

Before discussing specific positive results that these efforts revealed, it is first appropriate to discuss those things, as indicated by information available to the Air Force, that the "Roswell Incident" was not:

An Airplane Crash

Of all the things that are documented and tracked within the Air Force, among the most detailed and scrupulous are airplane crashes. In fact, records of air crashes go back to the first years of military flight. Safety records and reports are available for all crashes that involved serious damage, injury, death, or a combination of these factors. These records also include incidents involving experimental or classified aircraft. USAF records showed that between June 24, 1947, and July 28, 1947, there were five crashes in New Mexico alone, involving A-26C, P-51N, C-82A, P-80A and PQ-14B aircraft; however, none of these were on the date(s) in question nor in the area(s) in question.

One of the additional areas specifically set forth by GAO in its efforts was to deal with how the Air Force (and others) specifically documented ."..weather balloon...and other crash incidents." In this area, the search efforts revealed that there are no _air_ safety records pertaining to weather balloon crashes (all weather balloons "crash" sooner or later); however, there are provisions for generating reports of "crashes" as ground safety incidents in the unlikely chance that a balloon injures someone or causes damage. However, such records are only maintained for five years.

A Missile Crash

A crashed or errant missile, usually described as a captured German V-2 or one of its variants, is sometimes set forth as a possible explanation for the debris recovered near Roswell. Since much of this testing done at nearby White Sands was secret at the time, it would be logical to assume that the government would handle any missile mishap under tight security, particularly if the mishap occurred on private land. From the records reviewed by the Air Force, however, there was nothing located to suggest that this was the case. Although the bulk of remaining testing records are under the control of the US Army, the subject has also been very well documented over the years within Air Force records. There would be no reason to keep such information classified today. The USAF found no indicators or even hints that a missile was involved in this matter.

A Nuclear Accident

One of the areas considered was that whatever happened near Roswell may have involved nuclear weapons. This was a logical area of concern since the 509th Bomb Group was the only military unit in the world at the time that had access to nuclear weapons. Again, reviews of available records gave no indication that this was the case. A number of records still classified TOP SECRET and SECRET-RESTRICTED DATA having to do with nuclear weapons were located in the Federal Records Center in St. Louis, MO. These records, which pertained to the 509th, had nothing to do with any activities that could have been misinterpreted as the "Roswell Incident." Also, any records of a nuclear-related incident would have been inherited by the Department of Energy (DOE), and, had one occurred, it is likely DOE would have publicly reported it as part of its recent declassification and public release efforts. There were no ancillary records in Air Force files to indicate the potential existence of such records within DOE channels, however.

An Extraterrestrial Craft

The Air Force research found absolutely no indication that what happened near Roswell in 1947, involved any type of extraterrestrial spacecraft. This, of course, is the crux of this entire matter. "Pro-UFO" persons who obtain a copy of this report, at this point, most probably begin the "cover-up is still on" claims. Nevertheless, the research indicated absolutely no evidence of any kind that a spaceship crashed near Roswell or that any alien occupants were recovered therefrom, in some secret military operation or otherwise. This does not mean, however, that the early Air Force was not concerned about UFOs. However, in the early days, "UFO" meant Unidentified Flying Object, which literally translated as some object in the air that was not readily identifiable. It did not mean, as the term has evolved in today's language, to equate to alien spaceships. Records from the period reviewed by Air Force researchers as well as those cited by the authors mentioned before, do indicate that the USAF was seriously concerned about the inability to adequately identify unknown flying objects reported in American airspace. All the records, however, indicated that the focus of concern was not on aliens, hostile or otherwise, but on the Soviet Union. Many documents from that period speak to the possibility of developmental secret Soviet aircraft overflying US airspace. This, of course, was of major concern to the fledgling USAF, whose job it was to protect these same skies.

The research revealed only one official AAF document that indicated that there was any activity of any type that pertained to UFOs and Roswell in July, 1947. This was a small section of the July Historical Report for the 509th Bomb Group and Roswell AAF that stated: "The Office of Public Information was quite busy during the month answering inquiries on the 'flying disc,' which was reported to be in possession of the 509th Bomb Group. The object turned out to be a radar tracking balloon" (included with Atch 11). Additionally, this history showed that the 509th Commander, Colonel Blanchard, went on leave on July 8, 1947, which would be a somewhat unusual maneuver for a person involved in the supposed first ever recovery of extraterrestrial materials. (Detractors claim Blanchard did this as a ploy to elude the press and go to the scene to direct the recovery operations). The history and the morning reports also showed that the subsequent activities at Roswell during the month were mostly mundane and not indicative of any unusual high level activity, expenditure of manpower, resources or security.

Likewise, the researchers found no indication of heightened activity anywhere else in the military hierarchy in the July, 1947, message traffic or orders (to include classified traffic). There were no indications and warnings, notice of alerts, or a higher tempo of operational activity reported that would be logically generated if an alien craft, whose intentions were unknown, entered US territory. To believe that such operational and high-level security activity could be conducted solely by relying on unsecured telecommunications or personal contact without creating any records of such activity certainly stretches the imagination of those who have served in the military who know that paperwork of some kind is necessary to accomplish even emergency, highly classified, or sensitive tasks.

An example of activity sometimes cited by pro-UFO writers to illustrate the point that something unusual was going on was the travel of Lt. General Nathan Twining, Commander of the Air Materiel Command, to New Mexico in July, 1947. Actually, records were located indicating that Twining went to the Bomb Commanders' Course on July 8, along with a number of other general officers, and requested orders to do so a month before, on June 5, 1947 (Atch 14).

Similarly, it has also been alleged that General Hoyt Vandenberg, Deputy Chief of Staff at the time, had been involved directing activity regarding events at Roswell. Activity reports (Atch 15), located in General Vandenberg's personal papers stored in the Library of Congress, did indicate that on July 7, he was busy with a "flying disc" incident; however this particular incident involved Ellington Field, Texas and the Spokane (Washington) Depot. After much discussion and information gathering on this incident, it was learned to be a hoax. There is no similar mention of his personal interest or involvement in Roswell events except in the newspapers.

The above are but two small examples that indicate that if some event happened that was one of the "watershed happenings" in human history, the US military certainly reacted in an unconcerned and cavalier manner. In an actual case, the military would have had to order thousands of soldiers and airman, not only at Roswell but throughout the US, to act nonchalantly, pretend to conduct and report business as usual, and generate absolutely no paperwork of a suspicious nature, while simultaneously anticipating that twenty years or more into the future people would have available a comprehensive Freedom of Information Act that would give them great leeway to review and explore government documents. The records indicate that none of this happened (or if it did, it was controlled by a security system so efficient and tight that no one, US or otherwise, has been able to duplicate it since. If such a system had been in effect at the time, it would have also been used to protect our atomic secrets from the Soviets, which history has showed obviously was not the case). The records reviewed confirmed that no such sophisticated and efficient security system existed.

WHAT THE "ROSWELL INCIDENT" WAS

As previously discussed, what was originally reported to have been recovered was a balloon of some sort, usually described as a "weather balloon," although the majority of the wreckage that was ultimately displayed by General Ramey and Major Marcel in the famous photos (Atch 16) in Ft. Worth, was that of a radar target normally suspended from balloons. This radar target, discussed in more detail later, was certainly consistent with the description of July 9 newspaper article which discussed "tinfoil, paper, tape, and sticks." Additionally, the description of the "flying disc" was consistent with a document routinely used by most pro-UFO writers to indicate a conspiracy in progress--the telegram from the Dallas FBI office of July 8, 1947. This document quoted in part states: ."..The disc is hexagonal in shape and was suspended from a balloon by a cable, which balloon was approximately twenty feet in diameter. ...the object found resembles a high altitude weather balloon with a radar reflector. ...disc and balloon being transported..."

Similarly, while conducting the popular literature review, one of the documents reviewed was a paper entitled "The Roswell Events" edited by Fred Whiting, and sponsored by the

Fund for UFO Research (FUFOR). Although it was not the original intention to comment on what commercial authors interpreted or claimed that other persons supposedly said, this particular document was different because it contained actual copies of apparently authentic sworn affidavits received from a number of persons who claimed to have some knowledge of the Roswell event. Although many of the persons who provided these affidavits to the FUFOR researchers also expressed opinions that they thought there was something extraterrestrial about this incident, a number of them actually described materials that sounded suspiciously like wreckage from balloons. These included the following:

Jesse A. Marcel, MD (son of the late Major Jesse Marcel; 11 years old at the time of the incident). Affidavit dated May 6, 1991. " ... There were three categories of debris: a thick, foil like metallic gray substance; a brittle, brownish-black plastic-like material, like Bakelite; and there were fragments of what appeared to be I-beams. On the inner surface of the I-beam, there appeared to be a type of writing. This writing was a purple-violet hue, and it had an embossed appearance. The figures were composed of curved, geometric shapes. It had no resemblance to Russian, Japanese or any other foreign language. It resembled hieroglyphics, but it had no animal-like characters...."

Loretta Proctor (former neighbor of rancher W.W. Brazel). Affidavit dated May 5, 1991. ."..Brazel came to my ranch and showed my husband and me a piece of material he said came from a large pile of debris on the property he managed. The piece he brought was brown in color, similar to plastic...'Mac' said the other material on the property looked like aluminum foil. It was very flexible and wouldn't crush or burn. There was also something he described as tape which had printing on it. The color of the printing was a kind of purple..."

Bessie Brazel Schreiber (daughter of W.W. Brazel; 14 years old at the time of the incident). Affidavit dated September 22, 1993. ."..The debris looked like pieces of a large balloon which had burst. The pieces were small, the largest I remember measuring about the same as the diameter of a basketball. Most of it was a kind of double-sided material, foil-like on one side and rubber-like on the other. Both sides were grayish silver in color, the foil more silvery than the rubber. Sticks, like kite sticks, were attached to some of the pieces with a whitish tape. The tape was about two or three inches wide and had flower-like designs on it. The 'flowers' were faint, a variety of pastel colors, and reminded me of Japanese paintings in which the flowers are not all connected. I do not recall any other types of material or markings, nor do I remember seeing gouges in the ground or any other signs that anything may have hit the ground hard. The foil-rubber material could not be torn like ordinary aluminum foil can be torn..."

Sally Strickland Tadolini (neighbor of WW Brazel; nine years old in 1947). Affidavit dated September 27, 1993. ."..What Bill showed us was a piece of what I still think as fabric. It was something like aluminum foil, something like satin, something like well-tanned leather in its toughness, yet was not precisely like any one of those materials. ...It

14

was about the thickness of very fine kidskin glove leather and a dull metallic grayish silver, one side slightly darker than the other. I do not remember it having any design or embossing on it..."

Robert R. Porter (B-29 flight Engineer stationed at Roswell in 1947). Affidavit dated June 7, 1991. ."..On this occasion, I was a member of the crew which flew parts of what we were told was a flying saucer to Fort Worth. The people on board included...and Maj Jesse Marcel. Capt. William E. Anderson said it was from a flying saucer. After we arrived, the material was transferred to a B-25. I was told they were going to Wright Field in Dayton, Ohio. I was involved in loading the B-29 with the material, which was wrapped in packages with wrapping paper. One of the pieces was triangle-shaped, about 2 1/2 feet across the bottom. The rest were in small packages, about the size of a shoe box. The brown paper was held with tape. The material was extremely lightweight. When I picked it up, it was just like picking up an empty package. We loaded the triangle shaped package and three shoe box-sized packages into the plane. All of the packages could have fit into the trunk of a car. ...When we came back from lunch, they told us they had transferred the material to a B-25. They told us the material was a weather balloon, but I'm certain it wasn't a weather balloon..."

In addition to those persons above still living who claim to have seen or examined the original material found on the Brazel Ranch, there is one additional person who was universally acknowledged to have been involved in its recovery, Sheridan Cavitt, Lt Col, USAF, (Ret). Cavitt is credited in all claims of having accompanied Major Marcel to the ranch to recover the debris, sometimes along with his Counter Intelligence Corps (CIC) subordinate, William Rickett, who, like Marcel, is deceased. Although there does not appear to be much dispute that Cavitt was involved in the material recovery, other claims about him prevail in the popular literature. He is sometimes portrayed as a closed-mouth (or sometimes even sinister) conspirator who was one of the early individuals who kept the "secret of Roswell" from getting out. Other things about him have been alleged, including the claim that he wrote a report of the incident at the time that has never surfaced.

Since Lt Col Cavitt, who had first-hand knowledge, was still alive, a decision was made to interview him and get a signed sworn statement from him about his version of the events. Prior to the interview, the Secretary of the Air Force provided him with a written authorization and waiver to discuss classified information with the interviewer and release him from any security oath he may have taken. Subsequently, Cavitt was interviewed on May 24, 1994, at his home. Cavitt provided a signed, sworn statement (Atch 17) of his recollections in this matter. He also consented to having the interview tape-recorded. A transcript of that recording is at Atch 18. In this interview, Cavitt related that he had been contacted on numerous occasions by UFO researchers and had willingly talked with many of them; however, he felt that he had oftentimes been misrepresented or had his comments taken out of context so that their true meaning was changed. He stated unequivocally, however, that the material he recovered consisted of a reflective sort of material like aluminum foil, and some thin, bamboo-like sticks. He thought at the time, and continued

15

to do so today, that what he found was a weather balloon and has told other private researchers that. He also remembered finding a small "black box" type of instrument, which he thought at the time was probably a radiosonde. Lt Col Cavitt also reviewed the famous Ramey/Marcel photographs (Atch 16) of the wreckage taken to Ft. Worth (often claimed by UFO researchers to have been switched and the remnants of a balloon substituted for it) and he identified the materials depicted in those photos as consistent with the materials that he recovered from the ranch. Lt Col Cavitt also stated that he had never taken any oath or signed any agreement not to talk about this incident and had never been threatened by anyone in the government because of it. He did not even know the "incident" was claimed to be anything unusual until he was interviewed in the early 1980's.

Similarly, Irving Newton, Major, USAF, (Ret) was located and interviewed. Newton was a weather officer assigned to Fort Worth, who was on duty when the Roswell debris was sent there in July, 1947. He was told that he was to report to General Ramey's office to view the material. In a signed, sworn statement (Atch 30) Newton related that ."..I walked into the General's office where this supposed flying saucer was lying all over the floor. As soon as I saw it, I giggled and asked if that was the flying saucer...I told them that this was a balloon and a RAWIN target..." Newton also stated that ."..while I was examining the debris, Major Marcel was picking up pieces of the target sticks and trying to convince me that some notations on the sticks were alien writings. there were figures on the sticks, lavender or pink in color, appeared to be weather faded markings, with no rhyme or reason (sic). He did not convince me that these were alien writings." Newton concluded his statement by relating that ."..During the ensuing years I have been interviewed by many authors, I have been quoted and misquoted. The facts remain as indicated above. I was not influenced during the original interview, nor today, to provide anything but what I know to be true, that is, the material I saw in General Ramey's office was the remains of a balloon and a RAWIN target."

Balloon Research
The original tasking from GAO noted that the search for information included "weather balloons." Comments about balloons and safety reports have already been made, however the SAF/AAZ research efforts also focused on reviewing historical records involving balloons, since, among other reasons, that was what was officially claimed by the AAF to have been found and recovered in 1947.

As early as February 28, 1994, the AAZD research team found references to balloon tests taking place at Alamogordo AAF (now Holloman AFB) and White Sands during June and July 1947, testing "constant level balloons" and a New York University (NYU)/Watson Labs effort that used "...meteorological devices ... suspected for detecting shock waves generated by Soviet nuclear explosions"--a possible indication of a cover story associated with the NYU balloon project. Subsequently, a 1946 HQ AMC memorandum was surfaced, describing the constant altitude balloon project and specified that the scientific data be classified TOP SECRET Priority 1A. Its name was Project Mogul (Atch 19).

Project Mogul was a then-sensitive, classified project, whose purpose was to determine the state of Soviet nuclear weapons research. This was the early Cold War period and there was serious concern within the US government about the Soviets developing a weaponized atomic device. Because the Soviet Union's borders were closed, the US Government sought to develop a long range nuclear explosion detection capability. Long range, balloon-borne, low frequency acoustic detection was posed to General Spaatz in 1945 by Dr. Maurice Ewing of Columbia University as a potential solution (atmospheric ducting of low frequency pressure waves had been studied as early as 1900).

As part of the research into this matter, AAZD personnel located and obtained the original study papers and reports of the New York University project. Their efforts also revealed that some of the individuals involved in Project Mogul were still living. These persons included the NYU constant altitude balloon Director of Research, Dr. Athelstan F. Spilhaus; the Project Engineer, Professor Charles B. Moore; and the military Project Officer, Colonel Albert C. Trakowski .

All of these persons were subsequently interviewed and signed sworn statements about their activities. A copy of theses statements are appended at Atch 20-22. Additionally, transcripts of the interview with Moore and Trakowski are also included (equipment malfunctioned during the interview of Spilhaus) (Atch 23-24). These interviews confirmed that Project Mogul was a compartmented, sensitive effort. The NYU group was responsible for developing constant level balloons and telemetering equipment that would remain at specified altitudes (within the acoustic duct) while a group from Columbia was to develop acoustic sensors. Doctor Spilhaus, Professor Moore, and certain others of the group were aware of the actual purpose of the project, but they did not know of the project nickname at the time. They handled casual inquiries and/or scientific inquiries/papers in terms of "unclassified meteorological or balloon research." Newly hired employees were not made aware that there was anything special or classified about their work; they were told only that their work dealt with meteorological equipment.

An advance ground team, led by Albert P. Crary, preceded the NYU group to Alamogordo AAF, New Mexico, setting up ground sensors and obtaining facilities for the NYU group. Upon their arrival, Professor Moore and his team experimented with various configurations of neoprene balloons; development of balloon "trains" (see illustration, Atch 25); automatic ballast systems; and use of Naval sonobuoys (as the Watson Lab acoustical sensors had not yet arrived). They also launched what they called "service flights." These "service flights" were not logged nor fully accounted for in the published Technical Reports generated as a result of the contract between NYU and Watson Labs. According to Professor Moore, the "service flights" were composed of balloons, radar reflectors and payloads specifically designed to test acoustic sensors (both early sonobuoys and the later Watson Labs devices). The "payload equipment" was expendable and some carried no "REWARD" or "RETURN TO..." tags because there was to be no association between these flights and the logged constant altitude flights which were fully acknowledged. The NYU balloon flights were listed sequentially in their reports (i.e.,

A,B, 1,5,6,7,8,10 ...) yet gaps existed for Flights 2-4 and Flight 9. The interview with Professor Moore indicated that these gaps were the unlogged "service flights."

Professor Moore, the on-scene Project Engineer, gave detailed information concerning his team's efforts. He recalled that radar targets were used for tracking balloons because they did not have all the necessary equipment when they first arrived in New Mexico. Some of the early developmental radar targets were manufactured by a toy or novelty company. These targets were made up of aluminum "foil" or foil-backed paper, balsa wood beams that were coated in an "Elmer's-type" glue to enhance their durability, acetate and/or cloth reinforcing tape, single strand and braided nylon twine, brass eyelets and swivels to form a multi-faced reflector somewhat similar in construction to a box kite (see photographs, Atch 26). Some of these targets were also assembled with purplish-pink tape with symbols on it (see drawing by Moore with Atch 21).

According to the log summary (Atch 27) of the NYU group, Flight A through Flight 7 (November 20, 1946-July 2, 1947) were made with neoprene meteorological balloons (as opposed to the later flights made with polyethylene balloons). Professor Moore stated that the neoprene balloons were susceptible to degradation in the sunlight, turning·from a milky white to a dark brown. He described finding remains of balloon trains with reflectors and payloads that had landed in the desert: the ruptured and shredded neoprene would "almost look like dark gray or black flakes or ashes after exposure to the sun for only a few days. The plasticizers and antioxidants in the neoprene would emit a peculiar acrid odor and the balloon material and radar target material would be scattered after returning to earth depending on the surface winds." Upon review of the local newspaper photographs from General Ramey's press conference in 1947 and descriptions in popular books by individuals who supposedly handled the debris recovered on the ranch, Professor Moore opined that the material was most likely the shredded remains of a multi-neoprene balloon train with multiple radar reflectors. The material and a "black box," described by Cavitt, was, in Moore's scientific opinion, most probably from Flight 4, a "service flight" that included a cylindrical metal sonobuoy and portions of a weather instrument housed in a box, which was unlike typical weather radiosondes which were made of cardboard. Additionally, a copy of a professional journal maintained at the time by A.P. Crary, provided to the Air Force by his widow, showed that Flight 4 was launched on June 4, 1947, but was not recovered by the NYU group. It is very probable that this TOP SECRET project balloon train (Flight 4), made up of unclassified components; came to rest some miles northwest of Roswell, NM, became shredded in the surface winds and was ultimately found by the rancher, Brazel, ten days later. This possibility was supported by the observations of Lt Col Cavitt (Atch 17-18), the only living eyewitness to the actual debris field and the material found. Lt Col Cavitt described a small area of debris which appeared, "to resemble bamboo type square sticks one quarter to one half inch square, that were very light, as well as some sort of metallic reflecting material that was also very light ... I remember recognizing this material as being consistent with a weather balloon."

Concerning the initial announcement, "RAAF Captures Flying Disc," research failed to locate any documented evidence as to why that statement was made. However, on July

10, 1947, following the Ramey press conference, the Alamogordo News published an article with photographs demonstrating multiple balloons and targets at the same location as the NYU group operated from at Alamogordo AAF. Professor Moore expressed surprise at seeing this since his, was the only balloon test group in the area. He stated, "It appears that there was some type of umbrella cover story to protect our work with Mogul." Although the Air Force did not find documented evidence that Gen. Ramey was directed to espouse a weather balloon in his press conference, he may have done so because he was either aware of Project Mogul and was trying to deflect interest from it, or he readily perceived the material to be a weather balloon based on the identification from his weather officer, Irving Newton. In either case, the materials recovered by the AAF in July, 1947, were not readily recognizable as anything special (only the purpose was special) and the recovered debris itself was unclassified. Additionally, the press dropped its interest in the matter as quickly as they had jumped on it. Hence, there would be no particular reason to further document what quickly became a "non-event."

The interview with Colonel Trakowski (Atch 23-24) also proved valuable information. Trakowski provided specific details on Project Mogul and described how the security for the program was set up, as he was formerly the TOP SECRET Control Officer for the program. He further related that many of the original radar targets that were produced around the end of World War II were fabricated by toy or novelty companies using a purplish-pink tape with flower and heart symbols on it. Trakowski also recounted a conversation that he had with his friend, and superior military officer in his chain of command, Colonel Marcellus Duffy, in July, 1947. Duffy, formerly had Trakowski's position on Mogul, but had subsequently been transferred to Wright Field. He stated: ."..Colonel Duffy called me on the telephone from Wright Field and gave me a story about a fellow that had come in from New Mexico, woke him up in the middle of the night or some such thing with a handful of debris, and wanted him, Colonel Duffy, to identify it. ...He just said 'it sure looks like some of the stuff you've been launching at Alamogordo' and he described it, and I said 'yes, I think it is.' Certainly Colonel Duffy knew enough about radar targets, radiosondes, balloon-borne weather devices. He was intimately familiar with all that apparatus."

Attempts were made to locate Colonel Duffy but it was ascertained that he had died. His widow explained that, although he had amassed a large amount of personal papers relating to his Air Force activities, she had recently disposed of these items. Likewise, it was learned that A.P. Crary was also deceased; however his surviving spouse had a number of his papers from his balloon testing days, including his professional journal from the period in question. She provided the Air Force researchers with this material. It is discussed in more detail within Atch 32. Overall, it helps fill in gaps of the Mogul story.

During the period the Air Force conducted this research, it was discovered that several others had also discovered the possibility that the "Roswell Incident" may have been generated by the recovery of a Project Mogul balloon device. These persons included Professor Charles B. Moore, Robert Todd, and coincidentally, Karl Pflock, a researcher who is married to a staffer who works for Congressman Schiff. Some of these persons provided suggestions as to where documentation might be located in various archives, histories and libraries. A review of Freedom of Information Act (FOIA) requests revealed that Robert Todd, particularly, had become aware of Project Mogul several years ago and had doggedly obtained from the Air Force, through the FOIA, a large amount of material pertaining to it; long before the AAZD researchers independently seized on the same possibility.

Most interestingly, as this report was being written, Pflock published his own report of this matter under the auspices of FUFOR, entitled "Roswell in Perspective" (1994). Pflock concluded from his research that the Brazel Ranch debris originally reported as a "flying disc" was probably debris from a Mogul balloon; however, there was a simultaneous incident that occurred not far away, that caused an alien craft to crash and that the AAF subsequently recovered three alien bodies therefrom. Air Force research did not locate any information to corroborate that this incredible coincidence occurred, however.

In order to provide a more detailed discussion of the specifics of Project Mogul and how it appeared to be directly responsible for the "Roswell Incident," a SAF/AAZD researcher prepared a more detailed discussion on the balloon project which is appended to this report as Atch 32.

Other Research
In the attempt to develop additional information that could help explain this matter, a number of other steps were taken. First, assistance was requested from various museums and other archives (Atch 28) to obtain information and/or examples of the actual balloons and radar targets used in connection with Project Mogul and to correlate them with the various descriptions of wreckage and materials recovered. The blueprints for the "Pilot Balloon Target ML307C/AP Assembly" (generically, the radar target assembly) were located at the Army Signal Corps Museum at Fort Monmouth and obtained. A copy is appended as Atch 29. This blueprint provides the specification for the foil material, tape, wood, eyelets, and string used and the assembly instructions thereto. An actual device was also obtained for study with the assistance of Professor Moore. (The example actually procured was a 1953-manufactured model "C" as compared to the Model B which was in use in 1947. Professor Moore related the differences were minor). An examination of this device revealed it to be simply made of aluminum-colored foil-like material over a stronger paper-like material, attached to balsa wood sticks, affixed with tape, glue, and twine. When opened, the device appears as depicted in Atch 31 (contemporary photo) and Atch 25 (1947 photo, in a "balloon train"). When folded, the device is in a series of triangles, the largest being four feet by two feet ten inches. The smallest triangle section measures two feet by two feet ten inches. (Compare with descriptions provided by Lt Col Cavitt and others, as well as photos of wreckage).

Additionally, the researchers obtained from the Archives of the University of Texas-Arlington (UTA), a set of original (i.e. first generation) prints of the photographs taken at the time by the Fort Worth Star-Telegram, that depicted Ramey and Marcel with the

20

wreckage. A close review of these photos (and a set of first generation negatives also subsequently obtained from UTA) revealed several intesting observations. First, although in some of the literature cited above, Marcel allegedly stated that he had his photo taken with the "real" UFO wreckage and then it was subsequently removed and the weather balloon wreckage substituted for it, a comparison shows that the same wreckage appeared in the photos of Marcel and Ramey. The photos also depicted that this material was lying on what appeared to be some sort of wrapping paper (consistent with affidavit excerpt of crew chief Porter, above). It was also noted that in the two photos of Ramey he had a piece of paper in his hand. In one, it was folded over so nothing could be seen. In the second, however, there appears to be text printed on the paper. In an attempt to read this text to determine if it could shed any further light on locating documents relating to this matter, the photo was sent to a national level organization for digitizing and subsequent photo interpretation and analysis. This organization was also asked to scrutinize the digitized photos for any indication of the flowered tape (or "hieroglyphics, depending on the point of view) that were reputed to be visible to some of the persons who observed the wreckage prior to it getting to Fort Worth. This organization reported on July 20, 1994, that even after digitizing, the photos were of insufficient quality to visualize either of the details sought for analysis. This organization was able to obtain measurements from the "sticks" visible in the debris after it was ascertained by an interview of the original photographer what kind of camera he used. The results of this process are provided in Atch 33, along with a reference diagram and the photo from which the measurements were made. All these measurements are compatible with the wooden materials used in the radar target previously described.

CONCLUSION

The Air Force research did not locate or develop any information that the "Roswell Incident" was a UFO event. All available official materials, although they do not directly address Roswell *per se*, indicate that the most likely source of the wreckage recovered from the Brazel Ranch was from one of the Project Mogul balloon trains. Although that project was TOP SECRET at the time, there was also no specific indication found to indicate an official pre-planned cover story was in place to explain an event such as that which ultimately happened. It appears that the identification of the wreckage as being part of a weather balloon device, as reported in the newspapers at the time, was based on the fact that there was no physical difference in the radar targets and the neoprene balloons (other than the numbers and configuration) between Mogul balloons and normal weather balloons. Additionally, it seems that there was over-reaction by Colonel Blanchard and Major Marcel, in originally reporting that a "flying disc" had been recovered when, at that time, nobody for sure knew what that term even meant since the it had only been in use for a couple of weeks.

Likewise, there was no indication in official records from the period that there was heightened military operational or security activity which should have been generated if this was, in fact, the first recovery of materials and/or persons from another world. The post-War US Military (or today's for that matter) did not have the capability to rapidly identify, recover, coordinate, cover-up, and quickly minimize public scrutiny of such an event. The claim that they did so without leaving even a little bit of a suspicious paper trail for 47 years is incredible.

It should also be noted here that there was little mentioned in this report about the recovery of the so-called "alien bodies." This is for several reasons: First, the recovered wreckage was from a Project Mogul balloon. There were no "alien" passengers therein. Secondly, the pro-UFO groups who espouse the alien bodies theories cannot even agree among themselves as to what, how many, and where, such bodies were supposedly recovered. Additionally, some of these claims have been shown to be hoaxes, even by other UFO researchers. Thirdly, when such claims are made, they are often attributed to people using pseudonyms or who otherwise do not want to be publicly identified, presumably so that some sort of retribution cannot be taken against them (notwithstanding that nobody has been shown to have died, disappeared or otherwise suffered at the hands of the government during the last 47 years). Fourth, many of the persons making the biggest claims of "alien bodies" make their living from the "Roswell Incident."   While having a commercial interest in something does not automatically make it suspect, it does raise interesting questions related to authenticity. Such persons should be encouraged to present their evidence (not speculation) directly to the government and provide all pertinent details and evidence to support their claims if honest fact-finding is what is wanted. Lastly, persons who have come forward and provided their names and made claims, may have, in good faith but in the "fog of time," misinterpreted past events. The review of Air Force records did not locate even one piece of evidence to indicate that the Air Force has had any part in an "alien" body recovery operation or continuing cover-up.

During the course of this effort, the Air Force has kept in close touch with the GAO and responded to their various queries and requests for assistance. This report was generated as an official response to the GAO, and to document the considerable effort expended by the Air Force on their behalf. It is anticipated that that they will request a copy of this report to help formulate the formal report of their efforts. It is recommended that this document serve as the final Air Force report related to the Roswell matter, for the GAO, or any other inquiries.

RICHARD L. WEAVER, COL, USAF
DIRECTOR, SECURITY AND SPECIAL
PROGRAM OVERSIGHT

Attachments
1. Washington Post Article, "GAO Turns to Alien Turf in New Probe,"
January 14, 1994
2. GAO Memo, February 15, 1994
3. DoD/IG Memo, February 23, 1994
4. SAF/FM Memo, February 24, 1994, w/Indorsement

5. SAF/AA Memo, March 1, 1994, w/ March 16, 1994 Addendum
6. AF/IN Memo, March 14, 1994
7. AF/SE Memo, March 14, 1994
8. SAF/AQL Memo, March 22, 1994
9. AF/XOWP Memo, March 9, 1994
10. SAF/AAI Memo, March 10, 1994
11. AFHRA/CC Memo, March 8, 1994
12. AFOSI/HO Memo, May 11, 1994
13. List of Locations and Records Searched
14. HQ AAF "Issuance of Orders," June 5, 1947
15. Copy of Vandenberg's Appointment Book and Diary, July 7-9, 1947
16. July 9, 1947 Photos of Balloon Wreckage, Ft Worth Star Telegram
17. Signed Sworn Statement of Cavitt, May 24, 1994
18. Transcript of Cavitt Interview, May 24, 1994
19. Letter, July 8, 1946, Project Mogul
20. Signed Sworn Statement of Spilhaus, June 3, 1994
21. Signed Sworn Statement of Moore, June 8, 1994
22. Signed Sworn Statement of Trakowski, June 29, 1994
23. Transcript of Interview with Moore, June 8, 1994
24. Transcript of Interview with Trakowski, June 29, 1994
25. Illustration of Project Mogul "Balloon Trains"
26. Two Photos of Project Mogul "Balloon Trains"
27. Log Summary, NYU Constant Level Balloon Flights
28. List of Museums Contacted
29. Copy of Blueprint for "Pilot Balloon Target, ML-307C/AP Assembly"
30. Signed Sworn Statement of Newton, July 21, 1994
31. Photos of ML-307C/AP Device, With Vintage Neoprene Balloon and Debris
32. Synopsis of Balloon Research Findings by 1LT James McAndrew
33. "Mensuration Working Paper," With Drawing and Photo

STEVEN SCHIFF
FIRST DISTRICT, NEW MEXICO

CHAIRMAN
SUBCOMMITTEE ON BASIC RESEARCH
COMMITTEE ON SCIENCE

VICE CHAIRMAN
COMMITTEE ON GOVERNMENT REFORM
AND OVERSIGHT

COMMITTEE ON THE JUDICIARY

COMMITTEE ON STANDARDS OF
OFFICIAL CONDUCT

Doc. 7-3a Letter from Congressman Schiff, Aug 1, 1995

Congress of the United States
House of Representatives
Washington, DC 20515-3101

PLEASE REPLY TO:

WASHINGTON OFFICE
☐ 2404 RAYBURN BUILDING
WASHINGTON, DC 20515
(202) 225-6316

DISTRICT OFFICE
☐ 625 SILVER AVENUE, SW
SUITE 140
ALBUQUERQUE, NM 87102
(505) 766-2538

August 1, 1995

Clifford Stone
1421 E Tilden
Roswell, NM 88201

Dear Clifford:

I would like to sincerely thank you for having contacted my office in the past, expressing your support for my request to the General Accounting Office (GAO) regarding the "Roswell Incident."

Since you have indicated an interest in the final GAO report, which was formally issued on July 28, 1995, I am enclosing information which will allow you to obtain a copy of it, if you desire.

The GAO's final report, *Government Records: Results of A Search for Records Concerning the 1947 Crash Near Roswell, New Mexico,* can be obtained by contacting the GAO, by phone, fax, or mail.

Orders by Mail:
  U.S. General Accounting Office
  P. O. Box 6015
  Gaithersburg, MD 20884-6015

Orders By Phone:
    202/512-6000
Orders by fax:
    301/258-4066

Please reference the title of the document (see above), and document number GAO/NSIAD-95-187, when placing your request. The first copy requested will be provided at no charge. There will be a fee of $2 per additional copy; checks should be made out to the Superintendent of Documents. My Washington office and my Albuquerque office have only a limited number of reports available; these will be released on a first-come basis to people visiting my office(s).

I am also enclosing, for your information, a copy of the press release which I issued regarding the GAO report. Again, I thank you for your interest and expression of support.

Sincerely,

Steven Schiff

SS:mck

P.S. I want to alert you to the fact that a story reported by Richard Parker in the *Albuquerque Journal* of July 29, 1995, is inaccurate. I never said that the crash at Roswell was that of a device designed to monitor Soviet nuclear tests as claimed by the Air Force in their report of September 1994. As you can see from the enclosed press release, I only said that I rejected the original story of the weather balloon -- which the Air Force itself has disavowed. I have never offered a specific conclusion as to what crashed in Roswell in 1947; my official role has been to provide access to government documents relating to the subject.

News Release

Doc. 7-4a Press Release Concerning GAO
Report on Roswell, Jul 28, 1995

U.S. CONGRESSMAN
Steve Schiff
FIRST CONGRESSIONAL DISTRICT
NEW MEXICO

WASHINGTON OFFICE: 2404 Rayburn Building • Washington, D.C. 20515 • (202) 225–6316 • FAX (202) 225–4975
DISTRICT OFFICE: 625 Silver Ave., S.W., Suite 140 • Albuquerque, NM 87102 • (505) 766–2538 • FAX (505) 766–1674

Immediate Release
July 28th, 1995

J. Barry Bitzer
(202) 225-2245

Schiff Receives, Releases Roswell Report
(missing documents leave unanswered questions)

Washington: Congressman Steve Schiff today released the General
Accounting Office (GAO) report detailing results of a records
audit related to events surrounding a crash in 1947, near
Roswell, New Mexico, and the military response.

The 20 page report is the result of constituent information
requests to Congressman Schiff and the difficulty he had getting
answers from the Department of Defense in the now 48-year-old
controversy.

Schiff said important documents, which may have shed more light
on what happened at Roswell, are missing. "The GAO report states
that the outgoing messages from Roswell Army Air Field (RAAF) for
this period of time were destroyed without proper authority."
Schiff pointed out that these messages would have shown how
military officials in Roswell were explaining to their superiors
exactly what happened.

"It is my understanding that these outgoing messages were
permanent records, which should never have been destroyed. The
GAO could not identify who destroyed the messages, or why." But

-more-

Schiff pointed out that the GAO estimates that the messages were destroyed over 40 years ago, making further inquiry about their destruction impractical.

Documents revealed by the report include an FBI teletype and reference in a newsletter style internal forum at RAAF that refer to a "radar tracking device" - a reference to a weather balloon. Even though the weather balloon story has since been discredited by the US Air Force, Schiff suggested that the authors of those communications may have been repeating what they were told, rather than consciously adding to what some believe is a "cover up."

"At least this effort caused the Air Force to acknowledge that the crashed vehicle was no weather balloon," Schiff said. "That explanation never fit the fact of high military security used at the time." The Air Force in September, 1994 claimed that the crashed vehicle was a then-classified device to detect evidence of possible Soviet nuclear testing.

Schiff also praised the efforts of the GAO, describing their work as "professional, conscientious and thorough."

A two page letter discussing a related investigation into "Majestic 12" was also delivered.

Schiff will be available to the media Saturday, July 29th, from 10:00 AM to 2:00 PM at 2404 Rayburn HOB in Washington, DC and by telephone: (202) 225-6316.

A copy of the report may be obtained by calling (202) 512-6000 and referencing Document number GAO/NSIAD-95-187.

United States
General Accounting Office
Washington, D.C. 20548

National Security and
International Affairs Division

B-262046

July 28, 1995

The Honorable Steven H. Schiff
House of Representatives

Dear Mr. Schiff:

On July 8, 1947, the Roswell Army Air Field (RAAF) public information office in Roswell, New Mexico, reported the crash and recovery of a "flying disc." Army Air Forces personnel from the RAAF's 509th Bomb Group were credited with the recovery. The following day, the press reported that the Commanding General of the U.S. Eighth Air Force, Fort Worth, Texas, announced that RAAF personnel had recovered a crashed radar-tracking (weather) balloon, not a "flying disc."

After nearly 50 years, speculation continues on what crashed at Roswell. Some observers believe that the object was of extraterrestrial origin. In the July 1994 Report of Air Force Research Regarding the Roswell Incident, the Air Force did not dispute that something happened near Roswell, but reported that the most likely source of the wreckage was from a balloon-launched classified government project designed to determine the state of Soviet nuclear weapons research. The debate on what crashed at Roswell continues.

Concerned that the Department of Defense (DOD) may not have provided you with all available information on the crash, you asked us to determine the requirements for reporting air accidents similar to the crash near Roswell and identify any government records concerning the Roswell crash.

We conducted an extensive search for government records related to the crash near Roswell. We examined a wide range of classified and unclassified documents dating from July 1947 through the 1950s. These records came from numerous organizations in New Mexico and elsewhere throughout DOD as well as the Federal Bureau of Investigation (FBI), the Central Intelligence Agency (CIA), and the National Security Council. The full scope and methodology of our work are detailed at the end of this report.

Doc. 7-5b GAO Report to Congressman Schiff
Concerning Roswell, Jul 28, 1995

esults in Brief

In 1947, Army regulations required that air accident reports be maintained permanently. We identified four air accidents reported by the Army Air Forces in New Mexico during July 1947. All of the accidents involved military aircraft and occurred after July 8, 1947—the date the RAAF public information office first reported the crash and recovery of a "flying disc" near Roswell. The Navy reported no air accidents in New Mexico during July 1947. Air Force officials told us that according to record-keeping requirements in effect during July 1947, there was no requirement to prepare a report on the crash of a weather balloon.

In our search for records concerning the Roswell crash, we learned that some government records covering RAAF activities had been destroyed and others had not. For example, RAAF administrative records (from Mar. 1945 through Dec. 1949) and RAAF outgoing messages (from Oct. 1946 through Dec. 1949) were destroyed. The document disposition form does not indicate what organization or person destroyed the records and when or under what authority the records were destroyed.

Our search for government records concerning the Roswell crash yielded two records originating in 1947—a July 1947 history report by the combined 509th Bomb Group and RAAF and an FBI teletype message dated July 8, 1947. The 509th-RAAF report noted the recovery of a "flying disc" that was later determined by military officials to be a radar-tracking balloon. The FBI message stated that the military had reported that an object resembling a high-altitude weather balloon with a radar reflector had been recovered near Roswell.

The other government records we reviewed, including those previously withheld from the public because of security classification, and the Air Force's analysis of unidentified flying object[1] sightings from 1946 to 1953 (Project Blue Book Special Report No. 14), did not mention the crash or the recovery of an airborne object near Roswell in July 1947. Similarly, executive branch agencies' responses to our letters of inquiry produced no other government records on the Roswell crash.

eporting Air ccidents

According to press accounts from July 1947, Army Air Forces personnel from RAAF were involved in the recovery of an airborne object near Roswell. Therefore, if an air accident report was prepared, it should have

---

[1]According to Air Force regulation, an unidentified flying object is an airborne object that by performance, aerodynamic characteristics, or unusual features, does not conform to known aircraft or missiles, or does not correspond to Air Force definitions of familiar or known objects or unidentified aircraft.

been prepared in accordance with Army regulations. According to an Army records management official, in 1947 Army regulations required that air accident reports be maintained permanently. An Air Force official said there was no similar requirement to report a weather balloon crash.

According to an Air Force official who has worked in the records management field since the mid-1940s, air accident reports prepared in July 1947 under Army regulations should have been transferred to Air Force custody in September 1947, when the Air Force was established as a separate service.

The Air Force Safety Agency is responsible for maintaining reports of air accidents. We examined its microfilm records to determine whether any air accidents had been reported in New Mexico during July 1947. We identified four air accidents during this time period.[2] All of the accidents involved military fighter or cargo aircraft and occurred after July 8, 1947—the date the RAAF public information office first reported the crash and recovery of a "flying disc" near Roswell. According to the Army Air Forces' Report of Major Accident, these four accidents occurred at or near the towns of Hobbs, Albuquerque, Carrizozo, and Alamogordo, New Mexico. Only one of the four accidents resulted in a fatality. The pilot died when the aircraft crashed during an attempted take-off.

Search for Records

In searching for government records on the Roswell crash, we were particularly interested in identifying and reviewing records of military units assigned to RAAF in 1947—to include the 509th Bomb Group, the 1st Air Transport Unit, the 427th Army Air Force Base Unit, and the 1395th Military Police Company (Aviation).

Document disposition forms obtained from the National Personnel Records Center in St. Louis, Missouri, indicate that in 1953, the Walker Air Force Base (formerly RAAF) records officer transferred to the Army's Kansas City records depository the histories of units stationed at Walker Air Force Base. These histories included the 509th Bomb Group and RAAF for February 1947 through October 1947; the 1st Air Transport Unit for July 1946 through June 1947; and the 427th Army Air Force Base Unit for January 1946 to February 1947. We could not locate any documentation indicating that records of the 1395th Military Police Company (Aviation)

---

[2]These records do not include information regarding mishaps of air vehicles belonging to civilian or other government agencies. These records also do not include mishaps involving unmanned air vehicles such as remotely piloted aircraft, low-speed cruise missiles, and most balloons.

Doc. 7-5d GAO Report to Congressman Schiff
Concerning Roswell, Jul 28, 1995

were ever retired to the National Personnel Records Center or its predecessor depositories.

The July 1947 history for the 509th Bomb Group and RAAF stated that the RAAF public information office "was kept quite busy . . . answering inquiries on the 'flying disc,' which was reported to be in [the] possession of the 509th Bomb Group. The object turned out to be a radar tracking balloon." By his signature, the RAAF's commanding officer certified that the report represented a complete and accurate account of RAAF activities in July 1947. (Excerpts from the report are contained in app. I.)

In addition to unit history reports, we also searched for other government records on the Roswell crash. In this regard, the Chief Archivist for the National Personnel Records Center provided us with documentation indicating that (1) RAAF records such as finance and accounting, supplies, buildings and grounds, and other general administrative matters from March 1945 through December 1949 and (2) RAAF outgoing messages from October 1946 through December 1949 were destroyed. According to this official, the document disposition form did not properly indicate the authority under which the disposal action was taken. The Center's Chief Archivist stated that from his personal experience, many of the Air Force organizational records covering this time period were destroyed without entering a citation for the governing disposition authority. Our review of records control forms showing the destruction of other records—including outgoing RAAF messages for 1950—supports the Chief Archivist's viewpoint.

During our review of records at FBI headquarters, we found a July 8, 1947, teletype message from the FBI office in Dallas, Texas, to FBI headquarters and the FBI office in Cincinnati, Ohio. An FBI spokesperson confirmed the authenticity of the message.

According to the message, an Eighth Air Force headquarters official had telephonically informed the FBI's Dallas office of the recovery near Roswell of a hexagonal-shaped disc suspended from a large balloon by cable. The message further stated that the disc and balloon were being sent to Wright Field (now Wright-Patterson Air Force Base, Ohio) for examination. According to the Eighth Air Force official, the recovered object resembled a high-altitude weather balloon with a radar reflector. The message stated that no further investigation by the FBI was being conducted. (A copy of the teletype message appears in app. II.)

To follow up on the July 8th message, we reviewed microfilm abstracts of the FBI Dallas and Cincinnati office activities for July 1947. An abstract prepared by the FBI Dallas office on July 12, 1947, summarized the particulars of the July 8th message. There was no mention in the Cincinnati office abstracts of the crash or recovery of an airborne object near Roswell.

Because the FBI message reported that debris from the Roswell crash was being transported to Wright Field for examination, we attempted to determine whether military regulations existed for handling such debris. We were unable to locate any applicable regulation. As a final step, we reviewed Air Materiel Command (Wright Field) records from 1947 to 1950 for evidence of command personnel involvement in this matter. We found no records mentioning the Roswell crash or the examination by Air Materiel Command personnel of any debris recovered from the crash.

Queries to Federal Agencies Regarding Records on the Crash

We sent letters to several federal agencies asking for any government records they might have concerning the Roswell crash. In this regard, we contacted DOD, the National Security Council, the White House Office of Science and Technology Policy, the CIA, the FBI, and the Department of Energy.

The National Security Council, the White House Office of Science and Technology Policy, and the Department of Energy responded that they had no government records relating to the Roswell crash. (Copies of their responses appear in app. III, IV, and V.) The FBI, DOD, and the CIA provided the following information.

Federal Bureau of Investigation

The FBI informed us that all FBI data regarding the crash near Roswell had been processed under Freedom of Information Act (FOIA) requests previously received by the Bureau. We reviewed the FBI's FOIA material and identified the July 8, 1947, FBI teletype message discussing the recovery near Roswell of a high-altitude weather balloon with a radar reflector. (A copy of the FBI's response appears in app. VI.)

Department of Defense

DOD informed us that the U.S. Air Force report of July 1994, entitled Report of Air Force Research Regarding the Roswell Incident, represents the extent of DOD records or information concerning the Roswell crash. The Air Force report concluded that there was no dispute that something happened near Roswell in July 1947 and that all available official materials indicated the most likely source of the wreckage recovered was one of the project MOGUL balloon trains. At the time of the Roswell crash, project MOGUL was a highly classified U.S. effort to determine the state of Soviet nuclear weapons research using balloons that carried radar reflectors and acoustic sensors. (A copy of DOD's response appears in app. VII.)

Central Intelligence Agency

In March 1995, the CIA's Executive Director responded to our letter of inquiry by stating that earlier searches by the CIA for records on unidentified flying objects produced no information pertaining to the Roswell crash. The Executive Director added, however, that it was unclear whether the CIA had ever conducted a search for records specifically relating to Roswell. In the absence of such assurance, the Executive Director instructed CIA personnel to conduct a comprehensive records search for information relating to Roswell. On May 30, 1995, the CIA's Executive Director informed us that a search against the term "Roswell, New Mexico," in all CIA databases produced no CIA documents related to the crash. (A copy of CIA's response appears in app. VIII.)

Agency Comments

A draft of this report was provided to DOD for comment. DOD offered no comments or suggested changes to the report. The Chief Archivist, National Personnel Records Center offered several comments clarifying matters dealing with records management. These comments have been incorporated into the final report where appropriate.

The CIA, the Department of Energy, the FBI, the National Security Council, and the White House Office of Science and Technology Policy also received excerpts from the report discussing the activities of their respective agencies. They had no substantive comments and made no suggested changes to the report.

Scope and Methodology

To determine the requirements for reporting air accidents in 1947, we interviewed military service records management officials, reviewed military record-keeping regulations in effect during this time period, and examined Army Air Forces and Navy air accident reports.

We also sought to identify any government records related to the Roswell crash. In this regard, we visited and reviewed records at the locations listed in table 1.

Table 1: Locations Visited and Records Reviewed

Locations visited	Records reviewed
National Archives, Washington, D.C.	Air Force papers on unidentified flying objects Army Counterintelligence Corps historical files, 1947-49
National Archives II, College Park, Md.	Project Blue Book Special Report No. 14 National Security Council meeting minutes, 1947-48
National Archives, National Record Center, Suitland, Md.	Army Inspector General reports, 1947-58 Army staff intelligence correspondence, 1947-56 Headquarters Army Air Force message traffic, 1947-54 Army Air Force and Air Materiel Command (Wright Field) research and development files, 1947-50
National Personnel Records Center, St. Louis, Mo.	Morning reports for RAAF units, July 1947 Eighth Air Force messages, 1947-50 Eighth Air Force correspondence, 1947-51 Eighth Air Force weekly activity summaries, July 1947 Service records of key personnel assigned to RAAF, 1947 Project Sign[a] investigative reports, 1948 Army Adjutant General correspondence, 1947-49 Missile test firing reports at White Sands, N. Mex., 1947-54
Department of the Air Force, Washington, D.C.	Current and past records management regulations Report of Air Force Research Regarding the Roswell Incident, July 1994
Department of the Army, Washington, D.C.	Current and past records management regulations
Department of the Navy, Washington, D.C.	Air accident reports, July 1947
Air Force Safety Agency, Kirtland Air Force Base, N. Mex.	Air accident reports, July 1947
Air Force History Support Office, Bolling Air Force Base, Washington, D.C.	509th Bomb Group and RAAF monthly histories, July and August 1947
National Security Agency, Fort Meade, Md.	FOIA records, Citizens Against UFO Secrecy
Military History Institute, Army War College, Carlisle, Pa.	Army Counterintelligence Corps reports, 1947
Army Central Security Facility, Fort Meade, Md.	Army Counterintelligence Corps reports, 1947
Central Intelligence Agency, Langley, Va.	Scientific Advisory Panel on Unidentified Flying Objects (Robertson Panel) report FOIA records, Ground Saucer Watch, Inc.
Federal Bureau of Investigation, Washington, D.C.	FOIA records on unidentified flying objects
National Atomic Museum, Kirtland Air Force Base, N. Mex.	509th Bomb Group historical information, 1947 RAAF base newspaper Atomic Blast, July and August 1947

[a]Project Sign was the predecessor to Project Blue Book.

Our search of government records was complicated by the fact that some records we wanted to review were missing and there was not always an explanation. Further, the records management regulations for the retention and disposition of records were unclear or changing during the period we reviewed.

We also queried the National Security Council, the White House Office of Science and Technology Policy, the Department of Energy, the FBI, DOD, and the CIA to determine what government records they have on the Roswell crash. We did not independently verify the information provided to us in their written responses.

In addition to physically examining government records, we contacted the following federal activities to determine whether they had any information about the Roswell crash:

- Air Force Historical Research Agency, Maxwell Air Force Base, Alabama;
- Air Force Aeronautical Systems Center, Wright-Patterson Air Force Base, Ohio;
- Army Center for Military History, Washington, D.C.; and
- 509th Bomb Wing, Office of the Historian, Whiteman Air Force Base, Missouri.

We conducted our review from March 1994 to June 1995 in accordance with generally accepted government auditing standards.

Unless you publicly announce its contents earlier, we plan no further distribution of this report until 30 days after its issue date. At that time, we will make copies available to other interested parties upon request.

If you or your staff have any questions about this report, please call me on (202) 512-3504. A major contributor to this report is Gary K. Weeter, Assistant Director.

Sincerely yours,

Richard Davis

Richard Davis
Director, National Security
  Analysis

Contents

Contents

Abbreviations

CIA	Central Intelligence Agency
DOD	Department of Defense
FBI	Federal Bureau of Investigation
FOIA	Freedom of Information Act
RAAF	Roswell Army Air Field

Combined History for July 1947

Doc. 7-5k GAO Report to Congressman Schiff
Concerning Roswell, Jul 28, 1995

COMBINED HISTORY
509TH BOMB GROUP
AND
ROSWELL ARMY AIR FIELD
1 JULY 1947 THROUGH 31 JULY 1947

Doc. 7-5l GAO Report to Congressman Schiff
Concerning Roswell, Jul 28, 1995

RESTRICTED

The other three briefings were those which were given to the VIP
and a simulated briefing to a large group of Air Scouts representing
all of the troops in New Mexico which was given on 15 July 1947.

Several small projects were completed during the month including
signs on all the office doors, a building directory, and a world situation
map which is maintained on a day-to-day basis.

The Historical Section of S-2 has been seriously handicapped by
the removal of the regular stenographer with the reduction in force.

Due to the fact that the quality of the department reports has
in general been so inadequate, lectures are being prepared to be given
early in August to properly train the liaison representatives of each
department.

The Office of Public Information was kept quite busy during the
month answering inquiries on the "flying disc", which was reported to
be in possession of the 509th Bomb Group. The object turned out to be
a radar tracking balloon.

The main project of the month was making all arrangements for a
successful Air Force Day. Lt. Colonel Oliver LaFarge, Air Reserve Corps,
at Santa Fe, made arrangements for Colonel Blanchard to visit the Governor
of New Mexico and ask him to declare Air Force Day in New Mexico on
1 August.

RESTRICTED
39

FBI Teletype Message Dated July 8, 1947

Doc. 7-5m GAO Report to Congressman Schiff
Concerning Roswell, Jul 28, 1995

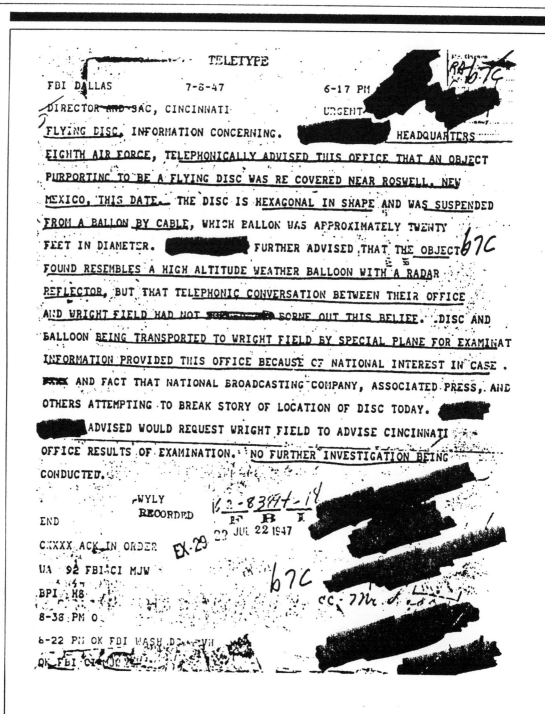

TELETYPE

FBI DALLAS   7-8-47   6-17 PM

DIRECTOR AND SAC, CINCINNATI   URGENT

FLYING DISC. INFORMATION CONCERNING.   HEADQUARTERS

EIGHTH AIR FORCE, TELEPHONICALLY ADVISED THIS OFFICE THAT AN OBJECT

PURPORTING TO BE A FLYING DISC WAS RE COVERED NEAR ROSWELL, NEW

MEXICO, THIS DATE. THE DISC IS HEXAGONAL IN SHAPE AND WAS SUSPENDED

FROM A BALLON BY CABLE, WHICH BALLON WAS APPROXIMATELY TWENTY

FEET IN DIAMETER.   FURTHER ADVISED THAT THE OBJECT

FOUND RESEMBLES A HIGH ALTITUDE WEATHER BALLOON WITH A RADAR

REFLECTOR, BUT THAT TELEPHONIC CONVERSATION BETWEEN THEIR OFFICE

AND WRIGHT FIELD HAD NOT BORNE OUT THIS BELIEF. DISC AND

BALLOON BEING TRANSPORTED TO WRIGHT FIELD BY SPECIAL PLANE FOR EXAMINAT

INFORMATION PROVIDED THIS OFFICE BECAUSE OF NATIONAL INTEREST IN CASE.

AND FACT THAT NATIONAL BROADCASTING COMPANY, ASSOCIATED PRESS, AND

OTHERS ATTEMPTING TO BREAK STORY OF LOCATION OF DISC TODAY.

ADVISED WOULD REQUEST WRIGHT FIELD TO ADVISE CINCINNATI

OFFICE RESULTS OF EXAMINATION. NO FURTHER INVESTIGATION BEING

CONDUCTED.

WYLY
RECORDED

END

CXXXX ACK IN ORDER   EX-29   22 JUL 22 1947

UA 92 FBI CI MJW

BPI H8

8-38 PM O

6-22 PM OK FBI WASH D

OK FBI CI

Comments From the National Security Council

Doc. 7-5n GAO Report to Congressman Schiff
Concerning Roswell, Jul 28, 1995

9K 2948

NATIONAL SECURITY COUNCIL
WASHINGTON. D.C. 20506

April 28, 1995

MEMORANDUM FOR MR. JOSEPH E. KELLEY
                Director-in-Charge, International
                  Affairs Issues
                General Accounting Office

SUBJECT: Request for NSC Records

I am responding to your April 12, 1995, request for information or NSC records related to the crash of an airborne object near Roswell, New Mexico in July 1947. The NSC has no records or information related to the incident at Roswell.

For information about any government records that may document the crash at Roswell, we suggest you contact the National Archives, Textual Reference Division, 8601 Adelphi Road, College Park, Maryland 20740. Their telephone number is (301) 713-7230.

                        Andrew D. Sens
                        Executive Secretary

Comments From the Office of Science and Technology Policy, Executive Office of the President

Doc. 7-5o GAO Report to Congressman Schiff
Concerning Roswell, Jul 28, 1995

EXECUTIVE OFFICE OF THE PRESIDENT
OFFICE OF SCIENCE AND TECHNOLOGY POLICY
WASHINGTON, D.C. 20500

April 26, 1995

Dear Mr. Hunt:

In response to your recent inquiry of April 12, 1995. The Office of Science and Technology Policy reviewed its records regarding the Roswell Incident. OSTP has no direct knowledge of what occurred at Roswell and no records, except for the information I received from the Air Force.

I look forward to receiving the GAO report.

Sincerely,

John H. Gibbons
Director

Enclosures
As stated

Mr. William Hunt
Director, Federal Management Issues
United States Government Accounting Office
Washington, DC 20548

Comments From the Department of Energy

Doc. 7-5p GAO Report to Congressman Schiff
Concerning Roswell, Jul 28, 1995

Department of Energy
Washington, DC 20585

June 8, 1995

Richard Davis
Director, National Security
  Analysis
General Accounting Office
Washington, D.C. 20538

Dear Mr. Davis:

This is in response to your request for records related to the crash of an airborne object near Roswell, New Mexico, in July 1947. We conducted an in-depth search for documents related to the crash and have found no such documents.

If you have any questions regarding this matter, please do not hesitate to contact Barry Uhlig of my staff on 202-586-1910.

Sincerely,

Joseph F. Vivona
Chief Financial Officer

Printed with soy ink on recycled paper

Comments From the Federal Bureau of Investigation

Doc. 7-5q GAO Report to Congressman Schiff
Concerning Roswell, Jul 28, 1995

U.S. Department of Justice

Federal Bureau of Investigation

Washington, D. C. 20535

April 24, 1995

Mr. Richard Davis
Director
Attn: Gary K. Weeter
National Security Analysis
General Accounting Office
Washington, D. C.

Dear Mr. Davis:

This is in response to a letter dated April 7, 1995, from Norman J. Rabkin, Director, Administration of Justice Issues, General Accounting Office, to John E. Collingwood, Inspector in Charge, Office of Public and Congressional Affairs, FBI, regarding government records concerning the crash of an airborne object near Roswell, New Mexico, in July 1947 (Code 701034).

A search of FBI indices for information relating to the crash of an airborne object near Roswell, New Mexico, in 1947, determined that all FBI data concerning the incident has been processed under the provisions of the Freedom of Information Act (FOIA) and is available for review in our FOIA Reading Room. A copy of the document forwarded to me by Gary Weeter is among the documents in the Reading Room. If your staff wishes to review the material, please call Margaret Tremblay, a member of my staff, at least 48 hours in advance of the desired appointment. She can be reached on 324-5292.

Sincerely yours,

Swanson D. Carter
Supervisory Special Agent
Office of Public and
      Congressional Affairs

Comments From the Department of Defense

Doc. 7-5r GAO Report to Congressman Schiff
Concerning Roswell, Jul 28, 1995

INSPECTOR GENERAL
DEPARTMENT OF DEFENSE
400 ARMY NAVY DRIVE
ARLINGTON, VIRGINIA 22202-2884

Analysis
and Followup

MAY - 4 1995

Mr. Richard Davis
Director, National Security Analysis
U.S. General Accounting Office
441 G Street N.W.
Room 5025
Washington, D.C. 20548

Dear Mr. Davis:

The Department of the Air Force July 1994 report is the DoD response to questions posed in your April 12 letter related to GAO Code 701034.

If you have any questions, please contact my action officer, Pattie Cirino, at 703-604-9631. If she is not available, please contact Ms. Merlene L. Scales at 703-604-9626.

Kathryn A. Truex
Deputy Assistant Inspector General
for GAO Report Analysis

Enclosure

Comments From the Central Intelligence Agency

Doc. 7-5s GAO Report to Congressman Schiff
Concerning Roswell, Jul 28, 1995

Central Intelligence Agency

Washington, D.C. 20505

30 May 1995

Mr. Richard Davis
Director, National Security Analysis
US General Accounting Office
Washington, D.C. 20548

Dear Mr. Davis,

In a letter dated 30 March 1995, this Agency advised you that it would conduct a comprehensive record search to aid in the completion of your investigation of the crash of an airborne object near Roswell, New Mexico, in July 1947. In accordance with your request, we have searched all of our data bases against the terms "Project Mogul" and "Roswell, New Mexico."

The search did not yield any documents related to either of these terms. Therefore, this Agency has no information, beyond those records already reviewed by Mr. Gary Weeter of your staff, relevant to your investigation.

Sincerely,

Nora Slatkin
Executive Director

CHAPTER EIGHT

A Final Word?

Initially, this chapter was not going to be included in this book. However, I feel that the information it contains is important and the American public have a right to know.

Had it not been for the tragic death of my son, Robert Francis Stone, on August 18, 1995, I would have carried much of this information to the grave. Instead, I will reveal some of it here, and more in a forthcoming book about my life and involvement within the Aerial Phenomena Field.

After my retirement from the United States Army in February, 1990, I was hired as a consultant to a Roswell, NM, security firm. On Friday night, August 18, 1995, I was working as Chief of Security at the Roswell Mall. Shortly after 8:00 P.M. we were notified that a motorcycle accident had occurred at the Mall entrance. I was the first officer to respond. Lying dead on the road beside his motorcycle was my son, Robert.

As Roswell Police officer Moore drove me home to inform my wife of our son's death, I heard an All Points Bulletin going out over the police radio for a small blue pickup truck in connection with the accident involving my son. Almost immediately, rumors began circulating about the accident.

About a week later, the News Manager for the local KBIM-TV News, David Gonzalez, called me and stated that he had heard there was more to my son's death than what was being reported. I informed him that I did not wish to discuss my son at that time—thus ending the conversation.

There exist many questions surrounding my son's death, and many reasons why I believe the police may have covered up various mechanical and medical facts about the incident. The police seem to have been acting on orders from higher up, and the whole cycle of denials and contradictions sounded all too familiar from my lifetime of chasing down evasive government sources. However, I will continue to search for the answers to those painful questions without the harsh glare of the media, until I am satisfied that I have the full truth.

I continue to ask myself each day if my involvement in this field had anything to do with the circumstances of my son's death. If foul play was involved, the two missions I have uncovered in my research that are revealed in this chapter might well be the reason why I was punished so severely. That said, I will continue to risk whatever repercussions may lie ahead by telling you what the U.S. Air Force does not wish you to know. This information has taken me more than thirty-five years to uncover.

Most, if not all, of the documents appearing in this chapter are being offered to the public for the first time. Many of these documents have not appeared in print in any other publication. And many of the governmental agencies involved were not even aware that I gained possession of the documents. But, I can assure you, they were all legally obtained.

★★★

To this very day the United States Air Force maintains that ±was the only agency of the federal government that had anything to do with UFOs. Furthermore, the Air Force maintains that its investigations of UFOs were carried out through Project Sign and Project Grudge, and ended with Project

Blue Book. This is a blatant lie and the Air Force knows it. (See doc. 8-1.)

The facts that I have uncovered are that the United States Army started its investigation of UFOs back during the Second World War. The Army's Counter Intelligence Corps (CIC) was charged with the responsibility of finding out what the "foo-fighters" being reported by the Allied aircrews were. After the war, this mission continued.

The CIC was very quietly investigating reports of unusual things being reported in the skies over America before the start of Project Sign (January 22, 1948). With the Kenneth Arnold sighting of June 24, 1947, in Roswell, NM, and the press picking up on it, more and more people started to report sightings of strange objects in our skies. With the outcry from the American public for answers, and in order to protect the secrecy of the real military investigations, Project Sign was established. However, the CIC quietly continued its own secret investigation—whose findings were not to be released to ordinary citizens.

The United States Air Force became a separate branch of the Armed Services in September 1947, as a result of the passing of the National Security Act by Congress. Those CIC individuals who remained in the Air Force after it separated from the U.S. Army became members of the Air Force's Office of Special Investigations (OSI), but were still working counterintelligence for the Air Force. Furthermore, they cooperated with the Army's CIC.

Further evidence of OSI involvement with UFO Investigations is provided in an FBI document dated October 9, 1950. This document states:

> Bureau liaison determined on the morning of October 9, 1950, from OSI Headquarters that the investigation of these aerial phenomena are being handled by OSI, Wright Field, Ohio. Their investigation of these phenomena fails to indicate that the sightings involved space ships or missiles from any other planet or country.

The reason given for the OSI failure to determine the origin of the phenomena was that

> the complaints received by them have failed to indicate any definite pattern of activity. (See doc. 8-3.)

But if these objects are interplanetary, would we have any idea as to what type of "pattern of activity" to really look for?

On January 22, 1948, Project Sign was established as a result of Air Force Letter (AFL) 200-5. Project Sign was assigned an A-2 priority at a Secret level, meaning that the project would not be totally inaccessible, as were Top Secret or security-sensitive information. However, we shall see that other directives placed other agencies with the responsibility for any information classified higher than Secret. Obviously, the Directorate of Air Intelligence was maintaining those files. Furthermore, as we have seen in Chapter One, those cases that could affect national security were not to become part of Project Sign, Project Grudge, or even the Project Blue Book system.

A letter from Headquarters, Air Defense Command, dated February 4, 1948, states:

> CIC personnel attached to the numbered air forces of this command may be utilized to prosecute the investigation of subject incidents (UFOs).

Here we have both the Air Defense Command and CIC being involved. (See doc. 8-2.)

The Directorate of Intelligence of the United States Air Force issued "Air Intelligence Requirements Memorandum Number 4," dated February 19, 1949. (See doc. 8-4.) The purpose of this memorandum was twofold:

> To enunciate continuing Air Force requirements for information pertaining to sightings of unconventional aircraft and unidentified flying objects, including the so-called "flying discs."

To establish procedures for reporting such information.

The investigation of UFOs, according to this document, was to include those reports from overseas commands and Air Attachés, as well as those reported in the United States. This is strange when one considers that, according to the Air Force at that time, the phenomenon was only being reported in the U.S. Also, officially we were not to investigate reports from overseas areas unless they were reported by military personnel. This, according to AFL 200-5.

★★★

On September 8, 1950, the Director of Air Force Intelligence issued a letter entitled "Reporting of Information on Unconventional Aircraft." (See doc. 8-5.) This letter stated:

> The United States Air Force has a continuing requirement for the reporting and technical analysis of observations of unconventional aircraft which might indicate an advance in progress of a foreign power. An unconventional aircraft, within the meaning of this directive, is defined as any aircraft or airborne object which by performance, aerodynamic characteristics, or unusual features, does not conform to any presently known aircraft type.

Please note the definition for unconventional aircraft given in this directive. Is it just coincidence that this is the same definition given for UFOs?

By mid-1953, the Air Defense Command (ADC) had taken over all field invesigations of UFOs. The reasons for this are simple. First, if UFOs proved hostile, it would be the Air Defense Command that would have to deal with the situation.

Second, in January 1953 the Air Defense Command activated the unit best suited to carry out investigations of Uniden-

tified Flying Objects: the 4602d Air Intelligence Service Squadron (AISS).

A CIA document, dated December 17, 1953, states:

> Of particular interest is the fact that ATIC [Air Technical Intelligence Center] is in the progress of transferring Project Bluebook to Hq., Air Defense Command. According to Lt. Col. Harry Johnston, Chief, Electronic Branch, the reason for the transfer was that ADC had been doing most of the investigative work of the project and "if it turns out that those things (UFOs) are space ships or long range aircraft from another country, ADC is the [Air Force] Command that would have to take action." (See doc. 8-6.)

On January 3, 1953, Air Defense Command Regulation 24-4 created the 4602d Air Intelligence Service Squadron. This special unit was given a wartime mission of exploiting downed enemy people, papers, and hardware. Outside of participating in simulated training problems, this unit had no peacetime mission. By March 1953, the decision was made to use the 4602d AISS in UFO investigations, and by the end of December 1953, a working agreement existed between the Air Techical Intelligence Center and the 4602d AISS. (See docs. 8-7 and 8-8.)

The members of the 4602d AISS who were to be involved in UFO investigations were given twenty hours of specialized training to better accomplish their assigned task. (See doc. 8-9.)

Since all UFO reports were to be forwarded to ATIC at Wright-Patterson Air Force Base, thus giving the impression that everything was going to Project Blue Book, it was extremely important to have in place at ATIC the means by which the truly good cases could be pulled and kept from the Project Blue Book Files. This would enable quick-response recovery teams to be dispatched. This was accomplished by the use of another secret military group organized under the name Operation Blue Fly, which is explained below.

Operation Blue Fly was established for the quick recovery of downed foreign equipment, papers, and personnel. Please keep in mind that this was a peacetime mission. Since there existed a belief that the flying discs might be some new device of the Soviet Union, they were included as an item of interest to Operation Blue Fly, the 4602d AISS being the operation's arms, legs, ears, and eyes.

Reports of UFOs were to be given to the 4602d AISS Detachment closest to the reported sighting. Then the detachment would determine if the case warranted follow-up investigation. The 4602d AISS was required to file a report to the Air Technical Intelligence Center within three days of receiving a report.

The reports did not go directly to the Project Blue Book office. First, a report was to go through the Operation Blue Fly Project Monitor Officer. A summary of the history of the Air Technical Intelligence Center for the period of July 1, 1954, through December 31, 1954, shows that problems with this quick-reaction program had been worked out and

In order to insure constant availability of qualified personnel for "Blue Fly," four ATIC officers were assigned duty as assistant project monitors. This assignment takes priority over other Operations Section projects when "Blue Fly" is alerted for travel. (See doc. 8-10.)

Those cases that were easily solved would be passed to the Project Blue Book office for proper filing. However, if the case was an unknown or diffcult in solving, a different course of action came into play.

If the case was truly a compelling unknown and the media had not become aware of it, it would be analyzed by Technical Intelligence (T-2) and the Electronics Division (T-3) of ATIC, while at the same time keeping it out of the Project Blue Book Files. These were the cases that could have some bearing on national security and "were

never meant to be part of the Project Blue Book system."

In order to aid the 4602d AISS in their investigations of UFOS, ATIC provided them with a document, dated January 14, 1955, entitled "UFOB Guide." (See doc. 8-11.) The intent of this document was to aid in the identification of known objects and phenomena, thus ruling out any confusion of experimental airborne materials with truely unidentified flying objects. The 4602d AISS was so impressed with this document, they created their own guide for use by the Ground Observer Corps: "Guide to UFO Identification." (See doc. 8-12.)

In 1957, the 4602d AISS was renamed the 1006th AISS and placed under Headquarters, U.S. Air Force, Directorate of Air Intelligence. With fewer personnel being assigned to the 1006th AISS than its older counterpart, the 1006th was granted the authority to investigate only those UFO cases appearing to have some intelligence value. (See doc. 8-13.)

Under Headquarters, U.S. Air Force Message #54322, dated December 23, 1957, a new Project was created called Project Moon Dust. The mission of Project Moon Dust was "to collect and analyze raw intelligence reports from the field on fallen space debris and objects of unknown origin." This Project also gave the Air Force the means to monitor the UFO investigation efforts of other nations. Some examples of how this activity was carried out are given in the history of the 39th Air Division, dated July 1, 1960, through December 31, 1960, and an OSI document dated August 16, 1962. (See docs. 8-14 and 8-15.)

In the early 1970s this project came under the control of the Department of State with monitorship responsibilities given to the Defense Intelligence Agency. However, well into the late 1980s the U.S. Air Force maintained its own Project Moon Dust.

Some excellent examples of how the Defense Intelligence Agency (DIA) carried out its responsibilities under Project Moon Dust are given in a DIA Message dated July 16, 1965, entitled "Unidentified Flying Objects Sighted in Antarctica"; a DIA Message dated August 26, 1966, entitled "Unidentified Flying Objects Over Taiwan"; a DIA Message dated April 3, 1967, entitled "Reported Sightings of Flying Saucers in Brazil"; a DIA Message dated January 19, 1968, entitled "Unidentified Flying Objects" and dealing with a Russian commission to study UFOs; a DIA Message dated August 9, 1968, entitled "UFO Newspaper Clippings" and dealing with reported UFO sightings in Argentina; and a DIA Message dated August 24, 1974, entitled "Spanish UFO Sightings."

Please note that the Defense Intelligence Agency considers all its records dealing with Project Moon Dust to still be classified in the interests of national security to this very day. The only records they have released to date are those that had already been released by the Department of State. (See docs. 8-16, 8-17, 8-18, 8-19, 8-20, and 8-21.)

According to the U.S. Air Force, none of the documents mentioned in this chapter exist. The Air Force states they were destroyed long ago. (See docs. 8-22 and 8-23.) To be sure, when a U.S. Senator asked the U.S. Air Force about these missions, the response was: "These missions never existed." (See Report to Congress in Appendix.)

Unfortunately for those seeking to cover up the truth, the documents attached to this chapter were all obtained legally from the U.S. Air Force, Defense Intelligence Agency, the FBI, and the Department of State—to name but a few. These missions, identified in this chapter, continue to this day. However, with the U.S. Air Force having no knowledge of what other government agencies had released to me, it was impossible for them to maintain any consistancy in their evasive, untruthful responses to my inquiries.

In a letter from the Air Force dated May 3, 1990, concerning a request from me on Moon Dust and Blue Fly, I was told:

We have two records responsive to your request. However, they are exempt from disclosure because the information contained in them is currently and properly classified.

Upon my appeal of this decision, the Air Force responded under a letter dated July 25, 1990:

The information responsive to your request that is being withheld is currently properly classified pursuant to Executive Order and is exempt from disclosure.... Release of the information could cause identifiable damage to the national security. Thus, a significant and legitimate governmental purpose is servied by its withholding, and discretionary release is not appropriate. (See Report to Congress in Appendix.)

In March 1991, the Department of State surfaced eleven documents pertaining to Project Moon Dust and Operation Blue Fly belonging to the U.S. Air Force. The Air Force responded, concerning these documents, with a letter dated June 5, 1991, stating:

We can neither confirm nor deny the existence or nonexistence of records responsive to your request regarding "Projects or Operations known as BLUE FLY, MOON DUST, AFCIN SOP, and ICGL#4," as any other response could reveal operations under section 1.3(a)(1) of Executive Order 12356, "National Security Information".

Once I started asking for congressional assistance, these documents known to exist disappeared. The Air Force could no longer locate them.

On September 29, 1994, I asked for the assistance of Senator Domenici's Office in getting the release of the above-mentioned documents. The Air Force responded with a letter dated December 7, 1994, stating:

The projects as such no longer exist, nor do their files. Classified

51

reports that existed, if any, presumably were destroyed.

Considering the Air Force's responses of May 3, 1990, July 25, 1990, and June 5, 1991, the above comment can only be considered as a statement made in a further attempt to cover up these missions.

On September 27, 1994, I requested that the Air Force do a "Mandatory Declassification Review" (MDR) of the Moon Dust and Blue Fly records. Once again, with a letter dated February 23, 1995, the Air Force denied the existence of any records. However, this time they sent me several records stating that they

> [were] previously provided to the Air Force by individuals seeking information on records relating to Projects MOONDUST and BLUEFLY.

An interesting point to this is that the records they sent me were taken directly from my previous book, UFOs: Let the Record Speak for Itself.

Finally, under a letter dated April 4, 1997, the Air Force admitted that Operation Blue Fly was, in fact, involved with the investigation of UFOs by stating:

> Its mission had been enlarged to include space objects and UFOs if any were reported available for recovery. No Soviet Bloc planes or personnel were ever downed in the United States, and no UFOs were ever reported downed or recovered in the United States or anywhere else. Operation Blue Fly was terminated because of the lack of activity. (See doc. 8-24.)

Once again, documents were attached to this letter—all taken from my previous book, along with its special reports. It was clear that the U.S. Air Force was one of my biggest fans, having purchased and repeatedly quoted from my book.

The Air Force statement "No Soviet Bloc planes or personnel were ever downed in the United States, and no UFOs were ever reported downed or recovered in the United States or anywhere else" is totally false.

On March 20, 1964, a Soviet-built Cuban HOUND Helicopter landed in Key West, Florida. The Air Force's Operation Blue Fly was assigned the primary responsibility for the intelligence exploitation of that helicopter. This case is taken directly from the official Air Force Intelligence files. (See doc. 8-25.)

On December 9, 1965, an object fell to earth in Acme, Pennsylvania. There exists in the official Project Blue Book file on this case, a hand-written note stating:

> A three man team has been dispatched to Acme, Pa. to investigate and pick up an object that started a fire.

This case is known within UFO circles as the Kecksburg Case. The "three man team" was not further identified and the object was never brought to Project Blue Book. This three-man team was, in fact, an Operation Blue Fly Team. (See doc. 8-26.)

The above examples present only two cases. To be sure, there exist many more. The Air Force insists these events never happened—even though they are taken from the Air Force's own official files. One can only guess how much more is being kept from the American people and their duly elected representatives.

If a nation of angry readers can help me launch a Congressional investigation of Air Force impropriety (we could call it UFOgate), a primary question to pose to the Air Force would be: How do known and classified documents allegedly "disappear?"

I am of the opinion that we are not encountering bureaucratic incompetence, but purposeful deceit, cover up and obstruction.

Conclusion

Like a crooked accountant preparing two sets of books, the United States Air Force maintained two separate UFO investigation programs. Operation Blue Book was the only program publicly known to exist, and is was conceived and prepared solely to mislead the public. The other program was given a higher classification, and its existence was kept secret from not only the general public but even from the congressional leaders of this country, who have a vital need to know.

Operation Blue Book's purpose was all public relations. It was a clearinghouse for UFO reports, and provided answers to questions from the general public. The highest classification ever given to Operation Blue Book (known in 1948 as Project Sign) was Secret, with an A-2 Priority. Operation Blue Book was never meant to be involved in the investigation of UFO reports that could have any possible effect on national security. Operation Blue Book was an officially sanctioned deception program to cover up the existence of the more highly classified UFO program that did investigate UFO cases with some bearing on national security.

The more highly classified program was the one with substance, concentrating on evidence of encounters with beings of vastly superior technical capabilities. The unit assigned to these "hot" UFO cases was a particular Air Intelligence Service Squadron that seemed to enjoy an unfair monopoly on UFO data, especially that which came in from Air Force pilots and NASA astronauts. This book, by the way, does not pretend to cover the NASA side of the UFO story, but one can find several books with compelling testimony from our astronauts. Relevant books coming out during this 50th anniversary of the 1947 Roswell Incident include William J. Birnes and Philip J. Corso's *The Day After Roswell*, Jim Marrs' *Alien Agenda*, and Bill Fawcett's *Making Contact*.

Even though I have described it as a prop, Operation Blue Book itself was terminated on December 17, 1969. This gave the public the impression that the U.S. Government was out of the business of investigating UFOs and no longer had any interest in the subject. However, the more highly classified program continued to investigate those cases considered to have vital technical intelligence data, and continues to do so to this day.

Do I have any flying saucers to show you at the UFO Enigma Museum in Roswell? No, but I'd be pleased to show you a good deal more than the best collection of government documents on the topic that you now hold in your hands. Without a doubt, much debris from and some intact specimens of unidentified aerial objects are being stored and examined at restricted government facilities. The Air Force, among other agencies, is actively gathering information on these objects from around the world. Even if the intelligence on these objects is relevant to industry, science, and medicine, the data still remain closed to the nation and the world "in the interests of national security."

★★★

The more highly classified UFO investigation program had been able to conceal its activities by hiding behind the Cold War. It used to be claimed that the program was looking for technical intelligence data on new types of Soviet aircraft and, later, on the Soviet space program. Many UFOs of the 1940s and 1950s were thus referred to as possible "unconventional aircraft" of the Soviet Union. Military budgets and secrecy were the fruits of this easy lie. A negligible amount of the material gathered in these investigations has yet to be explained as space junk from the USSR.

It is instructive here, in the conclusion, to review the U.S. Air Force's three officially held conclusions about UFOs: (1) UFOs are not a threat to national security; (2) UFOs do not represent technological developments or principles beyond the range of present-day scientific knowledge; and (3) there has been no evidence indicating that UFOs are of extraterrestrial origin.

My book is a direct counterattack on this fusillade of falsehood. Documentation released under the Freedom of Information Act by the Air Force and other government agencies clearly indicates that the first two of these conclusions are false by definition alone. While these documents from the Air Force and other agencies do not, by themselves, disprove the third conclusion, the existing evidence strongly suggests the existence of objects of unknown origin. The most logical conclusion is that these UFOs are not of our known world.

The purpose and origin of UFOs is yet to be ascertained, but it is evident that our government continues to stand ready to go anywhere in the world to recover possible objects of "unknown origin." My overriding concern is that the United States Congress has NEVER BEEN BRIEFED on the existence of a classified UFO investigation program or the existence of an UFO recovery program. It is my fervent hope that this book convinces even the biggest skeptics that *our government* has the real UFO problem! Whatever the UFOs really are, it is our democratic system that has been invaded by alien, tyrannical behavior on the part of Air Force intelligence and other government agencies.

I have found the UFO enemy, and it is us. Join me in writing to Congress, in insisting that there are governmental checks and balances missing on this issue. Whatever this awesome phenomenon is that has changed our lives forever, this career soldier insists that it is far too important to be left in the hands of the military.

Headquarters
Air Defense Command
Mitchel Air Force Base, New York

4 February 1948

D 333.5 (CIB)

SUBJECT: Investigation and Reporting of "Flying Disc" Incidents

TO: Commanding Generals, First, Second, Fourth, Tenth, Eleventh, and Fourteenth
           Air Forces, Air Defense Command
           ATTN: AC of S, A-2

        1. The numbered air forces of this command are responsible for the prompt
investigation and reporting of incidents relating to "flying discs" which occur
within their respective areas. Numbered air force A-2s, after evaluating disc
incidents, will determine the extent of investigation. Futile expenditure of military
funds and manpower must be avoided.

        2. "Flying discs" will be investigated as provided for in Counter Intelli-
gence Incident Cases, taking cognizance of the USAF Operating Intelligence Echelon
structure. Where it is evident that witnesses, who were together at the time of
incident but who are widely separated at the time of investigation would corroborate
each other's story, only one witness need be interrogated. If there is a reasonable
indication that a reported incident is a hoax or the fabrication of a publicity
seeking individual, no further investigative effort will be expended. However, a
report of such circumstances will be submitted to the FBI office concerned.

            a. CIC personnel attached to the numbered air forces of this command
may be utilized to prosecute the investigation of subject incidents.

            b. Investigations will be coordinated with the FBI Office concerned
in accordance with instructions contained in letter, this headquarters, D 333.3 EX,
subject, "Cooperation of FBI with AAF on Investigation of 'Flying Disc' Incidents,"
3 September 1947.

        3. Reports will be narrative in style and will cover only those facts
pertinent to the subject. Where source credibility cannot be established, or when
an incident lacks foundation, the report will merely state same. Two types of report
will be submitted on all incidents.

            a. Spot Reports (fragmentary reports) will be submitted on all incidents
and will be followed by a Letter Report.

            b. Letter Reports will be submitted to report the completed investigation
of all "flying disc" incidents.

        4. Reports will be submitted in duplicate promptly, usually be regular
mail. However, Spot reports on incidents of substantial character, i. e., those in
which the patent credibility of the witness is beyond challenge and whose technical

background is compatible with his observations of an occurrence obviously not atmospheric of celestial phenomena, may be transmitted by TWX. Reports will be submitted
directly to Headquarters, USAF, ATTN: Directorate of Intelligence, Air Intelligence
Requirements Branch. One informational copy of each report submitted will be forwarded to this command, ATTN: AC of S, Intelligence. Reports will be classified at
least CONFIDENTIAL.

BY COMMAND OF LIEUTENANT GENERAL STRATEMEYER:

                                        RICHARD W. GEUSS
                                        Captain, USAF
                                        Actg Asst Adj Gen

Office Memorandum • UNITED STATES GOVERNMENT

TO : THE DIRECTOR   SUBJECT: FLYING SAUCERS   DATE: October 9, 1950
FLYING DISCS
GREEN FIREBALLS

FROM : MR. D. M. LADD

PURPOSE   To advise you of the most recent information known to the Bureau concerning the captioned aerial phenomena.

BACKGROUND

You will recall that on August 23, 1950, I furnished to you a memorandum regarding Project Twinkle set up by the Department of the Air Force, with the assistance of Land-Air, Inc., at Vaughn, New Mexico, for the purpose of obtaining data regarding these unusual aerial phenomena which had been seen in the vicinity of sensitive installations in New Mexico. To date the Air Force has not advised us of any new developments in connection with this project.

_____, has been contacted by the Albuquerque Office and arrangements have been made in order that the Bureau will be advised in the event any information relative to these phenomena indicates any jurisdiction on the part of the Bureau.

According to Bureau files, an average of approximately three or four complaints have been received per month from June through September. These complaints were brought to the attention of OSI. A review of Bureau files does not indicate that there has been any increase in the sightings of these phenomena during or as a result of the war in Korea.

JURISDICTION FOR INVESTIGATION OF THESE PHENOMENA

You will recall the investigation to obtain information concerning these aerial phenomena is the jurisdiction of the Department of the Air Force. The Department of the Air Force is aware of our jurisdiction in matters relating to espionage, sabotage and internal security, and we have contacted OSI and requested them to advise us of any developments in connection with these phenomena which would be of interest to us as a result of our jurisdiction.

POSSIBLE ORIGIN OF THESE AERIAL PHENOMENA

The Bureau has been advised in the past by OSI that many of the sightings reported to them were determined by investigation to have been of weather balloons, falling stars, meteorological phenomena and other air-borne objects.

INFORMATION OBTAINED BY BUREAU LIAISON FROM OSI, WASHINGTON, D. C.
RE THE CAPTIONED MATTERS ON OCTOBER 9, 1950.

Bureau liaison determined on the morning of October 9, 1950 from OSI headquarters that the investigations of these aerial phenomena are being handled by OSI, Wright Field, Ohio. Their investigation of these phenomena fails to indicate that the sightings involved space ships or missiles from any other planet or country.

According to OSI, the complaints received by them have failed to indicate any definite pattern of activity. OSI further advised they are closely following the investigation of the captioned matters, and they will advise this Bureau of any matters of interest.

ACTION   None. The above is for your information.

DEPARTMENT OF THE AIR FORCE
HEADQUARTERS UNITED STATES AIR FORCE
DIRECTORATE OF INTELLIGENCE
WASHINGTON 25, D. C.

15 February 1949

AIR INTELLIGENCE REQUIREMENTS
MEMORANDUM NUMBER 4

UNCONVENTIONAL AIRCRAFT

PART I - GENERAL

1. **PURPOSE**

The purpose of this memorandum is twofold:

a. To enunciate continuing Air Force requirements for information pertaining to sightings of unconventional aircraft and unidentified flying objects, including the so-called "Flying Discs."

b. To establish procedures for reporting such information.

2. **RESCISSION**

Department of the Army Collection Memorandum Number 7, dated 21 January 1948, and letter, CSGID 425.1, dated 25 March 1948, both subject as above, which have been transferred to Air Force agencies for action, are herewith superseded.

3. **REPORTING**

a. **General**

(1) As complete an answer to the requirements enunciated in Part II, as may be procurable, should be dispatched by means of electrical transmission immediately after sightings.

(2) Supplementary reports should be forwarded as available by the most expeditious means consistent with the importance of the information reported.

b. **Major Air Commands (Overseas) and Air Attaches**

(1) Initial and supplementary cabled reports will be transmitted to the Director of Intelligence, Headquarters United States Air Force. Cables will contain the phase, "Pass to COMGENAMC WRIGHT-PATTERSON AFB, DAYTON, OHIO, ATTN: MCIAXO-3."

Classification (cancelled) (changed to ___ ___ ___
___), effective on ___ ___
___ under the authority of ACS I
by A/S/I USAF

ENCLOSURE

(2) Supplementary written reports, prepared on AF Form 112, will be forwarded to the Director of Intelligence, Headquarters United States Air Force.

(3) Commanding General, Air Materiel Command is authorized direct contact with major Air Commands (overseas) and organizations under their control in connection with the development of information on this subject.

c. Major Air Commands (ZI)

(1) Reports will be forwarded direct to the Commanding General, Air Materiel Command, Wright-Patterson Air Force Base, Dayton, Ohio, Attn: MCIAXO-3 by installations receiving information pertaining to the requirements enunciated in Part II.

(2) Copies of such reports may be supplied the Command Headquarters of the installation concerned.

(3) A copy of all reports sent to Air Materiel Command in accordance with these instructions will be forwarded at the same time to the Director of Intelligence, Headquarters United States Air Force.

(4) Written reports will be submitted on AF Form 112.

(5) Commanding General, Air Materiel Command is authorized direct contact with major Air Commands (ZI) and organizations under their control in connection with the development of information on this subject.

d. Non-Air Force Agencies

(1) Addressees other than those of the United States Air Force are requested to forward reports direct to the Commanding General, Air Materiel Command, Wright-Patterson Air Force Base, Dayton, Ohio, Attn: MCIAXO-3.

(2) In order to reduce the time factor involved in transmission of this type of information it is requested that, wherever communications facilities permit, subordinate elements be authorized to communicate reports direct to the Commanding General, Air Materiel Command.

PART II - REQUIREMENTS

General

1. Date of sighting.

2. Time of sighting (zonal by 24 hr. clock).

3. Where sighted (observer's position):

a. Ground

(1) City, town.

(2) Distance and direction from city or town, road, intersection, etc.

(3) From building (story), yard, etc.

(4) Map coordinates (if feasible) showing latitude and longitude.

RESTRICTED

b. **Air**

   (1) Type aircraft, speed, altitude, direction of flight.

   (2) Distance and direction from city, town or known landmark.

   (3) Clock position of object from observer's aircraft.

   (4) Latitude and longitude.

c. **Sea**

   (1) Latitude and longitude.

   (2) Proximity to land. (Name city, country, etc.)

4. Number of objects.

   Formation type (if any), sketch if possible.

5. Observable celestial phenomena or planets that may account for the sighting. (Local facilities or organizations which follow such celestial phenomena should be consulted for such information.)

6. Distance of object from observer.

   a. Laterally or horizontally.

   b. Angle of elevation from horizon.

   c. Altitude.

7. Time in sight.

8. Appearance of object.

   a. Color.

   b. Shape. (Sketch if possible)

   c. Apparent construction. (Of what material or substance)

   d. Size.

     (1) Estimated size.

     (2) Size as it appeared from observer's view. (Compared to known object)

9. Direction of flight.

10. Tactics or maneuvers.

   Vertical ascent or descent, horizontal, oscillating, fluttering, evasive, aggressive, erratic, etc.

11. Evidence of exhaust.

   a. Color of smoke.

   b. Length and width.

c. Odor (if any).

d. Rate of evaporation.

e. Does trail vary with sound? (spurts)

12. Effect on clouds.

  a. Opened path thru clouds.

  b. Forced cloud or mists.

  c. Reflected on cloud.

  d. Showed thru cloud.

13. Lights.

  a. Reflected or attached.

  b. Luminous

  c. Blinked on and off in relation to speed.

14. Support

  a. Wings.

  b. Aerodynamic list of fuselage.

  c. Vertical jet.

  d. Rotating cylinder or cone.

  e. Aerostatic lift (balloon or dirigible).

15. Propulsion.

  a. Propeller or jet.

  b. Rotor.

  c. Aerodynamic vanes (flapping or oscillating) (Katz Mayer effect).

  d. Visible exhaust or jet openings.

16. Control and stability.

  a. Fins

  b. Stabilizers (horizontal or vertical).

    (1) Size.

    (2) Shape.

    (3) Location.

- 4 -

17. Air ducts.

    a. Slots.

    b. Duct openings.

18. Speed - M.P.H.

19. Sound.

    a. Continuous whine or buzz.

    b. Roar, whistle, whoosh.

    c. Intermittent.

20. Manner of disappearance.

    a. Explode.

        (1) Possibility of fragments.

        (2) Other physical evidence.

    b. Faded from view.

    c. Disappeared behind obstacle.

Relative to the Observer

1. Name of observer.

2. Address.

3. Occupation.

4. Place of business.

    a. Employer or employee.

5. Pertinent hobbies.

    a. Is observer amateur astronomer, pilot, engineer, etc.

    b. Length of time engaged in hobby (experience).

6. Ability to determine:

    a. Color.

    b. Speed of moving objects.

    c. Size at distance.

7. Reliability of observer.

    a. Sources.

RESTRICTED

    (1) Neighbors.

    (2) Police Dept.

    (3) FBI records.

    (4) Employer.

8. Notes relative to observer on:

  a. Sightings in general.

  b. How attention was drawn to object(s).

    (1) Sound.

    (2) Motion.

    (3) Glint of light.

  c. Degree of fatigue and duration of flight at time of sighting in cases where observer is airborne.

9. Witnesses.

  a. Addressees.

  b. Occupation.

  c. Reliability.

10. Comments of interrogator regarding the intelligence and character of person interrogated.

Relative to Radar Sightings

1. Re radars operating on ground.

  a. Observations of range, speed, altitude and size of target.

  b. Did target executive any turn? If so, what angle (180°), etc. and what radius of turn. If radius of turn is not observable, how long did the target stay in the turn and what was its speed?

  c. Note particularly any separation of distant target into several targets upon approach. Track all if possible.

2. If airborne when object sighted.

  a. Were there any radar inductions or extra noise on radio circuits?

  b. Give estimates of size, speed, maneuvers, etc.

GENERAL

1. Teletype sequences of local weather conditions.

2. Winds aloft report.

RESTRICTED

RESTRICTED

3. Local flight schedules of commercial, private and military aircraft flying in vicinity at the time. (Check Canadian activity if close to that border.)

4. Possible releases of testing devices in vicinity sent aloft by Ordnance, Navy, Air Force, Army, Weather Units, Research Organizations or any other.

5. If object contacted earth, obtain soil samples within and without depression or spot where object landed (and then presumably departed) for purpose of making comparison of soils.

6. If object came sufficiently near other aircraft or known objects check surfaces with Geiger counters for possible radioactivity. Make comparisons with other unaffected aircraft objects, etc.

7. Obtain photographs (or original negatives) where available; if not, secure sketches of:

    a. Object.

    b. Surrounding terrain where observed.

    c. Place where it contacted earth (if this happened).

    d. Maneuvers.

    e. Formation if objects were more than two.

8. Secure signed statement.

9. Obtain fragments or physical evidence where possible.

10. Was any radio antenna to be observed, i.e., (any projections or extentions that might presumably be construed as such).

C. P. Cabell

C. P. CABELL
Major General, USAF
Director of Intelligence, Office of
Deputy Chief of Staff, Operations

DISTRIBUTION:

    Commanding Generals, Major Air Commands,
      ZI and Overseas
    All United States Air Attaches

    Director of Central Intelligence
    Special Assistant for Research and Intelligence,
      Department of State
    Director of Intelligence, GSUSA
    Chief of Naval Intelligence
    Commandant (INT), United States Coast Guard
    Director, Federal Bureau of Investigation

RESTRICTED

DEPARTMENT OF THE AIR FORCE
HEADQUARTERS UNITED STATES AIR FORCE
WASHINGTON 25, D. C.

> Doc. 8-5a Director of Air Intelligence Directive,
> Sept 8, 1950

AFOIC-CC-1   8 September 1950

SUBJECT: Reporting of Information on Unconventional Aircraft

TO: Commanding Generals, Major Air Commands, ZI and Overseas

           All United States Air Attaches

1. The United States Air Force has a continuing requirement for the reporting and technical analysis of observations of unconventional aircraft which might indicate an advance in technological progress of a foreign power. An unconventional aircraft, within the meaning of this directive, is defined as any aircraft or airborne object which by performance, aerodynamic characteristics, or unusual features, does not conform to any presently known aircraft type.

2. It is desired that information on unconventional aircraft be reported in the following manner:

a. A separate report of each incident will be forwarded. No information other than that bearing on the unconventional aircraft will be included in this report.

b. Priority of transmission accorded the report will be that appropriate in the judgment of the forwarding agency, according to its apparent authenticity and importance as intelligence.

c. Reports will be forwarded to Commanding General, Air Materiel Command, Attention: MCIS.

d. Reports forwarded by electrical transmission will include, as far as possible:

(1) A brief description of the object(s); its shape, size, color, number, formation if more than one, aerodynamic features, trail or exhaust, propulsion system, speed, sound, maneuvers, manner of disappearance, and other pertinent or unusual features.

(2) Time sighted in 24-hour clock zonal time, and length of time observed.

ENCLOSURE

Incl. 1   62-83594-249

CONFIDENTIAL

(3) Manner of observation; visual or electronic, from air
(give speed, altitude, and type of aircraft), or surface.
Any type of optical or electronic equipment used should
be described.

(4) Location of observer during sighting, giving exact latitude and longitude as closely as feasible, and/or reference
to a known landmark. Location of object(s) with respect to
observer, giving distance, direction, and altitude.

(5) Identifying information on observer(s) and witnesses,
estimate of reliability and experience, and any factors
bearing on estimated reliability of the sighting.

(6) Weather and wind conditions (teletype sequences) at time
and place of sightings.

(7) Any activity or condition, meteorological or otherwise,
which might account for the sighting.

(8) Existence of any physical evidence; fragments, photographs and the like, of the sighting.

(9) Interception or identification action taken. (Such
action should be taken whenever feasible, complying
with existing air defense directives.)

e. Reports forwarded by electrical transmission will be followed
up within ten (10) days by a written report on AF Form 112. This report
will contain the same information specified in subparagraph 2d above in
greater detail, and where feasible will include sketches and signed attested
narrative statements of observers.

f. Written reports of sightings, where no previous electrically
transmitted report has been submitted, will follow the same form as the
written follow-up report described in subparagraph 2e above.

g. Any physical evidence of the sighting will be forwarded by
most expeditious means to Commanding General, Air Materiel Command, Attn:
MCIS, under cover of a letter identifying the shipment with the report of
sighting. Mention of the method and time of shipping of this evidence
will be included in written report of the sighting.

3. It is desired that no publicity be given this reporting or
analysis activity.

BY COMMAND OF THE CHIEF OF STAFF:

Info copies to:
Dir/Int, G-2, Army
Dir/Naval Int.
Commandant (INT) US Coast Guard
Sp Asst for Research & Intel, State
Director FBI
Director of CIA

C. P. CABELL
Major General, USAF
Director of Intelligence

CONFIDENTIAL

Doc. 8-6a CIA Memorandum, Dec 17, 1953

17 December 1953

MEMORANDUM TO: Assistant Director, Scientific Intelligence

FROM   : Chief, Physics and Electronics Division, SI

SUBJECT   : Current Status of Unidentified Flying Objects
                  (UFOB) Project.

1. In accordance with the verbal request of Mr. Brent, Exec/SI, on 30 November, the following resume of the current status of unidentified flying objects activities has been prepared.

2. P&E Division assumed responsibility for the OSI project on unidentified flying objects as a result of your memorandum of 27 May 1953. The project has been confined to maintaining awareness of the activities of other agencies (notably the USAF) in the unidentified flying objects business and to maintenance of files.

3. Status of Department of Defense Activities.

a. Air Force. The Air Force continues to maintain, but with apparently decreasing emphasis, its interest in UFOB's. The present interest of the Directorate of Intelligence, Hq., USAF, is confined to a cursory cognizance of ATIC's project (Bluebook No. 10073). At ATIC the project is carried by one officer (Capt. Charles A. Hardin), one airman (A/1C Max G. Futch), and a secretary operating as the Aerial Phenomena Section of the Electronics Branch, Technical Analysis Division. In spite of this limited staff, as well as several changes of project officer, the project records appear to be up-to-date. ATIC personnel no longer conduct field investigations of UFOB sightings (these are requested from USAF intelligence officers [primarily Air Defense Command and Airways and Air Communications Service] nearer to the sightings), but confine their activities to receiving and checking reports as received, requesting additional field investigation where necessary, performing necessary checking against meteorological, astronomical, aircraft and balloon data, and recording their findings and conclusions in a cross-referenced system by date, location, source, type of observation and conclusion drawn. The Aerial Phenomena Section also deals directly with the Public Information Office of Hq., USAF, regarding information for public release. For about the past year, approximately ten percent of the reported sightings have been tagged as unsolved.

Of particular interest is the fact that ATIC is in the process of transferring project Bluebook to Hq., Air Defense Command. According to Lt. Col. Harry Johnston, Chief, Electronics Branch, the reason for the transfer was that ADC had been doing most of the

investigative work of the project and "if it turns out that these things (UFOB's) are space ships or long range aircraft from another country, ADC is the (Air Force) Command that would have to take action." Col. Johnston followed this concept with the somewhat contradictory statement that the project transfer did not reflect any change in Air Force policy. It is undoubtedly true that ADC is the Air Force Command primarily concerned with UFOB's at the present time in that their interceptors are occasionally dispatched "against" reported UFOB's and that their reporting stations and communications systems are involved in a considerable portion of the UFOB activity. ATIC will maintain liaison with the project.

Approximately a year and one half ago [ATIC initiated a program to purchase cameras for selected ADC radar sites and AACS control towers in locations where consistent UFOB reports were received in the hopes of photographing UFOB's. One lens of the camera (a stereoscopic type) was to be covered with a simple grating to record the spectrographic nature of the UFOB photographed. One hundred "Videon" 35 mm. cameras with "stereon" anastigmat f 3.5 lenses were purchased along with 100 gratings (15,000 line) from CENCO, Chicago. Seventy-four (74) cameras were distributed. Ninety percent of the gratings have "gone bad"--the actual grating separating from the plastic mounting plates. New gratings are expected shortly and ATIC expects to recall all of the 74 distributed cameras and re-equip them with the new gratings.]

Several months ago we were advised that ATIC planned to set up a concentrated instrumentation observational effort in the Albuquerque area. This has now been dropped.

[Project STORK (SECRET) has been preparing, at ATIC request, a comprehensive statistical report on UFOB sightings during the period 1947 through 1952. This study is now expected to be completed by 15 December 1953.

ATIC issues status reports on Project Bluebook on a tri-monthly basis the most recent being Report No. 12 30 September 1953.

b. Navy. The Navy in spite of press reports to the contrary, is presently devoting only part of one ONI analyst's time to maintaining cognizance of UFOB's.

c. Army. The Army has evidenced little or no interest in UFOB's other than cooperating with the Air Force in reporting sightings and pertinent data using the Air Force format.

4. Investigations or Interests of Foreign Governments.

d. Other. Aside from a few scattered reports, mostly old, which indicate interest in UFOB's by private individuals or groups, there is no information of concern or inquiries of consequence in other foreign countries.

5. Results of CSI Panel Recommendations. The consultants who considered this problem in January 1953 recommended that UFOB's be stripped of special status and aura of mystery and that policies on intelligence, training, and public education pertinent to true indications of hostile intent or action be prepared. The definite drop in the number of "sightings" reported during 1953 over 1952 could be attributed to actions following these recommendations. Two recent books ("Flying Saucers From Outer Space" by Keyhoe and "Flying Saucers Have Landed" by Leslie and Adamski) take full advantage of "official" UFOB reports released by the Air Force to develop a central theme that UFOB's are extraterrestrial in origin. Fortunately, the latter book is so nonsensical and obviously fraudulent that it may actually help calm down public reaction. These books do, however, illustrate the risk taken by the present policy. There are no other as yet apparent results of these recommendations.

TODOS H. ODARENKO

-3-

AIR TECHNICAL INTELLIGENCE CENTER
WRIGHT-PATTERSON AIR FORCE BASE
OHIO

In reply refer to
AFOIN-ATIAE-5

5 MAR 1953

SUBJECT: (Uncl) Utilization of 4602nd AISS Personnel in Project
Blue Book Field Investigations

TO: Commanding General
       Air Defense Command
       ATTN: Director of Intelligence
       Ent Air Force Base
       Colorado Springs, Colorado

1. During a recent conference attended by personnel of the 4602nd
AISS and Project Blue Book the possibility of utilizing 4602nd AISS field
units to obtain additional data on reports of Unidentified Flying Objects
was discussed. It is believed by this Center that such a program would
materially aid ATIC and give 4602nd AISS personnel valuable experience in
field interrogations. It would also give them an opportunity to establish
further liaison with other governmental agencies, such as CAA, other
military units, etc., in their areas.

2. To utilize these people the following plan is proposed:

a. When ATIC receives a report of an Unidentified Flying
Object that it deems advisable to further investigate, the Commanding
Officer, 4602nd AISS, will be notified by wire or phone. He will be
given the details of the report and suggestions for follow-up questioning that Project Blue Book personnel may believe pertinent. He will
then assign one of his units to the investigation.

b. If the investigation cannot be completed within three
calendar days of its request by ATIC, ATIC will be notified by wire.
This notification will briefly state the status of the investigation
and when it is expected to be completed. This wire will come directly
to the Commanding General, Air Technical Intelligence Center, Attn:
ATIAE-5, Wright-Patterson Air Force Base, Ohio, with an information
copy to whomever the Commanding Officer, 4602nd AISS deems necessary.

c. Upon completion of the investigation, or if the reported
object is identified during the investigation, ATIC will be notified as
to the pertinent facts by wire, the same as mentioned in paragraph 2b.
This wire will briefly state what courses of investigation were followed,
such as checking the locations of balloons and aircraft, the possibility
of meteors being observed, possible radar contacts, etc. The wire will
be followed by a complete written report.

10512

ATIC ATIAE-5 Subject: (Uncl) Utilization of 4602nd AISS Personnel in Project Blue Book Field Investigations

   3. Project Blue Book is acquainted with the physical location of all 4602nd AISS units and will use discretion in requesting investigations where long distance travel is required.

   4. If this proposed plan is concurred with, Project Blue Book will provide 4602nd AISS personnel with guidance material for investigations reports of Unidentified Flying Objects.

   5. Concurrence and/or comments on the plan proposed in paragraph 2 are requested.

       FOR THE COMMANDING GENERAL

                                        /S/ Robert C. Brown
                                          ROBERT C. BROWN
                                          Major, USAF
                                          Air Adj. Gen.

ADDRE 319.1 (5 Mar 53)   1st Ind

HQ AIR DEFENSE COMMAND, Ent AFB, Colorado Springs, Colorado

TO: Commanding General, Air Technical Intelligence Center, Wright-
     Patterson Air Force Base, Dayton, Ohio

     This headquarters concurs with plan as proposed in paragraph 2 of basic letter.

       FOR THE COMMANDING GENERAL:

                                        JOSEPH D. HORNER
                                        Lt Col,   USAF
                                        Asst Adj Gen,

2

10512

DIVISION OF RESPONSIBILITY ATIC-ADC

AGREEMENT:

An agreement was concluded in December 1953 between the Air Technical Intelligence Center and Air Defense Command whereby, in the future, the 4602d Air Intelligence Service Squadron will process and make on-the-spot investigations on all initial UFO reports originating in the ZI. The 4602d AISS is a definite intelligence activity which is widespread in the field. In some cases, ATIC will join ADC in field investigations.

UNKNOWNS:

At the conclusion of investigations by 4602d AISS, Air Defense Command will furnish information to ATIC on all closed (identified) cases and will forward all material and reports of investigations on the cases which remain as unknowns.

FINAL ANALYSIS:

The ATIC retains the responsibility for final analysis of these unknowns originating in the ZI, together with all cases from overseas.

AIR FORCE REGULATION 200-2 (NEW):

This program will be formally initiated with the publication of a new AFR 200-2 which is forthcoming.

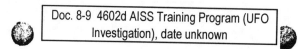

TRAINING PROGRAM
(UFO INVESTIGATION)
(20 Hours)

1. Introduction   3 Hours
   a. Background and History of the UFO Program   1
   b. Philosopy   1
   c. Public Relations   1

2. Investigation   5 Hours
   a. Procedures
   b. Techniques

3. Interrogation   5 Hours
   a. Philosophy
   b. Procedure
   c. Techniques
   d. Psychology

4. Equipment   5 Hours
   a. Geiger Counter   2
       (1) Purpose
       (2) Method of Operation
       (3) Operation
   b. Camera   1
       (1) Purpose
       (2) Operation
   c. Compass   45 Minutes
       (1) Purpose
       (2) Operation
   d. Binoculars   15 Minutes
       (1) Purpose
       (2) Operation
   e. Misc. Equipment   1 Hour

5. General Information   5 Hours
   a. Astronomy
   b. Balloons
   c. Satellites
           Etc.

6. Reporting   2 Hours

7. Summary   1 Hour

HISTORY OF
AIR TECHNICAL INTELLIGENCE CENTER

I JULY 1954 - 31 DECEMBER 1954

AIR TECHNICAL INTELLIGENCE CENTER
WRIGHT-PATTERSON AIR FORCE BASE
OHIO

Copy No.

T-55-211

EXCERPT
DECLASSIFIED BY
AFHRA/ISR NOV

(Uncl) "Blue Fly":[14]

This project remained in a "stand-by" status during this reporting

period and was not activated. (Uncl)

A problem arose as to the priority classification assigned to "Blue

Fly" project by the 18th Air Force. The liaison officer, Major Harold

M. Bergeson, and the ATIC Project Monitor met and resolved this and other

problems of minor importance. As a further result of this conference,

---

13. Project 40001, Collection of ATI Information - Specific Requests.

14. Project 40020, Collection of ATI Information - Foreign Equipment
     and Materiel.

47

Hq 62d Troop Carrier Wing (Heavy) put into effect an operations plan

which provides for complete support of "Blue Fly" within twelve hours

after receipt of an alert notice by that headquarters.

In order to insure constant availability of qualified personnel for

"Blue Fly," four ATIC officers were assigned duty as assistant project

monitors. This assignment takes priority over other Operations Section

projects when "Blue Fly" is alerted for travel.

ATIAE5/CAH/wm/69216

Doc. 8-11a UFO Reporting Guide, Jan 14, 1955

X-MGT-2
OFFICIAL FILE COPY
10073
ELECTRONICS BRANCH
Office of Record

SUBJECT: (U) Unidentified Flying Object Guide

TO: Commander
           4602d AISS (ADC)
           Ent Air Force Base
           Colorado Springs, Colorado

14 JAN 1955

1. Attached for your convenience is the "UFOB Guide" (Unidentified Flying Object Guide) which was prepared as a result of the conference held on 17 and 18 November 1954 between the commander and staff of the 4602d AISS and personnel of ATIC.

2. The "UFOB Guide" is divided into two parts. Part I contains the criteria for use in determining the feasibility of making follow-up investigations. Part II contains hypotheses or examples for use in identifying the objects or phenomena reported.

3. It is suggested that, after a reasonable period of use, a part III be added to the "UFOB Guide" incorporating the definitions and procedures as agreed upon in the conference and as outlined in your letter subject "Report of Visit of ATIC Representatives" dated 23 November 1954. This could then be printed or mimeographed and would serve both the 4602d AISS and the ATIC as standard operating procedure.

FOR THE COMMANDER

Incl
   UFOB Guide

MARY L. STORM
1st Lt. USAF
Assistant Adjutant

COORDINATION:

ATIAE-5 _C.A. Hardin_ DATE 1/12/55
        Capt C.A. Hardin

ATIAE   _____ DATE 12 Jan
        Lt Col H.C. Johnston

ATIA   _____ DATE 13 Jan
        Col W

UFOB GUIDE

This guide is designed for use in determining the feasibility

of follow-up investigation of Unidentified Flying Object reports

and in identifying the objects or phenomena concerned.

AIR TECHNICAL INTELLIGENCE CENTER
WRIGHT PATTERSON AIR FORCE BASE, OHIO

PART I

FOLLOW-UP INVESTIGATIONS

GENERAL

An UFOB report is worthy of follow-up investigation when it contains information to suggest that a positive identification with a well known phenomenon may be made or when it characterizes an unusual phenomenon. The report should suggest almost immediately, largely by the coherency and clarity of the data, that there is something of identification value and/or scientific value.

In general, reports which should be given consideration are those which involve several reliable observers, together or separately, and which concern sightings of greater duration than one quarter minute. Exception should be made to this when circumstances attending the report are considered to be extraordinary.

Special attention should be given to reports which give promise of a "fix" on the position and to those reports involving unusual trajectories.

RULES OF THUMB

Every UFOB case should be judged individually but there are a number of "rules of thumb," under each of the following headings, which should prove helpful in determining the necessity for follow-up investigation.

1. Duration of Sighting

When the duration of a sighting is less than 15 seconds, the probabilities are great that it is not worthy of follow-up. As a word of caution, however, should a large number of individual observers concur

on an unusual sighting of a few seconds duration, it should not be
dismissed.

When a sighting has covered just a few seconds, the incident,
when followed-up in the past, has almost always proved to be a meteor or
a gross mis-identification of a common object owing to lack of time in
which to observe.

2. <u>Number of Persons Reporting the Sighting</u>

Short duration sightings by single individuals are seldom worthy
of follow-up.

Two or three competent independent observations carry the weight
of 10 or more simultaneous individual observations. As an example, 25
people at one spot may observe a strange light in the sky. This,
however, has less weight than two reliable people observing the same
light from different locations. In the latter case a position-fix is
indicated.

3. <u>Distance from Location of Sighting to Nearest Field Unit</u>

Reports which meet the preliminary criteria stated above should
all be investigated if their occurrence is in the immediate operating
vicinity of the squadron concerned.

For reports involving greater distances, follow-up necessity
might be judged as being inversely proportional to the square of the
distances concerned. For example, an occurrence 150 miles away might
be considered to have four times the importance (other things being equal)
than one that is 300 miles away.

4. Reliability of Person or Persons Reporting

In establishing the necessity of follow-up investigation only "short term" reliability of individuals can be employed. Short term reliability is judged from the logic and coherency of the original report and by the age and occupation of the person. Particular attention should be given to whether the occupation involves observation reporting or technical knowledge.

5. Number of Individual Sightings Reported

Two completely individual sightings, especially when separated by a mile or more constitutes sufficient cause for follow-up, assuming previous criterion have not been violated.

6. The Value of Obtaining Additional Information Immediately

If the information cannot be obtained within seven days, the value of such information is greatly decreased.

It is of great value to obtain additional information immediately if previously stated criteria have been met. Often, if gathered quickly, two or three items (weather conditions, angular speed, changes in trajectory, duration, etc.) are sufficient for immediate evaluation.

If investigation is undertaken after weeks or months the original observers cease to be of value as far as additional new information is concerned. Generally, late interrogation yields only bare repetition of facts originally reported plus an inability on the part of the observer to be objective.

7. Existence of Physical Evidence (Photographs, Material, Hardware)

In cases where any physical evidence exists, a follow-up should

be made even if some of the above criteria have not been met.

CONCLUSION - Part I

It is understood that all above criteria must be evaluated in terms of "common sense." The original report, from its wording and clarity will almost always suggest to the reader whether there is any "paydirt" in the report.

PART II

IDENTIFICATION CRITERIA

GENERAL

When an UFO report meets, in large measure, the criteria projected in Part I and a follow-up investigation is instituted, then the interrogator should ask what physical object or objects might have served as the original stimulus for the report. The word "object" here includes optical phenomena such as reflections from clouds, sundogs, etc.

Frequently one or perhaps two solutions will be immediately suggested by the nature of the report. The word "solution" cannot be used here in the scientific sense. A solution in UFOB work means that a hypothesis has been arrived at which appears to have the greatest probability of having given rise to the given report.

Following is a group of hypotheses or examples which should prove helpful in arriving at solutions. A check should be made to see how many of the items are satisfied by the report and how many are missing. An effort should be made to obtain any missing items as soon as possible.

Each typical hypothesis is listed on a separate page.

5

AIRCRAFT

1. <u>Shape</u>: From conventional to circular or elliptical.

2. <u>Size</u>: Pinpoint to actual.

3. <u>Color</u>: Silver to bright yellow (night - black or color of lights).

4. <u>Speed</u>: Generally only angular speeds can be observed. This depends on distance but small objects crossing major portion of sky in less than a minute can be ruled out. Aircraft will not cross major portion of sky in less than a minute whereas a meteor certainly will.

5. <u>Formation</u>: Two to twenty. Numbers greater than 20 more likely birds than aircraft.

6. <u>Trails</u>: May or may not have (vapor and exhaust).

7. <u>Sound</u>: Zero to loud shrill or low depending on altitude.

8. <u>Course</u>: Steady, straight or gently curving (not erratic - may appear still if approaching head-on). Right angle turns and sudden reversals, changes in altitude ruled out. Note: Although report may indicate erratic course, if other items check, follow-up should proceed on basis of aircraft because of psychological tendencies of excited people to exaggerate course changes.

9. <u>Time In Sight</u>: More than 15 seconds, generally of the order of a minute or two.

10. <u>Lighting Conditions</u>: Night or Day.

11. <u>Radar</u>: Should show normal aircraft returns.

6

BALLOONS

1. Shape: Round to cigar or pinpoint.

2. Size: Balloons up to a hundred feet will generally appear from pinpoint to size of a pea held at armlength.

3. Color: Silver, white or many tints. It may possibly appear dark as when projected against the clouds.

4. Speed: Large scale erratic speed ruled out. In general hovering to slow apparent speed.

5. Formation: Single to cluster.

6. Trail: None.

7. Sound: None.

8. Course: Straight with a general gradual ascent, unless falling.

9. Time In Sight: Generally long. Note: Balloon may suddenly burst and disappear.

10. Lighting Conditions: Night or day but especially at sunset.

11. Radar: No return except when carrying sonde equipment.

METEOR

1.   Shape: Round to elongated.

2.   Size: Pinpoint to size of moon.

3.   Color: Flaming yellow with red, green or blue possible.

4.   Speed: Crosses large portion of sky in few seconds except if coming head-on.

5.   Formation: Generally single - can break into shower at end of trajectory. Occasionally (but rare) small groups.

6.   Trail: At night almost always a luminous train which can persist as long as a half hour (rarely). Daytime meteors are much less frequently observed. In daytime, leaves a whitish to dark smoke trail.

7.   Sound: None, although occasionally reported (believed psychological).

8.   Course: Generally streaking downward, but not necessarily sharply downward. Can on rare occasion give impression of slight rise.

9.   Time In Sight: Longest reported about 30 seconds, generally less than 10.

10. Lighting Conditions: Day or Night. Mostly night.

11. Radar: Return from meteor itself is highly improbable, however, the train left by a meteor, is a good radar reflector.

12. Other: An exceptionally bright meteor is called a fireball. These are rare but extremely spectacular and on occasion have been known to light surroundings to the brightness of daylight.

The planets, Venus, Mars, Jupiter, and Saturn are generally brighter than any star, but they twinkle very much less (unless very close to horizon). Stars twinkle a great deal and when near the horizon can give impression of flashing light in many colors.

1.   Shape: Pinpoint - starlike.

2.   Size: Never appreciable.

3.   Color: Yellow with rainbow variations.

4.   Speed: Stars apparent speeds carry them from east to west in the course of the night but they are often reported as erratic. The effect is psychological, most people being unable to consider a point as being stationary. Occasionally turbulence in the upper atmosphere can cause a star to appear to jump (rare) but somehow twinkling gives the impression of movement to many people. Note: Just because the report says the light moves does not rule out the possibility of it being a star unless motion is from one part of sky to another in relatively short time.

5.   Formation: There are no clusters of very bright stars but faint stars are grouped in their familiar constellations. Note: A report of 4 or 5 bright clustering lights would rule out stars.

6.   Trail: None.

7.   Sound: None.

8.   Course: Always describe 24 hour circle around pole of sky from east to west.

9.   Time In Sight: When clear, stars are always visible. Most stars rise or set during the course of the night. Stars low in western sky set within an hour or two. Stars in east, always go higher in sky.

10.   Lighting Condition: Night - Twilight.

11.   Radar: None.

OPTICAL PHENOMENA

GENERAL

This can cover a multitude of things. Original scanning of the report should be made to attempt to determine whether it more likely describes a material object or an optical phenomenon.

Optical phenomena which have been reported as UFOBs run from reflections on clouds and layers of ice crystals (sundogs) to the many types of mirages. No one set of optical phenomena can be set down as representation for the whole class.

There is no limit to the speed of optical phenomena. Reflections can travel from incredible speed, as in the case of a search-beacon on high clouds, to stationary.

These cases if well reported will almost always warrant follow-up. Their variety and connection with upper atmospheric conditions make these observations especially valuable scientifically.

1.   Shape: Generally round but can be elliptical or linear.

2.   Size: Starlike to large luminous glow.

3.   Color: Generally yellow.

4.   Speed: Stationary to fantastic.

5.   Formation: Any.

6.   Trail: None.

7.   Sound: None.

8.   Course: Any.

9.   Time In Sight: Any.

10. **Lighting Conditions:** Day and night.

11. **Radar:** No return. In special cases radar response will occasionally have to do with unusual clouds, and meteorological phenomena such as described in Minnaert's book "Light and and Color in the Open Air."

12. **Other:** One of the standard types is the "sundog." In this a large luminous halo is seen around the sun with one to four images of the sun placed along the halo circle at intervals of 90 degrees. Another report often has to do with a bright planet or even the moon shining through a light overcast. Mirages reflections are said to occur frequently when temperature inversions exists in the atmosphere. If an optical phenomena is suspected, routine check of the meteorological records should be made to establish whether such inversions existed.

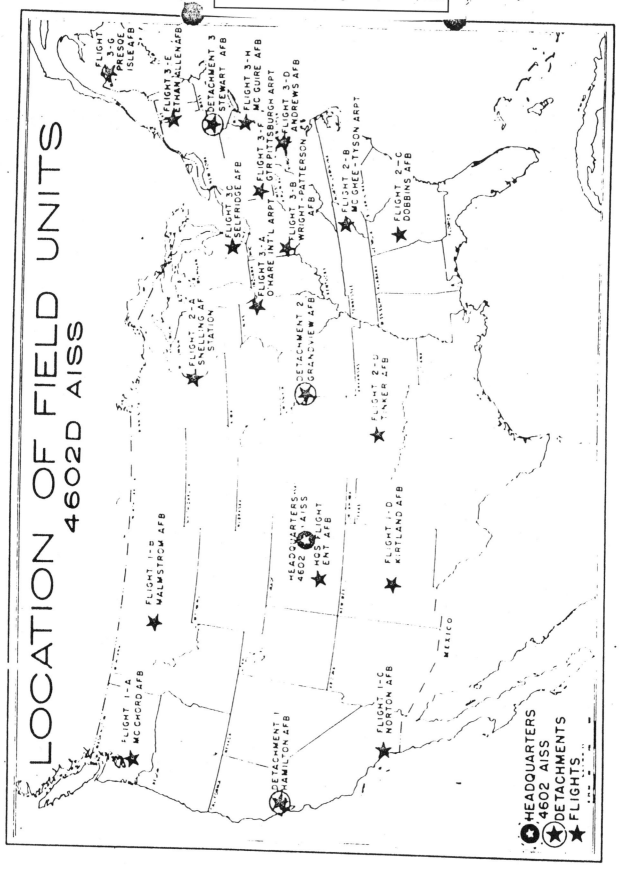

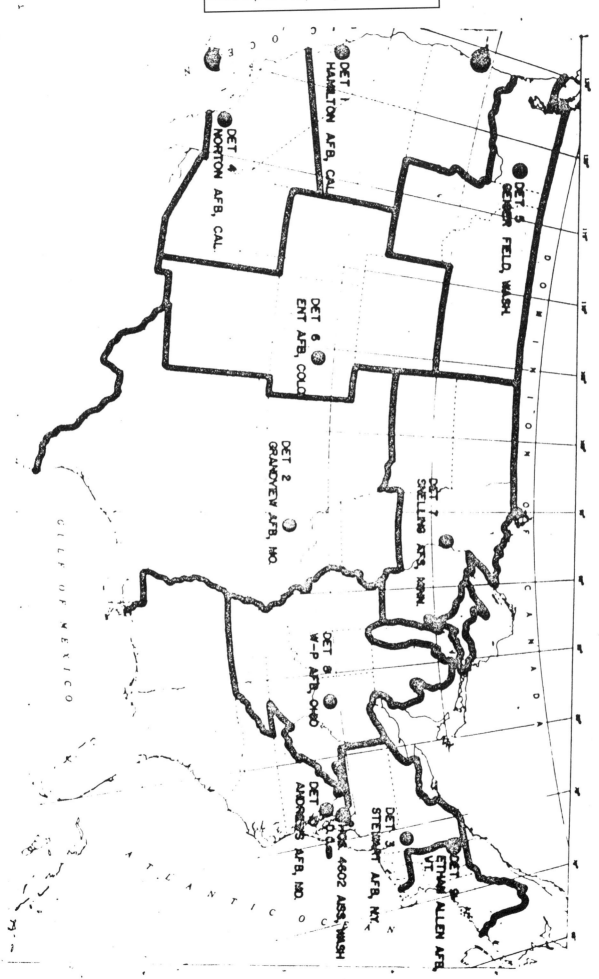

[handwritten notes: Rough Draft / Wilma - / Ref: Don't follow this / Partic's 400 w/ obj / Gen Harper ACD (GOC) / gives you --]

FOR

HEADQUARTERS 4602D AISS
Ent Air Force Base
Colorado Springs, Colorado

UFO

~~SIMPLE~~ GUIDE TO IDENTIFICATION

Unidentified Flying Objects

1. PURPOSE: This publication is designed for the use of Ground Observer Corps personnel, and is published to familiarize observers with common phenomena which are sometimes misinterpreted as Unidentified Flying Objects (UFOB's).

2. DEFINITIONS:

    a. Unidentified Flying Object (UFOB)-- Relates to any airborne object which by performance, aerodynamic characteristics, or unusual features does not conform to any presently known aircraft or missile type, or which cannot be positively identified as a familiar object.

    b. Familiar Objects-- Include balloons, astronomical bodies, birds, etc.

3. OBJECTIVE: Due to the prolonged observation of the sky during both daylight and night time hours, familiar objects such as meteors, aircraft, balloons, astronomical bodies, searchlights, birds, etc., will be frequently observed by GOC personnel. Due to atmospheric conditions (temperature inversions, dust, clouds, etc.,), reflections, sound (or

3. OBJECTIVE (Contd)

lack of sound), speed, position, etc., common phenomena may sometimes be misinterpreted as UFOB's. It is highly desirable that all UFO phenomena be identified or explained. In this respect, the observer requires some "rule-of-thumb" to assist him in this identification.

The object of this publication is to familiarize the Ground Observer with the appearance(s) of common objects under one or more of the circumstances listed above.

4. GUIDANCE: Attached is a list of common phenomena to which Ground Observers may be exposed during their tours of duty. It is recommended that you become thoroughly familiar with these criteria, as they may enable you to identify objects with a greater degree of accuracy.

BALLOONS

1. Shape: Round, cigar, pinpoint, or bowling pin,

2. Size: Balloons up to a hundred feet will generally appear from pinpoint to size of a pea held at armlength.

3. Color: Silver, white or many tints. It may possibly appear dark as when projected against the clouds. Sometimes transparent.

4. Speed: Large scale erratic speed ruled out. In general hovering to slow apparent speed,

5. Formation: Single to cluster.

6. Trail: None.

7. Sound: None

8. Course: Straight with a general gradual ascent, unless falling.

9. Time in Sight: Generally long. Note: Balloon may suddenly burst and disappear.

10. Lighting Conditions: Night or day but especially at sunset or sunrise.

WIND EFFECT: BALLOONS MOVE WITH THE SPEED AND DIRECTION OF THE PREVAILING WIND IN THE AREA AND ALTITUDE. IF BALLOON DETERMINED TO BE IN VICINITY WITHOUT REASONABLE DOUBT, AND CONSISTENT GENERALLY WITH THE DIRECTION AND SPEED OF THE WIND OBSERVED, THEN, THE PROBABILITY THAT THE OBJECT WAS A BALLOON IS HIGH.

AIRCRAFT

1. <u>Shape</u>: From conventional to circular or elliptical.

2. <u>Size</u>: Pinpoint to actual.

3. <u>Color</u>: Silver to bright yellow (night - black or color of lights).
   Jet exhaust yellow to red. Under certain conditions
   aircraft too far distant to be visible to the naked eye,
   will reflect sunlight from wings or fuselage.

4. <u>Speed</u>: Generally only angular speeds can be observed. This depends
   on distance but small objects crossing major portion of sky
   in less than a minute can be ruled out. Aircraft will not
   cross major portion of sky in less than a minute whereas
   a meteor certainly will.

5. <u>Formation</u>: Two to twenty. Numbers greater than 20 more likely
   birds than aircraft.

6. <u>Trails</u>: May or may not have (vapor and exhaust).

7. <u>Sound</u>: Zero to loud shrill or low depending on altitude and
   winds aloft. Under certain conditions, aircraft may be
   observed at high altitudes, without making any sound.

8. <u>Course</u>: Steady, straight or gently curving (not erratic - may
   appear still if approaching head-on). Right angle turns
   and sudden reversals, abrupt changes in altitude ruled out.

9. <u>Time in Sight</u>: More than 15 seconds, generally of the order of a
   minute or two.

10. <u>Lighting Conditions</u>: Night or Day.

METEOR

1. **Shape:** Round to elongated.

2. **Size:** Pinpoint to size of moon.

3. **Color:** Flaming yellow with red, green or blue possible.

4. **Speed:** Crosses large portion of sky in few seconds except if coming head-on.

5. **Formation:** Generally single - can break into shower at end of trajectory. Occasionally (but rare) small groups.

6. **Trail:** At night almost always a luminous train which can persist as long as a half hour (rarely). Daytime meteors are much less frequently observed. In daytime, leaves a whitish to dark smoke trail.

7. **Sound:** None

8. **Course:** Generally streaking downward, but not necessarily sharply downward. Can on rare occasion give impression of slight rise.

9. **Time In Sight:** Longest reported about 30 seconds, generally less than 10.

10. **Lighting Conditions:** Day or Night. Mostly night.

11. **Other:** An exceptionally bright meteor is called a "fireball". These are rare but extremely spectacular and on occasion have been known to light surroundings to the brightness of daylight.

STARS OR PLANETS

GENERAL

The planets, Venus, Mars, Jupiter, and Saturn are generally brighter than any star, but they twinkle very much less (unless very close to horizon). Stars twinkle a great deal and when near the horizon can give impression of flashing light in many colors.

1. Shape: Pinpoint - starlike.

2. Size: Never appreciable.

3. Color: Yellow with rainbow variations.

4. Speed: Stars apparent speeds carry them from east to west in the course of the night but they are often reported as erratic. The effect is psychological, most people being unable to consider a point as being stationary. Occasionally turbulence in the upper atmosphere can cause a star to appear to jump (rare) but somehow twinkling gives the impression of movement to many people.

5. Formation: There are no clusters of very bright stars but faint stars are grouped in their familiar constellations.
   Note: A report of 4 or 5 bright close clustering lights would rule out stars.

6. Trail: None.

7. Sound: None.

8. Course: Always describe 24 hour circle around pole or sky from east to west.

9. Time In Sight: When clear, stars are always visible. Most stars rise or set during the course of the night. Stars low in western sky set within an hour or two. Stars in east, always go higher in sky.

10. Lighting Condition: Night - Twilight.

Doc. 8-12h Headquarters, 4602d AISS Guide to
UFO Identification. date unknown

SEARCHLIGHTS

1. **Shape:** Round to elliptical.

2. **Size:** Pea at arms length to large luminous glow, dependent upon cloud height.

3. **Color:** White fluorescent.

4. **Speed:** Stationary to fantastic.

5. **Formation:** Usually only one but occasionally two or three.

6. **Trail:** None

7. **Sound:** None

8. **Course:** Circling, straight, stationary or erratic. **Note:** Scattered clouds can give impression of object disappearing and reappearing in a different portion of the sky in a few seconds.

9. **Time in Sight:** Generally long.

10. **Lighting Conditions:** Night

OPTICAL PHENOMENA

GENERAL

This can cover a multitude of things.

Optical phenomena which have been reported as UFOBs run from reflections on clouds and layers of ice crystals (sundogs) to the many types of mirages. No one set of optical phenomena can be set down as representation for the whole class.

There is no limit to the speed of optical phenomena. Reflections can travel from incredible speed, as in the case of a search-beacon on high clouds to stationary.

1. <u>Shape</u>: Generally round but can be elliptical or linear.

2. <u>Size</u>: Starlike to large luminous glow.

3. <u>Color</u>: Generally yellow

4. <u>Speed</u>: Stationary to fantastic.

5. <u>Formation</u>: Any.

6. <u>Trail</u>: None.

7. <u>Sound</u>: None.

8. <u>Course</u>: Any.

9. <u>Time In Sight</u>: Any.

10. <u>Lighting Conditions</u>: Day and night.

11. <u>Other</u>: One of the standard types is the "sundog". In this a large luminous halo is seen around the sun with one to four images of the sun placed along the halo circle at intervals of 90 degrees. Another report often has to do with a bright planet or even the moon shining through a light overcast. Mirages reflections are said to occur frequently when temperature inversions exists in the atmosphere.

DEPARTMENT OF THE AIR FORCE
HEADQUARTERS UNITED STATES AIR FORCE
WASHINGTON 25, D. C.

Doc. 8-13a U.S.A.F. Memorandum, Jul 21, 1959   2 1 JUL 1959

MEMORANDUM FOR MAJOR GENERAL CHARLES B. DOUGHER, ATIC

SUBJECT: UFO Program

1. Your letter of 22 June, subject as above, has been reviewed with interest. The problems involved in the reporting and investigating aspects of the ATIC UFO program are fully appreciated and it appears that steps of the type discussed in paragraph 2 of your letter will do much toward improving the reporting procedure. Utilization of the 1006th AISS, which you suggest as a means for improving the investigative function, however, presents some problems.

2. "Geographical deployment" is indicated in your letter as a primary reason for having the 1006th AISS perform the investigative function. Actually, the unit's present geographical deployment is considerably less extensive than it was, when, as the 4602d AISS (ADC), it had 19 field units available for UFO investigations. The total number of the 1006th AISS field units, now 10, is being reduced to 6, and whereas each of the 4602d AISS units was manned by 7 to 10 personnel, the 1006th AISS field detachments will have only one officer and two airmen each. Another important factor to be considered is that the smaller and fewer 1006th AISS field units perform extensive active peacetime functions in support of the AFCIN domestic collection program and the Air Intelligence reserve programs as opposed to the former 4602d AISS function of training for a wartime mission. The workload on the 1006th AISS field units is such that, if the scope of the squadron's present UFO investigative responsibilities were expanded to the extent suggested in your letter, the investigations would probably have to be accomplished by personnel from the headquarters at Fort Belvoir, Virginia.

3. In view of the sharply reduced personnel resources of the 1006th AISS and a limited advantage afforded by geographical deployment of a small number of field units performing full time intelligence functions, it is not considered advisable to increase the UFO investigative responsibilities currently assigned to the 1006th AISS by Air Force Regulation 200-2. It is suggested that measures of the type outlined in paragraph 2

of your letter, coupled with continued use of ATIC's existing authority to call upon the 1006th AISS for follow up or detailed UFO investigations might prove the most effective alternative to full time use of the 1006th AISS for UFO investigations.

Doc. 8-13b U.S.A.F. Memorandum, Jul 21, 1959

HAROLD E. WATSON
MAJOR GENERAL, USAF
DEPUTY ASSISTANT CHIEF OF STAFF,
INTELLIGENCE

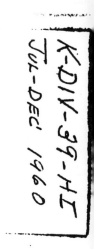

K-DIV-39-HI
JUL-DEC 1960

HISTORY OF THE

39TH AIR DIVISION

P.R.C.

1 July 1960 – 31 December 1960

Prepared by the Historical Division of the Office of Information
of 6139th Air Base Group, by Wilbert S. Higuchi, Historian

(Fifth Air Force – Pacific Air Forces)

RCS: AU-D5

Z- 8182751
0435015
1 390

responsible for training of aircrews and key personnel in current intelligence; the Target Support Section, responsible for maintaining materials for the targets function; the Air Targets Branch, responsible for mission briefings, supervision of target study, preparation, maintenance and issue of target folders; and the Administration Section, responsible for routine paperwork in support of the Intelligence Division.

Operational Intelligence

In intelligence, the pay-off comes when raw information has been collected, evaluated, interpretated, and disseminated as finished intelligence, reaching the right people at the right time. We realized this pay-off on several occasions during the period of this report.

The "Doughnut Cloud"

On 28 June 1960, we were alerted to look for signs of a Soviet missile shot to the mid-Pacific. The Navy was surveilling Soviet telemetry vessels which had moved into the usual Soviet test range in the Pacific; a test shot was expected to follow quickly.

Captain George L. Griffith, AO565506, was appointed project officer for Project "Moon Dust," a USAF-wide intelligence alert intended to sight and report Soviet missiles in flight or downed.

Upon his appointment, Captain Griffith contacted all possible sources at his disposal. This included the 43th District Office of Special Investigations, the Air Defense Control Center (ADCC), the tactical flying units, the Air Police, and all other organizations which were in a position to observe the night sky in their normal duties. These organizations were instructed to notify Captain Griffith the instant a sighting had been made.

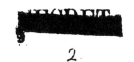

2

~~SECRET~~ DECLASSIFIED

109

The pay-off came at 0130 hours, 5 July 1960, when a phone call from the Division Operations Center (DOC) alerted him that a sighting had been made. At the DOC he met S/Sgt Thomas J. Sweeny of the Air Police. Sgt Sweeny summarized an account of the sighting ten air policemen and four Japanese civilian guards had made that night.

These fourteen men, at their different duty posts, had almost simultaneously witnessed a whitish luminous cloud, about 35 feet in diameter, slowly cross the airfield in a general northwest to southeast path under a scattered cloud layer at 36,000 feet. After five minutes the cloud seemed to spread open in the middle and a bright, reddish-orange glow, the size of a basketball, appeared. The "ball of fire" had streaks of flame darting out from its sides. The reddish center faded within a minute and the cloud assumed a doughnut shape with a dark center, and the cloud remained in this shape for about four minutes before it disappeared due east. [2]

Captain Griffith arranged to interrogate the witnesses later in the day. He interrogated six air policemen and one civilian guard to confirm the original report, then he reported his findings in accordance with "Moon Dust" directives. The whole operation was nicknamed "The Case of the Flying Doughnut." [3]

A TWX from Fifth Air Force to Pacific Air Forces headquarters on 6 July 1960 made it all seem worthwhile. [4] The object sighted was evaluated as a phenomenon which accompanied one of two Soviet missile shots from the Tura Tam test area to the mid-Pacific test range, six thousand miles away. Our sighting was backed up by a civilian airline pilot who had made an almost simultaneous sighting of the doughnut cloud.

~~SECRET~~ DECLASSIFIED

The "Suspended Star"

DECLASSIFIED

On 19 July 1960, within five minutes of each other, a helicopter pilot 400 feet in the air east of Hachinohe, and an NCO in a taxi heading toward the 6921st Radio Group Mobile area, both sighted an unidentified flying object.

According to the helicopter pilot, he saw what appeared to have been a star of great magnitude. It was white, with a blue tinge, and had a tail of whitish color. The "star" appeared to remain stationary during the five or six seconds he had glanced at it.

According to the NCO who had been in the taxi, the object fell slowly in a straight drop to the western horizon. He did not notice a tail, but otherwise his sighting closely coincided with that of the helicopter pilot. There is a good chance that the five minute time difference of the sightings was due to human error.

Intelligence had been alerted by USAF of the impending re-entry of the booster of the Soviet sattelite Sputnik IV during this immediate time period. Captain Griffith had made arrangements for relaying any sightings to him from wherever they were made.

Captain Griffith was notified by the DOC and he was soon in touch with the NCO. They met in the intelligence office and Captain Griffith interrogated him, relayed the information to Fifth Air Force, and contacted other likely sources. Then he interrogated the helicopter pilot and submitted a TMX report of the sightings. The report followed the format of USAF Special Request for Information A-2506 (Project Moon Dust), which was designed to facilitate reporting of re-entry or in-orbit earth sattelites.

DECLASSIFIED

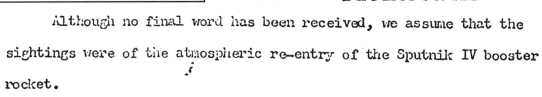
Although no final word has been received, we assume that the sightings were of the atmospheric re-entry of the Sputnik IV booster rocket.

Project Mood Dust was suspended on 4 August 1960.

The "Wavering Light"

On 18 August 1960, Captain Griffith called on an airman and three dependent wives in "B" Battery. They had reported an unidentified flying object to the Air Police, and Captain Griffith checked the sighting out. The "UFO" turned out to be the United States earth sattelite Echo I. Echo I was an earth orbiting balloon which was reflecting the sun's rays while at an altitude of over a thousand miles, circling the earth every 121 minutes.

To avoid further calls on the sattelite, and to reduce the chance of panic among those seeing it, Captain Griffith arranged for the Far East Network to announce the times that the sattelite could be seen from the Misawa area. [9]

The "Geyser"

On 30 September 1960, a TWX report was sent to Pacific Air Forces on a sighting of an unidentified object that entered the water off the coast of Hokkaido, near the village of Otaru. The report originated with the Japanese Ground Self Defense Force (GSDF) headquarters on Hokkaido, and was relayed to us by the Japanese Air Self Defense Force (JASDF) headquarters on Misawa Air Base. According to the report, a fiery object fell from the sky and into the sea, making a fountain of water which was described as looking like a "geyser" Technical Intelligence personnel from Tokyo took over the case, but were not able to locate or reclaim the object. [11]

DECLASSIFIED

Doc. 8-15a U.S.A.F. OSI Report, Aug 16, 1962

24-0   16 August 1962

Unidentified Flying Objects, Reference AFR 200-2, 22 Jul 62;
"Moon Dust", Reference Hq USAF Msg 54322, 23 Dec 57

Colonel William W. Jones
Commander
5010th Air Base Wing
APO 937, Seattle, Washington

1. Reference is made to our telephone conversation, 2100 hours,
15 August 1962.

2. On 14 August 1962, at 2200 hours, this office received a call
from Mr. Walt Gates, (Army CIC,) EL2-5453, who stated that a
Mr. ▓▓▓▓▓▓▓▓▓▓▓ Fairbanks▓▓▓▓▓▓▓ telephoned he had
observed an object sometime between 2230 and 2300 on 10 August
which he thought might be the booster to a Russian satellite.

3. On 15 August I interviewed Mr.▓▓▓▓▓▓▓▓▓▓▓▓ date of
birth - 1 December▓▓▓▓▓▓▓▓▓▓▓▓▓▓▓▓▓▓▓▓▓Fair-
banks, Alaska. Mr.▓▓▓▓▓said he was an engineer for the City
of Fairbanks, but lacked 30 hours towards his engineering degree
from the University of Alaska. He advised that in 1955 he worked
at Bethel, Bering Sea, for six months as an aviation weather
observer, and during his life he has seen numerous meteors, but
he has never seen an object such as the one he saw 10 August,
which he stated was definitely not a meteor. Mr.▓▓▓▓▓▓home
phone ▓▓▓▓▓▓▓▓and his office phone i▓▓▓▓▓▓▓▓

4. ▓▓▓▓▓▓said when he first sighted the round object it was the
size of a penny held in the hand at about arm's length and when
last sighted, it was the size of a silver dollar. The object was
white with a red and blue exhaust. The exhaust was similar to
a 4th of July skyrocket when first sighted. Next, he saw 3 or 4
white and blue streaked objects, one-fourth the size of the main
object, which appeared to drop from the main object and quickly
burn out. When last seen, the main object was all white. He
said the complete incident took place in four seconds. It was a
continuous sighting and he heard no sound. The object drew his
attention because it was extremely bright and appeared very close.

FOR OFFICIAL USE ONLY

It seemed to be dropping from the sky and heading toward him when it disappeared. Sighting from arm's length, the distance traveled was six to ten inches.

5. He saw the object sometime between 0830-0900 Zulu time, 11 August (2230 - 2300 local time, 10 August) and it was between twilight and night. The temperature was 65 degrees, clear visibility with a few scattered clouds. ~~████~~ said he was located at 148:31 E, 64:02 N or 50 miles southwest of Fairbanks when he made his ground visual sighting. When first sighted, the object was at a 30 degree angle above the horizon, azimuth 255 degrees and was last sighted 29 degrees 50 minutes, azimuth 253 degrees.

6. He roughly estimated the object may have been 500 or 1000 miles away, however, he could determine the distance by taking a sextant to the location since he knows exactly where he was when he saw the object.

7. ~~████~~ said ~~████~~ who is employed at the ~~████~~ Company ~~████~~ Fairbanks ~~████~~ saw the object for a longer period of time on the same nig~~████~~ saw it.

8. Brooks drew the attached drawings.

JONATHAN P. LAVERICK
Special Agent
Commander, OSI Det 8101

1 Atch
a/s

2

DEPARTMENT OF DEFENSE INTELLIGENCE INFORMATION REPORT

Doc. 8-16a DIA Intelligence Report, Jul 16, 1965

This report contains unprocessed information. Plans and/or policies should not be evolved or modified solely on the basis of this report.

(Classification and Control Markings)

1. COUNTRY: ARGENTINA/ANTARCTICA

2. SUBJECT: (U) Unidentified Flying Objects Sighted in Antarctica

3. ISC NUMBER:

4. DATE OF INFORMATION: 8 July 1965

5. PLACE AND DATE OF ACQ: Baires/8 July 1965

6. EVALUATION: SOURCE __B__ INFORMATION __2__

7. SOURCE:

OFFICIAL (Argentine Navy Hydrographic Service)

8. REPORT NUMBER: 5 804 0048 65

9. DATE OF REPORT: 16 July 1965

10. NO. OF PAGES: Three

11. REFERENCES: AIRATTACHE BAIRES MSG CITE AF-02 dtd 7 July 1965 (DTG 072110Z)(NOTAL)

12. ORIGINATOR: U.S. Naval Attaché, Buenos Aires, Argentina

13. PREPARED BY:

14. APPROVING AUTHORITY:

A. J. McEWAN, CAPT, USN

(Leave Blank)

8. SUMMARY:

Translation of four messages provided by the Chief, Argentine Navy Hydrographic Service concerning unidentified flying objects sighted recently in Antarctica is submitted. Message originators were Commander, Argentine Base at Deception Island (64 deg 59 min South 60 deg 32 min West), and Commander, Argentine Activity at Orcadas (Laurie Island, South Orkney Islands) (60 deg 45 min South 44 deg 43 min West). The messages summarize sightings by Argentine personnel, and reports that British and Chilean base personnel at Deception Island have also reported unidentified flying objects. Messages are quoted verbatim and have been provided without comment.

---

1. **First Message**   (Note: Times stated presumably LOCAL)

DTG 231459 JUNE 1965

ORIGINATOR: CO DECEPTION ISLAND

TO   CHIEF HYDROGRAPHIC SERVICE

INFO   CHIEF NAVY INTELLIGENCE SERVICE

UNIDENTIFIED FLYING OBJECTS SIGHTED SEVEN JUNE AT ONE NINE FIVE ZERO

16. DISTRIBUTION BY ORIGINATOR:

USCINCSO
USNAV90
COMSOLANT
CINCLANTFLT
USAFSO
AMEMB BAIRES
AIR ATTACHE BAIRES
DATT BAIRES

17. DOWNGRADING DATA:

18. ATTACHMENT DATA:

1 (U) Copies of four messages (in Spanish) *

Translated (as part of report)

REQUEST ATTACHMENT FROM DIAAP-1H2
* (FOREIGN LANGUAGE)

DD FORM 1396

(Classification and Control Markings)

REPLACES DA FORM 1048, 1 AUG 60, OPNAV FORM 3820 (Rev. 10-61), AF FORM 112, JUL 61, WHICH MAY BE USED UNTIL 1 JAN 62.

20

DEPARTMENT OF DEFENSE INTELLIGENCE INFORMATION REPORT

CONTINUATION SHEET

Doc. 8-16b DIA Intelligence Report, Jul 16, 1965

(Classification and Control Markings)

RPT NO: 5 804 0048 65

IS 2 OF 3 PAGES

ORIGINATOR
U.S. Naval Attache
Attache, Buenos Aires

(Leave Blank)

HOURS. OBJECTS SIGHTED BY CIVILIAN METEOROLOGIST JORGE STANICH AND OBSERVED DURING FIVE SECOND PERIOD. OBJECT STATIONARY, COLORED A CLEAR BRILLIANT YELLOW, APPARENT DIAMETER ONE POINT FIVE CENTIMETERS AND SURROUNDED BY AN IRIDISCENT HALO, APPEARING UNDER A THICK CLOUDY CONDITION 300 METER CEILING AT TWO THREE ZERO DEGREES FROM TRUE NORTH AT TWO FIVE DEGREES ABOVE THE HORIZON. SAME OBSERVOR OR SIGHTED ON EIGHT JUNE AT ZERO TWO TWO ZERO HOURS DURING A FOUR SECOND PERIOD SIMILAR OBJECTS WITH AN APPARENT DIAMTER OF ONE CENTIMETER WIDE APPEARING UNDER THICK CLOUDY CEILING OF 300 METERS AT POINT THREE THREE ZERO DEGREES FROM TRUE NORTH AT FOUR ZERO DEGREES ABOVE THE HORIZON. BOTH OBSERVATIONS MADE FROM METEOROLOGICAL CAMP THIS BASE. ON TWO ZERO JUNE THE CHILEAN BASE COMMANDER (AGUIRRE CERDA BASE) REPORTED THAT AT ONE SIX TWO ZERO HOURS A LUMINOUS OBJECT LARGER THAN A FIRST MAGNITUDE STAR WAS OBSERVED BY HIMSELF, JUAN BARRERA, LIEUTENANT BENAVIDEZ (BOTH AF PILOTS), METEOROLOGIST CONCHA AND SEVEN OTHER PERSONS. OBJECT MANEUVERED RAPIDLY FOR TWO FIVE MINUTES OVER DECEPTION ISLAND AREA. AMPLIFYING INFORMATION TO FOLLOW.

BT

2. Second Message.

DTG   041000 JULY.

ORIGINATOR   CO ORCADAS

TO   CHIEF HYDROGRAPHIC SERVICE

INFO   CHIEF NAVY INTELLIGENCE SERVICE

UNIDENTIFIED FLYING OBJECT SIGHTED ZERO THREE ONE SEVEN ZERO THREE BY TWO MEMBERS THIS BASE DURING ONE FIVE SECONDS. DESCRIPTION: WHITE LUMINOUS COLOR, NOT BRILLIANT, ROUND FORM, CLEAN OUTLINE, PARABOLIC TRAJECTORY WEST TO EAST, THREE ZERO DEGREES ABOVE THE HORIZON TOWARDS THE SOUTH, MOVED WITH INCREASING SPEED. VISUAL CONTACT LOST DUE TO CLOUDS.

3. Third Message.

DTG   041543 JULY.

ORIGINATOR   CO DECEPTION ISLAND

TO   CHIEF HYDROGRAPHIC SERVICE

INFO   CHIEF NAVY INTELLIGENCE SERVICE

UNIDENTIFIED FLYING OBJECTS SIGHTED OVER DECEPTION ISLAND ON TWO JUNE OBSERVED BY METEOROLOGIST AT ENGLISH BRAVO BASE AND FOUR PERSONS. SIGHTING LASTED FOR FIFTEEN DASH TWENTY MINUTE AT ONE NINE FOUR FIVE HOURS ON A CLEAR NIGHT WITH ONE EIGHTH STRATOCUMULUS CONDITION AND STARRY SKY, MOON IN FOURTH QUARTER. OBJECT WAS MOVING RAPIDLY AND OF A BRILLIANT COLOR, SOLID APPEARANCE AND NOISELESS, PREDOMINATE COLOR RED AND GREEN BUT AT TIMES YELLOW BORDERED,

(Classification and Control Markings)

DEPARTMENT OF DEFENSE INTELLIGENCE INFORMATION REPORT

CONTINUATION SHEET

Doc. 8-16c DIA Intelligence Report, Jul 16, 1965

T NO. 5 804 0048 65

OF 3 PAGES

NATOR

. Naval Attache
Buenos Aires, Argentina

(Classification and Control Markings)

(Leave Blank)

APPEARING AS A BRILLIANT STAR MOVING IN VARIABLE HEADINGS, SPEEDS, AND STOPS IN AN EASTERLY DIRECTION AT FOUR FIVE DEGREES ABOVE THE HORIZON. ON THREE JULY AT ONE NINE TWO ZERO HOURS THE METEOROLOGIST AND EIGHT OTHER PERSONS AT THE CHILEAN BASE AGUIRRE CERDA OBSERVED DURING TWO ZERO MIN (CLEAR NIGHT, TWO EIGHTS STRATOCUMULUS AND STARRY SKY, MOON FOURTH QUARTER) AN OBJECT APPEARING AS A STATIONARY LIGHT AT TIMES AND OF SOLID APPEARANCE LIKE A CELESTIAL BODY, NOISELESS, WHITE COLOR WITH BORDERS LIKE A BRILLIANT STAR, MOVING EAST TO WEST CENTRAL TRAJECTORY WITH OSCILLATIONS, DISAPPEARING IN THE CLOUDS, ELEVATION DUR ZERO DASH FOUR FIVE DEGREES OVER THE HORIZON. ON THREE JULY AT ONE NINE FOUR TWO HOURS METEOROLOGIST AND SIX PERSONS FROM THIS BASE OBSERVED BY NAKED EYE, BINOCULARS, AND THEODOLITE FOR A PERIOD OF ONE HOUR AND TWO MINUTES (CLEAR NIGHT, TWO EIGHTHS STRATUS, ONE EIGHTH CIRRUS, STARRY SKY, MOON FOURTH QUARTER) AN OBJECT DESCRIBED AS MORE BRILLIANT THAN A STAR OF THE FIRST MAGNITUDE WHICH WAS STATIONARY AT TIMES WITH FLASHING BRILLIANCE (APPEARING AND DISAPPEARING), MOVING ABOVE THE STRATUS AND BELOW THE CIRRUS AT TIMES, OF A SOLID APPEARANCE AND NOISELESS, ITS CENTER COLORED RED, BORDERS CHANGING FROM YELLOW TO GREEN TO ORANGE TO BLUE TO WHITE, AND LIKE A BRILLIANT IRRIDISCENT STAR, SMALL TRAJECTORY VARIATION, SIZE COMPARABLE TO THE HEAD OF A HALF INCH NAIL HEAD, FINALLY DISAPPEARING IN ALTITUDE AND DISTANCE. FORM WAS ROUND AND OVAL SHAPED. DIRECTION OBSERVED NORTH NORTHWEST APPROXIMATELY THREE THREE FIVE DEGREES FROM TRUE NORTH AND THREE ZERO DEGREES ABOVE THE HORIZON, APPROXIMATELY AT A DISTANCE OF ONE ZERO TO ONE FIVE KILOMTERS. SOME PHOTOGRAPHY TAKEN OF THIS SIGHTING.

4. Fourth Message.

DTG   062100.

ORIGINATOR   CO ORCADAS

TO   CHIEF HYDROGRAPHIC SERVICE

INFO   CHIEF NAVY INTELLIGENCE SERVICE

AMPLIFYING INFORMATION MY ZERO FOUR ONE ZERO ZERO ZERO. TWO VARIOMETERS WORKING AFFECTED BY MAGNETIC FIELD DISTURBANCE DURING THE TIME OBJECT SIGHTED.

Comment. Foregoing messages provided ALUSNA BAIRES by the Chief, Argentine Navy Hydrographic Service without comment. First information on UFOs appeared in local press of 6 July with ARG SECNAV PIO release. While information as provided carried no classification and is similar to that appearing in the press, ALUSNA BAIRES has classified ████████ until this point cleared with Chief, Hydrographic Service.

DEPARTMENT OF DEFENSE INTELLIGENCE INFORMATION REPORT

Doc. 8-17a DIA Intelligence Report, Aug 26, 1966

(Classification and Control Markings)

This report contains unprocessed information. Plans and/or policies should not be evolved or modified solely on the basis of this report.

1. COUNTRY: NATIONALIST CHINA	8. REPORT NUMBER: 1 818 0201 66
2. SUBJECT: ▮ Unidentified Flying Objects Over TAIWAN	9. DATE OF REPORT: 26 August 1966
3. ISC NUMBER:	10. NO. OF PAGES: 4
	11. REFERENCES: DIRM Chapter 4
4. DATE OF INFORMATION: 10 July 1966	12. ORIGINATOR: U S Air Attache, Rep of China
5. PLACE AND DATE OF ACQ: Taipei; 1 Aug 66	13. PREPARED BY: DONALD W MANSFIELD, MAJOR, USAF
6. EVALUATION: SOURCE B INFORMATION 2	14. APPROVING AUTHORITY: ROBERT G TOWER, CAPTAIN, USN DEFENSE ATTACHE
7. SOURCE: Chinese Air Force	

15. SUMMARY: ▮ This report forwards a translation of a Chinese Air Force special study of Unidentified Flying Objects over TAIWAN. The study reports and analyses seven sightings of unidentified flying objects over Taiwan and the Formosa Strait at 1800-1910 hours local time (1000 - 1110Z) 10 July 1966. Information contained in this study, such as times of sightings, physical location of observers, appearance of the objects and impact area of the one object that landed off the coast, should prove valuable to U.S. aerospace authorities in correlating re-entry data.

(Leave Blank) 0183

TIME	LOCATION	OBSERVATION	OBSERVER
1800/10 Jul	Southeast of Kuan-hsi, Hsin-chu County	A fleeting fireball	Unknown
1900/10 Jul	Over Heng-ch'un, Ping-tung County	Unidentified bluish flying object	Unknown
1900/10 Jul	Over Ch'eng Kung Chen, Tai-tung County	Unidentified flying object	Unknown
1905/10 Jul	Over Pi-nan Hsiang, Tai-tung County	Unidentified flying object	Unknown
1908/10 Jul	10,000 Yards East of Tung-yin Island at an altitude of 1,000 feet	Landed in sea in the shape of an arc	Seen by local garrison

16. DISTRIBUTION BY ORIGINATOR:	17. DOWNGRADING DATA:	18. ATTACHMENT DATA:
CINCPACAF (DIXAD), w/o Encl CINCPAC, w/o Encl		1 Enclosure Untranslated Chinese Document, 1 cy, 3 sheets

REQUEST ATTACHMENT FROM DIAAP-1H2

ENCLOSURE # 1 IS NOT REPRODUCIBLE

(Classification and Control Markings)

(22)

Doc. 8-17b DIA Intelligence Report, Aug 26, 1966	RT NO. 1 818 0201 66
	2 OF 3 PAGES
	NATOR U S Air Attache
	Rep of China

(Classification and Control Markings)

(Leave Blank)

1909/10 Jul	Control Tower, Kung-Kuan Air Base	A flashing reddish color resembling a falling rocket dropping vertically and disappeared instantly. Its position was 90-100° in relation to Kung-kuan. Distanced unknown.	Seen by Sino-American Tower Personnel
1910/10 Jul	Over the city of I-lan	The edge was red while the center was green and white It was 2 meters wide and approximately 4-5 meters long resembling a flying saucer in a very high speed fleeting from I-LAN to LO-TUNG	Seen by LIU and YEH, two policemen from YUAN-SHAN Police Station, I-LAN branch Police Station

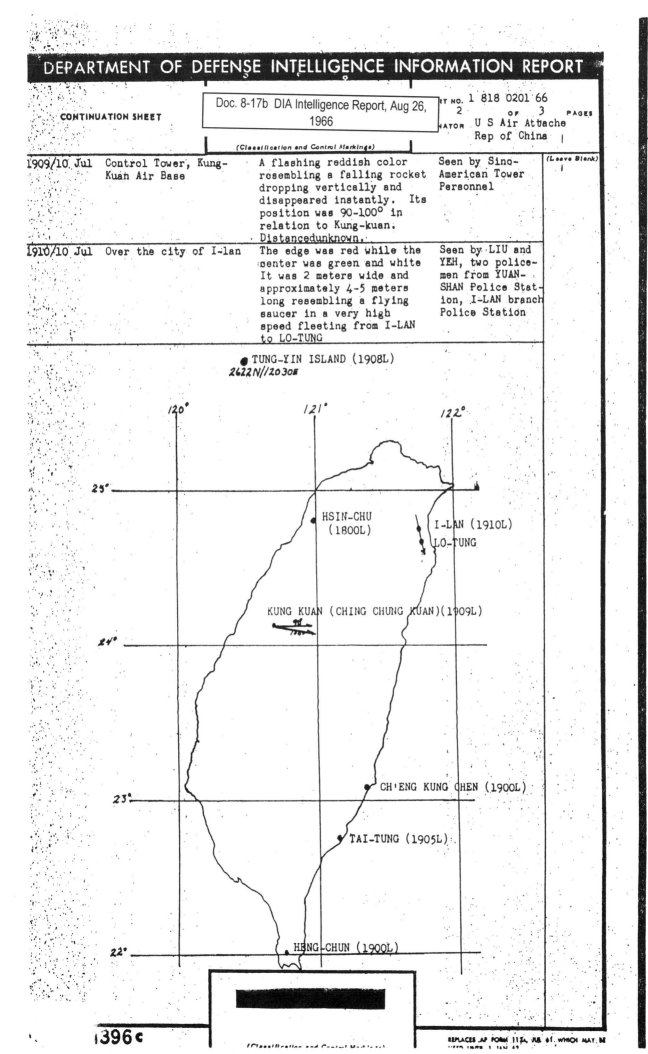

TUNG-YIN ISLAND (1908L)
2622N//12030E

120° 121° 122°

25°

HSIN-CHU
(1800L)

I-LAN (1910L)
LO-TUNG

KUNG KUAN (CHING CHUNG KUAN)(1909L)

24°

CH'ENG KUNG CHEN (1900L)

23°

TAI-TUNG (1905L)

HENG-CHUN (1900L)
22°

(Classification and Control Markings)

REPLACES AF FORM 112, FEB 61, WHICH MAY BE
USED UNTIL 1 JAN 62

CONTINUATION SHEET

Doc. 8-17c DIA Intelligence Report, Aug 26, 1966

REPORT NO. 1 818 0201 66
PAGE 3 OF 4 PAGES
ORIGINATOR U S Air Attache
Rep of China

(Classification and Control Markings)

1. ▇ General Situation:

a. The time of discovery was approximately several minutes after 1900 hours 10 July. The time of discovery over Hsin-chu was probably misquoted.

b. The points of discovery spread all over Taiwan.

c. The colors of the light objects included red, blue and white.

d. With the exception of Tung-yin, no altitude was indicated.

e. With the exception of I-lan and Kuan Kuang, no direction was indicated.

2. ▇ Study:

a. On the basis of their time of discovery over a wide area:

(1) The unknown flying objects discovered over Taiwan spread between east longitude 120.1 and 121.7 (between Tung-yin and I-lan), between north latitude 22 and 26.2 (between Heng-ch'un and Tung-yin). They covered an area 460 kilometers from north to south and 160 kilometers from east to west. It is felt that there must have been a greater number spread over a wide area on the nearby sea and ocean that were not seen. On the basis of the extent of the area over which these objects were discovered, they could not have come from any weapon that had been fired from the ground. Although they fell over a wide area, their time of descent was very short. Therefore, it is felt that they had descended from a common starting point at a very high altitude. They dispersed further and further apart as they descended. They could be seen with the naked eye as greater incandescence resulted from increased friction as they approached closer and closer to the earth through heavier atmospheric density.

b. On the basis of the colors of these unknown flying objects:

(1) The illuminated object must be made up of more than one substance. The light generated as a result of heat from friction was different due to differences in the degree of heat resistance and conductivity, and the difference in the smoothness of the surfaces of the disintegrated bodies during their descent.

(2) On the basis of the above statement, these unidentified flying objects were probably bodies-fallen satellites or second and third stage rockets that had entered orbits then disintegrated in the earth's atmosphere after they had either encountered a malfunction or had performed their ultimate mission.

3. ▇ Conclusion:

a. There are numberous unannounced American and Russian space satellites. It is possible that some of them may disintegrate in the earth's atmosphere.

b. On July 9, the Kung Shang Joh Pao, Hong Kong, published the following report on its second page: "Washington, July 7 (AFP) The United States announced today that the 29 ton satellite that went into orbit on Tuesday (July 5) had broken into pieces in space on the same day." Therefore, it seems possible that the unidentified flying objects discovered over Taiwan could be some of the broken pieces of the above mentioned 29 ton satellite:"

COMMENT:

1. ▇ The first four sightings list the observer as unknown. The last three sightings list officials (police, military) as observers. This is probably an indirect method to indicate source reliability of qualified vs unqualified rather than known vs unknown.

2. ▇ The 1800 time of sighting at Kuan-hsi may possibly be an even one hour error made either by the observer or by the people who prepared the study. The sightings

(Classification and Control Markings)

fall into two groups; a south grouping from 1900 to 1905 and a north group from 1908 to 1910. These groupings suggest a southeast to northwest path. There are two unaccountable discrepancies; the 1800 sighting being one hour off from the other six, and the mention of a north to south flight path at the I-lan sighting.

DEPARTMENT OF DEFENSE INTELLIGENCE INFORMATION REPORT

Doc. 8-18a DIA Intelligence Report, Apr 3, 1967

e report contains unprocessed information. no end/or policies should not be evolved or modified solely on the basis of this report.

(Classification and Control Markings)

COUNTRY: Brazil

2. SUBJECT: Reported Sightings of Flying Saucers in Brazil

3. ISC NUMBER:

4. DATE OF INFORMATION: March 1967
Rio de Janeiro, Brazil;

5. PLACE AND DATE OF ACQ: March 1967

6. EVALUATION: SOURCE ___C___ INFORMATION ___3___

7. SOURCE: DIRM 4.E.

8. REPORT NUMBER: IR 1 809 0112 67

9. DATE OF REPORT: 3 April 1967

10. NO. OF PAGES: 2

11. REFERENCES: DIRM 4.E.

12. ORIGINATOR: OAirA, Brazil

13. PREPARED BY:

14. APPROVING AUTHORITY:
VERNON A. WALTERS, Brig. Gen., USA
United States Defense Attache

8. SUMMARY:

Report briefly describes recent sightings of flying saucers in Brazil.

(Leave Blank)

1. On 22 March 1967 the crew of a Brazilian Air Force C-47 and the crew of a Cruzeiro do Sul photomapping aircraft reported having seen a flying saucer in the vicinity of Porto Alegre, Rio Grande do Sul. The object was initially sighted by the BAF crew who described it as a reddish colored full moon that appeared to be flying in circles. The BAF C-47 advised Salgado Filho Tower of the sighting, and the tower asked the Cruzeiro do Sul aircraft to intercept and identify the object. The Cruzeiro do Sul aircraft made contact with the object and pursued it for 15 minutes before it finally disappeared. No pictures were taken of the object. In addition to the reported sightings by the aircraft crews, the object was also reportedly seen by ground observers in the Porto Alegre area.

16. DISTRIBUTION BY ORIGINATOR:

USAFSO, Attn: Dir of Intel, Albrook AFB, C.Z.
USCINCSO, Attn: J-2, Quarry Heights, Canal Zone

17. DOWNGRADING DATA:

18. ATTACHMENT DATA:

(Leave Blank)

2. A more recent reported sighting occurred on 30 March 1967 in Rio Comprido. However, this one was reported only by ground observers. The object was described as completely white, silent, flying at low altitude, and would disappear and reappear at regular intervals. This particular sighting received very little publicity in the news media.

COMMENTS: As yet the Air Ministry has not issued any official comment on these sightings and is presently studying the statements of the aircraft crews and ground observers.

DEPARTMENT OF DEFENSE INTELLIGENCE INFORMATION REPORT

Doc. 8-19a DIA Intelligence Report, Jan 19, 1968

(Classification and Control Markings)

COUNTRY: USSR	8. REPORT NUMBER: 1 901 0007 68
SUBJECT: (U) Unidentified Flying Objects	9. DATE OF REPORT: 19 January 1968
	10. NO. OF PAGES: 2
SC NUMBER:	11. REFERENCES: DIRM: 1C1

DATE OF INFORMATION: 10 Nov 67 - 10 Jan 68

PLACE AND DATE OF ACQ: Moscow, USSR
20 Dec 67, to 11 Jan 68

EVALUATION: SOURCE ___A___ INFORMATION __2__

SOURCE: Official Liaison

12. ORIGINATOR: OUSAIRA MOSCOW USSR

13. PREPARED BY:

14. APPROVING AUTHORITY:
MELVIN J. NIELSEN
COLONEL, USAF
DEFENSE ATTACHE

REC'D GO-3 30 JAN 1968

388

SUMMARY:
(Leave Blank)

Report includes information on Russian commission set to study Unidentified Flying Objects. Of particular interest is the fact that first the Russians publicised the commission, but now claim the commission has en disbanded.

(U) In early November 1967 (exact date believed to be 10 Nov) Moscow TV esented a program on Unidentified Flying Objects. On 12 Nov 67 a Reuters lease in the U.K. press (believe article was in <u>Daily Telegraph</u>) reported the / program.

(U) The essence of the TV program, and Reuters report based on the TV program, s that the Russians had recently set up a commission to study UFOs. The airman of the Commission is retired SAF Major General A.P. STROLYAROV, a former chnical Services Officer. The group consisted of 18 astronomers and SAF officers lus 200 observers.

379180-4W
102300-4W
375700-4W

DISTRIBUTION BY ORIGINATOR:
USEUCOM
ARECR
AFE
NAVEUR
D, WPAFB, OHIO
A
Emb Moscow Science Attache,
2 cys

17. DOWNGRADING DATA:

18. ATTACHMENT DATA:
None

DD FORM 1396

(Classification and Control Markings)

39

O-443

DEPARTMENT OF DEFENSE INTELLIGENCE INFORMATION REPORT

CONTINUATION SHEET	Doc. 8-19b DIA Intelligence Report, Jan 19, 1968	DRT NO. 1 901 0007 68
		E 2 OF 2 PAGES
		INATOR

(Classification and Control Markings)

(Leave Blank)

3. ▓▓▓▓▓ A day or two after the TV program, the Reuters correspondent went to see General STROLYAROV. The General was very polite, confirmed the information about the commission, the 18 astronomers and SAF officers and the 200 observers. In addition, he said five (5) positive sightings had been made.

4. ▓▓▓▓▓ Approximately a week later the Reuters correspondent went back to see General STROLYAROV. However, this time the correspondent could not get past the General's secretary; was politely but firmly told the General was no longer available for interview.

5. ▓▓▓▓▓ On 12 December 1967, the British Embassy was directed by London to further investigate the subject with a view to cooperating with the Russians in observation teams for UFOs.

6. ▓▓▓▓▓ The Scientific Counselor of the British Embassy went to the State Committee for Science and Technology and inquired about the UFO Commission and the possibility of British-Russian cooperation in observation of UFOs. The British Counselor was politely received and the commission was freely discussed. The British were told they would receive a reply to their request about cooperation.

7. ▓▓▓▓▓ The British did not receive an answer and did not pursue the subject. However, on 8 January 1968 while on a routine visit to the Soviet State Committee for Science and Technology, the British Scientific Counselor was told the following: The commission for investigating UFOs had been set up in response to a popular demand. The commission had met twice, but since there was insufficient information to sustain it the commission would be disbanded after the next meeting.

8. ▓▓▓▓▓ The British Scientific Counselor believes the original announcement of the work of the commission on TV was an oversight on the part of the censors because the commission has not been reported or referred to anywhere else. He believes the commission has not been disbanded, but will continue under cover. This information was sent to London.

COMMENT: ▓▓▓▓

1. ▓▓▓▓▓ The preceding information was given to RO by source. RO also read confidential British files on this subject. RO did not approach Reuters correspondent because of delicate position of source. RO was unable to find anyone in Moscow who saw TV program or read article in UK press.

2. ▓▓▓▓ On 10 or 11 November 1967 the U.S. Science Attache received a telephone call from the Reuters correspondent and was asked if he had seen the TV program. When the Science Attache replied that he had not seen the program, the correspondent described it and asked the Science Attache if he thought the information was worth reporting. The Science Attache said yes. The Science Attache, like the RO, has not seen the UK press report. The U.S. Science Attache will receive two copies of this report and will forward one copy to the appropriate S & T Agency in Washington.

NOTE: This document contains information affecting the national defense of the United States within the meaning of the espionage laws, Title 18, U.S.C., Sec. 793 and 794. The transmission or the revelation of its contents in any manner to an unauthorized person is prohibited by law.

Doc. 8-20a DIA Intelligence Report, Aug 9, 1968

report contains unprocessed information. Plans and/or policies should not be evolved or modified solely on the basis of this report.

(Classification and Control Markings)

1. COUNTRY: ARGENTINA	8. REPORT NUMBER: 1 804 0123 68
2. SUBJECT: UFO Newspaper Clippings	9. DATE OF REPORT: 9 August 1968
	10. NO. OF PAGES: 2
3. ISC NUMBER:	11. REFERENCES: DIRM 1P1j IR 1 804 0121 68 DIRM 4E5f
4. DATE OF INFORMATION: 8 June to 8 August 1968	12. ORIGINATOR: USDAO, BUENOS AIRES, ARGENTINA
5. PLACE AND DATE OF ACQ: Buenos Aires, Argentina 8 August 1968	13. PREPARED BY:
6. EVALUATION: SOURCE ___B___ INFORMATION ___2___	
7. SOURCE: Local newspapers	14. APPROVING AUTHORITY: CHARLES V. GREFFET, COL, USAF U. S. Defense Attaché

RECD CO. 28 AUG 1968

5. SUMMARY:

This report transmits translated summaries of press articles on Unidentified Flying Objects (UFO's). It covers a general cross section occurring during the past 60 days. It is significant to note that a state of concern exists about the population in many parts of Argentina.

Following is a chronological summary of 23 articles, with numbers corresponding to numbers on clippings attached, last article in report is dated 8 August 1968.

1. La Razon (Buenos Aires), 8 Jun 68 - (Photo) Describes how two experienced pilots, 22 and 13 years with Aerolineas Argentinas, saw a UFO while flying over Punta Arenas.

2. La Razon (Buenos Aires), 1 July 68 - Describes findings of the Aerial Phenomena Research Organization of Tuscon, Arizona, with comments.

3. Los Principios (Cordoba), 5 July 68 - (Photo) Outlines details on the invention of a geomagnetic and light detector to warn of the presence of UFO's. Second article, same source, quotes Argentine Commander in Chief of Navy as suggesting that Argentine Armed Forces are participating in an investigation of UFO's.

4. Tribuna (San Juan), 9 July 68 - (Photo) Substantiates reality of UFO's and questions why, where and what for of their presence.

5. Diario del Pueblo (Tandil) 13 July 68 - Describes landing of a UFO at the Air Base at Tandil.

6. La Nacion (Buenos Aires) 15 July 68 - (Photo) Describes viewing a UFO on 23 June 68 at Mar del Plata.

7. La Prensa (Buenos Aires) 17 July 68 - Gives details of a speech by a Mr. Federico B. Kirbus, position unknown, which discounts UFO's.

8. La Cronica (Buenos Aires) 17 July 68 - Describes UFO sighting near Mendoza.

9. La Nacion (Buenos Aires) 17 July 68 - Cites two sightings - one in Tres Arroyos by a rancher and the other in Bolucato, Brazil. Latter gives good description of landing gear and mounting platform.

6. DISTRIBUTION BY ORIGINATOR:	17. DOWNGRADING DATA:	18. ATTACHMENT DATA:
USAFSO (w/enclosure) USCINCSO (w/o enclosure)		ENCLOSURE 23 newspaper clippings on UFO's

REQUEST ENC FROM DIAAP-10A

ENCL# 1 HAS NOT BEEN REPRODUCED

UNCLASSIFIED

DD FORM 1396
1 SEP 62

(Classification and Control Markings)

REPLACES DA FORM 1048, 1 AUG 50, OPNAV FORM 3820 (Rev. 10-61), AF FORM 112, JUL 61, WHICH MAY BE USED UNTIL 1 JAN 63.

(Classification and Control Markings)

(Leave Blank)

10. La Gente (Buenos Aires) 18 July 68 - (Photo) Explains Comision Abservadora de Objetos Voladores No Identificados (CODOVNI). Describes area of most common sightings.

11. La Nacion (Buenos Aires) 18 July 68 - Describes landing of UFO in Chos Malal on 16 July with forces emenating.

12. La Nacion, (Buenos Aires) 19 July 68 - Relates sightings by tower operator at Mendoza and pilot flying between Mendoza and Santiago, Chile. Also same source recounts sighting at Balboa, Spain.

13. La Razon (Buenos Aires) 26 July 68 - Describes attempt by five policeman in Olavanria to capture and later shoot three crewmembers of UFO.

14. La Cronica (Buenos Aires) 26 July 68 - Relates sightings of UFO's at San Carlos de Bariloche, Cordoba, and Coquimbo, Chile.

15. La Nacion (Buenos Aires) 27 July 68 - Describes sighting by persons in Laguna Paiva.

16. La Razon (Buenos Aires) 27 July 68 - (Photo) Relates new sightings near La Pastora, General Alvear and Tapalque. The latter describes the crew and inability of machine-gun bullets to affect them.

17. Cronica (Buenos Aires) 30 July 68 - Reports testimony of Dr. James McDonald of the U. S. House of Representatives, sighting at Punta del Este force from which caused motor of car to stall, near Cauquenes, Chile.

18. Clarin (Buenos Aires) 31 July 68 - (Photo) Describes and gives photos of a sighting in Lanus.

19. La Nacion (Buenos Aires) 1 Aug 68 - From Madrid, Fernando Sesma, president of the Association of Friends of the Visitors from Space, theorized that these visitors have picked Argentina as the place to begin the conquest of earth.

20. La Nacion (Buenos Aires) 2 August 68 - Describes a minute sighting near Rosario.

21. Asi (Buenos Aires) 3 Aug 68 - (Photo) Describes a sighting with photos near Trelew on 13 July 68.

22. La Razon (3 Aug 68) - Relates argument by a Professor Alexander Erú supporting theory of flying saucers.

23. Buenos Aires Herald (Buenos Aires) 8 Aug 68 - Describes in-space rendevous between two UFO's between Indio Rico and Tres Arroyos, Argentina.

COMMENTS: This report describes the rash of sightings of Unidentified Flying Objects (UFO's) presently occurring in Argentina and how this subject is the item of primary interest to the local populace. This report supplements IR 1 804 0121 68.

UNCLASSIFIED

DD 1396c

(Classification and Control Markings)

DEPARTMENT OF DEFENSE INTELLIGENCE INFORMATION REPORT

NOTE: This document contains information affecting the national defense of the United States within the meaning of the espionage laws, Title 18, U.S.C., Sec. 793 and 794. The transmission or the revelation of its contents in any manner to an unauthorized person is prohibited by law.

UNCLASSIFIED
(Classification and Control Markings)

A report containing unprocessed information. No and/or policies should not be evolved or modified solely on the basis of this report.

1. COUNTRY: SPAIN	8. REPORT NUMBER: 6 889 0174 74
2. SUBJECT: Spanish UFO Sightings	9. DATE OF REPORT: 22 August 1974
	10. NO. OF PAGES: Six
3. ISC NUMBER:	11. REFERENCES: DIRM 4K3g
4. DATE OF INFORMATION: September 1973 - June 1974	12. ORIGINATOR: USDAO MADRID SPAIN
5. PLACE AND DATE OF ACQ: Madrid Sep 73 - June 74	13. PREPARED BY: ▓▓▓▓▓▓▓▓
6. EVALUATION: SOURCE B INFORMATION 3	14. APPROVING AUTHORITY:
7. SOURCE: Local Press	*Richard T. Fox* RICHARD T. FOX, CAPTAIN, USN Acting Defense Attache

A

15. SUMMARY:

IR submits a list of 28 UFOs sighted in SPAIN during the period September 1973 to June 1974. Date and place sighted, observer, and description of UFO are given.

042263

RECEIVED DS-4D

5 SEP'74 12 54z

201

379180-SP

During the period September 1973 to June 1974 a rash of UFOs appeared over SPAIN and sightings were reported by various types of people. The following table summarizes these sightings.

NOTE: R.O. has no basis for checking validity of these reported UFO sightings. Data is forwarded strictly for information of those parties interested.

16. DISTRIBUTION BY ORIGINATOR:	17. DOWNGRADING DATA:	18. ATTACHMENT DATA:
USCINCEUR (ECJ2-R) USAFE CINCUSNAVEUR	NONE	NONE

(43)

44

UNCLASSIFIED
(Classification and Control Markings)

FORM 1396

DEPARTMENT OF DEFENSE INTELLIGENCE INFORMATION REPORT

| Doc. 8-21b DIA Intelligence Report, Aug 22, 1974 | | |

CONTINUATION SHEET

UNCLASSIFIED

(Classification and Control Markings)

ORT NO. ... 2 OF 6 PAGES

ORIGINATOR USDAO MADRID SPAIN

(Leave Blank)

Date	Location	Description	Observer	Remarks
11 Sep 73	El Ferrol del Caudillo (4.32°N-008.14W)	Bright, circular, with two humps, appeared to have feet on bottom part. Emitted a very powerful light.	Various.	Was immobile during time of observation.
11 Dec 73 (early morning)	Málaga (36.3N-004.25W)	Circular, like a flying saucer, had an intense red light	Various residents of Salitre and Cuartelos Streets, Málaga. (36.57N-004.30W)	Remained quiet for about 15 minutes, then departed suddenly towards Torremolinos.
17 Mar 74 (morning)	Sighted from football field of Guidad Jardin, Málaga.	N/A	Four youths.	
22 Mar 74 (early morning)	Arrecife, Lanzarote (37.3N-008.5W)	Yellow, longitudinal, like tail of a comet.	Fishermen.	
23 Mar 74 (early morning)	5 kilometers south of Castillo de las Guardas (37.3N-006.18W)	Mother ship – diameter 150-200 meters long. Three smaller ships resembling sombreros, flew silently, had no windows but towers above and below.	Travelling salesman from Sevilla (37.23N-005.59W)	Sighted for approximately 50 seconds, then it became violet in color, finally disintegrating.
23 Mar 74				Was pursued by one of the smaller ships, which disappeared as observer entered village of Castillo de las Guardas.
23 Mar 74 (3 a.m.)	On Highway near Sanlúcar de Barrameda (36.47N-006.21W)	Luminous, metal-like.	Chauffeur of President of Cádiz Provincial Commission.	Object moved upward with great brilliancy. As observer approached object, he felt a strange sensation. His car finally came practically to a stop, wavering back and forth like a feather.
24 Mar 74 (8:30 p.m.)	Córdoba (37.53N-004.46W)	Round, luminous, pink, not very large.	Two 13-year-old children.	Object moved upward with great speed at the two children, who fled behind a lamppost. Being further pursued, they ran into a house. Object ascended and flew away.

DEPARTMENT OF DEFENSE INTELLIGENCE INFORMATION REPORT

UNCLASSIFIED
(Classification and Control Markings)

(Leave Blank)

Date	Location	Description	Details
26 Mar 74 (3:30 a.m.)	Villa de Duo Hauros (4203N-0062W)	Large, oval, bluish green.	Hairdresser.	Ascended vertically, noiselessly.
26 Mar 74 (night)	Cádiz (3632N-0618W)	Luminous.	Various.	Object stationary according to an observer with binoculars.
26 Mar 74 (evening)	Jerez de la Frontera (3641N-0060W)	Revolving green and white lights, resembled a flying saucer.	Many people.	Made little noise, turned for several minutes.
26 Mar 74 (2 a.m.)	Valdeijadero (4025N-0055W)	Luminous. Strange object like a plate placed above another large, round object.	21-year-old truck driver.	Was motionless over the highway about 200 meters from observer. A similar object, also motionless, was seen 15-20 meters away. Two beings came out of the first vehicle, pointed to observer's truck, then went in again and both UFO's flew away.
27 Mar 74 (11:30 p.m.)	"	Silver.	"	Three silver ships parked on the highway with light similar to floodlight. Observer stopped motor of his car and some figures approached him. He ran, frightened, and they followed him. He threw himself into a gutter. His pursuers passed within 2 meters and he saw them. They were about 2 meters tall, had arms and legs but he did not see their faces. After they passed he returned to the truck. The beings returned to observe him again, then they entered their ships and left. Next day the Guardia Civil made an investigation. They found a hole in the ground, which the truck driver said he had not made.
27 Mar 74	Málaga	"	"	Big, luminous, moved slowly. Photographer. Photographed by 25 cm teleobjective lens, published in local paper. Later two more UFO's were discovered when the negative was developed. The UFO sighted disappeared slowly. Fifteen minutes later a small blue-violet mass was visible.

CONTINUATION SHEET	Doc. 8-21d DIA Intelligence Report, Aug 22, 1974	RT NO.	4 OF 0 PAGES
	UNCLASSIFIED (Classification and Control Markings)	ORIGINATOR	USDAO MADRID SPAIN

(Leave Blank)

Date	Location	Description	Observers	Behavior
27 Mar 74 (morning)	Córdoba	Not available.	Construction workers.	N/A
28 Mar 74 (daytime)	Córdoba	Luminous.	School children.	Appeared over Córdoba Sierra and disappeared shortly thereafter very rapidly.
31 Mar 74 (early morning)	Vigo (4221N-0084.3W)	Red.	Group of nurses.	Moving up and down over the Vigo inlet, then UFO disappeared behind mountains of the Morrazo peninsula.
2 Apr 74 (night)	La Unión (3737N-00052W)	Luminous, circular.	Ten persons on night shift at mining company.	Disappeared suddenly after having been seen several seconds.
4 Apr 74 (morning)	La Estrada (4241N-00829W)	Metallic, noiseless, size of a bus, had a reflector in turret. Gray or aluminum in color.	Two 12-year-old girls.	Stopped a few seconds about 10 or 12 meters from the ground and 100 meters from observers, then went out of sight.
11 Apr 74	San Pedro (4322N-00823W)	Oval, had no vapor trail.	Resident of San Pedro.	Was travelling at approximately 4,000 kilometers per hour, in sight for about 8 seconds.
14 Apr 74 (2 a.m.)	Herrera de Alcántara (3938N-0072W)	Rhomboid, formed by luminous, hoary lights. In upper lefthand part there was a pink-yellowish semicircle which became a circle as UFO came near ground level. Resident claims he heard a prolonged noise like that from an old alarm clock. Professor estimated size of smaller diagonal of rhomboid to be about 20 meters.	Professor, his wife and a student.	Was observed at ground level from a distance of 300 meters for 5 or 6 minutes, then flew northeast.

DEPARTMENT OF DEFENSE INTELLIGENCE INFORMATION REPORT

Doc. 8-21e DIA Intelligence Report, Aug 22, 1974

CONTINUATION SHEET

OF 6 PAGES

USDAO MADRID SPAIN

(Leave Blank)

Date	Location	Shape	Description
15 Apr 74	Ceuta (3552N-00520W) Algeciras (3608N-00530W)	Round, intense torch-like light.	Numerous passengers on ferry from Ceuta to Algeciras. Rose out of the water near a huge rock, traveled at low altitude, then fell into the water again. This happened twice.
15 Apr 74 (12:30 p.m.)	La Coruña (4322N-00823W)	Round.	Newspaper photographer. Four photographs were published in local newspaper.
21 Apr 74 (midnight)	Hogar de Arriola (Málaga)	Triangular or conical.	Astronomical group "Organización Juvenil Española" (Spanish Youth Organization). Was photographed by the group and photo appeared in local newspaper.
26 Apr 74 (near midnight)	Ceuta	Whitish-orange light.	Newspaper editor, his associates and printers of the paper. Was a great distance away and traveling at a speed that appeared to be slow, going from east to west and moving swiftly up and down. Disappeared after a few minutes.
8 May 74 (night)	Villanueva de la Vera (4008N-00528W)	40 or 50 centimeters in length, fish-like in form, bright-colored, had three powerful green lights, silent.	Guard (60 years old), a 62-year-old man and a young couple. Appeared over center of city for half a minute, then disappeared.
0 May 74 (shortly after 7 p.m.)	Alto de Cabrejas (Cuenca) (4204N-00503W)	Oval, reddish reflections	Three passengers on highway to Madrid from Cuenca - a businessman, his daughter and their chauffeur. Rotated over car for about 40 seconds, then flew higher and disappeared.
15 May 74 (4:30 a.m.)	Pedroche (3826N-00446W)	Round, size of a table.	Couple from Córdoba (businessman and a teacher). UFO pursued their car and when it intercepted their travel on the road, they turned around rapidly.
22 May 1974	Ibiza (3854N-00126E)	Somewhat like a top.	Wife of a reporter. Was photographed. Remained stationary in space for some time, then rose and disappeared.

DEPARTMENT OF DEFENSE INTELLIGENCE INFORMATION REPORT

CONTINUATION SHEET	UNCLASSIFIED	REPORT NO.
		PAGE ___ OF ___ PAGES
DD FORM 1396c	(Classification and Control Markings)	ORIGINATOR USDAO, MADRID SPAIN

(Leave Blank)

Doc. 8-21f DIA Intelligence Report, Aug 22, 1974

16 June 74
(5 a.m.)

Cáceres
(3929B-00622N)

46-year-old farm laborer.

Luminous, emitting brilliant light on the highway.

Was pursued by UFO for several kilometers at great speed. Saw three tall figures standing inside the ship. When observer extinguished the lights on his car, the object drew away. Then as he turned them on again, UFO approached again at enormous speed some 70 meters over his car. It followed his home and when he turned out his car lights, it slowly flew away.

COMMENTS OF EO: It is of interest to note that in April of this year teams of extra sensory perception specialists held a meeting in Málaga for the purpose of scientifically studying the UFOs seen in that vicinity. Results of this meeting unknown.

DEPARTMENT OF THE AIR FORCE
11TH SUPPORT WING

7 DEC 1994

11 MSS/MSIS (FOIA)
1000 Air Force Pentagon
Washington DC 20330-1000

Clifford E. Stone
1421 E. Tilden
Roswell, NM 88201

Dear Mr. Stone

This is in response to your September 29, 1994 Freedom of Information Act request addressed to Senator Domenici. We received it on October 17, 1994 from the Secretary of the Air Force Legislative Liaison.

The earlier, updated, reply to you via Senator Bingaman contains all the information the Air Force Intelligence community posses on Project Blue Fly and Moon Dust. The projects, as such no longer exist, nor do their files. Classified reports that existed, if any, presumably were destroyed. Therefore, a "no records" determination is made.

Project Blue Fly was classified because the Air Force did not wish the Former Soviet Union (FSU) to know whether it had captured and examined downed Soviet personnel, equipment, or aircraft. However, as no one or thing was ever downed or captured the mission was canceled, the Blue Fly teams disbanded, and in due course the files destroyed.

Project Moon Dust was initially classified because the Air Force did not wish the FSU to know which, if any, of its satellites or their components that had survived re-entry anywhere in the world may have been examined by the USAF before its return to the FSU. The program was declassified when the Department of State released a previously classified 1973 message: "Guidance for Dealing with Space Objects which have returned to Earth." As with Blue Fly, in due course the files were destroyed.

The Air Force continues to maintain an interest in
space objects that survive re-entry for purpose of
identification, liability, and treaty obligations. Such
objects are forwarded to the AF's National Air Intelligence
Center, Wright-Patterson AFB, OH, for analysis. If the item
is of foreign origin, the State Department notifies the
launching country per the Treaty governing such matters.

If you interpret this "no records" response as an
averse action you may appeal it to the Secretary of the Air
Force within 60 days from the date of this letter. Include
in your appeal your reasons for reconsideration and attach a
copy of this letter. Address your letter as follows:

> Secretary of the Air Force
> THRU: 11 MSS/MSIS (FOIA)
> 1000 Air Force Pentagon
> Washington DC 20330-1000

We regret the delay in responding to this request and
the confusion resulting from previous responses. We trust
this information is helpful.

Rhonda Jenkins is our action officer on (703) 695-4992.

Sincerely

LATRICIA D. GRACE
Freedom of Information Manager

94-1913

DEPARTMENT OF THE AIR FORCE
11TH SUPPORT WING

2 3 FEB 1995

11 MSS/MSISL (MDR)
1000 Air Force Pentagon
Washington DC 20330-1000

Mr. Clifford E. Stone
1421 East Tilden
Roswell New Mexico 88201-7955

Dear Mr. Stone

This is in response to your Mandatory Declassification Review (MDR) request dated September 27, 1994.

Attached are documents, that were previously provided to the Air Force by individuals seeking information on records relating to Projects MOONDUST and BLUEFLY. These documents were provided by an unknown source and they can not be authenticated. The Air Force dose not possess any documents either requested or relevant. Further, neither project now exists.

The recitation in Enclosure 3 to your letter is a factual statement of the history of Projects MOONDUST and BLUEFLY. The statement in the next-to-last paragraph still applies. For example if a space object were to be recovered and obtained by the Air Force, it would be forwarded to the National Air Intelligence Center (formerly Foreign Aerospace Science and Technology Center), Wright-Patterson AFB, OH, for analysis as noted. However, if a foreign government were to recover a space object and invite the US to examine and identify it, that nation's identity would be protected unless it agreed to release the story of the cooperation between us.

Questions concerning this review can be directed to the undersigned at DSN 225-4992 or COMM (703) 695-4992.

LATRICIA D. GRACE
Mandatory Declassification
Review Manager

Attachment:

Releasable Records

94-MDR-0057

DEPARTMENT OF THE AIR FORCE
WASHINGTON DC

OFFICE OF THE GENERAL COUNSEL

APR 0 4 1997

SAF/GCA
1740 AIR FORCE PENTAGON
WASHINGTON, D.C. 20330-1740

Mr. Clifford E. Stone
1421 East Tilden
Roswell, NM 88201-7955

Dear Mr. Stone:

This letter replies to your January 2, 1993 (JACL #93092) and December 13, 1994 (JACL #95052) appeals under the Freedom of Information Act (FOIA). Since the subject matter of the original requests was closely related, we decided to process these appeals together. I have been delegated the responsibility to conduct the Office of the Secretary of the Air Force review in your cases.

You were notified by a letter dated December 14, 1992 that "no records" were found in response to your September 25, 1992 request for records related to alleged UFO crashes and recoveries in the Roswell, New Mexico area on July 2, 1947, and the Kecksburg, Pennsylvania area on December 9, 1965. The Air Force has performed numerous searches for these documents over the years in response to requests by you and others. No responsive records have ever been found. Therefore, your January 2, 1993 appeal (JACL #93092) is denied.

As part of the above appeal, you questioned why there would be a denial authority and why appeal rights would be given if there were no records. The answer is that current laws dictate these procedures. Under the Freedom of Information Act, 5 U.S.C. § 552, a "no records" response is considered an adverse determination. A right to appeal is granted, and when it is exercised, a second search is conducted for responsive records.

Regarding the December 13, 1994 appeal, JACL #95052, a second search resulted in the discovery of responsive documents which are being released to you. The original records dealing with Operation Blue Fly and Project Moon Dust were destroyed quite some time ago. The Air Force Historical Research Agency and Air Force Intelligence discovered the enclosed records attached to previous requests for information on these programs. Some of the records were previously redacted, and some are of poor quality, however they represent the best remaining records available from these programs.

Operation Blue Fly was originated in the Air Defense Command during the Korean War to establish intelligence teams to visit crash sites in the United States to recover downed Soviet Bloc pilots and equipment, and existed until canceled in the 1970s. Its mission had been enlarged to include space objects and UFOs, if any were reported available for recovery. No Soviet Bloc planes or personnel were ever downed in the United States, and no UFOs were ever reported downed or recovered in the United States or anywhere else. Operation Blue Fly was terminated because of the lack of activity. As you know, the Air Force terminated its investigative interest in UFOs in 1969. The Air Force Special Activities Center at Fort Belvoir no longer exists, and no Operation Blue Fly or Project Moon Dust files were left.

Space objects have been recovered by U.S. civilians and turned over to the Air Force for inspection and analysis, but no Operation Blue Fly intelligence teams were involved in these transactions. Space objects come under Project Moon Dust, which is administered by the United States Department of State. Questions regarding these records should be directed to the Office of Freedom of Information, Privacy, and Classification Review, Bureau of Administration, U.S. Department of State, Washington, DC, 20520-1512; telephone: (202) 647- 6070; fax: (202) 736-7304.

This constitutes the final Air Force action on your appeals. The Freedom of Information Act, 5 U.S.C. § 552, provides for judicial review of this determination.

Sincerely,

Walter A. Willson
Deputy General Counsel
(Civilian Personnel & Fiscal)

Attachment:
Releasable records

(U) Project BLUE FLY

A BLUE FLY operation was initiated on 20 March 1964, when a Soviet built Cuban HOUND Helicopter landed at Key West, Florida. In accordance with the Defense Intelligence Agency Instruction Number 58-16, Subject (U) Exploitation of Foreign Aircraft, the USAF was assigned the primary responsibility for intelligence exploitation of this helicopter. The actual exploitation was jointly conducted with the Central Intelligence Agency, the Department of the Navy and the U.S. Army's Foreign Scientific and Technical Center. Air Force Systems Command (Foreign Technology Division) represented the Air Force during the on-site exploitation. The HOUND helicopter, with exception of the weapons system, was exploited at Key West. The weapons system was removed and evaluated at the Springfield Arsenal, Springfield, Massachusetts. The exploitation was completed on 4 April 1964. Three lengthy and detailed reports were published; one by Air Force Systems Command's (AFSC) Foreign Technology Division and two by the U.S. Army's Foreign Scientific and Technical Center. The helicopter is presently in storage at the U.S. Naval facility at Key West, Florida, pending disposal instructions from the Department of State.

> Doc. 8-25 U.S.A.F. Project (Operation) Blue Fly
> Report, Mar 20, 1964

I received a call from Maj Horkanf, USAF
Command Post, advising me to be prepared for a
possible UFO report. AP release 203 was the only
report at this time. AFLC Command Post called and
informed me that Maj. Livers, Detroit Air Defense Sector,
WO 26161, Ex. 741, called them and reported some
very unusual sightings. Reports came to Maj Livers
from Ohio, Indiana, Michigan, and Pennsylvania.

The time of sighting was relayed as 4.15 PM.
Some reports stated that the object was orange and
others stated it was white with a tail. I
called Maj. Quintanilla for his advice and
assistance. He came to the base and called
Maj. Liver. A further call was made to
the Oakdale Radar Site in Penna. A three
man team has been dispatched to Acme, Pa to
investigate and pick-up an object that started
a fire.

A call was received from Mr. ████████
████, Michigan (█ █████ █████ ████ or
█ █████ (some three) reporting fragments of
something. He works for a newspaper and
was looking for more info then he was giving.
He was advised to send any fragments to
Project Blue Book, WPAFB, Ohio.

Two calls have been received from newspapers.
Both have been referred to Washington, Secretary of the

Author's Updated Report on "Operation Blue Fly"
(Original Version Was Sent to the United States Congress in November 1993)

© 1993, 1997 by Clifford E. Stone

In early 1993, New Mexico Congressman Steven Schiff requested information on UFOs from the Department of Defense and the Air Force and received an unsatisfactory response. He then pounded the paper trail by publicly requesting any information on government documents that might exist concerning the Roswell Incident.

I responded to Congressman Schiff's appeal by sending him many of the documents I had amassed over 20 years of using the Freedom of Information Act to secure UFO information from various government agencies.

Congressman Schiff's Albuquerque office reviewed my files and contacted me, inquiring if I had any additional information. It was this request that encouraged me to prepare this report on the Air Force's Top Secret "Operation Blue Fly."

Besides sending this report to Congressman Schiff, I sent it to an additional twenty-seven congressmen and senators, as well as to the General Accounting Office, in November 1993.

The point of the report is to demonstrate to Congress that there were, and still are, active operations within the U.S. Intelligence Community to secretly gather information on "objects of unknown origin" and to recover any debris from such objects.

These operations are still ongoing, despite the denials of the Intelligence Community. I can only urge you to write your senators, congressmen, and members of the media, requesting the truth about what the military and intelligence agencies are doing with relevant information they possess on the subject of Unidentified Flying Objects.

The following is taken directly from an official U.S. Air Force document dated October 20, 1969, recommending the termination of Operation Blue Book:

> ...reports of unidentified flying objects which could affect national security are made in accordance with JANAP 146 or Air Force Manual 55-11, and are NOT part of the Blue Book system. The Air Force experience therefore confirms the IMPRESSION of the University of Colorado researchers "that the defense function could be performed within the framework established for intelligence and surveillance operations without the continuance of a special unit such as Operation Blue Book."

This quote clearly points out several items of interest concerning Operation Blue Book.

First, Blue Book was established to receive UFO reports from the public at large and act as a public relations unit. Blue Book was not to be involved with those cases considered to be of vital intelligence interest. For those cases, involving vital intelligence concerns, another entity or reporting channel had already been established outside the Blue Book reporting system.

Second, the Air Force, unknown to the public, had in place another reporting channel for UFO reports which they wished to keep away from the public's view. (The University of Colorado UFO researchers made just such a recommendation, not being aware of the existence of this other entity outside Operation Blue Book. Later, in this report, I identify this other entity and trace some of its history. However, for now, I would like to reflect upon some other interesting points made in this government document.)

> The termination of Operation Blue Book would leave no official federal office to receive reports of UFOs. However, as already stated, reports of UFOs which could affect national security would continue to be handled through the standard Air Force procedures designed for this purpose.

Read the above quote again, which is from the Air Force document in question, very closely. Here it is made very clear that while the termination of Operation Blue Book would give the impression that the U.S. Air Force was out of the UFO business by not having a clearinghouse, so to speak, for submission of UFO reports from the public, it would carry on its investigation of those UFO cases it deemed to have vital intelligence interest, without fear of any questions from the media or public at large. All the Air Force had to do, should anyone ask questions, was simply to state that the U.S. Air Force ceased its investigation of UFOs on December 17, 1969, as a result of the University of Colorado Study recommendation. Since the existence of this other reporting system was unknown to the media and public it was not required, nor did the Air Force wish, to make its existence known.

To this very day the U.S. Air Force does not want the American public to be made aware of any such UFO program currently in existence within its intelligence branch. Yet, I assure you that such a unit does, in fact, exist and one of its many duties is the gathering of information on UFO cases that it deems to have vital intelligence interest. This same unit is charged with the responsibility of forwarding the information it gathers on UFOs to other interested agencies.

There have been many explanations, both pro and con, given for this document, known as the "Bolender Memo." The pros have been that it "proves" the U.S. Air Force had, and still has, a highly classified UFO investigation program. The cons are that Brigadier General (B.G.) Bolender was pressed for time and had to say something. Not wanting to make "the powers that be" worry, that should a situation arise concerning UFOs and national security, we would be ill equipped to deal with such a contingency, he chose to declare that we already had that base covered—not really knowing what he was talking about.

Actually B.G. Bolender knew quite well what he was talking about. Bolender knew that Operation Blue Book did not investigate the really good UFO cases reported to the U.S Air Force. Bolender knew of that "special unit" located at Fort Belvoir, Virginia.

Under Air Defense Command Regulation 24-4, dated January 3, 1953, the 4602d Air Intelligence Service Squadron (AISS) was created. On August 26, 1953, this "special unit" was charged with the official investigation of UFOs under Air Force Regulation 200-2. All UFO reports were to go through the 4602d AISS prior to any transmission to Operation Blue Book at Wright-Patterson Air Force Base, Ohio.

AFR 200-2, dated August 12, 1954, stated:

The Air Defense Command has a direct interest in the facts pertaining to UFOBs [UFO reports] reported within the ZI [Zone of the Interior] and has, in the 4602d Air Intelligence Service Squadron [AISS] the capability to investigate these reports. The 4602d AISS is composed of specialists trained for field collection and investigation of matters of air intelligence interest which occur within the ZI. This squadron is highly mobile and deployed throughout the ZI.

Here we have an Air Force regulation making it clear that the Air Defense Command had a direct interest in UFOs, as well as the unit best suited to do the investigations: the 4602d AISS. It also indicated that another agency, outside of Operation Blue Book, was involved with UFO investigations.

We are aware that every Air Force Base was required to appoint an Operation Blue Book Officer, mostly as an additional duty, to handle UFO reports that came to the attention of the base. However, these officers were not permitted to report cases directly to Operation Blue Book at Wright-Patterson Air Force Base. They first had to bring the cases to the attention of—you guessed it—the 4602d AISS. Nor were they to conduct any investigation beyond a preliminary one, without a direct request to do so from the 4602d AISS.

AFR 200-2 stated:

All Air Force activities are authorized to conduct such preliminary investigation as may be required for reporting purposes; however, investigations should not be carried beyond this point, unless such action is requested by the 4602d AISS.

According to AFR 200-2:

The Air Technical Intelligence Center (ATIC) will analyze and evaluate: All information and evidence within the ZI after the Air Defense Command has exhausted all efforts to identify the UFOB; and all information and evidence collected in overseas areas.

I have several problems with the above quote from AFR 200-2. First, we now know, thanks to the Freedom of Information Act (FOIA), that many of the cases that should have been in the Operation Blue Book files were not there. However, they did show up in the Director of Air Intelligence's files with a clear indication that they had, in fact, gone through the 4602d AISS.

Second, many of the overseas cases, which should have been in the Operation Blue Book files, were also missing. However, many of these have also turned up in the Director of Air Intelligence's files, once again indicating they, too, had gone through the 4602d AISS.

Third, none of these missing files, which were located in the Office of the Director of Air Intelligence, gave any indication that they had been explained away by the 4602d AISS. Even if they had been explained, there should have been a paper trail of files and documents on these cases in the Operation Blue Book files.

In October 1989, the Office of the Director of Air Intelligence released several files to me. These files should have been in the Blue Book files also, but they were not. What I found interesting about this batch of files was that all technical information gathered by the aircraft that were involved was forwarded to the National Security Agency (NSA) by the 4602d AISS and not to Operation Blue Book. Of course, most of the aircraft involved in these cases were RB-47's and the National Security Agency would be the agency best suited to evaluate the electronic data gathered. However, the NSA will not, as of the publication date of this book, release any information on these cases, even though they occurred in the mid-1950s.

Over the years, as a result of Air Force reorganization, the 4602d AISS has been known by many names. In July 1957, the 4602d AISS became the 1006th AISS. In April 1960, it became known as the 1127th USAF Field Activities Group. Later, it would become known by such names as the 7602d Field Activities Group, the U.S. Air Force Special Activities Center, and today it exists as the 696th Air Intelligence Group, located at Fort Belvoir, Virginia.

Also, over the years, this unit maintained three of its peacetime functions. These were:

1. Unidentified Flying Objects (UFOs): to investigate reliably reported UFOs within the United States. From documents released under the Freedom of Information Act, it would, also, appear they collected information on UFOs from overseas and forwarded this information to "interested agencies."
2. Project Moon Dust: to recover non-U.S. objects or objects of unknown origin and debris of such objects that had survived re-entry from space to earth. Of course, some very earthly space objects are initially reported as UFOs or objects of unknown origin until closer examination is made.
3. Operation Blue Fly: to expeditiously retrieve MOONDUST and other items of vital intelligence interest. This included reports of allegedly downed UFOs, both within the United States and abroad.

These three peacetime missions all involve

a potential for employment of qualified field intelligence personnel on a quick reaction basis to recover or perform field exploitation of unidentified flying objects, or known Soviet/Bloc aerospace vehicles, weapons systems, and/or residual components of such equipment.

These missions were carried out by three-man intelligence teams. However, they could draw upon the resources of the closest military installation(s) in the area of operations both overseas and here in the United States.

We can ascertain from newspaper accounts and documents that have been released under FOIA requests that our government did, in fact, recover objects of unknown origin both overseas and in the United States. We can also ascertain that the military was involved in some aspects with these recoveries.

In December 1965, the military recovered an object of unknown origin in Kecksburg, Pennsylvania. In August 1967, we recovered an object of unknown origin, described as a satellite, in Sudan. In July 1968, we recovered an object of unknown origin in Nepal. This object was described as being in four pieces with one of the pieces said to be of a nose-cone shape.

What do all these cases have in common? Our government will not answer any questions concerning these cases. Neither will they identify the origin of the objects nor what these objects were. Surely, at this time in our world's history, there can be no useful purpose in keeping all of this information classified.

Debunkers will state that if these objects are anything, they are Soviet spacecraft which we recovered and do not want the Soviets to know came into our possession. If this were truly the case, why have the Soviets not filed an official protest with the United Nations for return of their property? The Soviets are just as capable to track down their fallen space objects as we are. They would surely be aware of where their space objects impacted on earth, should they survive re-entry.

In addition, we are a party to various space treaties and UN resolutions dealing with space objects which have returned to earth. Should we recover any object belonging to another country, and not return it, we would be in violation of international law. We should look very closely at any object or objects we might recover for technical intelligence purposes. However, in the end, we are compelled to return them to their launch authority or country of origin. In these cases mentioned above this has still not happened.

In December 1989, I decided to begin the process of gathering as much information as possible on the unit at Fort Belvoir, Virginia, Project Moon Dust, and Operation Blue Fly. The responses I received from the Air Force proved to be quite interesting in that they considered the release of any information to be so sensitive that in their response to me of June 5, 1991, they wrote:

> We can neither confirm nor deny the existence or nonexistence of records responsive to your request regarding "Projects or Operations known as BLUE FLY, MOON DUST, AFCIN SOP, and ICGL#4," as any other response could reveal classified information concerning military plans, weapons, or operations under section1.3(a)(1) of Executive Order 12356, "National Security Information." Therefore, pursuant to Title 5, United States Code (USC), Section 552(b)(1), and Air Force Regulation 12-30, paragraph 10a, your request is denied.

This statement indicated that these programs and regulations were current and still active.

Of course, I appealed this decision. All efforts, on my own, to gather information on the UFO History of the 4602d AISS, Project Moon Dust, and Operation Blue Fly have met with the Air Force ending all their replies with:

> Therefore, no further action is required and this matter is considered closed.

Considered closed by whom? I assure you, this matter was not, by any means, considered closed by me.

With the Air Force unwilling to release any information, I asked for the help of the office of Senator Bingaman. At first the Senator's Office was hesitant to become involved in such a nutty subject such as UFO cover-ups. However, after reviewing my documentation and listening to me explain that I was looking for the truth concerning these mystery missions and the 4602d AISS's involvement with them, and not necessarily UFOs or spacecraft from other planets, the Senator's Office made inquiries on my behalf.

In November 1992, the Air Force responded to Senator Bingaman's first inquiry. The Air Force stated:

> There is no agency nor has there ever been, at Fort Belvoir, Virginia, which would deal with UFOs or have any information about the incident at Roswell. In addition, there is no Project Moon Dust or Operation Blue Fly. These missions have never existed.

Armed with this response and believing that the Air Force had chosen to lie to a United States Senator in order to cover up the existence of these secret government agencies—Project Moon Dust and Operation Blue Fly—I challenged their reply.

In a letter dated April 14, 1993, the Air Force responded to my challenge to their earlier reply, stating:

Upon further review of the case (which was aided by the several attachments to Mr. Stone's letter), we wish to amend the statements contained in the previous response to your inquiry.

Also, the Air Force attempted to down play the 4602d AISS's involvement with UFOs by not naming the unit and by stating:

As the occasion never arose to use these air defense teams, the mission was assigned to Headquarters, United States Air Force, in 1957...

Furthermore, the Air Force wanted to suggest, in this letter, that it was the Headquarters of the United States Air Force, in 1957, that was expanded to include the investigations of UFOs through Project Moon Dust and Operation Blue Fly. However, the recorded history clearly shows this not have been the case.

Among the documents I sent to the Air Force to "educate" them were two documents dealing with UFO sightings in the Soviet Union. These documents were dated in the late 1980s.

This is what the Air Force had to say about these two documents:

Since the Air Force discontinued its investigative interest in UFOs in 1969, reports of UFO sightings are now recorded and forwarded only if there is a prior interest in the source of the UFO sighting. For example, Enclosures 3 and 4 of Mr. Stone's letter pertain to debriefings of two Soviet sources who were being interviewed for possible military information of interest. Their recounts of UFO sightings, even though they had occurred many years earlier, were included in the report for historical interest and were incidental to the main purpose of the report.

I would like to elaborate further on these two documents: Enclosure 3, dated November 25, 1987, and entitled "UFO Siting [Sighting] in Shadrinsk," deals with UFO sightings which took place in 1974. Enclosure 4, dated December 7, 1989, and entitled "Soviet Aircrew Sightings of Unexplained Phenomena," deals with UFO sightings which took place in 1984 and later.

These two reports seem to deal directly with UFO sightings in the U.S.S.R. They make no mention of anything controversial or secret, such as missile testing, technical information on a possible new Soviet MIG, or any type of military information (outside of the UFO sightings themselves) that I am aware of. My question is: What was the main purpose of these two reports if, as the Air Force claims, UFOs were allegedly "incidental"?

There exist many reasons for the Air Force to have a continued interest in UFOs. Among these are: to avoid technological surprise; searching out solutions to certain unanswered questions of atmospheric physics and radar propagation through the atmosphere which are involved with UFO reports; and the possible military exploitation of reported UFOs. All of these are of obvious intelligence interest and concern.

It does not require a believer in interplanetary visitors to understand why the Air Force would have an interest in UFOs. The reasons given above explain why much of the information might still be highly classified. However, this does not explain why the Air Force would deny any interest in UFOs, while, at the same time, the Air Force is continuing to collect information from around the world on UFO reports in the 1990s.

The United States Air Force has conducted, and continues to conduct, a highly classified UFO investigations program. Under this program, the Air Force has actively taken part in the recovery of objects of "unknown origin" and has chosen to remain silent about these recoveries. The special unit for these investigations and recoveries is located at Fort Belvoir.

The answers as to what our government really knows about UFOs, and whether they are of interplanetary origin, can only be learned through full disclosure of the records concerning these investigations by this special unit located at Fort Belvoir. This appears to be something the United States Air Force is not yet ready or willing to do.

During the existence of Operation Blue Book, Congress has held several hearings concerning UFOs. However, these hearings were always limited to just the records within the Blue Book files. No member of Congress has ever requested to hear testimony from other agencies or individuals within these other agencies which have knowledge of the existence of the more involved investigations into the subject of UFOs. The reason for this is very simple. Congress was not made aware of any agency, outside of the U.S. Air Force, that had any interest or involvement in UFO phenomena.

The release of classified information or material to Congress by any Department of Defense (DOD) agency is made in accordance with DOD Directive 5400.4. However, Congress must identify the information it is seeking—in writing. In addition, any DOD employee testifying before a congressional committee in executive session, in relation to a classified matter, must obtain the assurance of the committee that individuals present during the testimony have a security clearance commensurate with the highest classification of the information that may be discussed.

This seems to work well for information up to the Top Secret level. However, it gets much more involved for information protected under Special Access Programs, such as SCI or ESI material.

Department of Defense employees are briefed that members of Congress, by virtue of their elected positions, are not investigated or cleared by the DOD. They are further cautioned that while members of Congress might be cleared for information up to the Top Secret level, they may not be cleared for information protected under certain Special Access Programs; information considered as SCI or ESI material; or other information protected by executive directives. This is particularly true of congressional aids. Therefore, one can easily see the hesitation on the part of some who have testified before Congress; they have been less than candid and at times even less than truthful.

Once again the reason for this is simple. While Congress has passed laws to protect so-called whistleblowers, the congressional track record on protecting whistleblowers who have come forward and told what they knew on controversial matters has been poor. Therefore, a person testifying before a congressional committee is much more hesitant to volunteer any helpful information that is not specifically asked for. The rule of thumb is: If not asked, don't volunteer information.

To get to the truth, Congress should hold a congressional hearing in executive session to hear testimony concerning the classified aspects of the information that has and is being gathered by the various government agencies on reported UFOs, as alluded to by the documentation released under FOIA. A Congressional Committee should also inquire into the classified aspects of the recovery of "objects of unknown origin" under Project Moondust and Operation Blue Fly. This action would be of great benefit if for no other reason than to insure that Congress is made aware of such activities and their intended purpose. While some of the information gathered by this committee could not be made available to the public, as much as is possible should be considered for public disclosure.

In order to insure that a congressional hearing accomplishes its goals and to insure that all documentation is made available to Congress for review, the following guidelines should be required:

1. The best government documents gathered under FOIA by private researchers should be made available to the Congressional Committee.

2. The Congressional Committee should then meet in open session to explain the reasons for the hearing and to promote an open review of the documentation that was already released under FOIA. This should be done to remove any thought by the public of possible cover-up and to assure the public that this is not a search for "little green men" or "flying saucers" hidden away by the military. It should be made clear from the start that the committee is simply looking for the truth behind the alleged cover-up and is attempting to determine if various agencies were, in fact, withholding information from Congress and the American public concerning UFO phenomena, in violation of the law.

3. The Congressional Committee should follow up the open session with a closed executive session to hear testimony from witnesses within the various agencies involved. This, of course, should be done to protect legitimate national security concerns. It must be understood that while some information of interest to intelligence agencies might initially have been reported as UFOs or flying saucers, and documented in some released FOIA documents as such, there may be some legitimate national security concerns having nothing to do with UFO phenomena which justifies keeping those incidents classified.

4. Congress must demand that those government employees testifying before the committee behind closed doors be open and candid in their testimony. This would have to include both active and retired employees. These government employees are well aware of the poor record of Congress in protecting former whistleblowers. Unless there is full assurance that these people will not find themselves losing their jobs and retirement benefits as a result of trumped-up charges in the future, they will not be as open or candid as they should be.

5. Because of the various agencies involved, every effort should be made to insure that the members making up the Congressional Committee have security clearance commensurate with the highest classification of the information that might be discussed. Some of this information will be compartmented and may be considered extremely sensitive. Having a Top Secret clearance will not be enough to permit the revelation of the more interesting and sensitive discoveries.

6. A final written report should be made by Congress after the hearings, with as much public disclosure as possible. Again, the intent of this committee is not the proving or disproving of the existence of UFOs, but, rather, determining if these various government agencies have been completely candid and honest with members of Congress.

7. The intent of the Congressional Committee should simply be to establish the truth as to the alleged cover-up of UFO information by any governmental agency and the legality of any cover-up, should it be established that any such efforts were ongoing.